Formal Logic

WITHDRAWN

Formal Logic

A Model of English

Ronald Rubin, *Pitzer College*

Charles M. Young, *The Claremont Graduate School*

MAYFIELD PUBLISHING COMPANY
Mountain View, California

Library of Congress Cataloging-in-Publication Data

Rubin, Ronald.
    Formal logic : a model of English / Ronald Rubin, Charles M.
  Young.
      p.   cm.
    Includes index.
    ISBN 0–87484–891–1
    1. Logic. 2. Predicate (Logic)   I. Young, Charles M.   II. Title.
  BC71.R77   1989
  160 — dc19   88–33383

Manufactured in the United States of America

10 9 8 7 6 5 4 3 2 1

Mayfield Publishing Company
1240 Villa Street
Mountain View, California 94041

Sponsoring editor, James Bull; production editor, Sondra Glider;
manuscript editor, Carol Dondrea; text designer, Joan Greenfield.
The text was set in 10.5/12 Meridien No. 54 by Progressive
Typographers and printed on 50# Finch Opaque by Malloy
Lithographing, Inc.

To Susan and Nancy

Contents

Preface

This beginning text introduces students to a standard system of predicate logic. But it differs from most other such texts in its approach. Rather than viewing formal logic as an intrinsically interesting branch of mathematics, this text presents logical systems as models of English designed to illuminate reasoning of the sort that people encounter in everyday life. Even students with little previous training in logic, mathematics, or philosophy are (or can easily be brought to be) interested in the reasoning they find in discussions, editorials, ads, etc. Our strategy is to use that interest in ordinary reasoning to motivate the study of formal topics.

Accordingly, we have spent more time than authors of most other texts looking, without formalism, at English — the language in which our readers are most likely to find ordinary reasoning expressed. We motivate the introduction of the sentential calculus, for example, with the promise that it will help the reader understand the relation of sentential form to validity. So, before the introduction of sentential logic, we needed to introduce the idea of sentential form and to show our readers that some arguments in English are valid in virtue of their sentential forms. And, after presenting the sentential calculus, we devote a whole chapter to the justification for applying the lessons of the formal system to English.

This pattern is repeated throughout the book. Viewing systems of logic as simplified models of English, we motivate their introduction with the promise that they will help us to answer questions about ordinary reasoning. And, after we develop a formal point, we relate it back to English. (As we see it, the points we make are specifically about the English language, not — say — Chinese or Latin. Hence, the book's subtitle.)

Our approach grew out of our experience teaching logic. (One of us has taught twenty-five courses in logic over the last twenty years.) Like most other logic teachers, we have occasionally run across students who find formal logic intrinsically interesting. But most students in our classes have enrolled, not to be introduced to a branch of pure mathematics, but to gain some theoretical understanding of how people actually reason in everyday life. Students with this aim were disappointed by the more traditional logic texts, which offer little or no explanation of the relation of formal systems to conversational English. What *is* the relation of the English operator "if, then" to the formal arrow? What *do* formal derivations show us about the ways people reason in English? What *do* the formal quantifiers have to do with the English expressions like "all" and "some"? Most logic texts merely hint at answers to these difficult but important questions.

In this book, we provide fuller answers. As we have said, these answers can motivate students to study logic by connecting logical formalism to ordinary reasoning. Also, answers to questions about the relation of formalism to English can deepen students' understanding of English. What better way is there to develop students' understanding of the English operator "if, then", for example, than by comparing that operator to the formal arrow, noting *both* similarities *and* differences?

Our aim was to produce a text that works pedagogically. To this end, we conclude each chapter with a section summarizing the chapter's main line of thought and collecting its important definitions. All of the sections end with exercises, half of which are solved in the back of the book. Many of our exercises are problems of the "defend or criticize" sort. Such problems typically present the student with a metalogical statement; the student must decide whether the statement is true and to prove it or refute it accordingly. Because these exercises often require careful reading and thought, they challenge students to master, rather than simply to memorize, definitions of central concepts.

In the interests of simplicity, we have kept some familiar distinctions in the background — especially in the early chapters. Until Chapter 4, for example, we shy away from a discussion of use and mention, leaving the more alert students to wonder why certain expressions have been systematically italicized. Also, we have tended to slide over the distinction of sentences from statements, since the consequences of drawing this distinction would complicate our exposition. (Most students grasp the main lines of our thought when we say that an argument *in English* can owe its validity to the forms of the *sentences in it*. But, in our experience, only the most sophisticated would understand us if we said that an argument can owe its validity to the forms of some of the English sentences that can be used to express the statements of which the argument is composed.)

With unsophisticated, beginning students in mind, we start our discussion of logic from scratch, introducing in Chapter 1 the basic ideas of logical analysis — argument, premise, conclusion, validity, soundness, etc. Then, in

Chapter 2, we discuss at considerable length the problems involved in abstracting arguments from what people actually say and write. In these two chapters, there are few hints of the formal methods to follow.

In Chapter 3, we leave behind problems involved in the identification of arguments and move on to questions of evaluation. Here the central observation is that some arguments are valid simply in virtue of their forms. This observation naturally leads to an analysis of sentential form, to the development of a procedure for revealing sentential form, and to the discussion of common forms like *modus ponens, modus tollens,* the form of affirming the consequent, the form of the dilemma, and so on.

What exactly is the connection between form and validity? More generally, what is the relation of English syntax to English semantics? As a first step toward answering these questions, we develop a standard sentential calculus as a simplified model of the relevant aspects of English. After presenting this calculus in Chapter 4, we explicitly compare it to English in Chapter 5, noting both its strengths and weaknesses. The strengths help students to understand reasoning in English, while the weaknesses serve to motivate the refinements and extensions to come in subsequent chapters.

Noting that the construction of truth tables does not correspond to any process that people go through when reasoning in English, we devote Chapter 6 to developing a system of derivation for our logical system. Here again we keep constant, close contact with English. Even the formal rules of derivation, including those for conditional and indirect derivation, are presented as models of familiar moves in ordinary reasoning. (The first two sections of the appendix on trees, which do not keep such close contact with reasoning in English, can be used as an alternative to Chapter 6.)

Rather than moving directly from sentential to predicate logic, we ease the transition, using Chapter 7 to introduce a few of the important ideas on which the predicate calculus rests. In particular, we acquaint students with the basic ideas of set-theoretic semantics before they have a chance to be dazzled by the technical apparatus of quantification.

We add quantifiers to our system in Chapter 8, many-placed predicates in Chapter 9, and the identity sign in Chapter 10. As before, we keep constant contact with English, motivating changes in the system by reference to English, modeling formal rules of derivation on moves in ordinary argumentation, detailing procedures for translating from English into the formalism, and explicitly applying the lessons learned from the formal system to reasoning in English.

The ends of Chapters 5 and 6 are natural stopping places. (Chapter 2 takes much more time to cover than one might guess!) But instructors with well-prepared students may want to deal quickly with the first three chapters, leap into Chapter 4, and continue to the end of Chapter 9 or Chapter 10. Students who complete these late chapters may not be familiar with metalogical results like Church's and Gödel's theorems, but they will have a firm grasp of important metalogical concepts, an appreciation of the philosophical difficulties of relating formal systems to natural languages, and a sharpened awareness of how people actually reason.

Acknowledgements

While we of course accept full responsibility for any errors and omissions, we are pleased to thank those who provided help, encouragement, criticism, and advice at various stages of our project — especially Nancy Atkinson, Craig Ihara, Howard Katz, Edward Maine, John Perry, Susan Perry, Kiran Rana, and Walt Morris. Special thanks are due to David Sherry for his many helpful comments on the exercises.

Thanks are also due the Research and Development Committee of Pitzer College, which awarded Ronald Rubin a grant for the completion of this book.

Finally, our deep thanks to our families, who have shown more patience and understanding over the years than we ever dreamed might be necessary.

Ronald Rubin
Charles M. Young

Formal Logic

Chapter 1

Fundamentals of Identifying and Evaluating Arguments

1.1 Arguments, Premises, and Conclusions

A recent television commercial begins by pointing out several ways in which the warranties on American Motors cars are better than those on other companies' cars. It ends with the slogan, "If we didn't make 'em better, we couldn't back 'em better." American Motors runs this ad, of course, to get you to buy one of its cars. But what reason is there for thinking the ad will work?

Advertisers use a variety of different strategies to get you to buy their products. Some hire celebrities to speak for their products in the hope that your esteem for the celebrities will rub off on what they have to sell. Other advertisers show appealing people using their products or display the products in luxurious surroundings, hoping to influence you through your attraction to the people or the surroundings. Still others have an actor just tell you that their products are less expensive, or safer, or better made than their competitors' products, hoping that you will simply accept what the actor says.

But American Motors doesn't do any of these things in its ad. Rather than simply saying that its cars are better or trying to give you a vague feeling that you should buy one of its cars, American Motors presents evidence in the attempt to lead you to the belief that its cars are better than others: That is, it presents a *line of reasoning* designed to give you some grounds for thinking that you should buy one of its cars.

The systematic study of lines of reasoning like the one in the American Motors ad is called **logic,** and the people who engage in this study are called **logicians.** To help them in this study, logicians use the ideas of *premise* and

1

conclusion. When people reason, they move *from* some statements* *to* another. The statements from which they move are called **premises,** and the statements to which they move are called **conclusions.**

Logicians also use the term **argument.** As they use this term, an argument is a line of reasoning leading from premises to a conclusion. (Be careful not to confuse this technical sense of the term *argument* with the ordinary sense, in which it refers to verbal fights and heated disputes. As logicians use the term, an argument need not involve conflict of any sort.)

Let's see whether we can identify the premises and conclusion of the argument in the American Motors advertisement. First, what is the argument's conclusion? American Motors wants to persuade you to buy one of its cars, and it knows that you will be more likely to buy one if you believe that its cars are well made. Accordingly, it tries to persuade you that *American Motors cars are better made than other companies' cars.* By presenting you with a line of reasoning leading to this conclusion, American Motors hopes to persuade you that the conclusion is true. Hence, even though American Motors never explicitly makes this statement, it is the argument's conclusion.

Second, what are the argument's premises? Wanting to convince you that its cars are better made than other companies' cars, American Motors begins its ad with an extensive comparison of warranties. In its attempt to persuade you that its *cars* are better, American Motors tells you that its *warranties* are better. One premise of the argument, then, is that *American Motors warranties are better than other companies' warranties.*

Another premise is expressed with the words, "If we didn't make 'em better, we couldn't back 'em better." Obviously, American Motors uses this remark to connect the superiority of its warranties to the superiority of its cars. American Motors hopes that, because you know it would lose money offering good warranties on bad cars, you will readily believe that *if American Motors warranties are better than other companies' warranties, its cars are better made than other companies' cars.* And this is the second premise of its argument.

These two premises and the conclusion together make up the argument in the American Motors ad. In presenting the argument, American Motors hopes that you will accept both of the premises and that, as a result, you will come to accept the conclusion — namely, that *American Motors cars are better made than other companies' cars.* If you do accept this conclusion, you will be more likely to buy an American Motors car.

---

* Philosophers and logicians distinguish sentences from statements, saying that a sentence is a string of words that people use to make a statement. But, for reasons we explained in the preface, we will allow ourselves to slide freely over the sentence/statement distinction in this book.

Other people have other purposes for presenting arguments, and different arguments have different premises and different conclusions. But, in one respect, the American Motors argument is typical: *Every* argument is a line of reasoning leading from one or more premises to a conclusion.

Exercises 1.1

1. *Defend or criticize:** A line of reasoning leading from premises to a conclusion is called an arguement.

2. Try to identify the premises and conclusion of the arguments in the following passages. (Don't worry if you find this difficult. Detecting an argument's premises and conclusion is not an easy task, and later we will say much more about how to do it.)

    a. Alex can't be in New York. He was in Chicago a few minutes ago, and it takes at least an hour to get from Chicago to New York.

    b. Since all mice are animals, and since all animals die, all mice must die. Herman the mouse is therefore doomed.

    c. Either you will win the tennis match with Sally or you will lose to her. But, either way, you will regret having played. If you win, she will never talk to you again. If you lose, she'll never let you forget it.

    d. "Some people, quite properly appalled at the abuses that occurred, will say that Watergate demonstrated the bankruptcy of the American political system. I believe that precisely the opposite is true. Watergate represented a series of illegal acts and bad judgments by a number of individuals. It was the system that brought the facts to light and that will bring those guilty to justice." (former president Richard Nixon)

3. *Defend or criticize:* In an argument, all statements but one are premises.

4. *Defend or criticize:* The conclusion of an argument is the statement to which the argument's line of reasoning leads.

5. *Defend or criticize:* Every argument has exactly two premises.

6. *Defend or criticize:* Every argument has exactly one conclusion.

7. *Defend or criticize:* An argument is a line of reasoning leading from a conclusion to some premises.

---

* Exercises beginning with the words *Defend or criticize* contain a statement that may be true or false. If the statement is true, defend it by explaining why it is true. If the statement is false, criticize it by explaining why it is false. In some cases, the statement will be partly true and partly false; in such cases, defend the true part and criticize the false part. Often, it will be helpful to appeal to relevant definitions.

8. In a newspaper, magazine, or book, find a short passage that contains an argument. Quote the passage, and try to identify the argument's premises and conclusion.

▤   1.2 Distinguishing Arguments from Descriptions and Reports

As we defined *argument* in the last section, an argument is a line of reasoning leading from one or more premises to a conclusion. This definition tells us what arguments *are,* but it does not tell us how to recognize them when we see them. Given something that someone has said or written, how can we tell whether or not it contains an argument? In this section, we sketch an answer to this question.

Recall the American Motors ad that we used as an example in the last section. As we saw, American Motors tries in this ad to persuade its audience of the truth of a statement (namely, that *American Motors cars are better made than other companies' cars*). Generally, when an argument is used to persuade, the arguer begins with statements the arguer thinks the audience is likely to accept. Then, by presenting a line of reasoning leading from these initial statements to some other statement, the arguer tries to show the audience that, because they accept the initial statements, they should accept the other statement as well. In cases of this sort, the statements from which the arguer begins are the argument's premises, and the statement that the arguer is trying to persuade the audience to accept is the argument's conclusion.

This suggests a way to spot arguments. Given something someone has said or written, we can ask ourselves whether its author is presenting some statements in order to persuade an audience of the truth of some other statement. If the answer is yes, the author is in fact presenting an argument.

Of course, not everything that people say or write has an argument in it. Sometimes people merely *report* or *describe.* Consider, for example, this paragraph from A. F. Skutch's *The Life of the Hummingbird:*

> Certain hummingbirds, notably the hermits, fasten their nests beneath the arching tip of a palm leaf, which they always face while incubating eggs or brooding nestlings. To leave, they start beating their wings while still sitting, fly upward and backward until clear of the nest and leaf, then reverse and dart away.

Since Skutch wants his readers to accept what he says as true, one could say that he is writing to persuade. But, in the quoted passage, Skutch does not offer some statements with a view to convincing his audience of others; he simply reports some facts about hummingbirds. Accordingly, however informative and persuasive the passage may be, it does not contain an argument. In his attempt to persuade, Skutch does not reason *from* some statements *to* another.

In saying there is no argument in the quoted passage, we are not criticizing Skutch; for his purposes, description is all that is called for. We are simply pointing out that sometimes, in their attempts to persuade, people do not use arguments. Sometimes they simply tell us something, expecting us to believe them.

Since logic is the study of argument, it will be important for us to distinguish presentations of arguments from descriptions or reports. So far in this section, we have outlined a method for doing so. To see whether a person is presenting an argument, we try to figure out the person's motives — to discern what the person is trying to do. Is the person trying to persuade an audience of the truth of one statement on the basis of others? If so, the person is presenting an argument whose conclusion is the statement the arguer is trying to persuade the audience to accept and whose premises are the statements from which the arguer's line of reasoning begins.

But even a person who is not attempting to persuade anyone of anything may still be presenting an argument — for not all arguments are used to persuade. Consider, for example, the following passage from a biology text, *Birds of Prey*, by G. and D. Lloyd:

> Fights to the death over territory or for mates are very rare among birds of prey. This should not be surprising. For these birds, given their lethal armament, would long since have eliminated themselves from the animal kingdom if they regularly engaged in intraspecies combat.

Here the Lloyds are not trying to persuade anyone that fights to the death are rare among birds of prey. That such fights are rare is a fact established by observation, not argument. Since birds of prey seem ideally equipped for killing one another, however, some explanation is needed for *why* they rarely fight with one another. The Lloyds try to provide such an explanation in the quoted passage.

The explanation takes the form of an argument. One of the argument's premises, which the Lloyds explicitly state, is that *birds of prey would be extinct if they commonly fought to the death with one another.* Another premise, which the Lloyds do not explicitly state (at least not in the quoted passage), is that *natural selection eliminates from a species those behaviors that tend toward the species' extinction.* By reasoning from these premises to the conclusion that *birds of prey do not fight to the death with one another,* the Lloyds attempt to show that the birds' not fighting is a consequence of accepted biological theory. Thus, the Lloyds use an argument to explain.

In this book, we generally ignore arguments, like the Lloyds', that are used to explain. Indeed, following the practice of most logic texts, we generally ignore *all* arguments other than those used to persuade. Persuasion is a central use of argument — one of which all the other uses can be viewed as variations. And, in our study of persuasive arguments, we will touch on all the basic concepts of logic.

Exercises 1.2

1. Explain and illustrate the difference between an *argument,* as we are using the term in this text, and a *dispute.* How might a person use an argument *in* a dispute?

2. In a paper that you have written, find a passage that contains an argument. What are the argument's premises and what is its conclusion?

3. *Defend or criticize:* In general, when an arguer uses an argument to persuade, the arguer begins from the argument's premises and tries to persuade the audience of the truth of the argument's conclusion.

4. Say which of the following passages contains an argument:
  a. "Lye is another name for caustic soda. It is used to remove stubborn encrustations from [sea] shells. It gives good results, but it must be treated with caution." (Eugene Bergeron, *How to Clean Sea Shells*)
  b. When people understand something, they can explain it to others. But Hank can't explain algebra to anyone. So, you see that he doesn't really understand algebra after all.
  c. Surely all carp have scales. After all, carp are fish, and fish have scales.
  d. Teachers at The Willowberry School discuss each student's writing with each student individually. If students need to learn about punctuation, they are directed to books on grammar. If they can't spell very well, they are urged to get hold of a good dictionary.
  e. I see some tulips over there. This must be Holland!
  f. The address book is sitting on the desk. You can use it if you want, but please don't take it out of the office.
  g. Since Tommy cuts hair well, and since he doesn't charge very much, you get a good deal when you have him cut your hair.

5. The following passage contains an argument that is used to explain rather than to persuade. What is the argument's conclusion? What are its premises? (Think back to our discussion of the argument about birds of prey.)

> The balloons burst in his hands as John brought them into the house from the garage. He wondered why, until he thought about his high school chemistry. When he remembered that the room was warmer than the garage and that the air in balloons expands when heated, he realized that the balloons were bound to burst when brought in from the cold garage.

6. The following passage contains an argument that is used for a purpose other than to persuade or explain. What is the argument? To what use does the author of the passage put that argument? (Note that Crusoe did *not* write the passage and that he probably did not say anything, either aloud or to himself, when he saw the footprint.)

> Robinson Crusoe saw the fresh footprint in the sand and knew that he was not alone on the island. Only another man could have made a print like that. But he had seen no one, and a man could not have left the island unnoticed.

7. For what purpose might a person advance an argument one (or more) of whose premises the person knew to be false?

8. *Defend or criticize:* A person who accepts the premises of an argument should also accept its conclusion.

1.3 Making Arguments Explicit: Finding Their Premises and Conclusions

Suppose that, by applying the methods described in the previous section, we find an argument in what someone has said or written. What then? Often it is useful to lay the argument out in a way that makes it obvious exactly what its premises and conclusion are. To do this, we list the argument's premises and conclusion vertically and draw a line to separate the premises from the conclusion. (For the sake of convenient reference, we sometimes number the argument's premises and conclusion.) When we have described an argument in this way, we say that we have **made the argument explicit.**

To illustrate, we turn once again to the argument in the American Motors ad discussed at the beginning of this chapter. Made explicit, the argument is this:

> American Motors warranties are better than other companies' warranties.
>
> If American Motors warranties are better than other companies' warranties, its cars are better made than other companies' cars.
> _____
>
> So, American Motors cars are better made than other companies' cars.

If we had reversed the order of the premises, or if we had replaced the second premise with the equivalent statement *American Motors cars are better made than other companies' cars if its warranties are better than other companies' warranties,* the result would have been another way of presenting the very same argument. In general, there are various different, but equally good, ways of making a given argument explicit.

Why bother to make arguments explicit? Why not just leave them as we find them? The answer is that, in doing logic, we are interested in *evaluating* arguments — or, in other words, in determining which of them are good and which are not. As we will see later in this book, it is not possible even to begin evaluating an argument until we have clearly identified its premises and conclusion — until, that is, we have made the argument explicit.

Making arguments explicit is often very difficult. Arguers often fail to state all their premises, if only because they think that some are too obvious to bother mentioning. Sometimes they even fail to state their conclusions — this was true, remember, of the argument in the American Motors ad discussed at the beginning of this chapter. Furthermore, arguers sometimes speak informally, making statements that are neither premises nor conclusions — sometimes to provide support for their premises, sometimes to make their arguments easier to follow, and sometimes for no reason at all. In all these ways, then, arguers may fail to be as clear as they might be about the premises and conclusions of their arguments.

There are important reasons why arguers do not always make their arguments explicit. Sometimes, of course, arguers deliberately hide their premises or conclusions because they know that their arguments are not good ones. But people can have more honorable reasons for not making their arguments explicit. For example, they might think that, by presenting their arguments elegantly rather than explicitly, they will be more likely to persuade their audiences. They may want to impress their audiences, or to move people emotionally. They may not have very much time, or they may not want to bore people by saying aloud what everyone already knows. For these reasons, and for a great many others, most of the arguments we run across in our ordinary reading and conversation have not been made explicit.

Still, making arguments explicit is worthwhile and important. In making arguments explicit, we extract from what people actually say or write exactly those statements that make up their arguments, thereby exposing the arguments for study, criticism, and evaluation.

In Chapter 2, we will deal in detail with the process of making arguments explicit. Now we merely state two rules of thumb concerning arguments used to persuade. First, when we attempt to make an argument of this sort explicit, it is usually best to begin by asking ourselves, "What is the arguer trying to show?" The answer to this question will indicate the argument's conclusion. (Often it helps to look for phrases such as "hence," "so," "therefore," "thus," "it follows that," and so on.) Second, once we have identified the argument's conclusion, we should ask ourselves, "What is the arguer saying to persuade the audience that the conclusion is true?" (Here it sometimes helps to look for phrases such as "since," "because," "given that," and so on.) Typically, the answer to this question will indicate the argument's premises.

Exercises 1.3

Say which of the following passages have arguments in them. If you say that a certain passage does contain an argument, try to make that argument explicit.

1. Gerry must be sick today since he missed class this morning. He *never* misses class unless he's sick.

2. Any team in the league would be happy to have Dusty play for them. His batting average is over .300, and his defense is flawless. All teams dream of having a player like that.

3. In an attempt to discover the birth rate in Detroit, Dr. Maxwell spent three afternoons in the library. He looked at more than a hundred reference books, but none of them was helpful.

4. "As a challenge to Theism, the problem of evil has traditionally been posed in the form of a dilemma: If God is perfectly loving, he must wish to abolish evil; and if he is all-powerful, he must be able to abolish evil. But evil exists; therefore, God cannot be both omnipotent and perfectly loving." (J. Hick, *Philsophy of Religion*)

5. MARY: "You're an idiot, Tom, or you just don't care."
   TOM: "Then I'm a fool, because I *do* care."
                          (dialogue from the TV show *General Hospital*)

6. "[A]t the end of the Forties there were places, such as the one I remember in Munich, where you could drive in and have them take out your [Volkswagen's] motor and stick another one in the back, for an absurdly low price, about as easily and simply as you stop in for a refill of a ball-point pen." (A. Gingrich, "Some Dreams I've Driven")

7. Some of what is said in the White House ought to be kept secret. There are, for instance, many conversations about the weak spots in our nation's defenses. No sensible person would say that *these* conversations ought to be made public.

1.4 The Virtues of Arguments: Validity and Soundness

After we have made an argument explicit, we are in a position to *evaluate* it—that is, to determine whether it is a good argument or a bad one. In this section, we explain what makes an argument a good one, and in the next, we will take a few steps toward developing a method for finding out whether an argument is good or bad. (We will have much more to say about evaluation later on.)

Let's take an example for study from the debate on whether capital punishment is justified. Sometimes, those who believe that capital punishment *is* justified try to support their belief by saying that *capital punishment deters crime* and that, *because it does, it is justified.* In effect, these people advance an argument, which we can make explicit like this:

> Capital punishment deters crime.
>
> Capital punishment is justified if it deters crime.
> _____
>
> Therefore, capital punishment is justified.

With the first premise of the argument, supporters of capital punishment attempt to connect capital punishment to deterrence, and, with the second premise, they try to connect deterrence to justification.

Opponents of capital punishment can — and do — attack this argument on two distinct grounds. Some say that its first premise is false — that capital punishment does not in fact deter crime. And some say that its second premise is false — that capital punishment isn't justified even if it does deter crime.

Who is right about the truth of the argument's premises? This is a question that we will not even try to answer. Whether capital punishment really does deter crime is a complex question of sociology, not logic. Similarly, whether capital punishment would be justified if it did deter crime is a complex question of ethics, not logic.

Still, there remains an important role for logic in the argument's evaluation. While supporters and opponents of capital punishment may disagree about the truth of the argument's premises and about the truth of its conclusion, there is one fact about which they are in complete agreement. Both sides agree that, *if* the argument's premises are true, *then* its conclusion is true as well. It is their understanding of logic, not sociology or ethics, that allows them to see this important fact about the argument.

Ordinary English provides us with many different ways to describe the point of logic on which the supporters and opponents of capital punishment agree: We can say that the sample argument's premises *imply* or *entail* its conclusion, or we can say that the conclusion *follows from* or *is a consequence of* the premises. But logicians have a special way of putting the same point. They say that the argument is *valid.*

The idea of *validity,* which will be extremely important to us throughout the rest of this book, can be defined like this:

> An argument is **valid** just in case* it is impossible for its premises to be true while its conclusion is false.

An argument that is not valid is said to be **invalid.** That is, an argument is invalid just in case it *is* possible for its premises to be true while its conclusion is false.

Now, as we have said, the supporters and opponents of capital punishment agree that, if the premises of the sample argument are true, its conclusion must be true. They agree, in other words, that the argument is valid. While this agreement does not by itself settle the debate about capital punishment, it is very important to that debate. Since supporters of capital punishment know that anyone who accepts the argument's premises should also accept its conclusion, they know that they can persuade people that capital punishment is justified by convincing them that the argument's premises are true. On the other side, opponents of capital punishment also know that anyone who accepts the sample argument's premises ought to accept its conclusion. Because they don't want to accept its conclusion, they know that they must reject one or the other of its premises. Therefore, because the argument is valid, it shows supporters of capital punishment what they can do to defend their position, and it shows opponents of capital punishment what they must do to defend theirs.

Of course, supporters of capital punishment who offer the sample argument believe, not just that the argument is valid, but also that both of its premises are *true.* To describe valid arguments with true premises, logicians use the term *sound.* The idea of *soundness* can be defined like this:

> An argument is **sound** just in case it is valid and *all* of its premises are true.

An argument that is not sound is said to be **unsound.** That is, an argument is unsound if it is invalid or if it has one or more false premises. While there is general agreement that the sample argument about capital punishment is valid, there is a great deal of disagreement about whether it is sound because there is disagreement about the truth of its premises.

In general, arguers strive to construct sound arguments. It is important to see, however, that logic is *not* concerned with soundness. To tell whether an argument is sound, we may need to discover whether all of its premises are true. And, to discover whether an argument's premises are true, we may need to study science, theology, sociology, mathematics, ethics, or some other discipline.

---

* Often our definitions will contain the phrase *just in case* followed by a defining condition. Definitions of this sort say that the term being defined applies to everything that meets the condition, and to no others. Thus, the definition of validity says that the term *valid* applies to *all* those arguments, and to *only* those arguments, that meet a certain condition—namely, the condition that their premises cannot possibly be true while their conclusions are false.

Thus, logic is primarily concerned with validity rather than soundness. Indeed, for purposes of this book, logic may be defined as *the systematic study of valid argument.* As we go along in the book, we will develop more and more accurate ideas of validity and more and more powerful methods for telling whether particular arguments are valid.

Exercises 1.4

1. Arguments can be grouped as follows:

Group 1:   all true premises and a true conclusion
Group 2:   all true premises and a false conclusion
Group 3:   some false premises and a true conclusion
Group 4:   some false premises and a false conclusion

a. Are there arguments in all four groups?
b. Is there an argument that doesn't fall into any of the four groups?
c. In which of the groups are there valid arguments?
d. In which of the groups are there invalid arguments?
e. In which of the groups are there sound arguments?
f. In which of the groups are there unsound arguments?

2. *Defend or criticize:* Some valid arguments are unsound.

3. *Defend or criticize:* All sound arguments are valid.

4. *Defend or criticize:* All sound arguments have true conclusions.

5. *Defend or criticize:* All unsound arguments have false conclusions.

6. *Defend or criticize:* If an argument is valid, its premises follow from its conclusion.

7. *Defend or criticize:* A valid argument with a true conclusion must have at least one true premise.

8. *Defend or criticize:* A valid argument with a false conclusion must have at least one false premise.

9. *Defend or criticize:* Every invalid argument has at least one false premise.

10. *Defend or criticize:* If an argument is unsound, its conclusion must be false.

11. *Defend or criticize:* If an argument is sound, its premises infer its conclusion.

12. *Defend or criticize:* To show that deterrence does not justify capital punishment is to show that capital punishment is not justified.

1.5 A Method for Demonstrating Invalidity

As we defined validity in the last section, an argument is *valid* just in case it is not possible for its premises to be true while its conclusion is false. In this section, we move from this definition to a method for demonstrating invalidity.

Rather than describing the method abstractly, let's apply it to a sample argument:

Only residents of Maryland may vote in Maryland elections.

Young (an author of this book) is a resident of Maryland.

So, Young can vote in Maryland elections.

This argument is invalid; it is possible for its premises to be true while its conclusion is false. But how can we show this?

In answering this question, we will imagine that Young is a resident of Maryland who has not registered to vote. Since we know what it would be like for the imagined situation to exist, we should judge it *possible* that Young is an unregistered resident of Maryland. But, if Young were an unregistered resident of Maryland, the sample argument would have true premises and a false conclusion. So, it is possible for the argument's premises to be true while its conclusion is false. And the argument is therefore *invalid*.

In evaluating our sample argument, we imagined that Young is an unregistered resident of Maryland. In fact, Young is not a resident of Maryland; he lives in California. But finding this out does not force us to take back anything in our demonstration of the argument's invalidity. In particular, finding out that Young lives in California does not force us to change what we said about its being *possible* that Young is a resident of Maryland. For, as we are using the term *possible*, we can say that a situation is possible even if we are sure that the situation does not exist.

To help distinguish the way in which we are using the term *possible* from other, more common ways of using it, we introduce the idea of *logical possibility:*

A situation is **logically possible** just in case we can imagine what it would be like for that situation to exist.

Is it logically possible that Young lives in California? Yes; Young does in fact live in California, and so we can easily imagine that he does. Is it logically possible that Young lives in Maryland? Yes; while the supposition that Young lives in Maryland conflicts with known fact, it is logically possible that Young lives in Maryland since we can imagine what it would be like for him to live there. Is it logically possible that water runs freely uphill? Yes; while the supposition that water runs freely uphill conflicts with laws of nature, we can imagine what it would be like for water to run that way. Is it logically possible that there is a round square? No; since we cannot even imagine what it would be like for something to be both round and square, it is *not* logically possible that there is a round square.

With the idea of logical possibility in mind, consider the argument

Ben lives near Salt Lake City.

So, Ben lives in the United States.

Is it possible for this argument's premise to be true while its conclusion is false? Maybe not, as people ordinarily use the term *possible*. But, since we can imagine a situation in which Utah has seceded from the United States, such a situation is *logically* possible.

It was logical possibility that we had in mind in the last section when we defined validity. To make this clear, we will rewrite our definition of validity, like this:

An argument is *valid* just in case it is not *logically* possible for its premises to be true while its conclusion is false.

This definition says exactly the same thing as the old one, but it says it somewhat more precisely.

We now have a definition of validity that mentions logical possibility and a definition of logical possibility that mentions imagination. Together, these definitions justify our using imagination when evaluating arguments, as we have done in our examples. Given an argument that we believe to be invalid, we can try to imagine a situation in which its premises are true and its conclusion false. If we succeed, we may infer that it is logically possible for the premises to be true while the conclusion is false and, hence, that the argument is invalid.

Let's apply this method to the evaluation of another sample argument:

If Nancy has $50, she has more money than Bill.
Nancy doesn't have $50.

So, Nancy doesn't have more money than Bill.

To see that this argument is invalid, imagine a situation in which things are as they are now *except that* Nancy has $40 while Bill has $25. This situation is logically possible, since we can imagine what it would be like for it to exist. In this situation, both of the sample argument's premises are true: Nancy doesn't have $50, but she would have more money than Bill if she did. But, in this situation, the sample argument's conclusion is false: Nancy does have more money than Bill. It follows that it is logically possible for the argument's premises to be true while its conclusion is false and, hence, that the argument is invalid.

Our final example has to do with the argument

At least one house is brown.

At least one brown thing is beautiful.

_____

So, at least one house is beautiful.

To demonstrate this argument's invalidity, we will consider a situation in which there are only two things: an ugly brown house and a beautiful brown book. Again, since we can imagine what it would be like for this situation to exist, the situation is logically possible. But, in this situation, the sample argument's premises are true while its conclusion is false. Hence, the sample argument is invalid.

Our last two examples illustrate two common methods for describing possible situations. As the example about Nancy and Bill suggests, we can sometimes describe a logically possible situation by saying "It's just like the actual world *except that* . . . ." And, as our last example suggests, we can sometimes describe a logically possible situation by listing the objects in it and describing the properties of those objects. For purposes of demonstrating invalidity, either method will do. Having used either method to describe a logically possible situation in which a given argument's premises are true while its conclusion is false, we may infer that the argument is invalid.

Exercises 1.5

1. Is it *logically possible* that
   a. Young, the author of this book, can vote in Maryland elections?
   b. some dogs are not animals?
   c. a man born in 1670 is still alive?
   d. there is a whole number between 1 and 2?

2. *Defend or criticize:* Everything that is actual is logically posible. For example, it is logically possible that San Francisco is in California.

3. *Defend or criticize:* An argument is invalid just in case there is a logically possible situation in which its premises are true while its conclusion is false.

4. *Defend or criticize:* An argument is invalid if we can imagine a situation in which its premises are true while its conclusion is false.

5. *Defend or criticize:* An argument is valid just in case its conclusion is true in every logically possible situation in which its premises are true.

6. *Defend or criticize:* If we can imagine a situation in which an argument's premises are true while its conclusion is false, the argument is valid.

7. *Defend or criticize:* If we can imagine a situation in which an argument's premises are true while its conclusion is true, the argument is valid.

8. *Defend or criticize:* If we can imagine a situation in which the conclusion of a certain argument is false, the argument is invalid.

9. Using the methods described in this section, show that each of the following arguments is *invalid.*

    a. Miller is very tall. Miller is very wise. Therefore, Miller is both a tall and a wise man.

    b. All of the boxes are square, and all of the boxes are brown. Therefore, all square things are brown.

    c. Either Young is a resident of California or Young is a resident of Maryland. Either Young is a resident of Ohio, or Young is a resident of California. Therefore, either Young is a resident of Ohio or Young is not a resident of California.

    d. If a man is very rich, he can satisfy all his desires. Matt is a man, but he's not very rich. Therefore, Matt cannot satisfy all his desires.

10. *Defend or criticize:* If it is logically impossible for the premises of a given argument all to be true at the same time, then that argument is valid—but unsound.

1.6 A Note on Inductive Logic

As we said in the last section, we can test an argument for invalidity by trying to imagine a situation in which its premises are true although its conclusion is false. If we succeed, we may infer that there is a logically possible situation in which its premises are true while its conclusion is false and, hence, that the argument is invalid.

But what follows from the fact that an argument is invalid? Once we know that an argument is invalid, should we view it as completely useless and unacceptable? Or might an argument be invalid and still be useful in establishing the truth of its conclusion?

Faced with these questions, many philosophers and logicians sort arguments into two groups, calling some *deductive* and the others *inductive.*

In effect, a person who presents a deductive argument says to an audience, "Since you accept my premises, and since it is impossible for those premises to be true while my conclusion is false, you ought to accept my conclusion." Accordingly, if a deductive argument is to do its job well, it must be impossible for its premises to be true while its conclusion is false. In other words, if a deductive argument is to do its job well, it must be valid.

But, according to most philosphers and logicians, there are also inductive arguments, which work differently from deductive arguments. A person who presents an inductive argument seems to say this: "I admit that it is logically possible for my premises to be true while my conclusion is false and, hence, that my premises do not validly entail my conclusion. Still, since you accept those premises, and since the premises report *some evidence* in favor of my conclusion, you ought to accept the conclusion, too."

To see why philosophers think that there are inductive arguments, consider this passage written by a pollster:

> I asked 2% of the people in Springville whether they believed in life after death, and about 30% of those questioned said they did. It seems safe to conclude, then, that about 30% of the people in Springville accept the thought that people can survive the death of their bodies.

Making the argument in the passage explicit, we seem to get this:

> About 30% of the people in the pollster's sample believe in life after death.
>
> ---
>
> So, about 30% of the people in Springville believe in life after death.

There is no indication in the passage that the pollster's argument has any premise other than the one reporting the results of the poll.

Now, it clearly is logically possible for this argument's premise to be true while its conclusion is false; we can easily imagine that, while 30% of the pollster's small sample believe in life after death, the percentage of Springville's population that believes this is either much more or much less than 30%. So, if we try to evaluate the pollster's argument using the standards of deductive logic, we seem forced to say the argument is invalid. Yet the pollster's reasoning seems fairly *good:* While the results of the poll do not conclusively prove that 30% of Springville's population believe in life after death, they do seem to provide some evidence for this conclusion. Accordingly, many philosophers and logicians would say that we should classify the pollster's argument as inductive and that we should evaluate it by standards different from those we apply to deductive arguments.

Thought of this sort can be found in many logic books. Indeed, many introductory logic texts are divided into two sections — one labeled "Deduction" and the other "Induction."

In this book, however, we say very little about induction. How arguments like the pollster's work is the topic of an ongoing philosophical debate, and in writing this book we chose to stay out of the controversy. Instead, we have narrowed our attention to the uncontroversial theory of deductive logic. Those who want to learn about inductive logic should look elsewhere (for example, at Brian Skyrms's *Choice and Chance: An Introduction to Inductive Logic*). This text focuses on deduction.

1.7 Overview

In this chapter, we introduced the ideas of argument, premise, and conclusion:

> An *argument* is a line of reasoning leading from one or more statements, called *premises,* to a single statement, called a *conclusion.*

Often it is useful to describe an argument in a way that makes it clear exactly what its premises and conclusion are. When we have described an argument in this way, we have made that argument explicit:

> To *make an argument explicit,* we list its premises and conclusion vertically and draw a line separating the premises from the conclusion.

Once we have made an argument explicit, we are in a position to *evaluate* it — to determine whether it is good or bad. From the point of view of deductive logic, a good argument is valid:

> An argument is *valid* just in case there is no logically possible situation in which its premises are true while its conclusion is false.

And, as we have said:

> A situation is *logically possible* just in case we can imagine what it would be like for that situation to exist.

Accordingly, an argument is invalid if we can imagine what it would be like for its premises to be true while its conclusion is false.

> Valid arguments with true premises are said to be sound:

> An argument is *sound* just in case it is valid and all its premises are true.

Since discovering whether the premises of a given argument are true or false will typically take us outside logic, logic is concerned primarily, not with soundness, but with validity. Indeed, *deductive logic* can be defined as *the systematic study of valid argument.*

Chapter 2

Making Arguments Explicit: Identifying Premises and Conclusions

Logic has two main branches. One branch deals with the **identification** of arguments; the other with their **evaluation.** To *identify* an argument is to find its premises and its conclusion. To *evaluate* a (deductive) argument is to discover whether it is valid and whether its premises are true, though, as we have seen, logic rarely helps us in the latter task.* In this chapter, we deal with problems of identification, deferring to later chapters questions having to do with evaluation.

As we noted in Chapter 1, arguers sometimes fail to make their premises and conclusions clear. Often they do not state their premises explicitly, and sometimes they don't even state their conclusions. In addition, arguers typically speak informally, scattering their premises and conclusions among statements that are not truly parts of their arguments. They may make such statements to offer support for their premises or to make their arguments easier to follow, and they may make statements that are not relevant to their arguments at all. In consequence, even if we believe that there is an argument in what someone has said or written, we may have difficulty identifying its premises and conclusion.

But, if an arguer fails to state a conclusion, how can we tell what it is? If there are several different ways to make an argument explicit, how can we tell which is best? How can we tell whether an arguer has failed to state one or more

---

* There are some exceptions. For one thing, the premises of an argument might be *about* logic. For another, there are some statements — such as "All people are people" — that we can show to be true using the methods of logic alone.

premises? And, if we think that an arguer has failed to state a premise, how can we tell what the unstated premise is?

Although we address these questions in this chapter, we are not able to offer final answers. Making an argument explicit is not like following a cookbook recipe; following rules does not guarantee that we will be able to serve up an argument's premises and conclusion. To make arguments explicit, we need to look for patterns, to understand people's motives, and to make educated guesses. In these ways, making an argument explicit is somewhat like writing a poem or singing a song. To do it well requires artistry.

2.1 Finding Unstated Conclusions

Usually it is easy to see what an argument's conclusion is — the arguer tells us. After all, arguers typically want to convince us of the truth of certain statements, and they are more likely to succeed in this if they make it clear what those statements are. But, even when an arguer doesn't actually state a conclusion, it is usually a simple matter to figure out what the conclusion is. In most cases, we need only think about the context in which the argument is presented and about the arguer's likely aims in presenting the argument.

An example of an argument with an unstated conclusion is the one in the American Motors advertisement discussed at the beginning of Chapter 1. We found the argument's premises very easily. One premise was explicit: The words "If we didn't make 'em better, we couldn't back 'em better" expressed the premise that, *if American Motors warranties are better than other companies' warranties, its cars are better made than other companies' cars.* The argument's other premise was almost explicit: Because the ad began with an extensive comparison of warranties, we took the argument to rest on the further premise that *American Motors warranties are better than other companies' warranties.* But American Motors did not state their conclusion for us at all. We had to find it for ourselves.

This was easy. Since the argument occurred in the context of a television ad, it was clear that American Motors' aim in presenting it was to give us a reason for buying one of their cars. And the reason suggested by the content of the advertisement was that *American Motors cars are better made than other companies' cars.* Accordingly, we took this to be the argument's conclusion.

A somewhat more complicated example of an argument with an unstated conclusion is contained in this newspaper article:

SOUTH FLORIDA IN TROUBLE

Only the rains of a hurricane can save South Florida from a spring drought of catastrophic proportions, say the nation's weather scientists. But the chances of such a natural blessing are remote at this time of year.

At first glance, this article may not seem to contain an argument at all — only some assertions about the weather in Florida. But the context suggests otherwise. In particular, the headline "SOUTH FLORIDA IN TROUBLE" suggests that the statements in the article might be premises of an argument whose conclusion warns of some trouble facing South Florida.

Let's follow up this suggestion. What *sort* of trouble does South Florida face? The passage itself suggests two likely candidates: a hurricane and a drought. But the article says that a drought would be catastrophic, while it calls a hurricane a "natural blessing." The "trouble" of which the article warns, then, must be a drought, not a hurricane. And we may therefore regard the article as presenting an argument to the conclusion that *there will be a drought in South Florida.* (We will take up the problems involved in identifying this argument's premises later in this chapter.)

Our method for identifying the conclusion of the argument about South Florida was the same as our method for identifying the conclusion of the argument in the American Motors ad. In each case, we began by examining the argument's *context.* This context revealed the arguer's *aims,* and these aims revealed the argument's conclusion.

Exercises 2.1

1. State the conclusion of each of the following arguments:
   a. How smart is Alice? Well, the more education you have, the smarter you are, and she has more education than anyone I know.
   b. People with beards don't look like real Americans, and if you don't look like a real American you shouldn't be allowed to vote.
   c. "The key is blocking Nick Buoniconti. If you can block him you can run on the Dolphins. If you can run on them, you can beat them." (Johnny Unitas, football player)
   d. I'm not taking logic, because I'm only interested in courses that teach me something new. Logic doesn't.
   e. "Earl Butz says that in order to save money we should eat more fish. But what would be the point of that unless fish were cheaper than meat? In fact, meat is cheaper than fish." (from a newspaper column)
   f. "Belief in other minds and belief in God are in the same epistemological boat; hence if either is rational, so is the other. But obviously the former is rational; so, therefore, is the latter." (A. Plantinga, *God and Other Minds*)
   g. There are those who say that we should not regulate pornography or any other conduct of consenting adults. This is absurd. We should do whatever we can to preserve our society. And it is more than coincidence that societies that have decayed and collapsed — the Roman Empire is a perfect example — have generally done so in an atmosphere of steadily declining moral standards.

2. It is clear that American Motors wants you to accept the conclusion of its argument. Why, then, doesn't it state that conclusion explicitly? (To answer this, you'll need to guess.)

2.2 Finding Unstated Premises That Are Taken for Granted

We have seen that it is usually easy to determine the conclusion of an argument, even if the arguer does not state it explicitly. Accordingly, we now turn our attention from problems that arise in identifying unstated conclusions to those that arise in identifying unstated premises. The task of detecting unstated premises is much more difficult than that of detecting unstated conclusions, and we will devote most of the rest of this chapter to developing a procedure for coping with typical difficulties.

One reason why arguers leave premises unstated is that they take things for granted. For example, a person who argues from the premise that *this judge has decided a number of cases even-handedly* to the conclusion that *this judge is fair* may well think that the connection between even-handedness and fairness is too obvious to require explicit statement. Similarly, someone who argues from the premise that *this statue is made of gold* to the conclusion that *this statue is valuable* may not explicitly state the obvious fact that a statue made of gold is valuable. In cases like these, there may be no reason for arguers actually to assert obviously true statements, even if those statements are among their arguments' premises. Indeed, if an arguer does explicitly state a premise whose truth is obvious, it may only clutter up the argument, making it more difficult for the audience to follow the line of thought.

Still, in making arguments explicit we must take care to find even those premises too obvious for the arguer to state. Unstated premises are premises nonetheless, and we must identify *all* of an argument's premises — stated and unstated — if we are to evaluate the argument properly.

How can we tell, though, whether an arguer is relying on a premise too obvious to state? The answer to this question has to do with two general principles that will be central to our whole discussion of making arguments explicit: the principle of fidelity and the principle of charity.

The first of these principles has to do with fidelity to what arguers say or write. When we make arguments explicit, our aim is to bring to light arguments that people have actually constructed, not to repair deficiencies in their reasoning or to construct arguments of our own. Accordingly, our attempts to make arguments explicit should be guided by the **principle of fidelity:**

> When making arguments explicit, we should try faithfully and accurately to record the arguments people actually present, making additions only when there is very good reason for doing so.

This principle will incline us to suppose that arguers have completely and accurately presented their arguments in what they say or write.

The other principle has to do with charity. In addition to trying to represent arguments accurately, we also want to be as fair as possible to arguers when we make their arguments explicit. Accordingly, we should also be guided by the **principle of charity:**

> When making arguments explicit, we should try to find a *valid* argument in what arguers say or write.

The reason this principle is important is that most people (even those who have not studied logic) generally argue well — just as many people who have never studied grammar generally speak grammatically. To avoid making people appear to be worse reasoners than they actually are, then, we should be charitable and give them the benefit of the doubt. When we are making an argument explicit, charity will lead us to search for unstated premises if an argument's explicitly stated premises do not entail its conclusion.

To see how the principles of fidelity and charity work, think again about the person who argues from the premise that *this statue is made of gold* to the conclusion that *this statue is valuable.* If we only take account of what the arguer actually says, we will make the argument explicit in this way:

1. The statue is made of gold.
    _____
2. Therefore, the statue is valuable.

Clearly, this way of making the argument explicit accords with the principle of fidelity. We have recorded each of the statements that the arguer made, and nothing else.

But we have *not* been charitable. Since we can easily imagine a world in which gold is as common and worthless as mud, it is logically possible for (1) to be true while (2) is false, and the argument from (1) to (2) is therefore invalid. Thus, while the principle of fidelity leads us to say that we have correctly made the argument explicit, the principle of charity leads us to say that we have not.

How can we be charitable to the arguer? In this case, it is safe to assume that the arguer is taking for granted that *a statue made of gold is valuable.* Surely, the arguer takes the truth of this statement to be obvious and expects his audience to do the same. And the arguer clearly seems to be relying on the statement's truth in arguing that the statue is valuable. It seems, then, that we can make the arguer's reasoning explicit like this:

The statue is made of gold.

A statue made of gold is valuable.
_____
Therefore, the statue is valuable.

This argument seems to be — and in fact *is* — valid.

In this case, as in many others, fidelity and charity point in opposite directions. Fidelity inclines us to prefer the first version of the argument (the one with only one premise), since that version includes only what the arguer actually said. Charity inclines us to prefer the second version since — unlike the first one — the second version is valid. Charity tells us to add the second premise; fidelity tells us to leave it out. What should we do?

In a case like this, we should side with charity rather than fidelity. The reason is that the premise we must either add or omit — that *a statue made of gold is valuable* — is one that the arguer surely regarded as obvious and expected the audience to regard as obvious as well. Because the premise is of this sort, we can easily understand how it can be a part of the argument even though the arguer didn't explicitly state it. Thinking that the premise was too obvious to require explicit statement, the arguer simply took its truth for granted. We side with charity in this case, then, because we can see why the arguer might have chosen not to state the premise we want to add: The arguer took it to be too obvious to be worth mentioning.

This simple case illustrates a general procedure to follow in attempting to make arguments explicit. The first step, of course, is to look for a valid argument in what the arguer actually says. If we find one, there is generally no reason to suppose that something has been left out. But, if we don't find one, we should not immediately infer that the argument is invalid. Instead, we should be charitable and look for a statement that the arguer might be taking for granted. If we find such a statement, and if the arguer seems to be relying on it in moving from the argument's explicitly stated premises to its conclusion, charity requires us to suppose that the statement *is* one of the argument's premises.

In the argument about the golden statue, the unstated premise was an obvious truth. Notice, though, that in deciding to include the unstated premise as a part of the argument, we didn't appeal to the fact that the statement was true. It was the fact that the arguer thought the audience would take it to be obviously true, not the fact that it is true, that justified our including this statement as a premise when making the argument explicit.

Sometimes, we have to include as an unstated premise of an argument a statement that we know to be false. For example, if a child argues from the premise that *this trinket is shiny* to the conclusion that *this trinket is valuable,* we would be justified in including the premise that *shiny things are valuable* when making the child's argument explicit. Even though we know that this premise is false, there is every reason to suppose that the child views it as obviously true and expects the audience to do likewise. In general, then, we do not need to establish a statement's truth in order to show that it is an unstated premise of an argument. We need only establish that the arguer takes it to be obvious and expects the audience to accept it without question.

Of course, sometimes we won't really know what an arguer is taking for granted. This point emerges clearly when the arguer and the audience are from a culture different from ours. Consider, for example, the passage from Homer's *Iliad* in which Achilles laments,

> Now the son of Atreus, powerful Agamemnon, has dishonored me, since he has taken my prize and keeps it.

The word *since* indicates that Achilles is here giving a *reason* for thinking that he has been dishonored and, hence, that he is constructing an argument. One premise of the argument is, of course, that *Agamemnon has taken Achilles' prize.* Does the argument also have an unstated premise that links Agamemnon's actions to Achilles' loss of honor? Probably. But what might this premise be? Is it that Achilles is dishonored *whenever* his prizes are taken from him? Or that Achilles is dishonored whenever *Agamemnon* takes his prizes from him? Or that Achilles is dishonored if he no longer *has* a prize? To answer these questions, we would need to know what Achilles (or Homer) took for granted about prizes and honor, and, to know this, we would need to study the history of ancient Greece. Hence, the methods of logic will not, by themselves, reveal the argument's unstated premise. In the identification of arguments, as in many other endeavors, knowledge helps.

A final example. This one, which is richer and more interesting than any yet discussed, it taken from Shakespeare's play *Julius Caesar.* In this play, a band of conspirators kills Caesar, the famous Roman general and statesman. After the killing, various people address the outraged citizens of Rome.

The first to speak is Brutus, the leader of the conspiracy. Brutus defends his actions by saying that Caesar wanted to seize complete control of the government, to destroy the Roman republic, and to become emperor. At one point in his speech, Brutus asks the crowd,

> Had you rather Caesar were living, and die all slaves, than that Caesar were dead, to live all freemen? . . . [A]s Caesar was ambitious, I slew him.

Brutus clearly thinks that the crowd will regard the killing of Caesar as justified if he can convince them that *Caesar was ambitious.* To convince them of this, Brutus reminds them that, when Caesar had recently been offered the crown, he refused it *with reluctance.* Thus, Brutus attempts to construct an argument to the conclusion that *Caesar was ambitious,* one premise of which is that *Caesar refused the crown with reluctance.*

If this is all there is to Brutus's argument, it's clearly invalid; it's easy to imagine that its premise is true while its conclusion is false. Charity therefore requires us to look for an unstated premise. In this case, there is little doubt that Brutus is relying on the (quite reasonable) thought that Caesar's reluctance was a sign of ambition. When someone refuses something *reluctantly,* it's a sign that the person really wants that thing. Accordingly, Caesar's reluctance to refuse the crown was a sign that he really wanted to become emperor, and Brutus can take for granted the premise that *Caesar would not have refused the crown with reluctance unless he were ambitious.* When we make his argument explicit, we should include this premise as a part of it:

> Caesar refused the crown with reluctance.
>
> Caesar would not have refused the crown with reluctance unless he were ambitious.
>
> ———————————————————————————————————
>
> So, Caesar was ambitious.

With this argument, Brutus succeeds in convincing the crowd that he was right to kill Caesar.

Speaking after Brutus, Marc Antony challenges the idea that Caesar was ambitious and turns the crowd against Brutus. A crucial section of Antony's speech is this:

> You all did see that on the Lupercal
> I thrice presented [Caesar] a kingly crown
> Which he did thrice refuse. Was this ambition?

The context of Antony's speech and the way in which he asks his question make it clear that he thinks he has convinced the crowd that Caesar was *not* ambitious.

Antony convinces the crowd by suggesting an argument to the conclusion that *Caesar was not ambitious.* Clearly, Antony begins from the premise that *Caesar refused the crown when it was offered to him.* But Antony also relies on another thought, which he believes his audience will accept as obvious: the thought that ambitious people *accept* advancement when it is offered to them. In particular, Antony expects the crowd to believe that *Caesar would not have refused the crown if he had been ambitious.* Made explicit, then, Antony's argument is this:

> Caesar refused the crown.
>
> Caesar would not have refused the crown if he had been ambitious.
>
> ———————————————————————————————————
>
> So, Caesar was not ambitious.

This argument convinces the crowd, and they turn against Brutus.

The debate between Brutus and Antony is very interesting from a logical point of view because Brutus and Antony rely on the very same event, Caesar's refusal of the crown, to convince the crowd of opposite conclusions. Each draws the crowd's attention to a different aspect of the event, and each relies on a different unstated premise that he expects the crowd to accept as obvious. Highlighting the fact that Caesar refused the crown *with reluctance,* Brutus relies on the crowd's taking Caesar's reluctance as a sign of ambition. But, by deflecting the audience's attention from Caesar's reluctance to his refusal of the crown,

Antony is able to rely on their taking Caesar's *refusal* as a sign of a lack of ambition. Thus, in this exchange of arguments, some very important premises are ones that the arguers leave unstated.

Exercises 2.2

1. In Shakespeare's play *Julius Caesar*, the crowd first accepts the conclusion of Brutus's argument, and then the conclusion of Antony's. Can both of these arguments be sound? Can both of them be valid? Which of the arguments *should* the crowd have accepted? Why?

2. In your own words, state the principles of charity and fidelity discussed in this section.

3. *Defend or criticize:* It is always an error to leave a premise of an argument unstated.

4. *Defend or criticize:* When making an argument explicit, we may add as a premise any statement that is obviously true.

5. *Defend or criticize:* Sometimes, when making an argument explicit, we should add premises that are not already parts of that argument.

6. *Defend or criticize:* When trying to make an argument explicit, we should always assume that the argument is valid, since the occasions on which people argue invalidly are so rare that we can safely ignore them.

7. Make explicit the arguments in the following passages:
    a. Since Marcia was an avid Lakers fan and supporter, she hoped that the Lakers would make it to the play-offs.
    b. Susan can't possibly carry all of the packages home from the store by herself. To do that, she would need three arms.
    c. I'm certain that little Spot will love Burger Munchies, because *all* dogs love Burger Munchies.
    d. "I do know that this pencil exists; but I could not know this if Hume's principles were true; therefore, Hume's principles, one or both of them, are false." (G. E. Moore, *Some Main Problems of Philosophy*)

2.3 Finding Unstated Premises That Aren't Taken for Granted

In the last section we pointed out that, if an argument's explicitly stated premises do not entail its conclusion, charity inclines us to say that the argument has an unstated premise, while fidelity inclines us to say that it does not. Thus, the principle of fidelity and the principle of charity point in different directions.

In the cases discussed in the last section, the conflict was easily resolved. But, in the cases we examine in this section, the resolution is somewhat more difficult.

Consider, for example, this passage from an article by a newspaper columnist:

> It's clear that the committee will award the convention to Miami rather than Orlando. The only thing they care about is hotel rooms, and Miami has more of them.

There seems clearly to be an argument here — an argument to the conclusion that *the committee will award the convention to Miami rather than Orlando.* Since the argument's only explicitly stated premise is that *Miami has more hotel rooms than Orlando,* we might think that we should make the argument explicit in this way:

1.   Miami has more hotel rooms than Orlando.
     _____

2.   So, the committee will award the convention to Miami rather than Orlando.

Here we have recorded only statements that the columnist actually wrote, and there can therefore be no doubt that we have acted in accordance with the principle of fidelity.

But have we been charitable? It is easy to imagine that Miami has more hotel rooms than Orlando, but that the committee awards the convention to Orlando, even so. Thus, it is logically possible that (1) is true while (2) is false, and the argument from (1) to (2) is therefore invalid. Our first attempt to make the argument explicit thus seems to violate the principle of charity. At the very least, we ought to look harder for a valid argument in what the columnist has written.

In fact, there *is* a more charitable way to make the columnist's argument explicit. The columnist wrote that hotel rooms are *the only thing the committee cares about,* clearly suggesting that hotel rooms are especially important to the committee in making their decision. If we can formulate this special importance in a sentence, we may be able to regard the sentence as a premise of the argument and to include it when we make the argument explicit.

What, exactly, is the special importance the columnist thinks the committee attaches to hotel rooms? To say, in the context of a committee's making a decision, that one criterion is *the only thing the committee cares about* is to say that the committee will make the decision between Miami and Orlando solely on the basis of that criterion. It is to say, in other words, that *if Miami has more hotel rooms than Orlando, then the committee will award the convention to Miami rather than Orlando.*

Taking this to be one of the columnist's premises, we make the sample argument explicit like this:

1.   Miami has more hotel rooms than Orlando.

2'.   If Miami has more hotel rooms than Orlando, then the committee will award the convention to Miami rather than Orlando.

---

3.   So, the committee will award the convention to Miami rather than Orlando.

Unlike the argument we got on our first attempt to make the argument explicit, this one is valid. Charity therefore inclines us to prefer this way to the first.

At first glance, it may seem that what we have done here is similar to what we did in the last section, when we took the statement that *a statue made of gold is valuable* to be an unstated premise of the argument about the golden statue. It is not. Our justification for saying that the argument about the statue rested on the statement that a statue made of gold is valuable was that the arguer viewed it as obviously true and took it for granted. In contrast, there is no reason at all for thinking that the columnist views statement (2') as obviously true and takes it for granted; in making its decision, the committee might well take into account things other than hotel rooms. So, the reason for taking sentence (2') to be a premise of the columnist's argument is different from the one for taking the statement about the value of golden statues to be a premise of the argument about golden statues.

What does justify our taking (2') to be a premise of the columnist's argument? The answer is that there is a strong *hint* in what the columnist writes that the argument rests on this statement. By writing that *the only thing the committee cares about is hotel rooms,* the columnist strongly hints that *the committee will award the convention to Miami rather than Orlando if Miami has more hotel rooms than Orlando,* without quite coming out and saying so. It is this hint that justifies our going beyond what the columnist actually wrote when we make the argument explicit.

Our example illustrates an important general point. As we saw in the last section, if we find that an argument's explicitly stated premises do not entail its conclusion, we should look for premises that the arguer might be regarding as obviously true and taking for granted. The example of the columnist shows that, if we do not find any such premises, we should look for unstated premises that the arguer does *not* view as obviously true or take for granted. If we find some indication of such a premise in what the arguer actually said or wrote, and if the argument looks better with the premise than without it, we are justified in taking the premise to be part of the argument.

However, if we do not find any indication of such a statement in what the arguer said or wrote, the principle of fidelity should lead us to say that the argument is invalid. Consider, for example, this short newspaper article about a robbery:

> Thieves robbed the Morgans of over $5000 in cash and jewelry yesterday. Police reasoned that the thieves arrived by boat. "There's a dock in the backyard of the Morgans' house," said Sergeant Lewis.

Although this article does not present an argument of its own, the words "Police reasoned that . . ." indicate that the newspaper is reporting an argument that led the police to the conclusion that *the thieves arrived by boat.*

We might try to make the argument explicit like this:

1.   There is a dock in the backyard of the Morgans' house.
     _____

2.   So, the thieves arrived by boat.

Is this argument valid? Clearly not. We can easily imagine, for example, that the thieves drove to the Morgans' house. So, it's logically possible that (1) is true while (2) is false, and the argument is therefore invalid.

Having noted this, we should look for things that the police might be taking for granted. But, in this case, there do not seem to be any such things. If the argument rests on any unstated premises, they do not seem to be ones that the police think their audience will view as obvious truths.

Does the argument, then, rest on unstated premises that the police do *not* take for granted? The police might think, for example, that the Morgans' house cannot have been reached in any way other than by boat (because, say, the house is surrounded by an electrified fence, and none of the neighbors heard a helicopter). But, as we said earlier in this section, we should not take arguments to rest on premises of this sort unless there is some hint of the premises in what the arguer actually said or wrote. In the newspaper article about the theft, nothing at all is said about electric fences or helicopters. So, we have no reason to think the argument rests on an unstated premise. The argument does not seem to rest on any premise that the arguer judged obviously true and took for granted, and there is no hint in the passage of any other unstated premises.

Our first attempt to make the argument explicit was, therefore, as good as we can do. Although we tried to be as charitable as we could, we had in the end to be faithful and to judge that the police's argument is invalid. From what we can tell from the newspaper article, it seems the police should not have concluded the thieves arrived by boat.

Exercises 2.3

1. *Defend or criticize:* Whenever an argument has an unstated premise, that premise is a statement that the arguer believes to be obviously true.

2. *Defend or criticize:* In general, if an argument's stated premises entail its conclusion, we should not say that the argument has an unstated premise.

3. *Defend or criticize:* If an argument's stated premises do not entail its conclusion, we ought to say that the argument rests on an unstated premise. That is, whenever we can't be both charitable and faithful, we should be charitable.

4. *Defend or criticize:* Sometimes arguers *hint* at premises rather than explicitly state them.

5. Make explicit the arguments in the following passages:

    a. Malcolm's degree must not be in physics. This follows from the fact that Claremont Graduate School doesn't offer a Ph.D. in physics.

    b. "Students are not the best of judges; if they were, they should not have to be students." (Charles Frankel, *Education and the Barricades*)

    c. Norman Mailer won't win the Nobel prize for literature this year since an American won it last year.

    d. What do I think of him? My mother always told me that, if I have nothing good to say about someone, I should shut up. So I'm shutting up.

    e. "If you like the taste of gas, you'll hate the taste of Spark cigarettes." (from a TV ad)

    f. "According to Aristotle, justice in exchange is achieved when no one profits. As part of a theory of price, this is nonsense, and Aristotle knew it to be nonsense. Therefore, he was not seeking a theory of price." (M. I. Finley, from "Aristotle and Economic Analysis")

6. Make explicit the arguments in Exercise 2.1.1.

2.4 Extra Statements: Side Remarks, Supporting Assertions, and Connecting Links

So far, we have been examining cases in which an arguer leaves something unstated. There are also cases, however, in which arguers make statements that are neither premises nor conclusions. In this section, we classify some of these extra statements. Some we will call *side remarks,* some *supporting assertions,* and some *connecting links.*

A side remark occurs in the following passage:

> Thomas Jefferson must have been more than 57 years old when he died. No one under 35 can be president of the United States. In their wisdom, the country's founders ensured that this would be so when they wrote the Constitution. But Jefferson became president in 1801, and he didn't die until 1826.

Clearly, there is an argument here — an argument to the conclusion that Jefferson was more than 57 when he died. Leaving as an exercise the task of making the argument explicit, we look here only at the passage's third sentence, the one about the country's founders.

This sentence does not express the argument's conclusion, but there seems to be a good reason for saying that it doesn't express a premise either: We can ignore the sentence entirely and still find a valid argument in the passage. It seems, then, the sentence is not really part of the argument. It is merely a **side remark** — a statement appearing along with an argument that plays no role at all in the argument itself.

Not all the extra statements arguers make are side remarks, however. Consider another example:

> Prof. Krebbs is one of the foremost political thinkers alive, and he says that true peace will never come until there is complete nuclear disarmament. But disarmament will never come unless we bargain earnestly with the Soviets. Hence, if we bargain insincerely, peace will be beyond our reach.

Again we leave as an exercise for the reader the task of making the argument explicit. Our focus is on the statement that *Prof. Krebbs is one of the foremost political thinkers of our time.* What role does this statement play in the argument?

It seems clear that this statement about Prof. Krebbs is not the argument's conclusion; the conclusion is signaled by the word *hence* and is stated in the passage's very last sentence. It also seems clear that this statement is not one of the argument's premises; we can get a valid argument from the passage if we ignore the talk about Professor Krebbs altogether. But it seems clear that the statement about Krebbs is not just a side remark, either. For, while the statement about Krebbs's qualifications may not be a premise of the argument, it *does* play a role in the arguer's attempt to persuade his audience. One premise of the argument in the passage is that *peace will not come until there is complete nuclear disarmament,* and the statement about Krebbs is offered to get us to accept this premise. The arguer thinks that, if we are told that a leading political theorist, such as Krebbs, believes that peace will not come until there is complete disarmament, we will be more likely to believe it ourselves. Since the statement about Krebbs supports one of the arguer's premises, we call it a **supporting assertion.** Such statements help arguers to persuade by helping them to get their audiences to accept their premises.

An extra statement of yet another sort appears in this example:

> Chuck will win this year's chili contest if the contest is fair, and it *is* fair. It's clear, then, that Chuck is going to win. But, if Chuck wins, Andy will be outraged. So, this year, Andy is going to be outraged.

We can make this argument explicit like this:

1. Chuck will win if the contest is fair.
2. The contest is fair.
3. If Chuck wins, Andy will be outraged.

---

4. Therefore, Andy will be outraged.

This is a valid argument, and it accurately captures the line of reasoning in the original passage.

Yet, in our attempt to make the argument explicit, we have ignored the sentence, "It's clear, then, that Chuck will win." Despite the word *then,* this sentence does *not* state the argument's conclusion. And it doesn't state a premise, either; premises (1), (2), and (3) entail conclusion (4) by themselves. Then what *is* the sentence about Chuck's winning doing in the passage?

The function of this sentence is to show the audience that (4) does, in fact, follow from (1), (2), and (3). When one notices that (1) and (2) together entail

5. Chuck will win

one can easily see that (1), (2), and (3) together entail (4): Premises (1) and (2) clearly entail (5), and together (5) and (3) entail the conclusion (4). Accordingly, we call the sentence about Chuck's winning a **connecting link.** Though not itself a premise of the argument, a connecting link helps the audience link an argument's premises with its conclusion.

Sometimes we can choose which statements to view as premises and which to view as supporting assertions or connecting links. Consider, for example, the following passage:

> The Cafe is open unless Joe has stayed home. But Joe has not stayed home unless it's raining, and — as you can see for yourself — it's not raining. So, Joe has not stayed home. We can therefore be sure that the Cafe is open.

What are the premises and conclusion of the argument in this passage?

One way to make the argument explicit is this:

The Cafe is open unless Joe has stayed home.

Joe has not stayed home.

So, the Cafe is open.

In making the argument in the passage explicit in this way, we have ignored the statements that *Joe has not stayed home unless it's raining* and that *it's not raining.* In this way of making the argument explicit, the function of these statements is to support the premise that *Joe has not stayed home.* They support that premise by pointing to another, secondary argument whose conclusion is that premise:

> Joe has not stayed home unless it's raining.
>
> It's not raining.
> _____
>
> So, Joe has not stayed home.

In this way of making the argument explicit, then, the statements that *Joe has not stayed home unless it's raining* and that *it's not raining* are supporting assertions.

But we can also make the argument explicit in another way:

> The Cafe is open unless Joe has stayed home.
>
> Joe has not stayed home unless it's raining.
>
> It's not raining.
> _____
>
> So, the Cafe is open.

Here we view the statement that *Joe has not stayed home unless it's raining* and the statement that *it's not raining* as premises of the argument rather than supporting assertions. In this way of making the argument explicit, the sentence "So, Joe has not stayed home" is a connecting link, whose function is to help the audience see that the argument's premises do in fact entail its conclusion.

Both of our attempts to make the original argument explicit have been faithful, since they do not include anything other than what the arguer actually said. And both have been charitable, since both have yielded valid arguments. Accordingly, both are acceptable. We can take the statement *that Joe has not stayed home* as a premise of the argument, in which case we should view the statements that *Joe has not stayed home unless it's raining* and that *it's not raining* as supporting assertions. Or we can take the statements that *Joe has not stayed home unless it's raining* and that *it's not raining* as premises, in which case we should view the statement that *Joe has not stayed home* as a connecting link. While these two ways of making the argument explicit differ from each other in obvious ways, they are fundamentally equivalent.

Still, we must choose one way and stick to it. Statements other than an argument's premises and conclusion — such as side remarks, supporting assertions, and connecting links — have no place on the lists of statements that we use to represent the argument. Our sole aim in making an argument explicit is to identify its premises and conclusion.

Exercises 2.4

Make explicit the arguments in each of the following passages, noting any side remarks, supporting assertions, or connecting links that you may find.

1. Thomas Jefferson must have been more than 57 years old when he died. No one under 35 can be president of the United States. In their wisdom, the country's founders ensured that this would be so when they wrote the Constitution. But Jefferson became president in 1801, and he didn't die until 1826.

2. Professor Krebbs is one of the foremost political thinkers alive, and he says that true peace will never come until there is complete nuclear disarmament. But disarmament will never come unless we bargain earnestly with the Soviets. Hence, if we bargain insincerely, peace will be beyond our reach.

3. The temperature in San Diego was over a hundred yesterday. I read about it in the *Times.* People sure must have been uncomfortable!

4. "Yond Cassius has a lean and hungry look. He thinks too much; such men are dangerous." (Shakespeare, *Julius Caesar*)

5. There's life on Mars only if Mars's surface temperature is as warm as Earth's. But, as space probes have revealed, Mars's surface is much cooler than Earth's. So, there's no life on Mars. But, if there's no life, there are no canals. It's clear, then, that there are no canals on Mars.

6. Times are hard. Many people who want to go to college simply can't afford to do so. Of course, Howard can afford to go to any college he wants. But the fact is that no college will admit him; his high school grades are too low. And he can't be a doctor unless he goes to college. Despite his wealth, then, Howard can't be a doctor.

7. "I can never get married! Because I can never be faithful because if I'm looking, I'm dreaming; and if I'm dreaming, I'm wishing, and I could never stay married like that." (the singer Tiny Tim, as quoted in *TV Guide*)

2.5 What to Do about Qualified Statements

To complete our discussion of making arguments explicit, we now look at problems that arise when arguers qualify their premises with phrases like "probably," "it's likely that," and "it's clear that."

Our example for study will be the newspaper article about South Florida discussed earlier in this chapter:

SOUTH FLORIDA IN TROUBLE

Only the rains of a hurricane can save South Florida from a spring drought of catastrophic proportions, say the nation's weather scientists. But the chances of such a natural blessing are remote at this time of year.

As we saw earlier, this article warns that there will be trouble in South Florida, and the trouble of which it warns is a drought. Accordingly, we take the article to contain an argument to the conclusion that *there will be a drought in South Florida.* But what are the argument's premises?

Clearly, one premise is that *there will be a drought unless there is a hurricane;* the first sentence of the article straightforwardly states this premise. But the argument's other premises, if any, are not as easy to spot.

The second sentence of the article says that the chances of a "natural blessing" are slight, and (as we saw) the phrase "natural blessing" here refers to a hurricane. Could it be, then, that a second premise of the argument is that *a hurricane is unlikely?* If so, we should make the argument explicit as follows:

1. There will be a drought unless there is a hurricane.

2. A hurricane is unlikely.

   _____

3. So, there will be a drought.

This way of making the argument explicit is obviously faithful to what the article actually says.

There is a problem here, however. We can imagine that an *unlikely* hurricane hits and floods the southern part of Florida. After all, the unlikely sometimes does happen. But, if an unlikely hurricane were to flood southern Florida, premises (1) and (2) would be true while conclusion (3) would be false. Thus, if we have correctly identified the newspaper's premises and conclusion, its argument is *invalid.*

To see what went wrong in our attempt to make the newspaper's argument explicit, consider the statement

A hurricane is unlikely

which we took to be one of the argument's premises. In some contexts, this statement might be used to say something about likelihood or probability, but the author of the newspaper article does not seem to be doing this. Instead, the author seems to be making the statement that there will be *no* hurricane, and at the same time to be expressing some uncertainty about that statement's truth. That is, the author seems to be saying

There will be no hurricane (most likely)

where the author's premise is that *there will be no hurricane,* and the parenthetical remark is a confession of some doubt about that premise's truth. In making the argument explicit, though, we want to record its premises and conclusion and to ignore confessions of uncertainty. We can therefore ignore the parenthetical remark "most likely" and make the argument explicit as follows:

> There will be a drought unless there is a hurricane.
> There will be no hurricane.
> _____
> So, there will be a drought.

In making the argument explicit in this way, we treat the language of likelihood as the newpaper's comment on its own argument, and not as part of the argument itself.

While our first way of making the argument explicit yielded an invalid argument, our second way ignored the talk of chance and yielded a simple, valid argument. Hence, the second way is preferable.

The example illustrates a general point about qualifying expressions such as "probably," "it's likely that," and "it's clear that." Sometimes these expressions *are* part of an argument's content: People sometimes argue about probability, clarity, or certainty, just as they argue about everything else. But when people use such expressions merely to comment on their arguments, as in the case of the newpaper article, we should not include these expressions in our statements of their arguments' premises and conclusions. In cases of this sort, the qualifying phrases are not really parts of the arguments.

Exercises 2.5

1. Make explicit the arguments in the following passages:
   a. I'm confident that I'm going to get the job. I've heard that the other applicants are going to withdraw their applications. But the law says that if I'm the only applicant, I have to get the job.
   b. The Dodgers have a good chance of winning, so I'm going to watch the game. I watch whenever they have a good chance of winning.
   c. If the next card dealt to me is a face card, I'll win. But the next card dealt to me most probably *will* be a face card. I'm going to win! I'm going to win!
   d. George isn't on welfare. I'm certain that he lives at the Ritz, and it's a well-known fact that no one who lives at the Ritz is on welfare.
   e. I'm fairly sure that if Al makes an effort, he'll do well in the course. Almost certainly, though, he *will* make an effort. After all, he's tried hard in every course he's taken so far. So he'll probably do well in this course, just as he has in all the others.

2. Consider these two statements:

> There is gold in the mine.
> It's probable that there is gold in the mine.

Describe a situation in which the first is true while the second is false, and describe a situation in which the second is true while the first is false. Explain how someone might use the second sentence to make the qualified statement that there is gold in the mine.

2.6 Overview

In this final section, we pull together the various points made in this chapter and provide an outline of the entire process of making arguments explicit:

1. The principle of fidelity requires that, when making an argument explicit, we begin with the thought that the arguer has stated the argument completely. We should not suppose that an arguer has left a premise or conclusion unstated unless we are forced to do so by the principle of charity, which requires that we try to find a valid argument in what an arguer says or writes.

2. If we believe that an arguer has failed to state an argument's conclusion, thinking about the argument's context and about the arguer's aims in that context will generally reveal the conclusion to us.

3. When an argument's explicitly stated premises fail to entail its conclusion, we should begin to suspect that the argument rests on a premise that the arguer has found too obvious to state and has taken for granted. If we find that the arguer is relying on such a statement, the principle of charity justifies our saying that the statement is a premise of the argument.

4. Charity sometimes even justifies our saying that an argument has an unstated premise that the arguer does not regard as obvious — but this is so only when there is some hint of such a premise in what the arguer actually says or writes.

5. Since side remarks, supporting assertions, and connecting links are not parts of an argument, we should not include them when we make an argument explicit.

6. Whenever possible, we should regard qualifying phrases such as "it's likely that" and "it's possible that," not as parts of the argument itself, but as the arguer's comments on the argument.

Of course, these rules of thumb should be used with discretion, sensitivity, and care. As we noted at the outset, there are no rules that guarantee success in making arguments explicit.

Exercises 2.6

Say which of the following passages do and which do not contain arguments. If a passage does contain an argument, make that argument explicit.

1. Prof. Treadmill must be an unhappy man. After all, everyone who has just gotten a divorce is unhappy.

2. There will be at least three people at the meeting of the executive committee. It's almost certain that Scott and Morgan will be there; they told me that they would. And if Tom doesn't show up, Elise surely will.

3. We tend to think of antelopes as small, deerlike animals. And many antelopes do in fact fit this description. We should realize, however, that many antelopes do not.

4. Some analysts are optimistic about the economy. I am not. Unemployment is higher than it has been since the great depression. And, while inflation may be down, interest rates remain above 10%. Having studied economics for many years, I'm quite certain that these are bad signs.

5. Why didn't I order a steak? I'll tell you. I was told that I could order anything, and I always order pizza when I can.

6. Every Democratic president leads us to war, and every Republican president cuts back on social programs. Consequently, although we can't say exactly what the future holds, we can make at least one prediction with confidence: If the next president doesn't lead us to war, he or she will reduce spending for social programs.

Chapter 3

Sentential Form: How Sentences and Arguments Are Built Up from Smaller Parts

As we have said, logic has two main branches, one concerned with the identification of arguments and one concerned with their evaluation. In Chapter 2, we completed our treatment of logic's first branch by discussing the issues involved in detecting arguments and making them explicit. Turning now to the second branch of logic, we will occupy ourselves for the rest of this book with developing techniques for evaluating arguments.

Often, when evaluating an argument, we are interested in whether its premises are true. But, as we have seen, logic is of little help to us here. In general, logic helps us to determine whether an argument is valid, not whether its premises are true. From the point of view of deductive logic, then, to evaluate an argument is to find out whether it is valid or invalid.

Since Chapter 1, we have been using imagination to test for invalidity. To apply our test to a given argument, we try to imagine a situation in which the argument's premises are true while its conclusion is false. If we succeed, we infer that it is possible for the argument's premises to be true while its conclusion is false and, hence, that the argument is invalid.

This test, though often very useful, can require a great deal of thought and creativity. To apply the test to an argument with many premises, for example, we may be called upon to imagine very complicated situations. And even with simpler arguments, the test's success often depends on our ability to imagine strange and unlikely possibilities. It would be better to have a test for invalidity that depends less on our imaginative powers and that is easier to apply.

40

In addition, the test of imagination doesn't always tell us what we want to know. If we *succeed* in imagining a situation in which a given argument's premises are true while its conclusion is false, we can be confident that there is such a situation and, hence, that the argument is invalid. Suppose, though, that we *fail* in our attempts to imagine such a situation. May we infer that the given argument is valid? The answer is no. There are so many possible situations that we can never examine them all. Accordingly, no matter how much time and energy we spend on unsuccessful attempts to imagine situations in which an argument's premises are true while its conclusion is false, there may still be such a situation to be imagined. We may simply have given up too soon in our efforts to imagine one. So, by applying the methods of Chapter 1, we can sometimes show that arguments are invalid—but never that they are valid.

Fortunately, there *is* a satisfactory method for demonstrating validity, one that will work for a wide variety of English arguments. In this chapter, we take several important steps toward developing this method. We begin by observing that we can sometimes demonstrate the validity of an English argument by appealing to nothing more than its structure, or *form*. This observation will lead us to turn our attention away from the direct study of arguments themselves and to the study of their forms. And the study of forms will lead, in Chapter 5, to the development of a powerful method for demonstrating the validity of arguments.

3.1 Sentential Form: Clauses and Sentential Operators

In this section, we begin to explain what we mean by *form*. For much of the section, our example will be an argument that we call the McCoy argument:

McCoy's either a Platonist or an Aristotelian. He's plainly no Platonist. So he must be an Aristotelian.

We can make this argument explicit like this:

Either McCoy is a Platonist or McCoy is an Aristotelian.

It's not the case that McCoy is a Platonist.

_____

So, McCoy is an Aristotelian.

Most people see at a glance that this argument is valid (even if they don't know what a Platonist or an Aristotelian is, and even if they don't know who McCoy is). But suppose that someone *doesn't* see this. How could we go about convincing this skeptic that the McCoy argument really is valid?

We might point out that we have been unsuccessful in our attempts to imagine a possible situation in which the argument's premises are true while its conclusion is false, but this by itself should not convince the skeptic of the argument's validity. The skeptic would have to be convinced that we failed to imagine such a possible situation because there is none to be imagined, and not just because we gave up too quickly in our attempt to imagine one.

How can we prove that there is no such situation? The answer becomes clear when we notice that a situation in which the premises of the McCoy argument are true while its conclusion is false would need to satisfy three conditions. In such a situation,

a.   either a first thing or a second thing is true;

b.   the first of these things is false; and

c.   the second of these things is false.

Conditions (a) and (b) must be met for the McCoy argument's premises to be true, and condition (c) must be met for its conclusion to be false.

But no situation could possibly satisfy all three of these conditions at once. Condition (a) is met only if one of two things is true, but conditions (b) and (c) are met only if both of the things are false. Since there is no possible situation in which one of two things is true while both are false, there is no possible situation in which the McCoy argument's premises are true while its conclusion is false. And this shows that the argument is valid.

There is something surprising about this demonstration of the McCoy argument's validity. Before studying logic, most people think that an argument's validity somehow depends on what the sentences of the argument say, or, in other words, on the argument's *content*. But, as our demonstration of the McCoy argument's validity shows, this is not always so. The only fact about the argument's first premise that we mentioned in our demonstration of the argument's validity was that, for this premise to be true, one of two things must be true. The only fact about the second premise we mentioned was that, for it to be true, the first of these two things must be false. And the only fact about the conclusion we mentioned was that, for it to be false, the second of the two things must be false. It did not matter to our demonstration that the first of the two things was that McCoy is a Platonist, or that the second was that McCoy is an Aristotelian. Indeed, in the entire demonstration of the argument's validity, we did not once mention McCoy, or Platonism, or Aristotelianism. Hence, the validity of the McCoy argument does not rest on the content of its premises or conclusion.

Rather, the validity of the McCoy argument rests on the fact that the argument's sentences have a certain structure, or *form*. As we go along in this book, we will develop several different ideas of form, and we will describe precise methods for displaying the forms of English sentences and arguments. For the moment, however, we merely offer this:

> To see the **form** of a sentence or argument is to see how that sentence or argument has been built up from smaller parts.

So, for example, to see the form of the first premise of the McCoy argument — namely, *either McCoy is a Platonist or McCoy is an Aristotelian* — is to see how that sentence has been built up from the parts *McCoy is a Platonist, McCoy is an Aristotelian,* and *either — or* . . . . Similarly, to see the form of the McCoy argument is to see how the whole argument has been built up from certain smaller parts.

To make the idea of form more precise, we will introduce the technical terms *clause* and *sentential operator.* While these terms may seem strange at first, the ideas behind them are familiar and natural; only the labels are new. And the introduction of these terms will pave the way for a clear and precise definition of form in the next section.

Look first at the definition of *clause:*

> A **clause** is a string of words that can be a sentence by itself and that can be used by itself to make a statement.

The first premise of the McCoy argument — namely, *either McCoy is a Platonist or McCoy is an Aristotelian* — is a single, long clause. And within that long clause, there are two shorter ones: the clause *McCoy is a Platonist* and the clause *McCoy is an Aristotelian.* Note, though, that the strings *Is McCoy an Aristotelian?* and *Please tell me whether McCoy is an Aristotelian* are not clauses on our definition. Although these strings are sentences, they cannot be used to make statements — to say something true or false.

In addition to these short clauses, the McCoy argument contains the phrases "either — or . . . " and "it's not the case that — ." We call phrases such as these *sentential operators:**

> A **sentential operator** is a string of words that contains at least one gap. (We call the gaps *blanks* and indicate them with dashes, rows of dots, or other signs.) When the blanks in a sentential operator are filled with clauses, the result is a clause.

Thus, the sentential operator "either — or . . . " itself becomes a clause when the blanks in it are filled with the clauses *McCoy is a Platonist* and *McCoy is an Aristotelian.*

---

* We call them *sentential* operators because they can be used to make larger sentences out of smaller ones.

English has a great many sentential operators. Some that will be especially important to us in our study of logic are:

it's not the case that —

—, and . . .

—, or . . .

if —, then . . .

— only if . . .

— if and only if . . . *

Whenever we fill the blanks in one of these operators with clauses, the result is a clause, even if the clauses that we put into the blanks are themselves long and complicated.

Starting from a few short clauses and sentential operators, we can construct clauses as big as we please. The clauses may become too long and too complicated to understand, but each will be in grammatical English. Suppose, for example, that we begin with the short clauses *motorcycles are dangerous* and *cycle sellers are starving*. By putting the first of these clauses into the blank in the sentential operator "everyone believes that —", we can make the longer clause *everyone believes that motorcycles are dangerous*. Then, by putting the second of our short clauses into the blank in the operator "it's not the case that —", we can make the longer clause *it's not the case that cycle sellers are starving*. Finally, by putting the two long clauses that we have made into the blanks in the operator "although —, . . . ", we can form the even longer clause *although everyone believes that motorcycles are dangerous, it's not the case that cycle sellers are starving*. In this way, we can build long clauses using short clauses and sentential operators as building blocks.

If a clause can be constructed in this way, we call it *complex;* if it can't, we call it *simple:*

> A clause is **simple** just in case it contains no sentential operators; a clause is **complex** just in case it contains one or more sentential operators.

As we have said, every complex clause can be viewed as having been built up, step by step, from one or more simple clauses and one or more sentential operators.

Earlier in this section, we said that to see the form of a sentence is to see how the sentence has been made up from smaller parts. And as we have just seen, we can view some sentences as made up from simple clauses and sentential

---

* Sometimes we do not bother to include blanks when we mention sentential operators. Thus, we sometimes write "if and only if" instead of " — if and only if . . . ".

operators. Accordingly, we can define a certain sort of form, which we call *sentential* form, in this way:

> The **sentential form of a sentence** is the way that the sentence is made up from simple clauses and sentential operators.

We see forms of other sorts when we view sentences as made up from parts other than simple clauses and sentential operators, and we will examine some of these other forms later in this book. In this and the next few chapters, however, we will restrict our attention to *sentential* form.

In an obvious way, we can extend the idea of sentential form so that it applies to arguments:

> The **sentential form of an argument** is the way in which the argument's premises and conclusion have been made up from simple clauses and sentential operators.

With this understanding of *form*, we can begin to explain what we meant earlier when we said that the McCoy argument is valid in virtue of its form rather than its content. To demonstrate that argument's validity, we do not need to take note of what the simple clauses *McCoy is a Platonist* and *McCoy is an Aristotelian* say or mean. We need only note that, in the sentences of the argument, those simple clauses have been combined in a certain way with the sentential operators "either—or . . . " and "it's not the case that—". That is, to demonstrate the McCoy argument's validity, all we need to examine is the argument's sentential form.

Because the validity of an argument often rests on its sentential form, we will turn, in the next section, to the development of a precise method for revealing the sentential forms of sentences and arguments. What we learn there will lead us, in Chapter 5, to a powerful method for demonstrating the validity of English arguments.

Exercises 3.1

1. Which of the following strings of words are clauses? (Remember that, as we have defined *clause,* a clause can be used by itself to make a statement—to say something true or false.)

    a. Greece is on the Mediterranean Sea.
    b. If Greece is on the Mediterranean Sea
    c. Is Greece on the Mediterranean Sea?
    d. If cotton shrinks, then I should wash my shirt in cold water.
    e. cotton shrinks
    f. I should wash my shirt in cold water
    g. if—, then . . .
    h. Please wash this shirt in cold water.

2. Which of the following phrases are sentential operators?

a. —and . . .

b. if—, then . . .

c. —unless . . .

d. —even though . . .

e. my name is—

f. the cat is on the—

g. although—, . . . if __

h. it's not the case that—

i. . . . it is the case that—

j. —, implies . . .

k. —, John is ill

l. —; John is ill

m. —is taller than . . .

n. if today is Tuesday, —

o. —only if . . .

3. For each of the following complex clauses, describe the steps by which it could have been built up from simple clauses and sentential operators:

a. If John comes to the party, then Mary will be happy.

b. If it's not the case that John comes to the party, then it's not the case that Mary will be happy.

c. John will come to the party, or else Mary will come to the party.

d. It's not the case that it's not the case that John likes Mary.

e. John will bring his wife to the party or he will come alone, and he'll have a good time.

f. John will bring his wife to the party, or he'll come alone and he'll have a good time.

g. Although it's not the case that Bill was invited to the party, he refuses to stay home.

4. How many different complex clauses can a person construct using just the sentential operator "it's not the case that—" and the simple clause *fish swim?* (Explain your answer.)

5. Construct at least ten complex clauses using just the sentential operators "it's not the case that—" and "if—, then . . . " and the simple clauses *golf is fun* and *skiing is expensive.*

6. *Defend or criticize:* Any two arguments with the same content have the same form.

7. *Defend or criticize:* Any two arguments with the same form have the same content.

8. Recall the American Motors argument from Chapter 1:

American Motors warranties are better than other companies' warranties.

If American Motors warranties are better than other companies' warranties, American Motors cars are better made than other companies' cars.

So, American Motors cars are better made than other companies' cars.

Try, by examining this argument's form, to show that the argument is valid. Next, construct an argument with the same form as the American Motors argument. Is that argument valid or invalid? How do you know?

3.2 A Procedure for Revealing Sentential Form

As we said in the previous section, the sentential form of a sentence or argument is the way in which the sentence or argument is made up from simple clauses and sentential operators. In this section, we clarify this idea by describing a procedure for *revealing* sentential form.

The procedure is this:

> To reveal the sentential form of a sentence, we replace each of its simple clauses with an uppercase letter (the first, wherever it occurs, with ''*P*'', the second with ''*Q*'', and so on), leaving only its sentential operators in English.*

When we apply this procedure to a given sentence, we reveal the way that it has been made up from simple clauses and sentential operators, thus revealing its sentential form.

Let's apply the procedure, for example, to the first premise of the McCoy argument from the previous section:

> Either McCoy is a Platonist or McCoy is an Aristotelian.

As we have seen, this sentence is made up from the simple clauses *McCoy is a Platonist* and *McCoy is an Aristotelian* and the sentential operator ''either— or . . . ''. We can, therefore, reveal its sentential form simply by replacing its simple clauses with uppercase letters. Since the sentence's first clause is *McCoy is a Platonist* and its second is *McCoy is an Aristotelian,* we replace them, wherever they occur, with the letters ''*P*'' and ''*Q*'', respectively, leaving the sentential operators as they are. By making these replacements we get:

> Either *P* or *Q*

which is the sentential form of the McCoy argument's first premise.

Unfortunately, revealing sentential form is not always as easy as in our last example. Problems arise because, in *abbreviating* what they say, people often

---

* Notice that, on this definition, the sentential form of the sentence ''One graduate of the University of New Mexico is famous'' is not ''One graduate of *P*''. Although the expression ''the University of New Mexico is famous'' is a clause, the expression ''One graduate of . . . '' is not a sentential operator. If we put certain clauses other than ''the University of New Mexico is famous'' in its blank (''two plus two equals four,'' say) the resulting gibberish is not a clause.

make simple clauses and sentential operators difficult to spot. Consider, for example, the sentence:

> Tom ran ten miles, and so did his brother.

We can view this sentence as the result of putting two simple clauses into the blanks in the sentential operator "... , and —". Clearly, one of these simple clauses is *Tom ran ten miles*. But what is the other? Apparently, it can't be *so did his brother,* since that sequence of words can't be used by itself to make a statement. But the context makes it clear that the words *so did his brother* are used here, for reasons having to do with style, in place of *Tom's brother ran ten miles.* We can therefore view the original sentence as an abbreviation of the sentence:

> Tom ran ten miles, and Tom's brother ran ten miles.

Since this sentence has been made up from the simple clauses *Tom ran ten miles* and *Tom's brother ran ten miles,* and since our original sentence is an abbreviation of this second one, we say that the original sentence is made up from these same two simple clauses.

In general, then, the first step in analyzing a complex clause into its component simple clauses and sentential operators is to *expand all abbreviations.* This first step is crucial because the simple clauses and sentential operators from which a complex clause has been built up may have been hidden in the process of abbreviation. Thus, our full procedure for revealing a sentence's sentential form is this:

> To reveal the sentential form of a sentence, we
> a.   expand all abbreviations in the sentence; and
> b.   replace each of its simple clauses with an uppercase letter (the first, wherever it occurs, with "*P*", the second with "*Q*", and so on), leaving its sentential operators as they are.

Expanding abbreviations is particularly important when dealing with negation or denial. As English speakers, we have a variety of ways of denying that something is the case. Sometimes we use the sentential operator "it's not the case that —" (as in *it's not the case that Alfred is dressed*); sometimes we insert the word *not* in the clause (as in *Alfred is not dressed*); and sometimes we use a prefix such as *un-* (as in *Alfred is undressed*). To make life easier for ourselves, however, we will treat all of these methods of denial in the same way. Regardless of the method a person uses to deny the sentence *Alfred is dressed,* we will take the unabbreviated version of the denial to be:

> It's not the case that Alfred is dressed

and we will display the sentential form of this sentence with:

It's not the case that *P*.*

For a somewhat more complicated illustration of our procedure for revealing sentential form, suppose we want to reveal the form of this sentence:

1. Craig isn't a Democrat or a Republican.

Expanding all abbreviations, we get this:

2. It's not the case that Craig is a Democrat or Craig is a Republican.

But there is a problem here. Unlike sentence (1), sentence (2) can be read in two ways. On the one hand, we can see the simple clauses and sentential operators in sentence (2) as grouped like this:

It's not the case that (Craig is a Democrat or Craig is a Republican).

On the other hand, we can see them as grouped like this:

(It's not the case that Craig is a Democrat) or (Craig is a Republican).

Viewed in the first way, sentence (2) says that Craig is *neither* a Democrat *nor* a Republican. But viewed in the second way, sentence (2) says something very different—namely, that either Craig *is* a Republican, or he is *not* a Democrat.

When we expand the abbreviations in sentence (1), then, we make the groupings plain with parentheses, like this:

2. It's not the case that (Craig is a Democrat or Craig is a Republican).

This is the correct expansion of sentence (1) since, with its parts grouped this way, sentence (2) says exactly the same thing as sentence (1)—namely, that Craig is not in either of the major political parties.

The parentheses in (2) remain when we reveal its form:

It's not the case that (*P* or *Q*).

In thus revealing the form of sentence (1), we see how it has been made up from simple clauses and sentential operators: Two simple clauses have been joined with the operator "—, or . . . ", and the resulting complex clause has been put into the blank in the operator "it's not the case that —".

Sometimes, as in the last example, we can't accurately reveal a sentence's form without using parentheses. We don't want to leave the impression, however, that parentheses are *always* necessary. More often than not, we don't need to add any punctuation to a sentence when revealing its form.

---

* Often, in the interest of simplicity, we will write simply "not *P*" instead of "it's not the case that *P*."

Suppose, for example, that we want to reveal the form of this sentence:

Victor reads French and German, or he reads Japanese.

By expanding abbreviations and replacing simple clauses with uppercase letters, we reveal that its form is:

P and *Q*, or *R*.

The comma, which was present in the original sentence, indicates that everything to its left should be viewed as grouped together, just as though it were in parentheses. Hence, in revealing this sentence's form, there was no need to add parentheses. The punctuation present in the original sentence was enough.

We now have completely described our procedure for revealing the sentential form of sentences. To apply the procedure to an *argument,* we simply

a. make the argument explicit (see Chapter 2);
b. expand any abbreviations (adding parentheses to indicate grouping, if necessary); and
c. replace its first simple clause, wherever it occurs, with the uppercase letter "*P*", its second with "*Q*", and so on.

By following this procedure, we reveal the original argument's sentential form. Consider, for example, the following argument:

If I did well at the interview, I would have been offered the job. But no offer came. So, I must not have done well.

As preparation for revealing this argument's sentential form, we will make the argument explicit, like this:

If I did well at the interview, I was offered the job.
I wasn't offered the job.

So, I didn't do well at the interview.

Next, we expand all abbreviations:

If I did well at the interview, then I was offered the job.
It's not the case that I was offered the job.

So, it's not the case that I did well at the interview.

Finally, we replace the simple clause *I did well at the interview* with the letter *P* and the simple clause *I was offered the job* with the letter *Q*:

> If *P*, then *Q*.
> It's not the case that *Q*.
> ————————————
> So, it's not the case that *P*.

In revealing the form of this argument, we learn that it is made from two simple clauses, that the clauses are connected by the sentential operator "if —, then . . . " in the first premise, that the "then" clause of the first premise appears in the second premise, and so on.

Exercises 3.2

1. *Defend or criticize:* There really are only two steps to the procedure for revealing the sentential form of a given argument. First we make the argument explicit, and then we replace simple clauses with uppercase letters.

2. Make each of the following sentences more elegant by abbreviating:
    a. George is eating bread, and George is drinking water.
    b. It's not the case that Alice went to the store.
    c. Either Larry won the trophy, or Hal won the trophy, or Marsha won the trophy.
    d. Larry bought the book, Larry ran home, and Larry read the book.
    e. My brother said that, if my brother didn't get good grades in college, my brother wouldn't get into medical school.

3. Which of the following sentences contain abbreviations of complex clauses?
    a. The cat is on the mat, and the dog is near the fire.
    b. My father told me that, if I don't go to the store, then he will.
    c. Norman Mailer is tall and handsome.
    d. Norman Mailer is short.
    e. Norman Mailer is illiterate.
    f. Either Tom, Dick, or Harry is guilty.
    g. Students in this course, if any, will have a good time.

4. Consider the argument:

> Prices are rising and inflation is high, or the news reports are wrong.
> The news reports aren't wrong.
> ————————————
> So, the prices are rising.

Is the form of this argument any of the following?

a. *P* and *Q* or *R*

Not *R*

So, *P*

b. *P* and (*Q* or *R*)

Not *R*

So, *Q*

c. (*P* and *Q*) or *R*

Not *R*

So, *P*

d. *Q* and *R*, or *S*

Not *R*

So, *Q*

If not, what *is* the argument's form?

5. Reveal the form of each of the following sentences. (Don't forget to expand all abbreviations!)
   a. Jack walks up the hill just in case Jill does.
   b. Jack and Jill went up the hill, and Mary's little lamb wasn't far behind.
   c. Jack helped Jill to walk up a very steep hill on the top of which was an entirely dry well used for crop irrigation.
   d. Jack enjoyed the walk up the hill only if Jill didn't.
   e. If the Democrats lose, the Republicans win unless the party system collapses.
   f. Women attend both Harvard and Yale.
   g. Herbert and Yolanda talked for three hours.
   h. "And" has three letters, while "or" has only two.

6. Display the sentential forms of each of the following arguments.
   a. If elephants have wings, they can fly. Elephants do have wings. Therefore, they can fly.
   b. Elephants can fly unless they don't have wings. They do have wings. Hence, they can fly.
   c. Elephants can fly only if they have wings and aviators' licenses. Since they have neither, they can't fly.
   d. Either elephants can fly and they do have wings, or they can't fly and they don't have wings. Elephants have wings just in case they have aviators' licenses. Therefore, elephants have wings and can fly, if they have aviators' licenses.
   e. All elephants have wings. Everything with wings can fly. Therefore, elephants can fly.

3.3 Sentential Validity: A Connection of Sentential Form to Validity

In the last two sections, we defined *sentential form* and developed a precise method for revealing the sentential forms of sentences and arguments. Our motive for taking up the study of form was the belief that the study would help us to find an effective method for demonstrating the validity of arguments. In this section, we take another step toward developing such a method by linking sentential form to validity. The link will be the idea of *sentential validity,* which we define later in this section.

To see that form and validity are related, think back to the McCoy argument:

> Either McCoy is a Platonist or McCoy is an Aristotelian.
>
> It's not the case that McCoy is a Platonist.
> _____
>
> So, McCoy is an Aristotelian.

Using the procedure described in the previous section, we can reveal the argument's sentential form like this:

> Either *P* or *Q*
>
> Not *P*
> _____
>
> So, *Q*

This form shows how the simple clauses are arranged in the McCoy argument, what sentential operators appear in it, and where those sentential operators are placed.

As we saw in the first section of this chapter, it is exactly these facts that account for the McCoy argument's validity. Because the argument has this form, a possible situation in which its premises are true while its conclusion is false would be a situation in which one of two things is true while both of those things are false. Since there can be no such situation, the McCoy argument is valid — and what makes it valid is its sentential form.

Now consider another argument, which we call the *Miller argument:*

> Either Miller lives in Maryland or Miller lives in California.
>
> It's not the case that Miller lives in Maryland.
> _____
>
> So, Miller lives in California.

Although the Miller argument has completely different content from the McCoy argument, it has the very same sentential form:

> Either *P* or *Q*
>
> Not *P*
>
> ———
>
> So, *Q*

As with the McCoy argument, then, so with the Miller argument. A possible situation in which its premises are true while its conclusion is false would be a situation in which one of two things is true while both of those things are false. Since there can be no such situation, the Miller argument, like the McCoy argument, is valid.

Using the same reasoning, we can demonstrate the validity of *any* argument with the same sentential form as the McCoy argument, regardless of that argument's content. Hence, *every* argument with that sentential form is valid.

To describe this property of the McCoy argument's sentential form, we introduce the idea of *sentential validity:*

> An argument form is **sententially valid** (or **S-valid,** for short) just in case every argument of that sentential form is valid.

The opposite of sentential validity is *sentential invalidity.* An argument form is **sententially invalid (S-invalid)** just in case it is not S-valid—or, in other words, just in case at least *one* argument having that form is invalid.

Obviously, the ideas of S-validity and S-invalidity are closely related to the ideas of validity and invalidity. Indeed, S-validity and S-invalidity are *defined* in terms of validity and invalidity. Still, there is an important difference. Although validity and invalidity are properties of *arguments,* S-validity and S-invalidity are properties of arguments' *sentential forms.*

For any given S-invalid form, some arguments having that form are invalid. (This follows directly from the definition of S-invalidity.) Still, for any given S-invalid form, some arguments having that form are valid. Consider, for example, this simple form:

> *P*
>
> ———
>
> So, *Q*

Some arguments of this form are invalid (for example, "Goodman is a poet; therefore, Goodman is a novelist"). But other arguments of this form are valid (for example, "Goodman is a confirmed bachelor; therefore, Goodman is a bachelor"). Hence, from the observation that an argument has an S-invalid sentential form, nothing at all follows about the argument's validity or invalidity.

But suppose we find that the sentential form of a given argument is S-*valid*. Then it follows, from the definition of S-validity, that *every* argument having that form — including the given argument — is valid. Accordingly, if we had a method for demonstrating the S-validity of a given argument form, we would in effect have a method for demonstrating the validity of all the arguments having that form. The study of form thus promises to yield considerable dividends in our search for an effective method for demonstrating validity. Although we have so far been dealing with arguments one by one, the study of form promises to provide us with a way of demonstrating the validity of whole classes of arguments, all at once. In addition, since the form of an argument is independent of its content, the study of form promises to give us a method for demonstrating validity that, unlike the method for demonstrating invalidity from Chapter 1, is free of the limits of our imaginations.

As we will see, our new approach to demonstrating validity is astonishingly successful — so successful, in fact, that the formal test for validity is the principal test used by modern logicians. For this reason, the modern study of valid argument is often called *formal* logic.

Exercises 3.3

1. *Defend or criticize:* Just as we demonstrated the validity of the Miller argument in this section, we can demonstrate the validity of any argument with the same form as the McCoy argument, regardless of its content.

2. Demonstrate the validity of the following argument:

> Either Nixon was a liberal or Lenin was a Communist.
>
> Nixon wasn't a liberal.
>
> _____
>
> So, Lenin was a Communist.

3. *Defend or criticize:* The McCoy argument discussed in this section is S-valid.

4. *Defend or criticize:* The McCoy argument has a valid sentential form.

5. *Defend or criticize:* An argument has an S-invalid sentential form just in case some argument with that form is invalid.

6. *Defend or criticize:* If an argument form is S-invalid, every argument with that form is invalid.

7. *Defend or criticize:* To demonstrate the S-invalidity of a given argument form, we need only (i) find an argument having the given form and (ii) imagine a situation in which that argument's premises are true while its conclusion is false.

8. Using the method described in the previous exercise, demonstrate the S-invaldity of each of the following argument forms:

a. If *P*, then *Q*

   Q
   ―――――

   So, *P*

b. If *P*, then *Q*

   Not *P*
   ―――――

   So, not *Q*

c. *P* or *Q*

   P
   ―――――

   So, not *Q*

d. *P* only if *Q*

   Q
   ―――――

   So, *P*

e. If *P* and *Q*, then *R*

   P and *R*
   ―――――

   So, *Q*

f. *P* only if *Q*

   Q only if *R*
   ―――――

   So, *P* if *R*

g. Not *P*, and not *Q*

   R unless not *Q*
   ―――――

   So, *R*

h. Not (*P* and *Q*)
   ―――――

   So, not (*P* or *Q*)

3.4 Some Common Argument Forms

In this section, we describe eight argument forms that are so common they have been given special names. Most, but not all, of these forms are S-valid. Since arguments very often contain "if" clauses, we begin with some forms containing the sentential operator "if―, then . . . ". We then move on to forms containing the operators "either―or . . . " and "―, and . . . ".

modus ponens

A common form containing "if―, then . . . " is *modus ponens* (Latin for the *way of putting*):

If *P*, then *Q*

P
―――――

So, *Q*

Modus ponens is an S-valid argument form, and it is extremely important. In times gone by, logicians have viewed it as the fundamental form of argument, and even as the fundamental form of rational thought.

modus tollens

A second important argument form is *modus tollens* (Latin for the *way of taking*):

> If *P*, then *Q*
>
> Not *Q*
> _____
>
> So, not *P*

Like *modus ponens, modus tollens* is S-valid.

the fallacy of denying the antecedent

Another common argument form is this:

> If *P*, then *Q*
>
> Not *P*
> _____
>
> So, not *Q*

This form is S-invalid. But, because it looks like a cross between *modus ponens* and *modus tollens,* people often present or accept arguments of this form in the mistaken belief that the arguments are valid. Such people are said to have committed the *fallacy of denying the antecedent.* (The *antecedent* of an ''if—, then . . . '' sentence is the clause following the ''if''.)

the fallacy of affirming the consequent

Closely related to the fallacy of denying the antecedent is another S-invalid form:

> If *P*, then *Q*
>
> *Q*
> _____
>
> So, *P*

A person who presents or accepts an argument of this form in the mistaken belief that it is valid is said to have committed the *fallacy of affirming the consequent.* (The *consequent* of an ''if—, then . . . '' sentence is the clause following the ''then''.)

the hypothetical syllogism

In the Middle Ages, people gave the odd-sounding name *hypothetical syllogism* to the form:

If *P*, then *Q*

If *Q*, then *R*

_____

So, if *P*, then *R*

Consideration of a few examples should convince you that this form is S-valid.

dilemmas

Two final forms having to do with "if—, then . . . ":

Either *P* or *Q*	Either *P* or *Q*
If *P*, then *R*	If *R*, then not *P*
If *Q*, then *R*	If *R*, then not *Q*
_____	_____
So, *R*	So, not *R*

The form on the left is called the *constructive dilemma,* and the one on the right the *destructive dilemma.* Both are S-valid.

the conjunctive syllogism

A form having to do with the common operator "—and . . . ":

Not (*P* and *Q*)

P

_____

So, not *Q*

Clearly, this form, known as the *conjunctive syllogism,* is S-valid.

the disjunctive syllogism

Finally, an old friend, the *disjunctive syllogism:*

Either *P* or *Q*

Not *P*

_____

So, *Q*

Of course, this S-valid form is the form of the McCoy argument, which we discussed earlier in this chapter.

Exercises 3.4

1. *Defend or criticize:* If we find that an argument has one of the S-valid forms described in this section, we can infer that the argument is valid. So, for example, if we find that the argument has the form of the constructive dilemma, we can infer that the argument is valid.

2. Keeping the previous exercise in mind, show that each of the following passages contains a valid argument. (It will help to display the form of each argument.)

     a. Either it's raining or it's snowing. It's not the case that it's raining. So, it's snowing.

     b. If it's raining, the ground is wet. It's raining. So, the ground is wet.

     c. If Leonard has lots of money (and he does!), then Judy will go out with him. It follows that Judy will go out with him.

     d. Leonard doesn't have lots of money. If he did, Judy would go out with him. But she won't go out with him.

     e. Craig is not both a Democrat and a Republican. But he is a Democrat. So, he isn't a Republican.

     f. Either it's very cold outside or the heater isn't working. But I checked the heater myself, and I know that it is working. So, it must be very cold outside.

     g. Either Alice is a vegetarian or she eats steak. If she's a vegetarian, she likes potatoes. (What would a vegetarian diet be without potatoes?) On the other hand, if she eats steak, she also likes potatoes. (What would it be like to eat steak without potatoes?) So, Alice must like potatoes.

     h. I will vote for either Smith or Brown. If I vote for Smith, Brown won't win. And, if I vote for Brown, he still won't win. It's therefore inevitable: Brown won't win.

3. We have said that the following sentential forms are S-invalid:

    a. If P, then Q b. If P, then Q

       Not P Q

       ————   ————

       So, not Q So, P

Using the method described in Exercise 3.3.7, prove that each of these forms is S-invalid.

4. Consider the following passage:

    If the light bulb is burnt out, nothing will happen when we flip the switch. Hence, to discover whether the bulb is burnt out, we need only flip the switch. If the light doesn't go on, we know that the bulb is burnt out.

Do you think that the person who wrote this passage has made an error in reasoning? If so, why?

5. The S-valid forms that we listed in this section contain the sentential opera-tors "not — ", "if — , then . . .", "either — or . . .", and " —, and . . .". Are there also common S-valid forms containing the operator " — unless . . ."? Are there some containing the operator " — only if . . ."? If so, what are they? If not, why not?

6. Consider these argument forms:

      a. If P, then not Q

      P
      ———————

      So, not Q

      b. If not P, then Q

      P
      ———————

      So, not Q

      c. If P, then not Q

      Q
      ———————

      So, not P

      d. If not P, then not Q

      Not P
      ———————

      So, not Q

      e. If not P, then not Q

      Q
      ———————

      So, P

      f. P if Q

      Q
      ———————

      So, P

Which of these forms would you say are S-valid and which would you say are S-invalid? Why? (It may help to compare these forms with the various forms discussed in this chapter.)

7. *Defend or criticize:* Every argument of the form of the fallacy of denying the antecedent is invalid.

3.5 Overview

In this chapter, we viewed the premises and conclusions of arguments as made up from clauses and sentential operators:

> A *clause* is a string of words that can be a sentence by itself and that can be used by itself to make a statement. And a *sentential operator* is a string of words that contains one or more blanks and that becomes a clause when the blanks are filled with clauses.

As we saw, some clauses are simple while others are complex:

> A clause is *simple* just in case it contains no sentential operators, and a clause is *complex* just in case it contains one or more sentential operators.

If a clause is complex, we can view it as made from sentential operators and shorter clauses; if these shorter clauses are themselves complex, we can view them, in turn, as made up from sentential operators and still shorter clauses; and so on.

When we view the sentences of an argument as made up from simple clauses and sentential operators, we see the argument's sentential form:

> The *sentential form* of an argument is the way in which it is made up from simple clauses and sentential operators.

We can reveal the sentential form of an argument by following this procedure:

    a.   make the argument explicit;

    b.   expand all abbreviations in the argument; and

    c.   replace each of its simple clauses with an uppercase letter (the first, wherever it occurs, with "*P*", the second with "*Q*", and so on), leaving the sentential operators as they are.

There are concepts of form other than that of sentential form, but sentential form will be our focus for the next three chapters.

To connect sentential form to validity, we introduced the idea of sentential validity:

> An argument form is *sententially valid (S-valid)* just in case every argument of that sentential form is valid. Otherwise, it's sententially *in*valid (S-invalid).

If we can show that a given argument has an S-valid sentential form — for example, one of the common S-valid forms listed in the previous section — we can infer that *every* argument of that form, including the given argument, is valid. Accordingly, the study of sentential form promises to provide us with a reliable and efficient method for demonstrating the validity of arguments.

Chapter 4

Clause Logic: A Formal Model of English

With the introduction of a the idea of *form,* we have taken one important step toward the development of a decisive test for validity. If we can show that an argument has an S-valid sentential form, we may infer that the argument itself is valid. So far, though, we do not have any general method for demonstrating the S-validity of sentential forms. All we have is a short list of simple S-valid forms. What do we do when confronted with arguments whose sentential forms are more complex and less familiar?

Consider, for example, the argument:

> The roses are fresh if they are red. Therefore, either the roses are not red or they are fresh.

We can make this argument explicit like this:

1. The roses are fresh if they are red.

   ———————————————————————————————————————

2. So, either the roses are not red or they are fresh.

Eliminating abbreviations, we get:

1. The roses are fresh if the roses are red.

   ———————————————————————————————————————

2. So, either it's not the case that the roses are red, or the roses are fresh.

Replacing "the roses are fresh" with *"P"* and "the roses are red" with *"Q"*, we get the sample argument's sentential form:

1. *P* if *Q*.

    ———————————————————————————

2. So, either it's not the case that *Q*, or *P*.

If follows from the definition of S-validity that this argument is valid if its sentential form is S-valid. But *is* its form S-valid? At the moment, we don't have any systematic method for finding out.

Of course, if we happened to find an invalid argument with the same sentential form as the sample argument, we could infer that the form is S-invalid. But if our attempt to find such an argument is unsuccessful, we can't infer that the form is S-valid. There may be invalid arguments having the form that we didn't happen to hit on in our search. So, if we happen not to find an invalid argument with the sample argument's sentential form, we can't conclude anything at all about that form's S-validity or S-invalidity.

Then how *can* we demonstrate the S-validity of unfamiliar forms? Our answer to this question is based on the idea of *modeling English,* which we explain in the first section of this chapter. When we complete the task of actually modeling English in the remaining sections of the chapter, the result will be the system of logic that we call *clause logic,* or *CL,* for short. As we will show in Chapter 5, CL provides us with a powerful method for demonstrating the S-validity of argument forms and, hence, the validity of particular arguments.

4.1 Modeling English

In this section, we discuss the idea of *modeling* English — an idea that we apply in the rest of this chapter and, indeed, in the rest of this book.

Generally speaking, a **model** is a simplified representation that we can use to gain an understanding of the object or system it represents. Think, for example, about how we might go about teaching people the principles of military strategy. It wouldn't do much good to throw them into an actual battle. From the middle of the battlefield, they couldn't get a good view of what's actually going on. Also, since a real battle would be very complicated, they wouldn't be able to tell which parts of the outcome were the result of good decisions by the generals and which parts were due merely to superior numbers or chance. In fact, they would probably be too worried about survival to think about military principles at all.

A better approach — and one that is frequently adopted — is to use *war games.* In one of these games, aspects of real warfare are *simulated.* Students are told they are in certain battlefield situations, asked to respond, and then told or shown the consequences of their decisions. Thus, these games are simplified representations — or *models* — of warfare. The simplicity of the model allows students to see the whole picture more easily, to focus on strategy, and to recognize general principles — the structure and principles that the model shares with reality are much easier to detect in the simplified model than in the reality itself. (In using a model, though, one must constantly be aware of respects in which its reflection of reality is less than perfect and try to improve the model in these areas. Otherwise, using the model might lead one seriously astray.)

Since we want to study the features of English arguments relevant to questions of S-validity, we will develop a model of the language in which we express arguments. The virtue of the model will be its simplicity. English is a complicated and disorderly language. It has innumerable grammatical rules, including those applying to the use of "who" and "whom," those having to do with semicolons, and those governing verb tense. And the meanings of English sentences depend on the meanings of thousands and thousands of words, some of which are extremely difficult to define. Thus, someone who tried to say everything there is to say about English would quickly be buried in overwhelming detail and complexity. Fortunately, though, we are not interested in all the complexities of English. For the moment, we are interested only in the limited question of the S-validity of argument forms. In particular, we want to bring to light the features of English arguments relevant to the question of the S-validity of their sentential forms, and to come to some understanding of exactly what it is about arguments with S-valid forms that makes them valid. The model of English that we will construct will focus on the features of English relevant to these issues, thus enabling us to study S-validity without getting bogged down in the complexities of the language.

In developing our model of English, we will ignore spoken English and think of written English. Viewed in this way, English is a system of marks: letters and punctuation marks. It's clear, however, that a person who simply memorized the list of these marks wouldn't know very much about English. To learn how to read or write, a person would need to master the various *rules* for using these marks.

One set of rules — which we call **rules of vocabulary** — determines which sequences of marks are English *expressions*. These rules determine, for example, that the string of letters "the" is an English expression, while the string "hte" is not. Since the expressions of English are its words, the rules of vocabulary of English are given, in effect, by the list of words in a good dictionary.

A second set of rules — which we call **rules of formation** — determines how expressions can be strung together to make longer units. A string of expressions that has been put together in accordance with a language's rules of formation is called a **well-formed formula** — or, for short, a **wff** (pronounced "woof" or "wiff") — of that language. The wffs of English are its *sentences*. Thus, the rules of formation for English determine which strings of words (expressions) are grammatical sentences (wffs). It is, for example, a rule of formation for English that every sentence must contain at least one verb. Because they violate this rule, the strings "cat on mat" and "the dog loudly" are not counted as grammatical sentences.

Notice, though, that a person could master all the rules of vocabulary and formation for English and *still* not know how to read or write. These rules treat English as if it were *no more* than a system of marks on paper. They say nothing at all about the meanings of expressions, or about truth and falsity, or about the ways in which English expressions refer to things in the world. Logicians mark this point by saying that rules of vocabulary and formation are **syntactic rules**—the **syntax** of a sentence being the way that it has been put together.

In addition to syntactic rules, English also has rules that say how the expressions and wffs relate to the world. These rules are called **semantic rules**—the **semantics** of a sentence gives the conditions under which it is true or false. By way of illustration, consider the simple sentence

It's not the case that Rubin is swimming.

By examining the syntax of this sentence, we find only that it consists of two groups of words: a sentential operator (namely, "it's not the case that—") and a simple clause (namely, *Rubin is swimming*). When we examine the sentence's semantics, however, we notice that the simple clause *Rubin is swimming* is either true or false, and that the truth or falsity of the whole sentence is governed by the following rule:

A sentence formed by putting a clause in the blank of the operator "it's not the case that—" is *true* if the clause is *false*, and *false* if the clause is *true*.

This is a semantic rule. Unlike the syntactic rules we just discussed, this rule tells us something about the conditions under which the sentence would be true.

The semantic rules most important to us in our study of logic are those that describe the conditions under which sentences have certain *values*—truth or falsity. Accordingly, we will call these semantic rules **rules of valuation**.

By themselves, rules of valuation generally do not determine the values of English sentences. For example, although the sample rule of valuation for the sentence "It's not the case that Rubin is swimming" tells us something about the conditions that would have to be met for the sentence to be true, we would have to gather information about the world in order to tell whether those conditions are in fact met and to tell whether the sentence *is* true. In particular, we would have to know whether Rubin is swimming.

With the recognition of rules of valuation, we have completed our general characterization of English. According to our characterization, English is a system of marks (i.e., letters and punctuation marks) governed by three sets of rules. Rules of *vocabulary* determine which marks are English words. Rules of *formation* determine which strings of words are sentences. And rules of *valuation* determine the values (i.e., the truth or falsity) of English sentences in various possible situations. The rules of vocabulary and formation are *syntactic*, while the rules of valuation are *semantic*.

Like English, our simplified model of English will be a system of marks governed by rules of vocabulary, formation, and valuation. But what rules should our system have? Which features of English should we seek to capture in our system, and which should we let go?

When answering this question, we should remember that our reason for developing the system is to bring to light the features of English arguments relevant to the question of the S-validity of sentential forms. Since the sentential forms of English arguments are patterns of simple clauses and sentential operators, our model's vocabulary should include items corresponding to simple English clauses and to English sentential operators. Also, as the rules of formation for English allow us to build up long and complex clauses from simple clauses and sentential operators, our model's rules of formation should allow us to build up long wffs from the items that correspond to simple clauses and sentential operators.

Similarly, since S-validity is defined in terms of validity, and since validity is defined in terms of the truth or falsity of English sentences in possible situations, our model will need values corresponding to truth and falsity, and it will also need arrangements that correspond to possible situations.

Finally, if our model is to reflect accurately the relation of S-validity to sentential form, it must capture some of the *meanings* of particular English sentential operators. To see why, compare the S-valid argument form

Either *P* or *Q*

Not *P*

———

So, *Q*

to the S-invalid form

If *P*, then *Q*

Not *P*

———

So, *Q*

The first form is S-valid while the second is not, yet the two forms are very nearly identical. In fact, the *only* difference between them is that the first has the sentential operator "either—or . . ." where the other has "if—, then . . .". But, with respect to their syntax, these operators are the same: Each has two blanks, and each becomes a sentence when we fill in its blanks with clauses. Accordingly, the explanation of the fact that only one of the forms is S-valid must have to do with the semantics of these sentential operators. The meaning of "either — or . . ." is such that a sentence of the form "either *P* or *Q*" is true only if at least one of the clauses in it is true, and this is why arguments with the first sentential form are valid. Similarly, it is the meaning of "if —, then . . ." that accounts for the invalidity of arguments with the second form. Some sentences of the form "if *P*, then *Q*" are true even though both of the simple clauses in them are false. (Consider, for example, "If this is the last chapter of this book, this book has only four chapters.") Hence, there can be arguments of the second form that have true premises and false conclusions. The S-validity and S-invalidity of argument forms therefore depends on the *meanings* of the sentential operators appearing in those forms.

Accordingly, we will make sure that, for each of the important English sentential operators, there is an operator in our model corresponding to it, both syntactically *and* semantically. Of course, the correspondence will not always be exact; a simplified model cannot capture all the richness and variety of the language that it models. But we will at least try to ensure that the operators of our model resemble the corresponding English operators in those ways that bear on the S-validity of English argument forms. To the extent that we succeed, our model will provide us with a clear picture of the conditions under which sentential forms are S-valid.

Since the sentential form of an argument is a pattern of sentential operators and simple clauses, and since our first model of English will only model form of this sort, we call it **clause logic** (or **CL**). We will devote the rest of this chapter, as well as Chapters 5 and 6, to the development of CL and to the discussion of its relation to English.

Exercises 4.1

1. *Defend or criticize:* In the sense in which we are using the term *model,* the game of Monopoly is a model of real estate dealing.

2. *Defend or criticize:* When we say that an English clause is *complex,* we are describing its syntax, not its semantics.

3. *Defend or criticize:* While the idea of S-validity is a semantic idea, the idea of sentential form is a syntactic idea.

4. *Defend or criticize:* A person can know all the syntactic rules of a language without knowing any of its semantic rules, and a person can know all the semantic rules of a language without knowing any of its syntactic rules.

5. Suppose that we set up a secret code. In the code, a *cough* means "it's raining," a *sneeze* means "it's snowing," a *clap followed by* a *cough* means "it's not raining," and *a clap followed by a sneeze* means "it's not snowing."

Is this code a model of English? State the code's rules of vocabulary, formation, and valuation. What are the expressions of the code? What are its wffs?

4.2 The Syntax of Sentence Letters and Symbolic Operators

In this section, we begin our description of clause logic by stating its syntactic rules—its rules of vocabulary and rules of formation. In the next section we will state its semantic rules—its rules of valuation.

The expressions of English are words and punctuation marks, but CL has three different kinds of expressions:

E1.   Some expressions of CL are *sentence letters.* These are capital English letters.*

E2.   Some expressions of CL are *symbolic operators.* CL has exactly five:

the dash: —

the ampersand: &

the vel: ∨

the arrow: →

the double arrow: ↔

E3.   Some expressions of CL are *punctuation devices.* CL has two:

the left-hand parenthesis: (

the right-hand parenthesis:)

Only these marks are expressions of CL.

As the wffs of English are sentences, the wffs of CL are **symbolic sentences.** The following rules of formation tell us which strings of CL's expressions are symbolic sentences:

F1:   A sentence letter is a symbolic sentence all by itself.

F2:   The result of writing a dash in front of a symbolic sentence is a symbolic sentence.

---

* English has twenty-six such letters, more than we will ever need in this book. If we were to need more, we could get them by using numerical subscripts.

F3: The result of flanking* an ampersand with symbolic sentences and enclosing the whole in parentheses is a symbolic sentence.

F4: The result of flanking a vel with symbolic sentences and enclosing the whole in parentheses is a symbolic sentence.

F5: The result of flanking an arrow with symbolic sentences and enclosing the whole in parentheses is a symbolic sentence.

F6: The result of flanking a double arrow with symbolic sentences and enclosing the whole in parentheses is a symbolic sentence.

If a string of expressions can be put together in accordance with these rules, it is a symbolic sentence of CL. If it can't be put together in accordance with these rules, it's not a symbolic sentence. Thus CL's rules of formation completely determine the set of CL's symbolic sentences.

Consider, for example, the string

$(P \lor (Q \to R)$.

This string is *not* a symbolic sentence of CL. If it were, it would have been constructed in accordance with CL's rules of formation. But, then, it would contain *four* parentheses—two added with the vel (F4) and two with the arrow (F5). Since the string contains only *three* parentheses, it can't be a symbolic sentence.

Or consider the string:

$(-(P \lor Q) \to (R \leftrightarrow S))$.

To show that this string *is* a symbolic sentence, we can simply build it up, step by step, using the rules of formation:

Step 1: "P", "Q", "R", and "S" are all symbolic sentences (rule F1).

Step 2: "$(P \lor Q)$" is a symbolic sentence (step 1 and rule F4), and hence so is "$-(P \lor Q)$" (rule F2).

Step 3: "$(R \leftrightarrow S)$" is a symbolic sentence (step 1 and rule F6).

Step 4: "$(-(P \lor Q) \to (R \leftrightarrow S))$" is a symbolic sentence (steps 2 and 3, and rule F5).

Since we can build the original string in this way using the rules of formation, it is a wff of CL.

The symbolic sentence that we used as an example in the last paragraph consists of two long symbolic sentences—namely, "$-(P \lor Q)$" and "$(R \leftrightarrow S)$"—that have been linked together by an arrow. We therefore knew from the outset that the last rule used in the construction of the sample sentence was F5,

---

* To *flank* an operator with sentences is to put one sentence on its left and one on its right.

the rule having to do with the arrow. Indeed, we will *always* be able to tell which rule was used last in the construction of a given symbolic sentence. The trick is to look at the very first mark in the sentence, which must be a sentence letter, a dash, or a left-hand parenthesis. If the first mark in a given sentence is a sentence letter, the only rule used in constructing that sentence was F1. If the first mark is a dash, the last rule must have been F2. If the first mark is a parenthesis, the last rule must have been F3, F4, F5, or F6, depending on whether the parenthesis was introduced with an ampersand, a vel, an arrow, or a double arrow.

Accordingly, we can introduce the following terminology for describing symbolic sentences:

SENTENCE LETTER: A symbolic sentence is a **sentence letter** if the only rule used in its formation is F1.

PRINCIPAL OPERATOR: When we view a symbolic sentence as having been built up in steps from sentence letters and symbolic operators, the operator that is introduced last is the sentence's **principal operator.**

NEGATION: A symbolic sentence is a **negation** if the last rule used in its formation is F2. That is, a symbolic sentence is a negation if its principal operator is the dash.

CONJUNCTION: A symbolic sentence is a **conjunction** if the last rule used in its formation is F3. That is, a symbolic sentence is a conjunction if its principal operator is the ampersand. The sentences flanking a conjunction's ampersand are called its **conjuncts.**

DISJUNCTION: A symbolic sentence is a **disjunction** if the last rule used in its formation is F4 — in other words, if its principal operator is a vel. The sentences flanking a disjunction's vel are its **disjuncts.**

CONDITIONAL: A symbolic sentence is a **conditional** if the last rule used in its formation is F5 — in other words, if its principal operator is an arrow. The symbolic sentence to the arrow's left is the conditional's **antecedent;** the one to the arrow's right is the conditional's **consequent.**

BICONDITIONAL: A symbolic sentence is a **biconditional** if the last rule used in its formation is F6 — in other words, if its principal operator is a double arrow. The symbolic sentences flanking a biconditional's double arrow are called the **sides** of the biconditional.

We can use these new terms to classify symbolic sentences like this:

sentence letters	(1)	negations of sentence letters	(6)
conjunctions	(2)	negations of conjunctions	(7)
disjunctions	(3)	negations of disjunctions	(8)
conditionals	(4)	negations of conditionals	(9)
biconditionals	(5)	negations of biconditionals	(10)

negations of negations (11)

This grouping is *exclusive:* No symbolic sentence falls into more than one group. It is also *exhaustive:* Every symbolic sentence falls into at least one group.

This eleven-way grouping of symbolic sentences will be important to us in Chapter 6, when we develop a system of derivation for CL. To talk about the grouping conveniently, we say that, in finding a symbolic sentence's place in this grouping, we have identified the sentence's *basic form.*

Exercises 4.2

1. How many symbolic sentences are there in CL that don't contain any expressions except the sentence letter "P" or the dash? How many sentences are there in CL that don't contain any expressions except the sentence letter "P" or the vel?

2. For each of the following sequences of marks, prove either that it is a symbolic sentence or that it is not:

a. P
b. $-$P
c. $--$P
d. $-(-$P$)$
e. (p & q)
f. $(-$P & Q$)$
g. $-((P \lor Q) \lor (P \lor R))$
h. $((P \lor Q) \lor -P$ & R$)$
i.)P $\lor$ Q(
j. $(R \leftrightarrow (S \lor T) \rightarrow -Q)$
k. P $\rightarrow (Q \lor R)$
l. $(P \leftrightarrow (Q \rightarrow (R \lor P)))$
m. $((P \lor Q) \lor R)$ & $-P)$
n. $((P \lor Q) P$ & Q $(P \lor Q))$
o. $(P \lor Q \lor R)$
p. $(P$ & $(P$ & $(P$ & P$)))$

3. For each of the following symbolic sentences, identify its basic form:

a. $--$P
b. $---$P
c. $(-$P & $-$Q$)$
d. $-(-$P & $-$Q$)$
e. $((P \lor Q) \rightarrow R)$
f. $(P \lor (Q \rightarrow R))$
g. $(-(P \lor Q) \leftrightarrow (P \lor R))$
h. $-(-(P \lor Q) \leftrightarrow (P \lor R))$
i. $-(-((-P \lor (Q \lor R)) \rightarrow (Q \lor R))$ & P$)$
j. $((P \lor Q) \leftrightarrow -((P$ & Q$) \rightarrow (P \lor Q)))$

4. Construct each of the following:
  a. a conditional whose antecedent is a negation
  b. the negation of a conditional
  c. a biconditional whose sides are both the negations of disjunctions
  d. a conjunction whose conjuncts are both conjunctions
  e. a conditional whose antecedent is the negation of a negation and
     whose consequent is the negation of a biconditional.

5. *Defend or criticize:* To say that a sentence is a conditional is to describe that sentence's syntax, not its semantics.

6. *Defend or criticize:* Every exclusive grouping is also exhaustive, and every exhaustive grouping is also exclusive.

7. *Defend or criticize:* To identify a symbolic sentence's principal operator is to identify its basic form.

4.3 The Semantics of Sentence Letters and Symbolic Operators

Having stated CL's syntactic rules, we now turn to its semantic rules. Since we want the semantics of CL to correspond to the semantics of English, we need values corresponding to truth and falsity, and arrangements corresponding to possible situations.

As the values of English sentences are truth and falsity, the values of symbolic sentences of CL are *t* and *f*. There are logical systems with more (or fewer) than two values, but we will not discuss any of these systems in this book.

As English sentences are true or false in possible situations, CL's symbolic sentences have the value *t* or the value *f* in *valuations:*

A **valuation** is an assignment of values to sentence letters.

Some valuations are valuations for sentences:

A valuation *for a symbolic sentence* is the assignment of exactly one value, either *t* or *f*, to each of the sentence letters appearing in that symbolic sentence. (If a given sentence letter occurs more than once in the symbolic sentence, it is assigned the same value on all occurrences.)

And some valuations are valuations for groups—or, as we will say, *sets*—of sentences:

A valuation *for a set of symbolic sentences* is the assignment of exactly one value, either *t* or *f*, to each of the sentence letters appearing in the sentences in the set.

There are, for example, four valuations for the set of sentences containing "(P & Q)" and "−(P → Q)"—one in which both "P" and "Q" have the value *t*; one in which "P" has the value *t* while "Q" has the value *f*; one in which "P" has the value *f* while "Q" has the value *t*; and one in which both "P" and "Q" have the value *f*.

CL's rules of valuation determine which value a symbolic sentence has in a given valuation for it. There are six such rules:

> V1: In a given valuation, a sentence letter has whichever value the valuation assigns to it.
>
> V2: A negation has the value *t* when the negated sentence has the value *f*; otherwise, it has the value *f*.
>
> V3: A conjunction has the value *t* when both of its conjuncts have the value *t*; otherwise, it has the value *f*.
>
> V4: A disjunction has the value *f* when both of its disjuncts have the value *f*; otherwise, it has the value *t*.
>
> V5: A conditional has the value *f* when its antecedent has the value *t* and its consequent has the value *f*; otherwise, it has the value *t*.
>
> V6: A biconditional has the value *t* when its sides have the same value as one another; otherwise, it has the value *f*.

These are all of CL's semantic rules.

Just as the rules of valuation for English determine the values of English sentences in various possible situations, the rules of valuation for CL determine the values of symbolic sentences in various valuations for them. Yet CL's semantics differs in an important way from the semantics of English. If we consider a particular English sentence (say, "Babe Ruth was a better hitter than Ted Williams") and a particular situation (say, the actual one), there may be considerable disagreement about the value of the sentence in that situation. There may even be disagreement about the proper method to use for discovering the sentence's value in the situation. In the case of CL, though, disagreements of this sort cannot arise. Given a particular symbolic sentence and a valuation for it, we can always settle disputes about the sentence's value in that valuation simply by performing a calculation.

Consider, for example, the symbolic sentence

$$(-(-P \mathbin{\&} R) \lor Q)$$

and the valuation in which "R" has the value *t* while "P" and "Q" both have the value *f*. In this valuation, "R" has the value *t* (rule V1), and so does "−P" (rule V2). Accordingly, the conjunction

$$(-P \mathbin{\&} R)$$

has the value *t* (rule V3), and the negation of this conjunction,

$$-(-P \mathbin{\&} R),$$

has the value *f* (rule V2). Thus, in the given valuation, the disjunction

$$(-(-P \mathbin{\&} R) \lor Q)$$

has the value *f*, since both its disjuncts have the value *f* (rule V4).

This calculation provides us with a glimpse at the relation of CL's syntax to its semantics. In building the symbolic sentence

$$(-(-P \mathbin{\&} R) \lor Q)$$

from sentence letters, we use rules F2, F3, and F4 (in addition, of course, to rule F1). But for each of these rules of formation, there is a corresponding rule of valuation. The result of using rule F2 is a negation, and rule V2 tells us how the values of negations are determined by the values of their components. Similarly, the result of using F3 is a conjunction, and V3 tells us how the values of conjunctions are determined by the values of their components. The same sort of thing can be said of the remaining steps in the construction of the symbolic sentence. For *each* rule of formation that allows us to put components together to form a symbolic sentence, there is a rule of valuation telling us how the value of that symbolic sentence is determined by the values of its components.

Of course, every symbolic sentence, regardless of its length or complexity, is built up, step by step, in accordance with CL's rules of formation. So, it follows that, once we have chosen a valuation for a symbolic sentence (that is, once we have assigned values to its sentence letters), we can *always* use CL's rules of valuation to calculate the value of the sentence in that valuation. *The value of a complex symbolic sentence is completely determined by the values of the sentence letters in it.*

Exercises 4.3

1. Calculate the values of each of the following sentences in the valuation in which "P" and "Q" have the value *t* while "R" has the value *f*:

    a. $((P \mathbin{\&} Q) \mathbin{\&} -R)$
    b. $(P \to (Q \leftrightarrow R))$
    c. $((Q \to R) \to -(P \to Q))$
    d. $--((-P \to Q) \leftrightarrow ((P \lor -Q) \mathbin{\&} R))$
    e. $(R \to (((P \lor Q) \mathbin{\&} (-P \to P)) \to (Q \lor (P \lor R))))$

2. Calculate the values of sentences (a) through (e) from the previous exercise in the valuation in which "P", "Q", and "R" all have the value *f*.

3. *Defend or criticize:* If we find that one of a conjunction's conjuncts has the value *f*, we can infer that the entire conjunction has the value *f*.

4. *Defend or criticize:* If we find that one of a conjunction's conjuncts has the value *t*, we can infer that the entire conjunction has the value *t*.

5. *Defend or criticize:* If we find that one of a disjunction's disjuncts has the value *f*, we can infer that the entire disjunction has the value *f*.

6. *Defend or criticize:* If we find that one of a disjunction's disjuncts has the value *t*, we can infer that the entire disjunction has the value *t*.

7. *Defend or criticize:* If we find that a conditional's antecedent has the value *f*, we can infer that the entire conditional has the value *t*.

8. *Defend or criticize:* If we find that a conditional's consequent has the value *t*, we can infer that the entire conditional has the value *t*.

4.4 Constructing Truth Tables

There are four valuations for the symbolic sentence "(P & Q)"—one in which both "P" and "Q" have the value *t*; one in which "P" has the value *t* while "Q" has the value *f*; and so on. It is always possible to describe these valuations in words, but there is a better way. As we will show in this section, we can construct tabular diagrams called **truth tables.**

Table 4.1 shows the beginning of a truth table.

P	Q	Table 4.1
t	*t*	
t	*f*	
f	*t*	
f	*f*	

A horizontal row of "*t*"s and "*f*"s on the table is called a *line.* Each line of the table corresponds to one of the four valuations for "(P & Q)". The first line corresponds to the valuation in which "P" and "Q" both have the value *t*, the second to the valuation in which "P" has the value *t* while "Q" has the value *f*, and so on.

We can expand the truth table beyond this list of valuations, as shown in Table 4.2:

P	Q	(P & Q)	
t	t	t	Table 4.2
t	f	f	
f	t	f	
f	f	f*	

A vertical row of "*t*"s and "*f*"s on the table is a *column*. The column beneath "(P & Q)" shows, for each of the four lines of the table, the value of "(P & Q)" on that line. This column has a "*t*" on the first line because "P" and "Q" both have the value *t* on that line; it has an "*f*" on the second line because "Q" has the value *f* on that line; and so on. Thus, since each of the valuations for "(P & Q)" corresponds to exactly one of the table's lines, the table shows us at a glance the value of that sentence in each of the valuations for it.

We can expand the table still further, as in Table 4.3.

P	Q	(P & Q)	(P ∨ Q)	(P → Q)	(P ↔ Q)	−P	
t	t	t	t	t	t	f	Table 4.3
t	f	f	t	f	f	f	
f	t	f	t	t	f	t	
f	f	f	f	t	t	t	

When we expand the table in this way, we get a table for five different symbolic sentences, not counting "P" and "Q". (A table is a table *for* a given sentence if it shows the values that the sentence has in the various valuations for it.)

From Table 4.3, we can read off *all* of CL's rules of valuation. The first column to the right of the double line shows the rule of valuation for conjunctions (V3); the second shows the rule for disjunctions (V4); and so on. The table can therefore serve as a handy reminder of CL's semantics.

Tables of this sort are also useful in calculating the values of symbolic sentences in the various valuations for them. For example, if we want to know the value of the sentence

$$(P \rightarrow -(R \lor -Q))$$

---

* In constructing truth tables, we will always place "*t*"s and "*f*"s directly beneath the principal operator of any sentence that is not a sentence letter.

in each of its valuations, we can simply construct the table in Table 4.4.

P	Q	R	−Q	(R ∨ −Q)	−(R ∨ −Q)	(P → −(R ∨ −Q))	Table 4.4
t	*t*	*t*	*f*	*t*	*f*	*f*	
t	*t*	*f*	*f*	*f*	*t*	*t*	
t	*f*	*t*	*t*	*t*	*f*	*f*	
t	*f*	*f*	*t*	*t*	*f*	*f*	
f	*t*	*t*	*f*	*t*	*f*	*t*	
f	*t*	*f*	*f*	*f*	*t*	*t*	
f	*f*	*t*	*t*	*t*	*f*	*t*	
f	*f*	*f*	*t*	*t*	*f*	*t*	

The column on the far right of this table shows the value of the original conditional in each of the valuations for it. For example, the "*f*" at the top of this column shows that the conditional has the value *f* when "P", "Q", and "R" all have the value *t*, and the "*t*" at the bottom of this column shows that the conditional has the value *t* when "P", "Q", and "R" all have the value *f*.

Why does this table have eight lines when others have only four? A truth table for a given sentence has exactly one line for each of the sentence's valuations. If the sentence has only one sentence letter in it, there will be only two valuations for it and only two lines in its truth table. But if a sentence has two sentence letters in it, there will be four valuations for it and four lines in its truth table (as in the table for "(P & Q)"). And if a sentence has three sentence letters in it, there will be eight valuations for it and eight lines in its truth table (as in Table 4.4). Thus, the number of lines in a truth table *doubles* each time we add another sentence letter to the table. Mathematicians record this fact by saying that the number of lines in a truth table for a given symbolic sentence is 2^n, where *n* is the number of different sentence letters in that symbolic sentence.

The first step in constructing a truth table for a given sentence is to figure out the number of lines the table will have. Once we know this, we can mechanically fill in the part of the table to the left of the vertical double lines. First, we give each of the sentence letters in the given symbolic sentence its own column. Next we fill in the column immediately to the left of the double line, like this:

> Begin with a "*t*", alternate "*t*"s and "*f*"s, and end when the column has the right number of lines in it.

Then we fill in the next column to the left like this:

> Begin with a "*t*", alternate *pairs* of "*t*"s and "*f*"s, and end when the column has the right number of lines in it.

Then we fill in the next column to the left, like this:

> Begin with a *"t"*, alternate *quadruples* of *"t"*'s and *"f"*'s, and end when the column has the right number of lines in it.

If we continue this process (alternating groups of eight, then sixteen, then thirty-two, and so on) we will systematically list *all* the valuations for the given sentence.

Having set up the display of valuations in Table 4.4, we calculated the column for "−Q" as a step toward finding the column for "(R ∨ −Q)", and we calculated the column for "(R ∨ −Q)" as a step toward finding the column for "−(R ∨ −Q)". Since this sentence was the consequent of the conditional

$$(P \rightarrow -(R \vee -Q))$$

and since we already had a column for the conditional's antecedent (on the left of the double line), it was easy to calculate the column for the whole conditional. For, according to rule V5, a conditional's value is *f* when and only when its antecedent has the value *t* and its consequent has the value *f*.

The preceding example illustrates a typical pattern. When constructing truth tables, we generally prepare ourselves for finding the columns for complex sentences by finding the columns for their components. Thus, to find the column for a conjunction, we first find the columns for its conjuncts; to find the column for a negation, we first find the column for the negated sentence; to find the column for a conditional, we first find the columns for its antecedent and consequent; and so on. Working step by step in this manner, it is easy to calculate columns for any sentence, even one that is very long and complex.

Exercises 4.4

1. Although CL does not, some systems have the operators "|" (down-stroke) and "↓" (down-arrow), whose truth tables look like this:

P	Q	(P | Q)	(P ↓ Q)
t	*t*	*f*	*f*
t	*f*	*t*	*f*
f	*t*	*t*	*f*
f	*f*	*t*	*t*

State in words a rule of valuation for "|" and a rule of valuation for "↓".

2. In a truth table with just four lines, there can be no more than *sixteen* different columns.

    a. Construct a truth table for "P" and "Q" on which you show all sixteen different columns. (Number the columns from 1 to 16, beginning at the left.)

    b. Which column gives the values for "−P" on each of the table's four lines?

    c. Which for "(P → Q)"? For "(Q → P)"?

    d. For "(−P ↔ Q)"? For "−(P ↔ Q)"?

    e. For "(P & −P)"? For "(Q ∨ −Q)"?

    f. For "−(P → Q)"? For "(−P → Q)"? For "(P → −Q)"?

3. *Defend or criticize:* To calculate the column for a symbolic sentence on a truth table, we simply calculate the value of the sentence on each of the table's lines.

4. *Defend or criticize:* Each line on a truth table for a given symbolic sentence corresponds to exactly one valuation for that sentence, and each valuation for the sentence corresponds to exactly one line on the table.

5. Construct truth tables for each of the following sentences. (Save the tables; we will refer to them in the exercises for the next section.)

    a. (P ∨ (−P ∨ Q))   b. −(P → P)

    c. (((P → Q) → Q) → Q)   d. ((P → Q) ↔ (R → −P))

    e. ((P & −P) → (Q & −R))   f. −((P → Q) & (R → −P))

    g. (P & ((Q ∨ R) → −P))   h. (P & ((P & Q) → Q))

    i. ((P ∨ (Q ↔ R)) → −(R & P))   j. (−(P & Q) ∨ −(R → Q))

4.5 Using Truth Tables to Classify Symbolic Sentences

    Truth tables help us to categorize symbolic sentences, pairs of symbolic sentences, and sets of symbolic sentences. In this section, we introduce some common labels used in the categorization.

    As you may have noticed when doing Exercise 4.4.5, some symbolic sentences always have the value *t*, some always have the value *f*, and others sometimes have the value *t* and sometimes the value *f*. We will mark these distinctions with special terminology, as follows:

A symbolic sentence is a **CL-tautology** just in case it has the value *t* in every valuation for it.

A symbolic sentence is a **CL-contradiction** just in case it has the value *f* in every valuation for it.

A symbolic sentence is a **CL-contingency** just in case it has the value *t* in at least one valuation for it and the value *f* in at least one valuation.

Obviously, these definitions imply that every symbolic sentence of CL is a CL-tautology, a CL-contradiction, or a CL-contingency.

Each line on the truth table for a given symbolic sentence corresponds to exactly one valuation for that sentence, and each valuation for the sentence corresponds to exactly one line on the sentence's truth table. We can therefore discover which of our new terms applies to a given symbolic sentence simply by examining that sentence's column on a truth table. A symbolic sentence is a CL-tautology just in case its column contains a "*t*" on each line; it is a CL-contradiction just in case its column contains an "*f*" on each line; and it is a CL-contingency just in case its column contains both "*t*"s and "*f*"s. Thus, we can use truth tables to tell whether given sentences are CL-tautologies, CL-contradictions, or CL-contingencies.

We also can use truth tables to test *pairs* of symbolic sentences for *CL-equivalence:*

> Two symbolic sentences are **CL-equivalent** just in case they have the same value in every valuation for them.

To tell whether two symbolic sentences are CL-equivalent, we need only put them both on the same truth table and compare their columns. If the columns are identical, the sentences are CL-equivalent. If the columns differ in any way, the sentences are not CL-equivalent.

Finally, we can use truth tables to tell whether *sets* of sentences are *CL-consistent:*

> A set of symbolic sentences is **CL-consistent** just in case there is a valuation for those sentences in which they all have the value *t* together; otherwise, the set is **CL-inconsistent.**

To tell whether a set of sentences is CL-consistent, we need only put all the sentences on the same truth table and examine the table's lines. If there is a line on which all the sentences in the set have the value *t*, the set is CL-consistent; otherwise, the set is CL-inconsistent.

Exercises 4.5

1. *Defend or criticize:* The negation of any CL-tautology is a CL-contradiction, the negation of any CL-contradiction is a CL-tautology, and the negation of any CL-contingency is a CL-contingency.

2. By examining their truth tables, discover which of the symbolic sentences listed in Exercise 4.4.5 are CL-tautologies, which CL-contingencies, and which CL-contradictions.

3. *Defend or criticize:* Every CL-contradiction is the negation of a CL-tautology.

4. By examining truth tables,
   a. find a short symbolic sentence that is CL-equivalent to "(((P → Q) → Q) → Q)" (see Exercise 4.4.2.a),
   b. find a short sentence that is CL-equivalent to "((P ∨ Q) & (P ↔ Q))" (see Exercise 4.4.2.a),
   c. show that "−(P ↔ Q)" is equivalent to "(−P ↔ Q)",
   d. show that "(P ∨ Q)" is CL-equivalent to "−(−P & −Q)" and that "(P & Q)" is CL-equivalent to "−(−P ∨ −Q)".

5. *Defend or criticize:* Two symbolic sentences are CL-equivalent just in case the biconditional of which they are the sides is a CL-tautology.

6. Using truth tables, find out whether the following sets of symbolic sentences are CL-consistent:

   Set a: "(P → Q)", "P", and "−Q"

   Set b: "(P ∨ Q)", "P", "Q"

   Set c: "(−P ∨ Q)", "(R ∨ −Q)", and "(−P ↔ Q)"

7. *Defend or criticize:* If every sentence in a given set is a CL-contingency, the set is CL-consistent.

8. *Defend or criticize:* A set containing only one symbolic sentence is CL-inconsistent just in case that sentence is a CL-contradiction.

4.6 Using Truth Tables to Test Symbolic Arguments for CL-Validity

Our primary purpose in developing a simplified model of English is to bring to light the features of arguments relevant to questions of the S-validity of their sentential forms. If we are going to use CL to illuminate these features, we must find items of CL corresponding to arguments in English, and we must find some property of those items corresponding to S-validity. We do this in this section. As you might have guessed, the items of CL that correspond to arguments in English will be called *symbolic arguments,* and the property that corresponds to S-validity will be called *CL-validity.*

Since Chapter 1, we have been representing arguments with lists of sentences. At the top of one of these lists are the argument's premises, beneath the list of premises is a horizontal line, and beneath the line is the argument's conclusion, preceded by the word "so". We can easily duplicate this pattern in

CL using symbolic sentences in place of English sentences. We might, for example, write this:

$$(P \rightarrow (Q \vee R))$$
$$-((Q \vee R) \mathrel{\&} -P)$$

So, $(P \leftrightarrow (Q \vee R))$

We call such a list of symbolic sentences a **symbolic argument.** The sentences above the line are the argument's *premises,* and the one below the line is its *conclusion.*

Strictly speaking, the concept of validity does not apply to symbolic arguments. Validity is defined in terms of truth and falsity, and symbolic sentences do not have these values. Still, symbolic sentences can have the values *t* and *f*, which correspond to truth and falsity in some obvious ways. We can therefore define a new notion of validity — CL-validity — that is closely related to the validity of arguments in English:

> A symbolic argument is **CL-valid** just in case there is no valuation in which its premises have the value *t* while its conclusion has the value *f*.

Roughly speaking, CL-validity stands to symbolic arguments as validity stands to English arguments.

A valuation in which a symbolic argument's premises have the value *t* and its conclusion the value *f* is called a **counterexample** to that symbolic argument. We can say, then, that a symbolic argument is CL-valid just in case there is no counterexample to it.

Since truth tables provide us with a way of finding counterexamples to symbolic arguments, they provide us with a test for CL-validity. Consider, for example, Table 4.5, which shows the truth table for the symbolic argument we used as an example earlier in this section.

P	Q	R	$(P \rightarrow (Q \vee R))$	$-((Q \vee R) \mathrel{\&} -P)$	$(P \leftrightarrow (Q \vee R))$
t	*t*	*t*	*t*	*t*	*t*
t	*t*	*f*	*t*	*t*	*t*
t	*f*	*t*	*t*	*t*	*t*
t	*f*	*f*	*f*	*t*	*f*
f	*t*	*t*	*t*	*f*	*f*
f	*t*	*f*	*t*	*f*	*f*
f	*f*	*t*	*t*	*f*	*f*
f	*f*	*f*	*t*	*t*	*t*

Table 4.5

Is there a line of this truth table on which the argument's premises have the value *t* while its conclusion has the value *f*? No. The only lines on which the premises all have the value *t* are the first, second, third, and eighth. But, on each of these lines, the conclusion has the value *t* as well. There are, to be sure, lines on which the conclusion has the value *f*: the fourth, fifth, sixth, and seventh. But these lines don't show that the argument is CL-invalid, since they are not lines on which the premises have the value *t*. So, there are no lines on which the premises have the value *t* while the conclusion has the value *f*.

Since every valuation for the symbolic argument corresponds to a line of the truth table, it follows that there is no valuation in which the argument's premises have the value *t* while its conclusion has the value *f*—or, in other words, that there is no counterexample to the argument. From this it follows that the symbolic argument is CL-valid.

Consider another symbolic argument:

1. P
2. ((−P & R) → Q)
3. (−Q ∨ R)
   _____
4. So, −R

To test this argument for CL-validity, we can construct the truth table in Table 4.6.

Table 4.6

(1)					(2)	(3)		(4)
P	Q	R	−P	(−P & R)	((−P & R) → Q)	−Q	(−Q ∨ R)	−R
t	*t*	*t*	*f*	*f*	*t*	*f*	*t*	*f*
t	*t*	*f*	*f*	*f*	*t*	*f*	*f*	*t*
t	*f*	*t*	*f*	*f*	*t*	*t*	*t*	*f*
t	*f*	*f*	*f*	*f*	*t*	*t*	*t*	*t*
f	*t*	*t*	*t*	*t*	*t*	*f*	*t*	*f*
f	*t*	*f*	*t*	*f*	*t*	*f*	*f*	*t*
f	*f*	*t*	*t*	*t*	*f*	*t*	*t*	*f*
f	*f*	*f*	*t*	*f*	*t*	*t*	*t*	*t*

Here the columns for the argument's premises are numbered (1), (2), and (3), and the column for its conclusion is numbered (4).

On the first and third lines of this table, the argument's premises all have the value *t*, while its conclusion has the value *f*. There are therefore two counter-examples to the symbolic argument—one (corresponding to the first line of the table) in which "P", "Q", and "R" all have the value *t*, and one (corresponding to the third line) in which "P" and "R" have the value *t* while "Q" has the value *f*. Hence, the symbolic argument is CL-invalid.

Finally, consider this symbolic argument:

A

$((-A \ \& \ C) \rightarrow B)$

$(-B \lor C)$

_____

So, $-C$

If we are observant, we can tell that this argument is CL-invalid without bothering to construct a truth table. This symbolic argument is exactly the same as the last one except that it has "A" wherever the last one had "P", "B" wherever the last one had "Q", and "C" wherever the last one had "R". In consequence, the pattern of "*t*"s and "*f*"s in this argument's truth table will be exactly the same as the pattern in Table 4.6. Hence, the table for this argument, like the table for the last one, will reveal counterexamples on its first and third lines. Without constructing another truth table, then, we can tell that the sample argument is CL-invalid.

Exercises 4.6

1. *Defend or criticize:* There is a counterexample to a symbolic argument only if that argument is CL-invalid.

2. *Defend or criticize:* If an English argument has an S-valid sentential form, that English argument is CL-valid.

3. *Defend or criticize:* When "P" and "Q" both have the value *t*, the symbolic argument:

$(P \rightarrow Q)$

Q

_____

So, P

is CL-valid.

4. Using truth tables, check the following symbolic arguments for CL-validity:

a. $((P \ \& \ Q) \rightarrow R)$

  $(R \rightarrow Q)$

  _____

  So, $(R \lor -Q)$

b. $-P$

  _____

  So, $(P \rightarrow (Q \lor R))$

c. $((P \rightarrow Q) \rightarrow R)$

  $-(-R \rightarrow (P \ \& \ Q))$
  _____

  So, $(P \rightarrow R)$

d. $(P \rightarrow -(Q \rightarrow R))$

  $-Q$

  $(-P \rightarrow R)$
  _____

  So, R

e. $(P \leftrightarrow (Q \lor R))$

  $(Q \rightarrow (R \lor -P))$
  _____

  So, $-Q$

f. $-(P \rightarrow Q)$

  $(P \leftrightarrow Q)$
  _____

  So, $(Q \ \& -Q)$

5. *Defend or criticize:* If the conclusion of a symbolic argument is a CL-tautology, the argument is CL-valid, regardless of its premises.

6. *Defend or criticize:* If the premises of a symbolic argument are CL-inconsistent, the argument is CL-valid, regardless of its conclusion.

7. *Defend or criticize:* If a symbolic argument has exactly two premises, and if we form the conditional whose antecedent is the conjunction of those premises and whose consequent is its conclusion, then the conditional will be a CL-tautology just in case the symbolic argument with which we began is CL-valid.

8. *Defend or criticize:* A symbolic argument is CL-valid just in case the set containing its premises and the negation of its conclusion is CL-inconsistent.

4.7 Object Languages and Metalanguages

If we write an essay about the moon, it's highly unlikely that we will confuse our object of study with the language in which we are writing. The moon, after all, is a bright object in the night sky, while English is a system of marks governed by syntactic and semantic rules. But when we write about a language, such as CL, which is also a system of marks, it is all too easy to confuse the language that we are describing with the one in which we are describing it.

To see this, consider again the definition of CL-validity:

A symbolic argument is CL-valid just in case there is no valuation in which its premises have the value *t* while its conclusion has the value *f*.

Noticing that the terms "CL-valid", "the value *t*", and "the value *f*" don't usually appear in English dictionaries, many people reason that this definition must be a sentence of the language CL. But this reasoning is wrong. If the definition were a sentence of CL, it would contain nothing but sentence letters, symbolic operators, and parentheses. In fact, the definition is in *English* — English that we have jazzed up with special terminology.

To avoid confusion, then, we should carefully distinguish CL from English. CL is the language that we have been writing *about*, while English is the language that we have been writing *in*. That is (in logician's jargon), CL has been our **object language**, while English has been our **metalanguage** for CL.

Typically, what makes it possible for us to use a language to talk *about* things is that it contains names that pick the things out, as if by pointing to them. For instance, what makes it possible for us to use English to talk about poets is that English contains names—such as "Milton," "Donne," and "Shakespeare"—that are used to pick out poets. Similarly, what makes it possible for us to use English to talk about CL is that English contains names that pick out CL's expressions and wffs. In the third section of this chapter, for example, we introduced names for CL's symbolic operators, as shown in Table 4.7.

Operator of CL	English Name for Operator	Table 4.7
—	dash	
&	ampersand	
∨	vel	
→	arrow	
↔	double arrow	

On the left of this table are expressions of CL; on the right are expressions of English, our metalanguage for CL.

To ensure that every well-formed formula (wff) of CL has an English name, logicians have made up a special convention. According to this convention, we can make an English name for any wff simply by enclosing that wff in quotation marks, as shown in Table 4.8.

Wff of CL	English Name for Wff	Table 4.8
P	"P"	
(P → Q)	"(P → Q)"	
(P ↔ (R ∨ −S))	"(P ↔ (R ∨ −S))"	

Here, as in Table 4.7, the items on the left are in the language CL, while those on the right are in our metalanguage for CL—namely, English.

Were we to mix CL with English, we might get something like this:

(P & Q) is a conjunction whose first conjunct is P.

What we mean here is clear enough, but it is not well put: "(P & Q)" and "P" are expressions of the symbolic language CL, while the rest of the sentence is in English. Since the sentence is about expressions of CL, we should attend to the distinction between metalanguage and object language and use our convention about names, like this:

"(P & Q)" is a conjunction whose first conjunct is "P".

But what happens when we talk *about* English *in* English — as we did, for example, in the last chapter? Must we distinguish our object language from our metalanguage even then? Logicians say yes.

Suppose, for example, that a person reads the sentence:

1. Spot is the smartest dog in the world

and that he then writes the sentence:

2. The sentence I just read contains two noun phrases — namely "Spot" and "the smartest dog in the world."

While it may seem odd to say that sentence (1) is in a different language from sentence (2), this is exactly what logicians do say. Sentence (1) is in object-English, while sentence (2) is in meta-English. The expressions of object-English — such as "Spot" and "the smartest dog in the world" — pick out animals, but the expressions of meta-English — such as "the sentence that I just read", " "Spot" ", and " "the smartest dog in the world" " — pick out expressions of object-English.

In the early chapters of this book, where we used English to talk about English, we often (deliberately) overlooked the distinction of object-English from meta-English. Our aim there was to introduce the basic concepts of logic before raising subtle issues about the use of quotation marks. But from now on we will be merciless, putting quotation marks wherever they belong.

Exercises 4.7

1. Numerals are the names of numbers. Thus, the Arabic numeral "2", the Roman numeral "II", and the English word "two" are all names for the whole number between one and three.

Bearing this in mind, say which of the following sentences are true and which false:

a. 2 is a name.
b. "2" is a number.
c. "Two" is the name of a number.
d. "II" is the name of a numeral.
e. "Two" is a name for "2".
f. " "2" " is the name of a number.

 g. " "2" " is the name of the name of a number.

 h. "Two" names the same number as "2".

 i. " "Two" " names the same name as " "2" ".

2. The following argument seems to be valid and to have true premises, but its conclusion is absurd. Where does the argument go wrong?

 1. Lions eat meat and fish.

 2. Meat and fish are words.

   ———————————

 3. So, lions eat words.

3. The following argument seems to be valid and to have true premises, but its conclusion is false. Where does the argument go wrong?

 1. $\frac{1}{2} = \frac{2}{4}$.

 2. The numerator of $\frac{1}{2}$ is 1.

   ———————————

 3. Therefore, the numerator of $\frac{2}{4}$ is 1.

4. Look back to the last sentence of the second to the last paragraph of this section. Does this sentence have the proper number of quotation marks in it? Why do the quotation marks sometimes double up?

4.8 Overview

 In this chapter, we introduced a simplified model of English, CL. The vocabulary of this model includes an infinite stock of sentence letters, five symbolic operators (the dash, the ampersand, the vel, the arrow, and the double arrow), and two punctuation devices (the left- and the right-hand parentheses).

 Using CL's rules of formation, we can construct symbolic sentences. Some of these symbolic sentences are sentence letters:

 A symbolic sentence is a *sentence letter* just in case it consists of one expression—a capital letter.

All other symbolic sentences contain a principal operator:

 When we view a symbolic sentence as having been built up in steps from sentence letters and symbolic operators, the operator that is introduced last is the sentence's *principal operator*.

The idea of a principal operator allowed us to develop terms for sorting symbolic sentences:

NEGATION: A symbolic sentence is a negation just in case its principal operator is a dash.

CONJUNCTION: A symbolic sentence is a conjunction just in case its principal operator is an ampersand. The sentences flanking the ampersand are the conjunction's *conjuncts*.

DISJUNCTION: A symbolic sentence is a disjunction just in case its principal operator is a vel. The sentences flanking the vel are the disjunction's *disjuncts*.

CONDITIONAL: A symbolic sentence is a conditional just in case its principal operator is an arrow. The symbolic sentence to the arrow's left is the conditional's *antecedent;* the one to the arrow's right is the conditional's *consequent.*

BICONDITIONAL: A symbolic sentence is a biconditional just in case its principal operator is a double arrow. The symbolic sentences flanking the double arrow are the biconditional's *sides.*

These terms apply to symbolic sentences according to their *syntax.*

The central idea in CL's *semantics* is that of a valuation:

A *valuation* for a set of symbolic sentences is an assignment of exactly one value — either *t* or *f* — to each of the sentence letters appearing in the sentences of the set.

The idea of a valuation gave us a new set of terms for describing symbolic sentences and collections of symbolic sentences:

CL-TAUTOLOGY: A symbolic sentence is a CL-tautology just in case it has the value *t* in every valuation for it.

CL-CONTRADICTION: A symbolic sentence is a CL-contradiction just in case it has the value *f* in every valuation for it.

CL-CONTINGENCY: A symbolic sentence is a CL-contingency just in case it has the value *t* in at least one valuation and the value *f* in at least one valuation.

CL-EQUIVALENCE: Two symbolic sentences are CL-equivalent just in case they have the same value as one another in every valuation for them.

CL-CONSISTENCY: A set of symbolic sentences is CL-consistent just in case there is a valuation for them in which they all have the value *t* together; otherwise, the set is CL-inconsistent.

Just as English sentences go together to form arguments, symbolic sentences can be viewed as forming *symbolic arguments*. And, as arguments in English are valid or invalid, symbolic arguments are CL-valid or CL-invalid:

> A symbolic argument is *CL-valid* just in case there is no valuation in which its premises have the value *t* while its conclusion has the value *f*. Otherwise, it is *CL-invalid*.

In effect, this definition says that a symbolic argument is CL-valid just in case there is no *counterexample* to it, a counterexample to a symbolic argument being a valuation in which the argument's premises have the value *t* while its conclusion has the value *f*.

Given a symbolic argument, we can construct a *truth table* for it. The *lines* of the table (i.e., the horizontal rows of "*t*"s and "*f*"s) correspond one to one with the valuations for the given symbolic argument, and the *columns* (that is, the vertical rows of "*t*"s and "*f*"s) therefore show the values of the argument's premises and conclusion in every valuation for them. Accordingly, by looking at the table for a given symbolic argument, we can tell whether the argument is CL-valid. If there is a line on the table on which the argument's premises have the value *t* while its conclusion has the value *f*, the line represents a counterexample to the argument, and the argument is therefore CL-invalid. However, if there is no such line, there is no counterexample to the argument, and it is therefore CL-valid.

In the discussion of this chapter, CL was our object language, and English was our metalanguage:

> On a given occasion, our *object language* is the language that we are talking *about*, and our *metalanguage* is the language we are talking *in*.

Chapter 5

CL and English

As we saw in Chapter 3, if we can show that a given argument has an S-valid sentential form, we can correctly infer that every argument of that form—including the given argument—is valid. In the hope of developing a general method for demonstrating the S-validity of argument forms and of learning what it is about arguments with S-valid forms that makes them valid, we introduced the system CL, a simplified model of English. Our plan was to capture in CL those features of English relevant to the S-validity of argument forms.

The time has now come to assess the extent to which we have succeeded in our plan. How well does CL model English? Does CL provide us with a reliable and efficient method for demonstrating the S-validity of argument forms? And does CL yield any insight into why English arguments with S-valid sentential forms are valid?

5.1 Connections between Sentential Operators and Symbolic Operators

CL provides us with a simple model of English syntax. Its sentence letters correspond to the simple clauses of English, and its symbolic operators correspond to some of the sentential operators of English. Furthermore, as English sentences are made up from simple clauses and sentential operators, CL's symbolic sentences are made up from sentence letters and symbolic operators.

Finally, as English arguments are made up from English sentences, CL's symbolic arguments are made up from CL's symbolic sentences. So, we have these connections between English syntax and the syntax of CL:

ENGLISH	CL
simple clauses	sentence letters
sentential operators	symbolic operators
sentences	symbolic sentences
arguments	symbolic arguments

CL also provides us with a simple model of English semantics. Typically, a declarative English sentence is either true or false (but not both) in a given possible situation. Similarly, a symbolic sentence of CL has either the value t or the value f (but not both) in a given valuation for it. Thus, we have these semantic correspondences between English and CL:

ENGLISH	CL
truth	the value t
falsity	the value f
possible situation	valuation

In addition, particular sentential operators of English correspond, both syntactically and semantically, to particular symbolic operators of CL. In the rest of this section, we examine some of these correspondences. Our primary objects of study are the English operators "it's not the case that", "and", "but", "although", "or", "unless", "if, then", "only if", and "if and only if". For sentences containing these operators, we will discover the relation of the sentence's value (truth or falsity) to the values of its simple clauses, and we will identify operators of CL that mirror that relation.

it's not the case that

The sentence "It's not the case that it's raining" is true when the simple clause "it's raining" is false, and false when the clause "it's raining" is true. Similarly, the symbolic sentence "−R" has the value t when "R" has the value f, and the value f when "R" has the value t. Thus, the English operator "it's not the case that" corresponds to CL's dash. In fact, the correspondence is so complete that, if an English sentence begins with "it's not the case that," we call that sentence a *negation*.

and

The sentence "It's raining and the ground is wet" is true when and only when the clauses "it's raining" and "the ground is wet" are both true. Similarly, the symbolic sentence "(R & W)" has the value *t* when and only when the sentence letters "R" and "W" both have the value *t*. Thus, the operator "and" corresponds both syntactically and semantically to CL's ampersand. In light of this correspondence, we use the term "conjunction" to refer to English sentences whose principal operator is "and".

The correspondence of the ampersand to "and" is not exact. In a symbolic conjunction, it makes no difference which conjunct comes first: "(P & C)" and "(C & P)" are CL-equivalent. But, in an English conjunction, it may make a real difference which conjunct comes first. For example, the sentence "I gave my professor a present and passed the course" differs in what it suggests, if not in what it says, from the sentence "I passed the course and gave my professor a present."

But this difference should not prevent us from saying that CL's ampersand corresponds to the English "and". Because CL is a *simplified* model of English, it cannot be nearly as subtle as English. When we are using English, the order in which we mention events often suggests the order in which they actually occurred; that's why the two sentences about giving the professor a gift suggest very different things. But in the move from English to CL, subtleties such as this are lost.

Still, in those respects that are important to us as students of logic, the English operator "and" *is* accurately represented by CL's ampersand. While "and" does not correspond to the ampersand in all respects, it does correspond to the ampersand in the respects that are important for our purposes.

but and *although*

Consider the sentences

> It's raining, but the sky is blue.
> Although it's raining, the sky is blue.

These sentences have somewhat different uses. A person who says "It's raining, but the sky is blue" expresses some surprise that it's raining while the sky is blue. And a person who says "Although it's raining, the sky is blue" expresses the same surprise, but emphasizes the point that the sky is blue while deemphasizing the point that it's raining.

Still, both of the sample sentences have something important in common with the sentence "It's raining, and the sky is blue": each is false unless the clauses "it's raining" and "the sky is blue" are both true. Since a symbolic conjunction has the value *f* unless both of its conjuncts have the value *t*, the English operators "but" and "although" both correspond to CL's ampersand— just as does the operator "and".

If the operators "and", "but", and "although" have different uses, how can they all correspond to the same operator of CL? Here again it's important to remember that CL is a *simplified* model of English. CL's operators cannot capture subtleties having to do with time, or tension, or emphasis. They can only represent facts about how the operators work in English arguments. And with respect to *these* facts, the operators "and", "but", and "although" are indistinguishable. That's why all of these operators correspond to the very same operator of CL: the ampersand.

or

The sentence "It's raining, or the ground is wet" is true when and only when at least one of its simple clauses is true. Similarly, the symbolic sentence "(R ∨ W)" has the value *t* when and only when at least one of its disjuncts has the value *t*. Hence, "or" corresponds to CL's vel. The correspondence is so complete that, if the principal operator in an English sentence is "or", we call the sentence a *disjunction*.

Some people are reluctant to believe that an English disjunction is true when *both* its disjuncts are true. To see what lies behind this reluctance, suppose that a friend says, "I owe you a dinner; I'll take you out on Tuesday or Thursday." Plainly, your friend doesn't plan to take you to dinner on *both* days, and some people infer from this that — contrary to what we have said — the disjunction "I'll take you out on Tuesday, or I'll take you out on Thursday" is *false* when both of its disjuncts are true.

In fact, however, we ought not to accept that inference. In effect, your friend made *two* statements. The first is that you are owed one dinner, and the second is that he will buy you a dinner either on Tuesday or on Thursday. It is the first of these statements, together with some obvious assumptions about your friend's generosity, that carries the implication that your friend will take you out to dinner only once. By itself, the disjunction "I'll take you out on Tuesday or Thursday" leaves open the possibility that your friend *will* take you out twice. It is because you know that your friend owes you only one dinner, and not because your friend uses the sentential operator "or", that you know you will receive only one dinner. Here — as in all other cases — a disjunction is true when one *or* both of its disjuncts is true.

unless

Your professor says, "You'll fail the course unless you take the exams." The professor's statement isn't proven false if you take the exams and pass the course; that's what your professor wants. Nor is the statement proven false if you skip the exams and fail the course. Indeed, it was probably to warn you of this possibility that your professor made the statement in the first place. Nor is the statement proven false if you take the exams and fail the course — you might take the exams and fail them, after all. But the professor's statement *is* proven false if you pass the course without taking the exams — the professor said you would *fail* unless you took the exams. Thus, the sentence "You'll fail the course unless you take the exams" is false when and only when the simple clauses "you'll fail the course" and "you take the exams" are both false. Similarly, the symbolic sentence "(C ∨ E)" has the value *f* when and only when the sentence letters "C" and "E" both have the value *f*. We say, therefore, that "unless", like "or", corresponds to CL's vel.

Of course, in saying that you'll fail unless you take the exams, the professor suggests that there is a *connection* between your not taking the exams and your failing. More precisely, the professor suggests that, if you skip the exams, you will fail *as a result* of your not having taken them. But, just as CL's operators cannot capture subtleties about time or tension or emphasis, they also cannot capture subtleties about what produces what. There is thus a nuance to "unless" that the vel does not capture.

This is not an objection to our saying that "unless" corresponds to the vel, for the nuance is not relevant to the aspects of "unless" that matter to us as students of logic. In those aspects, the vel corresponds well to "unless". The symbolic arguments

$$
\begin{array}{ccc}
(P \lor Q) & & (P \lor Q) \\
-P & \text{and} & -Q \\
\hline
\text{So, } Q & & \text{So, } P
\end{array}
$$

are both CL-valid, and the argument forms

$$
\begin{array}{cc}
P \text{ unless } Q & P \text{ unless } Q \\
\text{not } P & \text{not } Q \\
\hline
\text{So, } Q & \text{So, } P
\end{array}
$$

are both S-valid.

if, then

Relating the operator "if, then" to CL's symbolic operators raises special problems. To see why, consider the pair of sentences:

> If today is Tuesday, then tomorrow is Wednesday.
> If today is Tuesday, then tomorrow is Thursday.

Suppose, for the sake of the example, that today is in fact Monday. Then each of our sample sentences begins with a false "if"-clause and ends with a false "then"-clause. But the first sentence is true and the second is false.

As our pair of sample sentences illustrates, the truth or falsity of an "if, then" sentence is not, in general, determined simply by the truth or falsity of the clauses from which the sentence is made up. But CL's operators work differently. Whenever we use one of CL's operators to join two symbolic sentences together, the value of the result is *completely* determined by the values of its parts. So, for example, the value of a symbolic conditional is completely determined by the values of its antecedent and its consequent. So, no operator of CL corresponds very well to the English operator "if, then".

Still, the operator "if, then" corresponds well enough to CL's arrow for the purposes of logicians. For this reason, an English "if, then" sentence is called a *conditional,* the clause after the "if" is called the conditional's *antecedent,* and the clause after the "then" is called the conditional's *consequent.*

To see why the arrow is indeed the operator of CL that corresponds best to "if, then", imagine that CL has an operator, the asterisk ("*"), whose syntax is exactly the same as the ampersand's, the vel's, the arrow's, and the double arrow's. What rule of valuation should we establish for the asterisk if we want this operator to correspond as closely as possible to "if, then"?

We can break this question up into four parts: Given that we want the asterisk to correspond to "if, then", what do we want the value of "(P * Q)" to be (1) when both "P" and "Q" have the value t; (2) when "P" has the value t and "Q" has the value f; (3) when "P" has the value f and "Q" has the value t, and (4) when both "P" and "Q" have the value f? The answer to this four-part question will tell what rule of valuation we should establish for the asterisk.

For the answer to the first part of the question, notice that there are some sound English arguments of the form *modus ponens* ("if P, then Q; P; so, Q"). The premises and conclusions of such arguments are all true, since all sentences in sound arguments are true. Thus, some true English conditionals have true antecedents and true consequents. If the asterisk is to mirror this important fact about "if, then", then

"(P * Q)" must have the value t when "P" and "Q" both have the value t.

For the answer to the second part of the question, notice that all arguments of the form *modus ponens* are valid. Notice also that, if there were a true English conditional with a true antecedent and a false consequent, some argument of the form *modus ponens* would be invalid. From these observations, it follows that all English conditionals with true antecedents and false consequents are false. And if the asterisk is to mirror this important fact about "if, then", then

"(P * Q)" must have the value f when "P" has the value t and "Q" has the value f.

For the answer to the third part of our question, consider the true English sentence "If Los Angeles is in Ohio, then Los Angeles is in the United States." This sentence illustrates the fact that some true English conditionals have false antecedents and true consequents. (If there were no such conditionals, the fallacies of affirming the consequent and denying the antecedent wouldn't be fallacies!) If the asterisk is to mirror this important fact about "if, then," then

> "(P * Q)" must have the value *t* when "P" has the value *f* and "Q" has the value *t*.

For the answer to the fourth part of our question, notice that there are some sound English arguments of the form *modus tollens* ("if *P*, then Q; not *Q*; so, not *P*"). The premises and conclusions of such arguments are all true, since all sentences in sound arguments are true. Thus, some true English conditionals have false antecedents and false consequents. If the asterisk is to mirror this important fact about "if, then," then

> "(P * Q)" must have the value *t* when "P" and "Q" both have the value *f*.

Putting the answers to our four questions together, we see that the asterisk will mirror the English operator "if, then" semantically only if "(P * Q)" has the following truth table:

P	Q	(P * Q)	Table 5.1
t	*t*	*t*	
t	*f*	*f*	
f	*t*	*t*	
f	*f*	*t*	

But Table 5.1 is just the truth table for "(P → Q)"!

There is therefore no need to make up a new operator to correspond to "if, then". Although the correspondence of the arrow to "if, then" isn't perfect, the arrow does capture some important facts about "if, then", mirroring its semantics as well as possible for an operator of CL.

only if

Suppose your professor says, "You'll pass the course only if you take the exams." What would prove this statement to be false? If you take the exams, the statement isn't proven false even if you fail the course; the professor has merely said that your taking the exams is *one* of the course's requirements. Nor is the statement proven false if you skip the exams and fail the course. But the statement *is* proven false if you pass the course without having taken the exams: The professor said that you had to take the exams to pass the course. Similarly, the symbolic sentence "(P → Q)" has the value *f* when and only when "P" has the value *t* while "Q" has the value *f*. Thus, the operator "only if" corresponds to CL's arrow.

There is, however, a puzzle here. Clearly the sentence

You'll pass the course only if you take the exams

does not say the same thing as the sentence

If you pass the course, then you take the exams.

The first makes perfectly good sense; the second seems silly. How can it be, then, that both the sentential operator "if, then" and the operator "only if" correspond to CL's arrow?

By now, the outline of the answer should be familiar. The sentence "If you pass the course, then you take the exams" suggests that your passing the course could somehow *precede* and *result in* your taking the exams, and this is what seems silly. In contrast, the sentence "You'll pass the course only if you take the exams" suggests that your not taking the exams will *result in* your not passing the course, and this is probably true. Thus, the ways in which "if, then" and "only if" differ have to do with time and with what might produce what. But CL, being a simplified model of English, cannot mark differences of these sorts.

The distinctions that CL *can* mark are those having to do with the ways in which sentential operators work in arguments. And in this respect, the operator "only if" does not differ from "if, then". As the forms *modus ponens* and *modus tollens* are S-valid, so are the forms

> *P* only if *Q*
>
> *P*
> ———
> So, *Q*

and

> *P* only if *Q*
>
> Not *Q*
> ———
> So, not *P*

And, as the forms of denying the antecedent and affirming the consequent are S-invalid, so are the forms

> *P* only if *Q*
>
> Not *P*
> ———
> So, not *Q*

and

> *P* only if *Q*
>
> *Q*
>
> ———
>
> So, *P*

Thus, while the operators "if, then" and "only if" differ in what they suggest, they are strikingly similar in the ways they work in arguments. Because of these similarities, "if, then" and "only if" correspond to the same operator of CL: the arrow.

if and only if

Clearly the operator "if and only if" is closely related to the operators "if, then", "and", and "only if", and hence to CL's arrow and ampersand. But, postponing an exploration of these relations until the next section, we now view "if and only if" as a single operator and ask which of CL's operators most closely corresponds to it.

Let's imagine a professor who says, "When I grade, I don't think about anything but the final exam. You'll pass the course if and only if you pass the final." In effect, the professor says that there are only two possibilities: Either you will pass both the final and the course, or you will fail both. In other words, what the professor is *denying* is that you can pass one and fail the other. Thus, the sentence "You'll pass the course if and only if you pass the final" is false if one of the simple clauses in it is true while the other is false, and it is true otherwise.

Accordingly — since the symbolic sentence "(P ↔ Q)" has the value *f* when and only when "P" has one value and "Q" the other — the operator of CL that corresponds to "if and only if" is the double arrow. This warrants our using the term *biconditional* to refer to English sentences whose principal operator is "if and only if". The clauses flanking the "if and only if" are, of course, the English biconditional's *sides*.

Another sentential operator that corresponds to CL's double arrow is "just in case" — an operator that appears in many of the definitions in this book.

Exercises 5.1

1. *Defend or criticize:* Although we have said that the value *t* corresponds to truth and the value *f* to falsity, we could just as easily have said that the value *f* corresponds to truth and the value *t* to falsity.

2. Memo writers like to use the operator "and/or" because it sounds official. Say which of CL's operators corresponds to "and/or" and defend what you say.

3. *Defend or criticize:* The operator "because" corresponds to CL's double arrow.

4. I say, "You'll miss the plane unless you run." Is my statement proven false if you run but still miss your plane?

5. *Defend or criticize:* The operator "if, then" corresponds syntactically more closely to the arrow than to the vel.

6. *Defend or criticize:* The operator "if, then" corresponds as closely to the double arrow as it does to the arrow.

7. *Defend or criticize:* Some true English conditionals have true antecedents and true consequents. If this weren't so, there wouldn't be any sound arguments with the form *modus ponens.*

8. *Defend or criticize:* If the antecedent of an English conditional is true while its consequent is false, the conditional itself must be false. If this weren't so, some arguments with the form *modus ponens* would be invalid.

9. *Defend or criticize:* Some true conditionals have true consequents and false antecedents. If this weren't so (that is, if all true conditionals with true consequents had true antecedents), the fallacy of affirming the consequent wouldn't be a fallacy.

10. *Defend or criticize:* Some true conditionals have false antecedents and false consequents. If this weren't so, there wouldn't be any valid arguments with the form *modus tollens.*

11. In Chapter 3, we said that the form of the constructive dilemma and the form of the hypothetical syllogism are S-valid. If we take the operator "if, then" out of these forms and replace it with "only if", are the resulting forms S-valid?

12. Which of CL's operators corresponds most closely to the operator "when and only when"?

5.2 Standard English and Translating into CL

In the last section, we pointed to correspondences between particular sentential operators of English and particular symbolic operators of CL. These correspondences are permanent. To set up correspondences between particular English sentences and particular sentences of CL, though, we also need to establish *temporary* correspondences, which associate particular simple clauses of English with particular sentence letters of CL.

We set up such correspondences by means of **schemes of correspondence,** like this one:

L: the match is lit

O: there is oxygen present

S: the match was struck

To set up such a scheme, we simply associate simple English clauses with sentence letters of CL, making sure that no two different clauses are associated with the same letter.

Once we have set up a scheme of this sort, we can find complex symbolic sentences of CL that correspond, both syntactically and semantically, to complex sentences of English. We say that, in finding such symbolic sentences, we *translate* the English sentences into CL, and we call the symbolic sentences *translations* of the corresponding English sentences.

In this section, we focus on the translation of sentences that are in *Standard English:*

A sentence is in **Standard English** just in case it contains no sentential operators except "it's not the case that", "and", "or", "unless", "if, then", "only if", and "if and only if", and all of these operators are used in the usual ways.

If a sentence is in Standard English, we can translate it into CL without difficulty. We simply set up a scheme of correspondence and then replace the parts of the English sentence, including its sentential operators, with the corresponding expressions of CL.

Consider, for example, the Standard English sentence

If the match was struck, then the match is lit.

We know from the last section that the operator "if, then" corresponds to the arrow, and our scheme of correspondence associates the clauses "the match was struck" and "the match is lit" with the sentence letters "S" and "L", respectively. The symbolic sentence

$(S \rightarrow L)$

is therefore a translation of the original English sentence.

For a second example of translation from Standard English, notice that the symbolic sentence

$(L \rightarrow O)$

translates the sentence

The match is lit only if there is oxygen present.

Here again the symbolic sentence corresponds part by part to the English sentence that it translates, for (as we saw in the last section) "only if" corresponds to the arrow.

This translation may seem odd. In saying, "the match is lit only if there is oxygen present," we suggest that there must be oxygen present *before* the match will light, but the direction of the arrow in "(L → O)" seems to suggest that the match lights *before* there is oxygen present. Yet the translation is correct. As we pointed out in the last section, the direction of CL's arrow has nothing to do with the direction of time. Don't be misled by the arrow's shape; simply replace the parts of the English sentence with corresponding expressions of CL, leaving the order as it is.

As a final example, we translate the Standard English sentence

If the match is lit, then the match was struck and there is oxygen present.

Because this sentence is complex, it's useful to translate in stages. In the first stage, we identify the sentence's principal sentential operator and replace it with the corresponding operator of CL, leaving the rest of the sentence in English. The comma clearly shows that "if, then" is the sentence's principal operator. Hence, the first stage of our translation is

(the match is lit → the match was struck and there is oxygen present).

In the next stage, we work inward until we reach simple clauses:

(the match is lit → (the match was struck & there is oxygen present)).

By replacing simple clauses with the corresponding sentence letters, we get

(L → (S & O)),

which is our translation of the original sentence.

Exercises 5.2

1. *Defend or criticize:* In setting up a scheme of correspondence, we abbreviate simple English clauses with sentence letters, and the sentence letters take on the meanings of the simple clauses they abbreviate.

2. *Defend or criticize:* In our schemes of correspondence, we associate symbolic operators of CL with sentential operators of English.

3. Say which of the following sentences are in Standard English. Translate those that are in Standard English into CL, providing your own scheme of correspondence.
    a. I'm Chevy Chase, and you're not.
    b. If Sally turns in a good paper, then her teacher will be happy.
    c. Sally will get an A unless she turns in a bad paper.

d. It may rain, but Bill doesn't care.

e. It will rain, or it will be windy and the temperature will drop.

f. It will rain or it will be windy, and the temperature will drop.

g. If Jack went up the hill, then it's not the case that Jill went up the hill.

h. Since Bill won't play, Sally won't play either.

i. If Jack went up the hill, Jill did too; otherwise, she didn't.

j. The settlement of the West could only take place if the Indian problem was solved.

k. The Indian problem could be solved if an agreement could be reached on water rights.

l. Although Bill is kind to her, Mary doesn't like him.

5.3 Paraphrasing from English into Standard English

If a given sentence is in Standard English, we can use the method described in the previous section to translate it directly into CL. If a given sentence is not in Standard English, however, we must translate it in two steps. The first step is to *paraphrase* the sentence into Standard English, and the second is to translate the paraphrase into CL. The translation of the paraphrase will serve as a translation of the original sentence.

Consider, for example, the sentence

The match was not struck.

This is, of course, an abbreviation of the complex clause

It's not the case that the match was struck,

which is in Standard English. Translating the unabbreviated paraphrase of our original sentence, we get

−S,

a translation of the original sentence. To translate the original sentence into CL we had to paraphrase it into Standard English.

In the last example, we paraphrased into Standard English simply by expanding an abbreviation. But sometimes paraphrasing requires a little more thought. Imagine, for instance, a politician who says this:

Are subsidies to the dairy industry justified? I say No! Such subsidies are justified if subsidies to the tobacco industry are. But only a fool would believe *that*.

The argument in the politician's remark can be made explicit like this:

1. Subsidies to the dairy industry are justified if subsidies to the tobacco industry are.
2. Only a fool would believe that subsidies to the tobacco industry are justified.

   ---

3. So, subsidies to the dairy industry are not justified.

But how can we paraphrase the premises and conclusion of this argument into Standard English?

Let's focus for a moment on the politician's first premise. Here there are no abbreviations to expand. But since the operator " — if . . ." is not in Standard English, the sentence is not in Standard English, and we must paraphrase it as a first step toward translation.

The key to the paraphrase is that every sentence of the form "*P* if *Q*" is equivalent to the corresponding sentence of the form "if *Q*, then *P*"; an "if" clause is a conditional's antecedent regardless of where it appears in a sentence. So, we can paraphrase the politician's first premise with the equivalent sentence

> If subsidies to the tobacco industry are justified, then subsidies to the dairy industry are justified.

This sentence *is* in Standard English, and (using the obvious scheme of correspondence) we can translate it as

$$(T \rightarrow D).$$

Clearly, this translation of our paraphrase of the politician's initial sentence can serve as a translation of the sentence itself.

Let's now turn to the politician's second premise, "But only a fool would believe that subsidies to the tobacco industry are justified." A first glance might indicate that this premise is about the beliefs of fools, but a closer look reveals that its real force is to *deny* that subsidies to the tobacco industry are justified; to say that only a fool would hold a certain belief is to say, with a rhetorical flourish, that the belief is false. Accordingly, the politician's second premise can be paraphrased as

> It's not the case that subsidies to the tobacco industry are justified.

This paraphrase can be translated by the symbolic sentence

$$-T,$$

which we can therefore regard as a translation of the politician's second premise.

Both times that we paraphrased the politician, our paraphrases were *perfect:*

> A paraphrase of a sentence is **perfect** just in case it means exactly the same as the paraphrased sentence.

But it often is impossible to attain perfection in paraphrasing, and we have to settle for mere *adequacy:*

> A paraphrase of a sentence is **adequate** just in case it captures as much of what the paraphrased sentence says as we can represent in CL.

Consider, for example, the sentence:

> Mary is poor but honest.

This sentence may not seem to contain any sentential operators, but it is in fact an abbreviation of the sentence:

> Mary is poor, but Mary is honest.

Since the operator "but" is not in Standard English, we need to paraphrase further before translating into CL.

We can complete the paraphrase by moving from "Mary is poor, but Mary is honest" to the Standard English sentence

> Mary is poor, and Mary is honest.

The justification for replacing "but" with "and" is that a sentence of the form "*P* but *Q*" — like the corresponding sentence of the form "*P* and *Q*" — is true only if its component clauses are both true. Of course, the paraphrase loses the *contrast* between poverty and honesty implied by the original sentence. But since there is no way to capture this contrast in CL, the paraphrase is adequate for our purposes. All that we lose in the paraphrase is something that wouldn't have shown up in a translation anyway.

Once we have paraphrased "Mary is poor but honest" with "Mary is poor, and Mary is honest," it's easy to see that (under the obvious scheme of correspondence) its translation is

> (P & H).

Here, as in all of the other examples in this section, translation has been a two-step process. In the first step, we move from an English sentence to its paraphrase in Standard English. In the second, we move from the paraphrase directly to a symbolic sentence of CL. The result of following the process is a translation of the original English sentence.

Exercises 5.3

1. *Defend or criticize:* Standard English has only five operators: "it's not the case that", "and", "or", "if, then", and "if and only if".

2. *Defend or criticize:* Often translation is a two-step process. In the first step, we translate into Standard English, and in the second, we paraphrase the translation into CL.

3. Paraphrase each of the following sentences into Standard English, indicating whether your paraphrase is perfect or merely adequate. Then supply your own schemes of correspondence and translate the sentences into CL.

    a. The patient will die unless we operate.
    b. The patient will die if we operate.
    c. The patient will die if we don't operate.
    d. Hamlet is an unexciting play.
    e. Tom, Dick, and Harry are all politicians.
    f. Tom, Dick, and Harry talked for two hours.
    g. Jack and Jill went up the hill, and Mary's little lamb wasn't far behind.
    h. Not both Jack and Jill went up the hill.
    i. This woman is either mad or drunk.
    j. Both men are mad and drunk.
    k. Romance is the province of the rich, not the profession of the unemployed.
    l. When Hal's hot he's hot, and when he's not he's not.
    m. Sunlight not only stimulates the mind, it also cures diarrhea.
    n. A cigar store Indian is neither a cigar, a store, nor an Indian.
    o. "And" has three letters in it, while "or" has but two.
    p. Since George is dumb, he's happy.
    q. Tom keeps calling Mary even though she refuses to talk to him.
    r. Tom will keep calling Mary even if she refuses to talk to him.
    s. With a copy of our new book, you can save a lot of money on food.

4. *Defend or criticize:* Every English sentence can be paraphrased perfectly into Standard English.

5. Imagine that CL doesn't have a double arrow and that "if and only if" is not an operator of Standard English.

    a. How would you translate "Jack went up the hill if and only if Jill did" into CL? (*Hint:* Expand the sentence using "if, then", "and", and "only if".)
    b. How does the translation that you produced in part (a) relate to the one that you would have gotten using the double arrow?

5.4 Special Problems in Translation: Deviance and Intractability

The general correspondences that we have outlined between certain sentential operators of English and certain symbolic operators of CL sometimes break down. They break down, in particular, when an English operator is used in an unusual — or, as we will say, a **deviant** — way. Faced with a deviant use of an operator of Standard English, we may need to replace it with another operator of Standard English before we can translate into CL.

Suppose, for example, that Alice says to Fred,

You take my car and I'll call the police.

If we're not thinking carefully, we might notice the word "and" in this sentence and leap to the translation

(C & P).

But this would be wrong. Alice is not saying that Fred *will* take her car, and she isn't saying that she will call the police either. Rather, she is warning Fred that she will call the police *if* he takes her car. Accordingly, a correct translation of Alice's remark would be

(C → P).

Hence, the use of "and" in the original sentence is deviant. In the context of Alice's remark, the operator "and" corresponds more closely to the arrow than to the ampersand.

Here is another example of deviance:

There is coffee on the stove if you want some.

This sentence may look like a conditional, but it isn't. A person would naturally use this sentence to say that there *is* coffee on the stove. The phrase "if you want some" simply serves as an indication that the speaker is *offering* the coffee to those who may want some. But, in translating a person's remarks into CL, we should focus on what is said and ignore polite gestures. The correct paraphrase of the original sentence is therefore

There is coffee on the stove,

and its translation is simply

C.

Here, then, is another case of deviance. Although the original sentence contains an "if", its translation does not contain an arrow.

In addition to problems of deviance, translators sometimes face problems of *intractability*. These problems arise because some operators of English don't correspond to *any* operator of CL.

Consider, for example, the sentence

Tarski doubts that Secretariat won the Kentucky Derby.

The first step in translating this sentence into CL, it seems, is to paraphrase it into Standard English. But how can we paraphrase the operator "Tarski doubts that — "? The only sentential operator in Standard English with one blank in it is "it's not the case that — ", which transforms true sentences into false ones and vice versa. But the operator "Tarski doubts that — " doesn't work that way. We can know the values of simple clauses without having any clue as to the values of the sentences we get by putting those clauses into the blank in the operator "Tarski doubts that — ". Thus, *no* operator of Standard English, and no symbolic operator of CL, corresponds semantically to "Tarski doubts that — ".

Because we are unable to paraphrase the sentence "Tarski doubts that Secretariat won the Kentucky Derby" into Standard English, we must translate it into CL with a single sentence letter, like this:

W.

This is not a very revealing or interesting translation. But, given the intractability of the operator "Tarski doubts that — ", we can do no better.

Partly because of the problems of deviance and intractability, translating English into CL is an art rather than a science. In particular, it is not possible to state rules that will guarantee success on every occasion. When we translate from English into CL, it is important to be flexible and, above all, to be sensitive to what people might mean by what they say and write.

Exercises 5.4

1. Translate each of the following sentences into CL, providing your own schemes of correspondence.
   a. I'll punch you in the stomach if you stand on your head.
   b. Some men are dishonest.
   c. I'll forget about the incident — provided that you do too.
   d. The sun was not created until the fourth day.
   e. Truth is beauty, beauty truth.
   f. Although Keats thinks that truth is beauty, Shelley doesn't.
   g. If John comes to the party, I'll eat my hat.
   h. John wondered whether it's raining.
   i. I think that I have enough money, but I'll take my Visa card just in case.

j. I like bourbon as well as Scotch.

k. Stand on your head and I'll punch you in the stomach.

l. When I work a logic problem without grumbling, you can be sure that it's one I can solve.

2. *Defend or criticize:* The operator "it's possible that" is intractable, since no operator of CL corresponds to it semantically.

5.5 CL-Validity, S-Validity, and Validity

In Chapter 4, we developed the system CL in the hope that it would provide us with an effective method for demonstrating the S-validity of argument forms and show us why arguments with S-valid forms are valid. Now that we have discussed the process of translating arguments into CL, we turn to the question of what we can learn about an argument by looking at its CL-translation. Suppose, in particular, that we have succeeded in translating an argument from English into CL and that, using a truth table, we have demonstrated the translation's CL-validity. What, if anything, follows about the S-validity of the English argument's sentential form or about that argument's validity?

In answering these questions, we once again consider the McCoy argument, which we used as an example in Chapter 3:

Either McCoy is a Platonist or McCoy is an Aristotelian.

It's not the case that McCoy is a Platonist.

So, McCoy is an Aristotelian.

Under the obvious scheme of correspondence, we can translate the argument into CL like this:

$(P \lor A)$

$-P$

So, A

Then, using a truth table, we can establish that there is no valuation in which the translation's premises have the value *t* while its conclusion has the value *f* and, hence, that the translation is CL-valid. But, having shown this, what may we infer about the S-validity of the McCoy argument's sentential form or about the validity of the McCoy argument itself?

As we saw, this argument has the sentential form

P or *Q*

Not *P*

———————

So, *Q*

Suppose, just for the moment, that this argument form is S-invalid—that some sample argument of this form is invalid. On this supposition, there must be a possible situation in which the sample argument's premises are true while its conclusion is false. And, in this situation,

    a.   either the first simple clause in the sample argument is true or the second is,

    b.   the first simple clause is false, and

    c.   the second simple clause is false.

Conditions (a) and (b) must be met if the sample argument's premises are true in the situation, and condition (c) must be met if its conclusion is false in the situation.

Now, as we have seen, items of the model CL correspond to items of English. The sentence letters "P" and "A" correspond to simple clauses, the symbolic operator "∨" to the sentential operator "or", and the values *t* and *f* to truth and falsity. Accordingly, if there were a situation meeting conditions (a), (b), and (c), there would be a valuation for the sentence letters "P" and "A" in which

    a'.   "(P ∨ A)" has the value *t*,

    b'.   "P" has the value *f*, and

    c'.   "A" has the value *f*.

Clearly, such a valuation would be a counterexample to our symbolic translation of the McCoy argument. So, we now know that, if there is an invalid argument with the same sentential form as the McCoy argument, there is a counterexample to the McCoy argument's symbolic translation.

However, having demonstrated this translation's CL-validity with a truth table, we know that there is *no* counterexample to it! It follows that our original supposition was false; *there is no invalid argument with the same sentential form as the McCoy argument, and the form is therefore S-valid.* Thus, from the fact that the McCoy argument has a CL-valid translation, we may infer that it has an S-valid sentential form. And, from the fact that the argument has an S-valid form, we may infer that *every* argument of this form, including the McCoy argument itself, is valid.

This illustrates a general truth. Normally, if we find that the symbolic translation of an English argument is CL-valid, we may infer that the English argument has an S-valid sentential form and, hence, that the argument itself is valid.

Since CL's operators do not always perfectly mirror the semantics of the English operators they translate, however, there are exceptions to this general rule. Consider, for example, this argument:

Jim has red hair on his head.

So, if Jim is completely bald, then he has red hair on his head.

This argument seems plainly invalid. Suppose that Jim does have red hair on his head and, hence, that the premise of the argument is true. It still seems that he wouldn't have any hair on his head if he were completely bald and, hence, that the conclusion is false. Yet, the argument has this CL-valid translation:

R

So, $(B \rightarrow R)$

In this case, then, it seems that an invalid argument has a CL-*valid* translation.

What went wrong? The answer has to do with the fact, noted earlier, that CL's arrow does not correspond very well to the English operator "if . . , then — ". While symbolic conditionals always have the value *t* when their antecedents have the value *f*, some English conditionals — such as the conclusion of our sample argument — are *false* even though their antecedents are false. As a result, the sample argument's translation does not accurately mirror the argument's semantics. And that's why the argument is an exception to the general rule that arguments with CL-valid translations are valid.

Such exceptions need not bother us, though, since they do not occur very often in ordinary English argumentation. In logic, as in other systematic inquiries, one is interested in what typically occurs, and the procedure we have developed works very well for ordinary argumentation. Except for odd cases that are easy to spot, if we translate an English argument into CL and demonstrate the translation's CL-validity, we may infer that the argument has an S-valid sentential form and, hence, that it is valid. Thus, CL provides us with an effective and reliable method for demonstrating the S-validity of argument forms and the validity of particular arguments in English.

What's more, CL gives us some insight into *why* certain arguments are valid. As we have shown, we may infer that an argument is valid if we find that it has a CL-valid translation. This would not be the case unless, in translating the argument into CL, we captured everything relevant to its validity. But, in translating an argument from English into CL, *all* that we preserve are facts about patterns of clauses and sentential operators and facts about the ways in which the values of complex clauses are determined by the values of the simple clauses in them. Accordingly, if we can demonstrate an argument's validity with the methods of CL, its validity must be due entirely to these facts. In other words, if we can demonstrate an argument's validity with the methods of CL, its validity is due entirely to its sentential form.

CL has therefore done more than to provide an effective method for demonstrating the S-validity of argument forms and the validity of particular arguments. It has also isolated for us the features on which the validity of such arguments depend, helping us to understand *why* those arguments are valid.

Exercises 5.5

1. *Defend or criticize:* If an English argument has a CL-valid translation, the argument is valid.

2. *Defend or criticize:* If an English argument has a CL-invalid translation, the argument is invalid.

3. *Defend or criticize:* An English argument is valid just in case its symbolic translation is CL-valid.

4. Using truth tables, test each of the following (silly) English arguments for validity.
   a. Either logic is hard or it's nice. It's not hard. So, it's nice.
   b. If logic is hard, it's nice. It's not nice. So, it's not hard.
   c. Logic is hard if it's nice. But, if it isn't nice, it's not fun. Therefore, logic is fun only if it's hard.
   d. Logic is nice although it's not hard. Logic isn't fun unless it's hard. Therefore, either logic is hard or it's fun.
   e. If logic is nice, it's either hard or it's fun. Logic isn't hard unless it's nice. Logic is no fun at all. Therefore, logic is nice just in case it's hard.
   f. Logic is nice unless it's hard, but it's fun only if it's not hard. Therefore, logic is either nice or it's fun, if it's not hard.
   g. Logic is nice unless it's hard. But it's hard only if it's not fun. Therefore, if logic is fun, it's hard if and only if it's nice.

5. For each of the following passages, (i) make the argument in the passage explicit, (ii) paraphrase the argument into Standard English, (iii) translate the Standard English version of the argument into CL, (iv) test the translation for CL-validity using a truth table, and (v) draw an inference, if possible, about the validity of the original English argument.
   a. If it's raining, the ground is wet. It's raining. So, the ground is wet.
   b. If Al is happy, lunch was good. If lunch was good, there's a new cook. It follows that, if Al is happy, there's a new cook.

c. Sarah won't like the pizza unless it has pepperoni on it. But it doesn't have any pepperoni on it. Can you guess what Sarah is going to think of it?

d. If you try the casserole that I cooked for you, you'll like it. So, if you try it and don't like it, there's something wrong with your taste buds.

e. You will either stay up late tonight or get up early tomorrow, but not both. You'll stay up late tonight, just like you always do. So, I guess you won't be getting up early.

f. I'm opposed to the idea, which has been expressed by Senator Zipp and others, that we would be justified in sending marines into Monaco. Sending marines into Monaco would be justified only if there were a threat of war. Otherwise, we would merely be increasing the tension in the area. But, as Mr. Zipp himself admits, there is no threat of war. Indeed, the area is perfectly peaceful and likely to remain so.

g. If Mike goes to the party, he'll have a good time. For, he'll take Sara if he goes, and he'll have a good time if he does.

h. Prof. Beecham is on leave for the whole year. That means that the calculus class will be taught either by Prof. Puff or by Prof. Bor. But the class will be small if it's taught by Prof. Puff, and the same will be true if it's taught by Prof. Bor. Both of them are very hard graders. So, the calculus class will be small this year.

i. You ask how I can be so sure that Mr. Badmouth is a liar. Well, either he knew what was going on, in which case he is a liar, or he's a fool. But it seems clear to me — and to you, too, I hope — that whatever Mr. Badmouth's shortcomings, he's not a fool.

5.6 Overview

We began this chapter by discussing correspondences between particular sentential operators of English and particular symbolic operators of CL. Among the important correspondences were these:

OPERATORS OF ENGLISH	OPERATORS OF CL
it's not the case that	−
and	&
or	∨
unless	∨
if, then	→
only if	→
if and only if	↔

Although these correspondences are not perfect, the symbolic operators generally do capture the important facts about the ways that the corresponding sentential operators work in arguments.

In light of these correspondences, we developed a method for demonstrating the S-validity of argument forms and, hence, the validity of particular English arguments. We can outline the method step by step, in this way:

1. Given a passage containing an argument, *make the argument explicit.*

2. *Paraphrase the argument into Standard English.* (As we said, an argument is in Standard English just in case it contains no sentential operators other than "it's not the case that", "and", "or", "unless", "if, then", "only if", and "if and only if", and these operators are used in their usual ways.)

3. *Set up a scheme of correspondence.* (Such a scheme associates each simple clause in an argument with a different sentence letter of CL.)

4. *Translate into CL.* (To translate from Standard English into CL, replace simple clauses with the corresponding sentence letters and sentential operators with the corresponding symbolic operators, changing punctuation where necessary.)

5. *Find out whether the translation is CL-valid using a truth table.*

If the table shows that the translation is CL-*in*valid, we may draw no inference at all about the validity or invalidity of the original English argument. On the other hand, if the table shows that the translation is CL-valid, we may infer that the original English argument has an S-valid sentential form and, hence, that the argument is valid.

Chapter 6

A System of Derivation for CL

Using the method of Chapter 5, we can construct a truth table for any symbolic argument, and the truth table will show us whether the argument is CL-valid. Still, the method of truth tables leaves much to be desired. The construction of a large truth table can be tedious and uninteresting, and clerical errors are hard to avoid and to detect, when made. Besides, although our aim in developing CL has been to study reasoning in English, the process of constructing truth tables does not correspond to anything people actually do when presenting arguments to one another.

We therefore devote this chapter to developing a new test for CL-validity. The test will involve **derivations** — lists of symbolic sentences constructed in accordance with precise syntactic rules. Typically, we will be able to demonstrate a symbolic argument's CL-validity just as well with a short and elegant derivation as with a large and clumsy truth table. And, since the moves we make in constructing derivations will often resemble those that people naturally and spontaneously make when presenting arguments to one another, our system of derivation will shed light on the ways in which people actually reason in everyday life.

The inspiration for our system of derivation comes from a reexamination of the sentences that we called *connecting links* (Chapter 2). By developing ways of using symbolic connecting links that parallel the ways people use connecting links in the presentation of real arguments, we will create a system of derivation for CL. Then, to strengthen this system, we will add methods of *conditional derivation* and *indirect derivation*. The resulting method of demonstrating validity will be easier to use than the method of truth tables and will correspond more closely to reasoning in English.

6.1 How Connecting Links Work in the Presentation of English Arguments

In Chapter 2, we observed that arguers often include with their premises and conclusions sentences that help others to see their arguments' validity — sentences that we called *connecting links.* In this section, we take a closer look at how connecting links work. What we learn will help us later to develop a system of derivation for CL.

An example of an English connecting link appears in the following passage from an investigator's report of a plane crash:

> Evidence indicates that, at the time of the crash, the pilot Capt. Knapp was asleep. If Capt. Knapp had noticed that the plane was on fire, he surely would have radioed for help. We know, however, that he never touched the radio. So, he must not have noticed the fire. But he would have noticed a fire of that size had he been awake.

The passage contains an argument, which we can make explicit like this:

1. If Knapp had noticed the fire, then he would have radioed for help.
2. He didn't radio for help.
3. He would have noticed the fire if he had been awake.

    _____

4. Therefore, he wasn't awake.

Since sentences (1), (2), (3), and (4) accurately paraphrase sentences that the investigator actually wrote, this way of making the argument explicit is faithful to the investigator's words. And, since the argument from (1), (2), and (3) to (4) is valid (see Exercise 6.1.1), we can be confident that this way of making the argument explicit is charitable, too.

Notice, though, that in making the argument explicit we seem to have ignored the sentence

5. So, he must not have noticed the fire.

Since the investigator's primary aim was to show that Capt. Knapp was asleep, sentence (5) is not the main argument's conclusion. And sentence (5) does not seem to be one of the argument's premises either. The argument does not need sentence (5) as a premise, since sentences (1), (2), and (3) entail sentence (4) by themselves.

But, if sentence (5) is neither one of the argument's premises nor its conclusion, why did the investigator bother to include it? What is the role of this sentence in the investigator's reasoning? The answer, of course, is that sentence (5) is a connecting link. Without itself being a part of the main argument, sentence (5) helps the investigator show the audience that the argument's conclusion follows from its premises.

To see that sentence (5) does indeed help in this way, notice what the investigator's prose would have been like without it:

> Evidence indicates that, at the time of the crash, the pilot Capt. Knapp was asleep. If Capt. Knapp had noticed that the plane was on fire, he surely would have radioed for help. We know, however, that he never touched the radio. But he would have noticed a fire of that size had he been awake.

Presented with *this* prose, most readers would have a hard time telling whether the investigator's argument is valid or invalid; here the movement of the investigator's thought simply is not clear. Of course, people who have studied logic can stop, make the argument explicit, and construct a truth table. But the investigator, not wanting anyone to take the time and trouble to do this, tried to present the argument in a way that makes its validity obvious.

Sentence (5) is crucial to this strategy. To see why, notice that, while we can view sentences (1) and (2) as premises of the investigator's main argument, we can also view them as premises of another (obviously valid) argument whose conclusion is sentence (5):

1. If Knapp had noticed the fire, he would have radioed for help.
2. He didn't radio for help.

   ───

5. So, he didn't notice the fire.

Clearly, this is not the investigator's main argument; as we have said, the conclusion of the main argument is that Knapp was not awake. Still, sentence (5) begins with the word "so", and it obviously follows from sentences (1) and (2). So, clearly, the investigator wanted us to infer sentence (5) from those before it. Accordingly, we may regard sentence (5) as the conclusion of a *subargument* whose premises are sentences (1) and (2).

After presenting this subargument, the investigator went on to use its conclusion as a premise of another:

5. Knapp didn't notice the fire.
3. He would have noticed the fire if he had been awake.

   ───

4. Therefore, he wasn't awake.

Both of the investigator's subarguments have the familiar form of *modus tollens,* and, since this form is S-valid, both of the subarguments are obviously valid. When the readers of the investigator's report see that these subarguments are valid, they will see that the main argument is also valid. Thus, by using a connecting link to break up the main argument into two obviously valid subarguments, the investigator can easily convince the audience of the main argument's validity.

Furthermore, the investigator's audience is *right* to be convinced. Since (4) follows from (5) and (3), (4) must be true if (5) and (3) are. And, since (5) follows from (1) and (2), (5) must be true if (1) and (2) are. It follows that (4) must be true if (1), (2), and (3) are—or, in other words, that the argument from (1), (2), and (3) to (4) is valid. Thus, from the fact that both of the investigator's subarguments are valid, it follows that the main argument is valid as well.

This example provides us with a general understanding of the use of connecting links. With the aid of connecting links, an arguer can turn the task of evaluating a long or complex argument into that of evaluating several simple and obviously valid subarguments. If the subarguments are valid, the main argument must be valid, too.

We say that an arguer who uses connecting links in this way *derives* a conclusion from premises, and we call a collection of sentences that contains an argument's premises and conclusion, together with some connecting links, a *derivation* for that argument.

In the rest of this chapter, we will develop a formal system of derivation for CL. Since CL is a simplified model of English, its methods of derivation will generally be simplified models of methods that we use to construct derivations in English. Thus, in addition to providing us with an elegant procedure for demonstrating CL-validity, our system of formal derivation will provide us with some insight into the ways that people actually reason in English.

Exercises 6.1

1. Using the method of truth tables, show that the argument about the plane crash is in fact valid.

2. *Defend or criticize:* While we can take sentence (5) to be a connecting link (as we did in the text), we can also take it to be a premise of the investigator's main argument. If we do this, however, we should take sentences (1) and (2) to be supporting assertions. (See the section of Chapter 2 on extra statements.)

3. *Defend or criticize:* All arguments are derivations, and all derivations are arguments.

4. *Defend or criticize:* If one can use connecting links to move from a set of statements to another statement by means of small, obviously valid subarguments, then the argument from the set of statements to the other statement must be valid.

5. *Defend or criticize:* If one uses connecting links to move from a set of premises to a conclusion by means of small subarguments, some of which are invalid, then one's main argument must be invalid.

6. *Defend or criticize:* One derives a conclusion from a set of premises only if all of one's subarguments are valid.

7. Say which of the following passages contains a derivation. If you say that a passage does contain a derivation, identify the subarguments by which the arguer moves from the main argument's premises to its conclusion. Do any of these subarguments have familiar S-valid forms?

> a. There is an important connection between rainfall and the growth rate of scrub vegetation. If the spring rains are heavy, the scrub grows tall. But, as the reports of the weather bureau show, the rainfall has been heavy this spring. So, the scrub will grow tall. But mud slides are very unlikely when the scrub is tall. Therefore, we can safely conclude that there will be no mud slides.
>
> b. A year made up of twelve lunar months is about eleven days short of a solar year. That is, when the moon has gone through twelve full cycles, the sun will still have eleven days to go before it completes its full cycle through the heavens. On the other hand, a year consisting of thirteen lunar months would be about nineteen days longer than the solar year.
>
> c. If Sally has the day off, she will go to either the beach or the park. And Sally does in fact have the day off. Thus, Sally must be at either the beach or the park. I'm sure that she's having a great time if she's at the beach. And, if she's at the park, she's having a great time there. Any way you look at it, then, Sally's having a great time.
>
> d. Tony will major in either chemistry or English. But, judging from what he says about his English professors, I don't think that he's going to stick with English. It seems, then, that Tony will major in chemistry. But, if he majors in chemistry, he has to take lots of lab courses. So, I guess that Tony's afternoons are going to be busy for a while.

8. For each of the following arguments, construct a derivation in which you move from the argument's premises to its conclusion in small, obviously valid steps. (Keep in mind the common S-valid forms described in Chapter 3.)

> a. Either I'll drive my car or I won't go to the store.
>
> If I don't go to the store, there won't be milk in the morning.
>
> I won't drive my car.
>
> _____
>
> So, there won't be milk in the morning.
>
> b. The class is meeting.
>
> If the class is meeting, the teacher is present.
>
> If the teacher is present, homework has been assigned.
>
> _____
>
> So, homework has been assigned.

    c. Either the cat or the dog is out.

      The cat isn't out.

      If the dog is out, the gate is unlatched.

      If John was the last person to leave the house, the gate is latched.

      So, John wasn't the last person to leave the house.

    d. If the party was loud, Mr. Murphy called the police unless the party ended before 10:00 P.M.

      The party was loud.

      The party didn't end before 10:00 P.M.

      It's not the case that both Mr. Murphy and Mrs. McNaughty called the police.

      So, Mrs. McNaughty didn't call the police.

6.2 Rules of Inference for Negations, Conjunctions, and Disjunctions

As we said in the previous section, an English derivation is a list of sentences in which an arguer moves from premises to a conclusion in small, obviously valid steps. With this definition in mind, we begin in this section to develop a formal system of derivation for the system CL. The system will allow us to construct **symbolic derivations** — lists of symbolic sentences that move from arguments' premises to their conclusions in accordance with rules called **rules of inference**.

Which rules of inference apply to a given symbolic sentence will depend on the sentence's *basic form.* Indeed, that's why we developed the eleven-way grouping of symbolic sentences in Chapter 4. Some rules will apply to conjunctions, some to biconditionals, some to the negations of disjunctions, some to the negations of negations, and so on.

In this section, we limit ourselves to nine rules, which primarily have to do with conjunctions and disjunctions, with their negations, and with the negations of negations. In the next section, we will discuss rules having to do with symbolic sentences of other basic forms.

The full and abbreviated names of our first nine rules are as follows:

FULL NAME	ABBREVIATION
Premise Introduction	Prem
Double Negation Introduction	DNI
Double Negation Elimination	DNE
Simplification	Simp
Conjunction	Conj
The Conjunctive Syllogism	CS
The Disjunctive Syllogism	DS
Adjunction	Adj
The DeMorgan Rule	DM

We now examine each of these rules. (Diagrams illustrating the rules appear in Section 6.7 at the end of the chapter.)

Premise Introduction (Prem)

The rule Prem is this:

> If we are using a derivation to test a given symbolic argument for CL-validity, we may write any of that argument's premises as a line of the derivation.

This rule allows us to get derivations started.

Double Negation Introduction (DNI)

The rule DNI tells us how to create double dashes at the beginnings of symbolic sentences:

> If a symbolic sentence appears as a line of a derivation, we may write the negation of the negation of that sentence as a subsequent line.

DNI allows us to move, for example, from "A" to "− − A", or from "− (A & B)" to "− − − (A & B)".

Double Negation Elimination (DNE)

DNE tells us how to get rid of double dashes at the beginnings of sentences:

> If the negation of the negation of a symbolic sentence appears as a line of a derivation, we may write the sentence itself as a subsequent line.

DNE allows us to move, for example, from "−−A" to "A", or from "−−−(A & B)" to "−(A & B)".

Simplification (Simp)

The rule Simp allows us to take conjunctions apart:

> If a conjunction appears as a line of a derivation, we may write either of its conjuncts as a subsequent line.

Simp allows us to move, for example, from the conjunction "(A & (B ∨ C))" either to "A" or to "(B ∨ C)".

Conjunction (Conj)

The rule Conj allows us to create conjunctions:

> If both of a conjunction's conjuncts appear as lines of a derivation, we may write the conjunction itself as a subsequent line.

Conj allows us to move, for example, from "A" and "(B ∨ C)" to "(A & (B ∨ C))".

The Conjunctive Syllogism (CS)

The rule CS allows us to construct symbolic subarguments whose forms resemble that of the conjunctive syllogism:

> If the negation of a conjunction appears as a line of a derivation, and one of the conjunction's conjuncts appears as another, we may write the negation of its other conjunct as a subsequent line.

This rule allows us to move, for example, from "− ((A → B) & C)" and "C" to "− (A → B)".

The Disjunctive Syllogism (DS)

The rule DS allows us to construct symbolic subarguments whose forms resemble that of the disjunctive syllogism:

> If a disjunction appears as one line of a derivation and the negation of one of its disjuncts as another line, we may write the other disjunct as a subsequent line.

DS allows us to move, for example, from "(− (A → B) ∨ C)" and "−C" to "−(A → B)".

Adjunction (Adj)

The rule Adj allows us to produce disjunctions:

> If either of a disjunction's disjuncts appears as a line of a derivation, we may write the disjunction itself as a subsequent line.

With the rule Adj, we may move in a derivation from a symbolic sentence to *any* disjunction of which that sentence is a disjunct. Adj allows us to move, for example, from "A" to "(A ∨ B)", or to "(B ∨ A)", or even to "((C → (B ↔ A)) ∨ A)".

The DeMorgan Rule (DM)

Named after the logician Augustus DeMorgan (1806 – 1871), this rule allows us to construct symbolic subarguments that mirror English arguments of the S-valid form "Not (*P* or *Q*); so, not *P*". The rule is this:

> If the negation of a disjunction appears as a line of a derivation, we may write the negation of either of its disjuncts as a subsequent line.

Using this rule, we can move in a derivation, say, from "−((P ∨ Q) ∨ R)" to either "−(P ∨ Q)" or "−R".

We will add more rules of inference later, but in this section we limit ourselves to the nine just described: Prem, DNI, DNE, Simp, Conj, CS, DS, Adj, and DM.

To construct a derivation for a given symbolic argument, we simply use these rules to move from the argument's premises to its conclusion. Consider, for example, the symbolic argument

(−A ∨ B)

−B

(C ∨ A)

_____

So, C

Using our rules of inference, we can move from this argument's premises to its conclusion like this:

1.	(−A ∨ B)	Prem
2.	−B	Prem
3.	−A	1,2 DS
4.	(C ∨ A)	Prem
5.	C	3,4 DS

This is a symbolic derivation for the sample argument — a list of symbolic sentences constructed in accordance with our rules of inference.

The symbolic derivation consists of numbered lines. On each line is a symbolic sentence and, to the sentence's right, an annotation which states our justification for writing that sentence. In these annotations, numerals refer back to previous lines of the derivation, and letters refer, through our abbreviations, to rules of inference. Thus, the annotation "Prem" on line (1) indicates that the symbolic sentence on that line is a premise of the symbolic argument whose CL-validity we are demonstrating, and the annotation "1,2 DS" on line (3) indicates that the symbolic sentence on that line has been produced by applying rule DS to the symbolic sentences on lines (1) and (2). Each line of a derivation should have an annotation of this sort.

For another example of a derivation, consider the symbolic argument:

$$(-A \mathrel{\&} B)$$
$$-((B \lor C) \mathrel{\&} -A)$$
_____

So, $(-C \lor -B)$

As we have said, to construct a symbolic derivation for this argument is to move from its premises to its conclusion in accordance with our rules of inference. How can we do this?

In approaching problems of this sort, it is best to have a plan. A common way of developing such a plan is to "work backwards" from the conclusion to the premises from which it is to be derived. We might begin, for example, by asking how we might produce the conclusion "$(-C \lor -B)$". Well, if we had "$-C$" as a line of symbolic derivation, we could produce "$(-C \lor -B)$" by using the rule Adj. But how might we get "$-C$"? If we could get "$-(B \lor C)$" from the symbolic argument's second premise, we could get "$-C$" by using DM. And how can we get "$-(B \lor C)$" from the argument's second premise? We can get "$-A$" by applying Simp to the argument's first premise, and, from "$-A$" and the argument's second premise, we can get "$-(B \lor C)$" using CS.

With this plan in mind, we can construct a symbolic derivation for the sample symbol argument like this:

1.	$(-A \mathrel{\&} B)$	Prem
2.	$-((B \lor C) \mathrel{\&} -A)$	Prem
3.	$-A$	1 Simp
4.	$-(B \lor C)$	2,3 CS
5.	$-C$	4 DM
6.	$(-C \lor -B)$	5 Adj

If we had started without a plan, we might have gone on and on in the symbolic derivation without getting any nearer to the sample argument's conclusion.

Because we derived the sample symbolic argument's conclusion from its premises, we can be sure that the argument is CL-valid. To see why, let v be any valuation in which both of the sample argument's premises have the value t. Since the symbolic sentences on lines (1) and (2) of the sample derivation are the premises of the sample symbolic argument, both of these sentences must have the value t in valuation v. But the symbolic sentence on line (3) follows from those on lines (1) and (2) by one of our rules of inference, and *every inference constructed in accordance with these rules is CL-valid*. So, the sentence on line (3) must also have the value t in valuation v. Similarly, the symbolic sentence on line (4) must have the value t in valuation v. (Again, the sentences from which it is inferred all have the value t in v, and every inference constructed in accordance with our rules is CL-valid.) By the same reasoning, *every* sentence in the symbolic derivation — including the last one, which is the sample argument's conclusion — must have the value t in valuation v. Hence, the fact that we have constructed a symbolic derivation for the sample argument shows that, in any valuation in which the sample argument's premises have the value t, so does its conclusion. And it follows from this that the sample symbolic argument is CL-valid.

More generally, since every inference constructed in accordance with our rules is CL-valid, symbolic derivations provide us with a way to demonstrate the CL-validity of symbolic arguments. Given a symbolic argument, we can try to derive its conclusion from its premises using our nine rules of inference. If we succeed, we can be sure that the argument is CL-valid.

Of course, we already had a method for demonstrating CL-validity: the method of truth tables from Chapter 4. To demonstrate a given symbolic argument's CL-validity with a truth table, we need only work away, mechanically grinding out "t"s and "f"s in accordance with CL's rules of valuation. Eventually, we will come to the end of the table, and the table will tell us whether the given symbolic argument is CL-valid or CL-invalid. In contrast, if we start off wrong in a symbolic derivation for a CL-valid symbolic argument, or if we apply the method to a symbolic argument that our rules can't handle (such as one whose validity has to do with the use of the arrow), we can go on forever, generating line after line in accordance with the rules of inference but never reaching the argument's conclusion. Unlike the method of truth tables, then, the method of derivation doesn't always tell us what we want to know.

Still, the method of derivation has several things to be said in its favor. First, symbolic derivations are shorter and more elegant than truth tables. Second, the symbolic derivations are more challenging and, hence, more interesting to construct than truth tables. Third, although we will need to abandon truth tables when we move on in later chapters to more sophisticated models of English, the method of derivation will continue to provide us with a useful tool for evaluating symbolic arguments. Finally, as we pointed out at the beginning of this chapter, symbolic derivations — unlike truth tables — provide us with some insight into the ways that people reason in English. As we said in the previous section, people often demonstrate the validity of English arguments by moving from their premises to their conclusions in small, obviously valid steps. Similarly, we can demonstrate a symbolic argument's CL-validity by moving from its premises to its conclusion in small steps, each of which is CL-valid.

Exercises 6.2

1. *Defend or criticize:* The rule DNE allows us to move in derivations from the sentence "(A & −−B)" to the sentence "(A & B)".

2. *Defend or criticize:* In effect, every time we use one of our nine rules of inference in the course of constructing a derivation, we construct a CL-valid subargument — since every inference constructed in accordance with our rules is CL-valid.

3. *Defend or criticize:* If we move in a derivation from a symbolic argument's premises to its conclusion, we can be sure that the argument is CL-valid.

4. *Defend or criticize:* If we try but fail to construct a derivation for a given symbolic argument, we can be sure that the argument is CL-*in*valid.

5. Using derivations, demonstrate the CL-validity of each of the following arguments:

> a. (A & (B & C))
> _____
> So, ((A & B) & C)

> b. −(A ∨ B)
> _____
> So, (−A & −B)

> c. −(A & B)
>   (C ∨ A)
>   −C
> _____
> So, −B

> d. −((A ∨ B) ∨ C)
> _____
> So, ((−A & −B) & −C)

> e. A
> _____
> So, ((−(A ∨ B) ∨ A) ∨ C)

f. $-((A \& B) \lor -C)$

  $(C \lor -A)$
_____

So, $-A$

g. $-(-A \lor B)$

  $-((A \lor C) \& D)$

  $(-(-D \lor A) \lor C)$
_____

So, C

h. $(-(-A \& -B) \& -(B \lor C))$

  $(-(A \& -C) \lor (-A \lor D))$
_____

So, $(-A \lor D)$

i. A

  $-A$
_____

So, B

6.3 Rules of Inference for Conditionals and Biconditionals

In the previous section, we introduced nine rules of inference, which have primarily to do with negations, conjunctions, and disjunctions. In this section, we add some more rules to our system of derivation: rules for dealing with conditionals and biconditionals. With these new rules, we will be able to construct symbolic derivations for more symbolic arguments than we could in the previous section. Yet, if we are able to derive a symbolic argument's conclusion from its premises using our new rules, we may still infer that the argument is CL-valid.

Here is a list of the full and abbreviated names of the new rules:

FULL NAME	ABBREVIATION
Modus Ponens	MP
Modus Tollens	MT
The Dilemma	D
The Hypothetical Syllogism	HS
Elimination of the Negations of Conditionals	ENC
Biconditional Introduction	BCI
Biconditional Elimination	BCE
Elimination of the Negations of Biconditionals	ENB

We discuss these eight rules one by one. (Again, diagrams illustrating the rules appear in Section 6.7 at the end of this chapter.)

Modus Ponens (MP)

Named after the form of *modus ponens,* the rule MP is this:

> If a conditional appears as a line of a derivation and its antecedent as another, we may write its consequent as a subsequent line.

This rule tells us, for example, that we may write "−A" as a line of a derivation if "(−B → −A)" and "−B" appear as previous lines.

Modus Tollens (MT)

Named after the form of *modus tollens,* the rule MT is this:

> If a conditional appears as a line of a derivation and the negation of its consequent as another, we may write the negation of its antecedent as a subsequent line.

This rule tells us, for example, that we may write "−A" as a line of a derivation if "(A → B)" and "−B" appear as previous lines.

The Dilemma (D)

The rule D, which is named after the form of the (constructive) dilemma, is this:

> If two lines of a derivation contain conditionals with identical consequents, and if another line contains a disjunction whose left disjunct is the antecedent of one of the conditionals and whose right disjunct is the antecedent of the other, we may write the conditionals' (shared) consequent as a line of the derivation.

According to this rule, if "((A ∨ B) ∨ −C)", "((A ∨ B) → (D → E))", and "(−C → (D → E))" all appear as lines of a derivation, we may write "(D → E)" as a subsequent line.

The Hypothetical Syllogism (HS)

The rule HS, which is named after the form of the hypothetical syllogism, is this:

> If two conditionals appear as lines of a derivation and the consequent of one is the same as the antecedent of the other, we may write as a subsequent line of the derivation a conditional whose antecedent is the antecedent of the one and whose consequent is the consequent of the other.

Thus, if "(A → −B)" and "(−B → (C ∨ −D))" both appear as lines of a derivation, we may write "(A → (C ∨ −D))" as a subsequent line.

Elimination of the Negations of Conditionals (ENC)

As its name suggests, this rule helps us to *eliminate* the *negations* of conditionals from derivations:

> If a conditional's negation appears as a line of a derivation, we may write as a subsequent line of the derivation a conjunction whose first conjunct is the conditional's antecedent and whose second conjunct is the negation of the conditional's consequent.

This rule allows us to move in a derivation, say, from "−((A ∨ B) → (A ↔ C))" to "((A ∨ B) & −(A ↔ C))".

Biconditional Introduction (BCI)

In stating this rule, it is useful to regard biconditionals as made up from *component conditionals:*

> A conditional is a **component** of a biconditional just in case its antecedent is one of the biconditional's sides and its consequent is the other.

Thus, "((A & B) → −C)" and "(−C → (A & B))" are the components of the biconditional "((A & B) ↔ −C)".

The rule BCI allows us to construct biconditionals from their components:

> If both of a biconditional's component conditionals appear as lines of a derivation, we may write the biconditional itself as a subsequent line.

For example, BCI allows us to write the biconditional "(A ↔ B)" as a line of a derivation if both of its component conditionals—namely, "(A → B)" and "(B → A)" —appear as previous lines.

Biconditional Elimination (BCE)

The rule BCE allows us to break biconditionals apart into their component conditionals:

> If a biconditional appears as a line of a derivation, we may write either of its component conditionals as a subsequent line.

This rule allows us to move, say, from "(A ↔ B)" to either "(A → B)" or "(B → A)".

Elimination of the Negations of Biconditionals (ENB)

ENB, which allows us to eliminate the negations of biconditionals from derivations, is this:

> If the negation of a biconditional appears as a line of a derivation, we may erase its first two marks, which will be a dash and a left-hand parenthesis (in that order), replace them with a left-hand parenthesis and a dash (in that order), and write the result as a line of the derivation.

This rule allows us to move, for example, from the negation "$-(A \leftrightarrow B)$" to the CL-equivalent biconditional "$(-A \leftrightarrow B)$".

To illustrate these new rules, we consider the symbolic argument

$(-(A \rightarrow B) \rightarrow D)$

$-(D \lor E)$

$(B \leftrightarrow -C)$

_____

So, $(A \rightarrow -C)$

Limited to just the nine rules of inference from the previous section, we could never derive the conclusion of this symbolic argument from its premises. But, using our new rules along with the old, we can construct a symbolic derivation for the argument, like this:

1.	$(-(A \rightarrow B) \rightarrow D)$	Prem
2.	$-(D \lor E)$	Prem
3.	$(B \leftrightarrow -C)$	Prem
4.	$-D$	2 DM
5.	$--(A \rightarrow B)$	1,4 MT
6.	$(A \rightarrow B)$	5 DNE
7.	$(B \rightarrow -C)$	3 BCE
8.	$(A \rightarrow -C)$	6,7 HS

Here the old rules DM and DNE help us to deal with the negation of a disjunction and the negation of a negation, while the new rules MT, BCE, and HS help us to deal with conditionals and biconditionals.

In one important respect, our new rules are like the old ones: Every inference constructed in accordance with the rules is CL-valid. Accordingly, we may continue to use the system of derivation to demonstrate CL-validity, just as we did before we added the new rules. That is, if we can derive a symbolic argument's conclusion from its premises using our rules of inference, we can correctly infer that the argument is CL-valid.

Exercises 6.3

1. *Defend or criticize:* CL now has one rule of inference corresponding to each of the S-valid forms discussed in Chapter 3. MP corresponds to *modus ponens,* MT to *modus tollens,* and so on.

2. *Defend or criticize:* In this section, we introduced exactly six new rules of inference: MP, MT, HS, D, BCI, and BCE.

3. *Defend or criticize:* Every inference constructed in accordance with the rules that we introduced in this section is CL-valid.

4. *Defend or criticize:* If we can derive a symbolic argument's conclusion from its premises using our rules of inference, we can be sure that the argument is CL-valid.

5. Using truth tables, show that "$-(A \rightarrow B)$" is CL-equivalent to "$(A \,\&\, -B)$" and that "$-(A \leftrightarrow B)$" is CL-equivalent to "$(-A \leftrightarrow B)$", but that "$-(A \rightarrow B)$" is not CL-equivalent to "$(-A \rightarrow B)$".

6. Demonstrate the CL-validity of each of the following arguments using a derivation:

   a. $(A \leftrightarrow B)$
   $((C \lor D) \rightarrow B)$
   C
   _____
   So, A

   b. $((A \lor B) \rightarrow C)$
   $(-B \leftrightarrow -C)$
   $(A \lor D)$
   $-D$
   _____
   So, B

   c. $(A \rightarrow (-B \rightarrow (C \rightarrow D)))$
   $(A \,\&\, -B)$
   $-D$
   _____
   So, $(-C \lor B)$

   d. $(A \,\&\, (B \lor C))$
   $(A \rightarrow (B \rightarrow -D))$
   $(-(C \rightarrow -D) \rightarrow -A)$
   _____
   So, $-D$

e. $(-(A \rightarrow B) \rightarrow C)$
$(A \And -C)$
___
So, $(B \lor C)$

f. $(A \lor (B \lor C))$
$((A \rightarrow D) \And -D)$
$(-D \leftrightarrow -B)$
___
So, C

g. $(A \lor B)$
$-B$
$(-C \rightarrow B)$
$(D \rightarrow -(A \And C))$
___
So, $-D$

h. $-(A \rightarrow B)$
$-(-C \rightarrow -D)$
___
So, $(A \And D)$

i. $(C \lor -(B \leftrightarrow C))$
$(B \leftrightarrow C)$
$((B \lor D) \rightarrow (E \And (F \And -G)))$
$((C \And -G) \rightarrow H)$
___
So, H

j. $-(A \leftrightarrow -B)$
$-(B \leftrightarrow -C)$
___
So, $(-A \rightarrow -C)$

6.4 Conditional Derivation

In the previous two sections, we developed a system of derivation that provides us with an elegant method for demonstrating CL-validity. If we can move in a derivation from a symbolic argument's premises to its conclusion in accordance with these rules, we can correctly infer that the argument is CL-valid.

If we fail in our attempt to derive an argument's conclusion from its premises, however, we should *not* infer that the argument is CL-*in*valid. The cause of our failure may have been our own lack of persistence or cleverness. In addition, there are CL-valid arguments whose CL-validity we can *never* demonstrate with our current rules, no matter how persistent or clever we are. An example is the CL-valid argument

$(-P \lor Q)$

$(R \lor -Q)$

So, $(P \rightarrow R)$

We can begin a symbolic derivation by writing the argument's premises, and we can go on indefinitely by using the rules we already have. But, however long we continue in this way, we will never reach the symbolic argument's conclusion.

In this section, we will correct this shortcoming by adding new rules specially designed to aid us in the derivation of conditionals: the *Rule of Supposition for Conditional Derivation* (SuppCD) and the *Rule of Conditional Derivation* (CD). Together, SuppCD and CD will give us a powerful method of derivation called *conditional derivation.*

The inspiration for conditional derivation comes from a strategy that people often use when reasoning in English. Consider, by way of illustration, the following letter and reply:

> Dear Addie:
>
> I am planning on getting married to John and would like to invite my old boyfriend Bill to the wedding. Unfortunately, John is very jealous, and he doesn't like Bill very much. What should I do?
> —*Perplexed in Peoria*

> Dear Perplexed:
>
> Suppose you do invite Bill to the wedding. As you say, John is jealous, so he'll surely start a fight. But a fight at a wedding always spells disaster. Your wedding, which should be the most beautiful moment in your life, will be a horror.
> So don't invite your old beau. If you do, your wedding will be ruined.

Clearly, Addie advises Perplexed not to invite Bill to the wedding, and her advice is based on her assertion of the conditional, "If you do invite Bill, your wedding will be ruined."

To establish the truth of this conditional, Addie adopts the strategy of conditional derivation. She gets her derivation started by supposing—for the sake of the argument—that Perplexed does invite Bill to the wedding. From this supposition, together with other premises (such as that *John is jealous of Bill*), Addie reaches the connecting link, "John will start a fight." Then, from this connecting link, together with the premise that *a fight would ruin the wedding,*

Addie infers that *the wedding will be ruined*. Of course, Addie doesn't know whether her original supposition is true; that is, she doesn't really know whether Perplexed will invite Bill. So, her reasoning does not establish that the wedding *will* be ruined. But Addie can take her reasoning to establish the truth of the conditional "*If* Perplexed invites Bill to the wedding, *then* the wedding will be ruined."

This example illustrates a common method of reasoning in English. Often, to establish the truth of an English conditional, one

(a)   supposes, for the sake of the argument, that the conditional's antecedent is true,

(b)   derives the conditional's consequent, using the supposition as if it were a premise, and

(c)   infers that the conditional itself is true.

Thus, in our example, Addie (a) supposes that Perplexed does invite Bill to the wedding, (b) derives from this supposition that the wedding will be ruined, and (c) infers that the conditional "*If* Perplexed invites Bill, *then* the wedding will be ruined" is true.

Of course, Addie could have derived the same conclusion without resorting to this tactic. She could, for example, have constructed an argument with the form of the hypothetical syllogism, like this:

If you invite Bill, John will start a fight. If John starts a fight, the wedding will be ruined. So, if you invite Bill, the wedding will be ruined.

But, given the choice between this method for reaching her conclusion and the method of conditional derivation, Addie had good reason to choose the latter. The method of conditional derivation allowed her to highlight, in the form of direct assertions, the consequences of her supposition. Instead of simply saying to Perplexed, "If you invite Bill, John will start a fight," Addie supposes that Perplexed *does* invite Bill, and then asserts, "John *will* start a fight." Presented in this graphic way, the argument is easier for an audience to follow and has more persuasive force.

Our aim in this section is to build a procedure similar to Addie's into our formal system of derivation. To do this, we will need two new rules of inference. The first of these new rules — the **Rule of Supposition for Conditional Derivation (SuppCD)** — allows us to make the suppositions that get conditional derivations started. And the second of our new rules — the **Rule of Conditional Derivation (CD)** — allows us to end conditional derivations by writing the desired conditionals once we have derived their consequents.

To see how the new rules work, think again about the CL-valid argument that we mentioned at the outset of this section:

$(-P \lor Q)$

$(R \lor -Q)$

So, $(P \to R)$

As we have noted, we cannot derive this symbolic argument's conclusion from its premises if we are limited to the rules of derivation described in the previous sections. With the aid of our two new rules, however, we can easily derive the argument's conclusion from its premises, like this:

1. $(-P \lor Q)$ — Prem
2. $(R \lor -Q)$ — Prem
3. P — SuppCD
4. $--P$ — 3 DNI
5. Q — 1,4 DS
6. $--Q$ — 5 DNI
7. R — 2,6 DS
8. $(P \to R)$ — 3–7 CD

Here, the lines in the box form a **conditional derivation** — a subderivation that begins with a supposition like the one on line (3), and ends with a use of CD like the one on line (8).

The full statement of the rule SuppCD is this:

When attempting to derive a symbolic conditional, we may write that conditional's antecedent as a supposition.

And the full statement of the rule CD is this:

If a conditional's antecedent appears as an (unboxed) line of a derivation with the annotation "SuppCD" and its consequent appears as a subsequent (unboxed) line, we may write the conditional itself as a line — provided that we draw a box enclosing the line with the annotation "SuppCD" and all subsequent lines up to, but not including, the one with the annotation "CD".

These rules may never be used independently of one another. For every use of SuppCD, there must be a subsequent use of CD, and for every use of CD, there must be a prior use of SuppCD.

The boxes that we draw when using CD do more than point out conditional derivations. *Once a sentence is in a box, we cannot derive other sentences from it or cite it in annotations.* To see the reason for this restriction, think back to the derivation in Dear Addie's reply to Perplexed from Peoria. Here Addie makes the supposition that Perplexed will invite Bill to the wedding, even though she doesn't know whether the supposition is true, and she then infers from this supposition (together with other premises) that the wedding will be ruined. Yet, if the wedding is not ruined — say, because Perplexed *takes* Addie's advice — no one would say that Addie had made a mistake in her reasoning. This is because Addie does not really assert that the wedding *will* be ruined; she merely derives the sentence "The wedding will be ruined" from a supposition that she makes *temporarily* and *for the sake of her argument.* It is her intention, once she has reached the conclusion "The wedding will be ruined *if* Bill is invited," to withdraw her supposition and to take back everything that she derived from it.

Similarly, in our sample symbolic derivation, we made the supposition on line (3) temporarily and for the sake of the derivation. When we made the supposition, our plan was to cancel it and to withdraw everything that we had derived from it once we had finished our conditional derivation. Boxes help us to carry out this plan — for, as we have said, once a sentence is in a box, we cannot derive other sentences from it or cite it in annotations. To enclose lines of a derivation in a box is, in effect, to erase the sentences on those lines from the derivation.

Of course, there were no boxes in the simple system of derivation that we introduced in the previous sections. The addition of the rules SuppCD and CD has thus forced us to make important changes in how symbolic derivations look. The fact is, however, that none of these changes affects the system's reliability as a test for CL-validity. If we can derive a symbolic argument's conclusion from its premises, we can be sure that the argument is CL-valid — even if we have used SuppCD and CD.

To see this, look once again at the sample argument

$(-P \lor Q)$

$(R \lor -Q)$

_____

So, $(P \rightarrow R)$

Imagine that we have been given the task of demonstrating this symbolic argument's CL-validity using the system of derivation from the previous two sections — a system that lacks the method of conditional derivation. At first, the task might seem impossible; as we have said, we cannot move from this argument's premises to its conclusion in such a system. Still, there is a roundabout method for using a derivation to demonstrate the sample argument's CL-validity.

To see what this method is, notice that a valuation is a counterexample to our sample symbolic argument just in case, in it, the symbolic sentences "$(-P \lor Q)$" and "$(R \lor -Q)$" have the value *t* while "$(P \rightarrow R)$" has the value *f*.

But, according to our rule of valuation for conditionals (V5), the symbolic sentence "(P → R)" has the value *f* when and only when "P" has the value *t* while "R" has the value *f*. So, a valuation is a counterexample to our sample argument just in case, in it, "(−P ∨ Q)", "(R ∨ −Q)", and "P" have the value *t* while "R" has the value *f*. And any valuation in which these symbolic sentences have these values would also be a counterexample to the symbolic argument

(−P ∨ Q)

(R ∨ −Q)

P

———

So, R

It follows that, if a valuation is a counterexample to our *original* sample argument, then that valuation is also a counterexample to this *variation* of it. Accordingly, by showing that there is no counterexample to the variation, we show that there is no counterexample to the original. In establishing the CL-validity of the variation, we establish the CL-validity of the original symbolic argument.

This provides us with our roundabout method for demonstrating the sample symbolic argument's validity: We can demonstrate the variation's CL-validity with a symbolic derivation and infer that, since the variation is CL-valid, the original argument must be CL-valid, too.

In effect, this is what we did when we constructed the symbolic derivation:

1.	(−P ∨ Q)	Prem
2.	(R ∨ −Q)	Prem
3.	P	SuppCD
4.	− −P	3 DNI
5.	Q	1,4 DS
6.	− −Q	5 DNI
7.	R	2,6 DS
8.	(P → R)	3–7 CD

On line (3) of this derivation, we wrote "P" as a supposition, resolving to treat it as if it were one of our premises, and we then set out to derive the sentence "R". That is, we temporarily changed our problem from that of constructing a derivation for the original symbolic argument to that of constructing one for the variation. At line (8), however, we switched back to the original problem — for here we boxed up the conditional derivation and wrote the conclusion of the original symbolic argument. It is as if, faced with the problem of constructing a derivation for the original argument, we went off to the side, demonstrated the CL-validity of the variation, noted that the variation is CL-valid only if the original argument is, and inferred that the original argument must be CL-valid, too.

In our sample derivation, we used CD only once. There is nothing in the rules, however, to prevent a derivation's having two or more conditional derivations in it, one after the other. Consider, for example, this symbolic derivation:

1.	$(A \rightarrow -(B \lor C))$	Prem
2.	$(B \& -A)$	SuppCD
3.	B	2 Simp
4.	$((B \& -A) \rightarrow B)$	2–3 CD
5.	B	SuppCD
6.	$(B \lor C)$	5 Adj
7.	$--(B \lor C)$	6 DNI
8.	$-A$	7,1 MT
9.	$(B \& -A)$	5,8 Conj
10.	$(B \rightarrow (B \& -A))$	5–9 CD
11.	$(B \leftrightarrow (B \& -A))$	4,10 BCI

Here, to derive a biconditional, we constructed two conditional derivations, one for each of the biconditional's component conditionals. Then, having succeeded in deriving these conditionals on lines (4) and (10), we put them together with BCI on line (11).

In addition to symbolic derivations in which one box occurs *after* another, there are some in which one box occurs *inside* another. An example is this:

1.	$(A \rightarrow (-B \& C))$	Prem
2.	$(-B \rightarrow (-D \rightarrow E))$	Prem
3.	A	SuppCD
4.	$-E$	SuppCD
5.	$(-B \& C)$	3,1 MP
6.	$-B$	5 Simp
7.	$(-D \rightarrow E)$	6,2 MP
8.	$--D$	4,7 MT
9.	D	8 DNE
10.	$(-E \rightarrow D)$	4–9 CD
11.	$(A \rightarrow (-E \rightarrow D))$	3–10 CD

Here, wanting to derive the conditional on line (11), we wrote its antecedent as a supposition on line (3) and set out to derive its consequent, "$(-E \rightarrow D)$". Then, noticing that "$(-E \rightarrow D)$" is itself a conditional, we wrote *its* antecedent as a supposition on line (4) and set out to derive *its* consequent, "D". Having reached "D" on line (9), we completed the symbolic derivation with the uses of CD on lines (10) and (11).

We now have an example in which conditional derivations occur one after another and an example in which they occur one inside another. It is important to note, however, that conditional derivations *cannot* overlap. To see why, consider the following attempt at derivation:

1.	$(A \rightarrow B)$	Prem
2.	$(B \rightarrow C)$	Prem
3.	A	SuppCD
4.	D	SuppCD
5.	B	1,3 MP
6.	C	2,5 MP
7.	$(A \rightarrow C)$	3–6 CD

To finish this symbolic derivation, we would need another line with the annotation "CD"—a line whose annotation would cite the supposition on line (4). But, since line (4) is already in a box, we are not allowed to derive other sentences from it or cite it in annotations. So, we can never finish this attempt at derivation.

Problems of this sort are easy to avoid. If, in the course of constructing a symbolic derivation, we have two unboxed lines with the annotation "SuppCD", we should box up the second *before* we box up the first. By doing this, we ensure that we never box ourselves into a corner.

One final point has to do with the derivation:

1.	P	SuppCD
2.	$--P$	1 DNI
3.	P	2 DNE
4.	$(P \rightarrow P)$	1–3 CD

This symbolic derivation *has* been constructed in accordance with our rules, but it is awkward. Although we already had written "P" on line (1), we had to play a little trick with DNI and DNE in order to write it again on line (4).

So that we won't need tricks of this sort, we will add a new rule of inference—the **Rule of Repetition (R):**

> If a symbolic sentence appears as an unboxed line of a derivation, we may write that sentence again.

This rule will not allow us to do anything that we couldn't have done with DNI and DNE, but it will help to keep our conditional derivations short and simple.

Exercises 6.4

1. *Defend or criticize:* According to the rule CD, if a conditional's consequent appears as one line of a symbolic derivation with the annotation "SuppCD", and if the conditional's antecedent appears as a subsequent line of the derivation, we may write the conditional itself as a line.

2. *Defend or criticize:* A given symbolic argument whose conclusion is a conditional is CL-valid just in case the symbolic argument we get when we add the conditional's antecedent to the set of premises and replace the conditional with its consequent is CL-valid.

3. What, if anything, is wrong in the following attempts at derivation?

a. 1. $(-A \rightarrow -B)$ Prem
   2. $--B$ SuppCD
   3. $--A$ 1,2 MT
   4. $(--B \rightarrow --A)$ 2–3 CD
   5. A   3 DNE

b. 1. $\boxed{P}$ SuppCD
   2. $\boxed{P}$ 1 R
   3. $(P \rightarrow P)$ 1–2 CD

c. 1. $(A \rightarrow B)$ Prem
   2. A   Prem
   3. B   1,2 MP
   4. C   SuppCD
   5. $(B \, \& \, C)$ 3,4 Conj

4. Demonstrate the CL-validity of the following symbolic arguments by deriving their conclusions from their premises:

a. $(A \lor B)$
   $(A \rightarrow C)$
   $(B \rightarrow D)$
   ———————
   So, $(-C \rightarrow D)$

b. A
   ——————————————
   So, $((-A \lor -B) \rightarrow (A \, \& -B))$

c. $((A \, \& \, B) \lor -(A \lor B))$
   ————————————
   So, $(A \leftrightarrow B)$

d. $(A \rightarrow (B \lor C))$
$\quad (-A \rightarrow -D)$
——————
So, $(D \rightarrow (-B \rightarrow C))$

e. $(A \rightarrow (B \mathbin{\&} C))$
$\quad ((B \lor D) \rightarrow E)$
$\quad ((E \rightarrow F) \mathbin{\&} G)$
——————
So, $(A \rightarrow (F \mathbin{\&} G))$

f. $(A \rightarrow (B \rightarrow C))$
$\quad ((B \rightarrow C) \rightarrow (A \mathbin{\&} D))$
——————
So, $(A \rightarrow D)$

g. $(((A \lor B) \mathbin{\&} C) \leftrightarrow D)$
$\quad (E \rightarrow (B \mathbin{\&} C))$
——————
So, $(E \rightarrow D)$

h. $(A \leftrightarrow B)$
——————
So, $((A \leftrightarrow C) \leftrightarrow (B \leftrightarrow C))$

i. $(A \leftrightarrow B)$
$\quad (B \rightarrow C)$
$\quad (-C \lor B)$
——————
So, $(A \leftrightarrow C)$

j. $(A \rightarrow (B \lor C))$
$\quad -(-(B \rightarrow D) \lor E)$
$\quad -(-(C \rightarrow D) \mathbin{\&} -E)$
——————
So, $(A \rightarrow D)$

5. Demonstrate the validity of the following English arguments by constructing derivations for their symbolic translations:

    a. Alice will go to law school if and only if her husband gets a job. Therefore, Alice won't go to law school if and only if her husband doesn't get a job.

    b. Carl will go skiing if either Mary or Paula asks for a ride. Dwight will stay home just in case Carl doesn't go skiing. Hence, Dwight will not stay home if Paula asks for a ride.

6. *Defend or criticize:* Unlike most of CL's rules of inference, the Rule of Repetition does not correspond to anything people do when they try to persuade others.

6.5 Indirect Derivation

Earlier in this chapter, we developed a simple system of symbolic derivation based on simple rules of inference, such as CS and MP. Then, noting that there were CL-valid arguments for which we could not construct derivations, we added the rules SuppCD and CD. As we saw, adding these rules strengthened our system of derivation considerably.

Yet there remain some CL-valid arguments for which we still cannot construct symbolic derivations. An example is

$$(-A \rightarrow B)$$
$$(A \leftrightarrow C)$$
$$(B \rightarrow C)$$
_____

So, C

Although this symbolic argument is CL-valid, we cannot derive its conclusion from its premises with just the rules we now have. In this section, therefore, we add two new rules of derivation: the *Rule of Supposition for Indirect Derivation* (SuppID) and the *Rule of Indirect Derivation* (ID).

As with the methods of direct and conditional derivation, our new rules are inspired by a method that people use when reasoning in English. For an example of this method, consider this passage from a math text:

> Is zero an odd number? Well, suppose that it is. Then two is also odd. (Proof: The result of adding two to zero is two, and the result of adding two to an odd number is always odd.) But two, being the number of the pair, clearly is not odd. So, zero is not odd, either.

In this passage, the author makes a supposition *contrary* to the argument's conclusion. That is, in an attempt to show that zero is *not* odd, the author supposes — for the sake of argument — that zero *is* odd. Then, using the supposition as if it were a premise, the author derives a statement (namely, that *two is odd*) that conflicts with the known truth that *two is not odd*. Finally, having done this, the author concludes that *zero is not odd*.

The pattern here is a common one. Often, to show that a given sentence is true, an arguer will attempt to derive a falsehood from that sentence's negation. If the arguer succeeds in this attempt, the sentence's negation must be false and the original sentence must therefore be true. The pattern is thus one of *indirect* derivation. Rather than arguing for a sentence's truth directly, an arguer does so indirectly, by arguing for the falsity of its negation.

We will model this pattern of reasoning in CL by adding two new rules of derivation to our system. One is the **Rule of Supposition for Indirect Derivation (SuppID):**

If we want to derive a symbolic sentence, we may write its negation as a supposition.

And the other is the **Rule of Indirect Derivation (ID):**

If a sentence and its negation both appear as (unboxed) lines of a derivation, and if a previous (unboxed) line of the derivation is a supposition with the annotation "SuppID", we may delete the initial dash from the supposition and write the result as a subsequent line and annotate it with "ID" — provided that we draw a box enclosing the original supposition and all subsequent lines up to, but not including, the one with the annotation "ID".

This rule stands to SuppID as CD stands to SuppCD. In particular, just as every use of SuppCD must be followed by a corresponding use of CD, every use of SuppID must be followed by a corresponding use of ID.

To construct an indirect derivation in English, we make a supposition, derive something that conflicts with a known truth, and conclude that our supposition is false. Similarly, in using rules SuppID and ID, we write a sentence as a supposition, derive the negation of an (unboxed) sentence in the derivation, and then write the sentence of which our supposition is the negation. In view of this similarity, we say that, when we use SuppID and ID, we construct a **symbolic indirect derivation.**

For an example of such a derivation, consider the symbolic argument that we mentioned at the beginning of this section:

$(-A \rightarrow B)$

$(A \leftrightarrow C)$

$(B \rightarrow C)$

———————

So, C

When we first looked at this argument, our rules of inference did not allow us to derive its conclusion from its premises. But now that we have added SuppID and ID to those rules, we can easily construct a symbolic derivation for the argument, like this:

1.	$(-A \rightarrow B)$	Prem
2.	$(A \leftrightarrow C)$	Prem
3.	$(B \rightarrow C)$	Prem
4.	$-C$	SuppID
5.	$-B$	3,4 MT
6.	$--A$	1,5 MT
7.	$(A \rightarrow C)$	2 BCE
8.	$-A$	7,4 MT
9.	C	4–8 ID

Since the supposition of "−C" on line (4) leads us to a sentence on line (6) and to that sentence's negation on line (8), rule ID allows us to write the conclusion "C" on line (9).

In the sample symbolic derivation, lines (4) through (8) are boxed. The rule ID requires that we draw a box *whenever* we complete an indirect derivation. And the effect of these boxes is just the same as that of the boxes we draw when we use the rule CD: Once a sentence is in a box, we should not cite it in subsequent annotations. The boxes thus have the effect of canceling suppositions and retracting everything that we derived from those suppositions.

Even so, the fact that SuppID allows us to make suppositions whenever we want may raise doubts about our system's reliability as a test for CL-validity. Does our sample derivation really demonstrate that the sample symbolic argument is CL-valid?

To see that is does, consider the following set of symbolic sentences, which we will call S:

$(-A \rightarrow B)$
$(A \leftrightarrow C)$
$(B \rightarrow C)$
$-C$

This set contains the sample argument's premises and the negation of the sample argument's conclusion.

If old rules such as MT and BCE allow us to derive a sentence and that sentence's negation from S, then S must be CL-inconsistent. But a symbolic argument is CL-valid just in case the set containing its premises and the negation of its conclusion is CL-inconsistent. Hence, to demonstrate the sample argument's CL-validity, we need only derive a sentence and its negation from the sentences in S.

This is exactly what we did in our sample symbolic derivation. Since we wrote the sample argument's premises on lines (1), (2), and (3), and the negation of its conclusion on line (4), the sentences that we had to work with at line (5) were those in the set S. Therefore, when we derived both "−A" and "−−A" from these sentences, we could be sure that S was CL-inconsistent. But, as we just showed, the fact that the set S is CL-inconsistent shows that the sample symbolic argument is CL-valid. Accordingly, the rule ID allowed us to write the sample argument's conclusion, "C", on line (10).

Generalizing from this example, we can see that — even when we allow ourselves to use SuppID and ID — our system of symbolic derivation provides us with a reliable test for CL-validity. If we can derive a symbolic argument's conclusion from its premises using SuppID and ID, we can be certain that the argument is CL-valid. In addition, now that we have added SuppID and ID to our rules of derivation, we can (in theory) construct a symbolic derivation for *any* CL-valid argument whatever. Hence, a symbolic argument is CL-valid just in case our rules allow us to derive its conclusion from its premises.

Exercises 6.5

1. *Defend or criticize:* If a sentence appears in a symbolic derivation with the annotation "SuppID," the sentence's first mark must be a dash.

2. *Defend or criticize:* If we can derive a sentence and its negation from a given set of sentences without using SuppCD, CD, SuppID, or ID, that set must be CL-inconsistent.

3. *Defend or criticize:* A symbolic argument is CL-valid just in case the set containing its premises and the negation of its conclusion is CL-inconsistent.

4. *Defend or criticize:* Suppose that lines (1) and (2) of a finished derivation both have the annotation "Prem", that line (3) has the annotation "SuppID", and that line (4) has the annotation "SuppCD". Then at least one subsequent line of the derivation must have the annotation "ID". But, *before* any line with the annotation "ID", there must be a line with the annotation "CD".

5. *Defend or criticize:* In a single symbolic derivation, conditional derivations and indirect derivations may appear one after another or one inside another.

6. Identify the errors, if any, in the following attempts at derivation:

a. 1. $(A \rightarrow B)$ Prem
   2. A Prem
   3. $\boxed{-C}$ SuppID
   4. $\boxed{B}$ 1,2 MP
   5. $\boxed{-B}$ SuppCD
   6. C 1–4 ID

b. 1. $(-A \rightarrow A)$ Prem
   2. $\boxed{-A}$ SuppID
   3. $\boxed{A}$ 1,2 MP
   4. $\boxed{-A}$ 2 R
   5. A 2–4 ID

c. 1. $(C \rightarrow (-A \,\&\, B))$ Prem
   2. A Prem
   3. $\boxed{C}$ SuppCD
   4. $\boxed{(-A \,\&\, B)}$ 1,3 MP
   5. $\boxed{-A}$ 4 Simp
   6. $\boxed{A}$ 2 R
   7. $-C$ 3–6 ID

d. 1.   B   Prem
   2. $\boxed{A}$ SuppCD
   3. $\boxed{A}$ 2 R
   4.   (A → A)   2–3 CD

7. Construct a derivation for each of the following symbolic arguments:

a. (A ∨ −B)
   (−C → −A)
   (−C → B)
   ─────────
   So, C

b. −(−A & −B)
   ───────────
   So, (A ∨ B)

c. (A ∨ B)
   (−C → −A)
   ──────────
   So, ((B → A) → C)

d. (A → B)
   (C → B)
   ─────────────────
   So, ((A ∨ C) → −(−D & − B))

e. ((A → B) → C)
   (−D ∨ −A)
   (B ↔ −D)
   ──────────
   So, C

f. ((A → B) & D)
   (B → −C)
   ──────────
   So, (C → −(A ∨ B))

g. ((A → B) → C)
   (D → (−B → E))
   ───────────────
   So, ((C ∨ −E) → (D → C))

h. (A → (B → (C & −C)))
   ────────────────────
   So, (A → −B)

i. $(A \rightarrow B)$
$\quad (C \rightarrow D)$
$\quad ((B \vee D) \rightarrow E)$
$\quad -E$
$\quad \overline{}$
$\quad$ So, $-(A \vee C)$

j. $(A \rightarrow (B \rightarrow C))$
$\quad (-D \rightarrow (A \vee C))$
$\quad (A \rightarrow B)$
$\quad \overline{}$
$\quad$ So, $(D \vee C)$

k. $((-A \vee B) \vee C)$
$\quad -(B \leftrightarrow -C)$
$\quad \overline{}$
$\quad$ So, $(C \vee -A)$

6.6 Derivation in CL and in English

With the introduction of the rules SuppID and ID in the previous section, we completed CL's system of symbolic derivation. In this section, we briefly reflect on what this system shows us about English.

We can derive a symbolic argument's conclusion from its premises using CL's rules of inference only if the argument is CL-valid. And, as we saw in Chapter 5, if an argument has a CL-valid translation, it generally follows that the argument has an S-valid form and, hence, that it is valid. Accordingly, we can demonstrate an argument's validity by constructing a derivation for its symbolic translation. Since symbolic derivations tend to be less clumsy than truth tables, our new method for demonstrating validity is more elegant than the old one described in Chapter 4.

But the refinement of our method for demonstrating validity has not been our only aim in developing CL's system of symbolic derivation. We have also sought to deepen our understanding of the relation of English syntax to English semantics and to shed some light on the ways that people reason in English. How has the addition of a system of derivation to CL furthered us in these aims?

Central to the answer to this question are the ideas of derivability and entailment. Applied to CL, the idea of *derivability* is this:

A symbolic argument's conclusion is **derivable** from its premises just in case, using CL's rules of inference, we can move in a finished derivation from those premises to that conclusion.

And, applied to CL, the idea of *entailment* is this:

A symbolic argument's premises **entail** that argument's conclusion just in case the argument is CL-valid.

These ideas are familiar; we have been using them all along in this chapter. Only the names are new.

In our definition of *derivability*, we mention CL's rules of inference. These rules say that we may write sentences of certain kinds in symbolic derivations if we already have sentences of certain other kinds, but these rules say nothing at all about values or valuations. Hence, CL's rules of inference are syntactic rules. To say that a symbolic argument's conclusion is derivable from its premises is to comment on the argument's syntax, not its semantics.

In contrast, to say that a symbolic argument's premises *entail* its conclusion is to say that the argument is CL-valid — or, in other words, that there is no valuation in which its premises have the value *t* while its conclusion has the value *f*. Unlike the idea of derivability, then, the idea of entailment is semantic. In saying that a symbolic argument's premises entail its conclusion, we say something about the argument's semantics, not its syntax.

Despite this difference between the ideas of derivability and entailment, the ideas are closely related. As we indicated when introducing CL's rules of inference, a symbolic argument's conclusion is derivable from its premises only if the argument is CL-valid. And, as we said after introducing the rules SuppID and ID, a symbolic argument is CL-valid only if its conclusion is derivable from its premises. We can record these points in a single sentence, like this:

A symbolic argument's conclusion is *derivable* from its premises if and only if those premises *entail* that conclusion.

Logicians sometimes express the same thing by saying that CL's system of derivation is logically *adequate*.

We have not really proven CL's adequacy, of course. We have merely hinted at a proof that the system never allows us to construct symbolic derivations for CL-invalid arguments, and we have not even gone that far toward demonstrating that we can always derive the conclusions of CL-valid symbolic arguments from their premises. But, as one can see by looking at texts on mathematical logic, the adequacy of CL's system of derivation *can* be proven. In fact, since all of CL's rules have been explicitly stated, CL's adequacy can be demonstrated with mathematical rigor and precision.

When we turn to English, however, things are not nearly so clear-cut. It would be difficult, if not impossible, to list all the syntactic and semantic rules of English. And even if we did make such a list, our definition of validity would still rest on the hazy and controversial idea of logical possibility. So, there is no chance of demonstrating the adequacy of the English system of derivation with anything like mathematical precision.

Yet, typically, people accept an English argument as valid just in case the arguer can move from its premises to its conclusion with small inferences that seem obviously valid. And, often, an English inference seems obviously valid because it has a familiar form, such as *modus ponens* or *modus tollens.* So, although we cannot rigorously prove the adequacy of the system of derivation for English, we can still make the general observation that, in English as in CL, the ideas of derivability and entailment go hand in hand. As a general rule, an English argument's conclusion is derivable from its premises just in case the argument is valid.

Since CL is a simplified model of English, CL's system of symbolic derivation helps us to understand this important fact about English. As we have indicated in this chapter, many of CL's rules of inference (for example, MP, CD, and ID) mirror English rules of inference. And, as we showed in Chapter 5, CL's rules of valuation mirror English rules of valuation. Hence, by studying the relation of derivability to entailment in CL, we can gain some understanding of the relation of derivability to entailment in English.

CL's system of symbolic derivation has therefore lived up to its promise. Not only has it provided us with an elegant formal method for demonstrating the validity of English arguments, it has also shed some light on the relation of English syntax to English semantics.

Exercises 6.6

1. *Defend or criticize:* In CL, the ideas of derivability and entailment go hand in hand.

2. By constructing symbolic derivations, demonstrate the validity of the following English arguments:
   a. Logic is pleasant if the exercises are nice, and easy if the exercises are short. Therefore, if the exercises are short or nice, logic is either pleasant or easy.
   b. If logic is pleasant, it's not easy. On the other hand, if logic isn't pleasant, the exercises aren't nice. But the exercises aren't nice only if they aren't short. Therefore, either logic isn't easy or the exercises aren't short.

    c. The exercises are short. If the exercises are short and nice, then logic is pleasant. If logic is pleasant unless the exercises aren't nice, then students work hard. Therefore, students work hard.

    d. Students work hard only if the exercises are short, and they do well only if the exercises are nice. But students work hard only if the exercises are not nice, and they do well only if the exercises are not short. Either students do well or they work hard. Therefore, students do well when and only when the exercises are not short.

    e. Logic is both easy and pleasant — but only if the exercises are short. If students work hard and the exercises are short, then if students do not do well either logic is not pleasant or the exercises are nice. Therefore, if logic is pleasant and students work hard, logic is easy only if either students do well or the exercises are nice.

3. *Defend or criticize:* The rule Simp tells us that, if a conjunction appears on a line of a derivation, we may write either of its conjuncts on a subsequent line. So, the rule Simp is a syntactic rule of CL, not a semantic rule.

4. In this section, we made two assertions about CL's rules of inference:

    a. If there is a (known or unknown) way to derive a symbolic argument's conclusion from its premises, the argument is CL-valid.

    b. If a symbolic argument is CL-valid, there is a (known or unknown) way to derive its conclusion from its premises.

Describe a change in CL's rules of inference that would leave (a) true but make (b) false. Next, describe a change in CL's rules of inference that would leave (b) true but make (a) false. Finally, describe a change in CL's rules of inference that would make both (a) and (b) false.

5. *Defend or criticize:* The adequacy of CL's system of derivation can be rigorously demonstrated, as can the adequacy of the system of derivation for English.

6.7 Overview

    In this chapter, we have introduced a number of rules of inference. We now summarize these rules (with the exception of Prem) using diagrams. The diagram for each rule shows one or two simple inferences that have been constructed in accordance with that rule:

DNI

$$\frac{P}{\text{So, } --P}$$

DNE

$$\frac{--P}{\text{So, } P}$$

Simp

$$\frac{(P \& Q)}{\text{So, } P} \quad \text{or} \quad \frac{(P \& Q)}{\text{So, } Q}$$

Conj

$$\frac{\begin{array}{c} P \\ Q \end{array}}{\text{So, } (P \& Q)} \quad \text{or} \quad \frac{\begin{array}{c} P \\ Q \end{array}}{\text{So, } (Q \& P)}$$

CS

$$\frac{\begin{array}{c} -(P \& Q) \\ P \end{array}}{\text{So, } -Q} \quad \text{or} \quad \frac{\begin{array}{c} -(P \& Q) \\ Q \end{array}}{\text{So, } -P}$$

DS

$$\frac{\begin{array}{c} (P \lor Q) \\ -P \end{array}}{\text{So, } Q} \quad \text{or} \quad \frac{\begin{array}{c} (P \lor Q) \\ -Q \end{array}}{\text{So, } P}$$

Adj

$$\frac{P}{\text{So, } (P \lor Q)} \quad \text{or} \quad \frac{P}{\text{So, } (Q \lor P)}$$

DM

$$\frac{-(P \lor Q)}{\text{So, } -P} \quad \text{or} \quad \frac{-(P \lor Q)}{\text{So, } -Q}$$

MP

$$\frac{\begin{array}{c} (P \to Q) \\ P \end{array}}{\text{So, } Q}$$

MT

$$\frac{\begin{array}{c} (P \to Q) \\ -Q \end{array}}{\text{So, } -P}$$

D

$$\frac{\begin{array}{c} (P \lor Q) \\ (P \to R) \\ (Q \to R) \end{array}}{\text{So, } R}$$

HS

$$\frac{\begin{array}{c} (P \to Q) \\ (Q \to R) \end{array}}{\text{So, } (P \to R)}$$

ENC

$$\frac{-(P \to Q)}{\text{So, } (P \& -Q)}$$

BCI

$$\frac{\begin{array}{c} (P \to Q) \\ (Q \to P) \end{array}}{\text{So, } (P \leftrightarrow Q)} \quad \text{or} \quad \frac{\begin{array}{c} (P \to Q) \\ (Q \to P) \end{array}}{\text{So, } (Q \leftrightarrow P)}$$

BCE

$$\frac{(P \leftrightarrow Q)}{\text{So, } (P \to Q)} \quad \text{or} \quad \frac{(P \leftrightarrow Q)}{\text{So, } (Q \to P)}$$

ENB

$$\frac{-(P \leftrightarrow Q)}{\text{So, } (-P \leftrightarrow Q)}$$

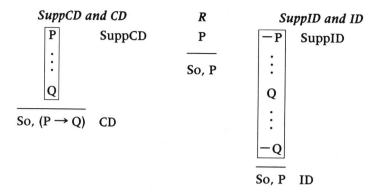

Of course, these are very simple examples. Using Simp, for instance, we may not only move from "(P & Q)" to "P" but also from "(P & (Q → −R))" to "(Q → −R)".

To construct a symbolic *derivation* for a symbolic argument is to move from its premises to its conclusion in accordance with these rules of inference. And, as we have said, if we can construct a symbolic derivation for a given symbolic argument, we can be certain that the argument is CL-valid.

Chapter 7

Predicate Logic: Constants and Predicate Letters

With the development of the system of symbolic derivation in the last chapter, we completed our discussion of the system CL. What has CL done for us, and what remains to be done?

The path to the development of CL began in Chapter 1 with the definition of validity:

> An argument is *valid* just in case there is no logically possible situation in which its premises are true while its conclusion is false.

With this definition in mind, we set out to find a reliable and efficient method for demonstrating the validity of particular arguments — ideally, one that would shed some light on what it is about valid arguments that accounts for their validity.

We took a large step toward the development of such a method in Chapter 3, with our examination of the McCoy argument:

McCoy is either a Platonist or an Aristotelian.

McCoy is not a Platonist.

So, McCoy is an Aristotelian.

As we saw, this argument owes its validity not to the content of the sentences in it, but to their form.

To clarify our idea of form, we distinguished clauses from sentential operators:

A *clause* is a string of words that can be a sentence by itself and that can be used by itself to make a statement.

A *sentential operator* is a string of words that contains one or more blanks and that becomes a clause when the blanks are filled with clauses.

These definitions led to the definition of sentential form:

The *sentential form* of a sentence or argument is the way it is made up from simple clauses and sentential operators.

To reveal the sentential form of a given sentence or argument, we expand abbreviations and replace simple clauses with uppercase letters (the first, wherever it occurs, with *"P"*, the second with *"Q"*, and so on).

It is because of its sentential form that our example, the McCoy argument, is valid. Any other argument with the same form, we noted, would be valid as well. Accordingly, we introduced the notion of sentential validity (S-validity):

An argument's sentential form is *sententially valid* (S-valid) just in case every argument of that form is valid.

The study of sentential form promised to yield a method for demonstrating the validity of whole groups of arguments, all at once.

In an attempt to find such a method, we developed the system CL, a simplified model of English. CL's vocabulary includes sentence letters, which correspond to simple clauses of English, and symbolic operators, which correspond to sentential operators. In virtue of these correspondences, CL captures important facts about the sentential forms of arguments in English. It also captures important facts about validity. As arguments in English are either valid or invalid, symbolic arguments of CL are either CL-valid or CL-invalid:

A symbolic argument is *CL-valid* just in case there is no valuation in which its premises have the value *t* while its conclusion has the value *f*. Otherwise, it is *CL-invalid*.

CL's symbolic arguments thus correspond to arguments in English, both syntactically and semantically.

Because of these correspondences, CL provides us with a method for demonstrating the S-validity of argument forms and, hence, the validity of particular arguments. Given an argument in English, we can translate it into CL and try to demonstrate the translation's CL-validity with a truth table or a symbolic derivation. If we succeed, we may infer that the sentential form of the original argument is S-valid. And, knowing that an argument's form is S-valid, we may infer that the argument itself is valid. CL thus allows us to make practical use of the observation that some arguments owe their validity to their sentential forms.

Then hasn't CL done everything a system of logic *can* do? No! There are still some valid arguments whose validity CL does not help us either to demonstrate or to understand. An example is contained in this, seemingly uncomplicated, reasoning:

> There should be no doubt about Hatfield's being an M.D.; *all* psychiatrists are M.D.s.

Assuming the arguer takes it for granted that Hatfield *is* a psychiatrist, we can make the argument explicit like this:

> All psychiatrists are M.D.s.
>
> Hatfield is a psychiatrist.
> _____
>
> So, Hatfield is an M.D.

This argument (which we call the *Hatfield argument*) seems valid, and in fact it is. But what accounts for its validity? How can we demonstrate that there is no possible situation in which its premises are true while its conclusion is false?

Here the methods of CL are no help. We can do no better at translating the argument into CL than this:

> P
>
> Q
> _____
>
> So, R

But this symbolic argument is CL-*in*valid. So, CL's methods are not up to the task of demonstrating the Hatfield argument's validity. The reason is that, while CL's methods have to do with sentential form, it is not in virtue of its sentential form that the Hatfield argument is valid.

Though not valid in virtue of its *sentential* form, the Hatfield argument is nonetheless valid in virtue of its form. So, to demonstrate this argument's validity, we need to sharpen our understanding of the form of English sentences and arguments and to reflect this understanding in the syntax and semantics of our model of English.

We accomplish these tasks in this chapter and the next, thus moving from CL to the more sophisticated system called **predicate logic** or **PL**. We begin in the next section by examining the form of the Hatfield argument's second premise and conclusion: "Hatfield is a psychiatrist" and "Hatfield is an M.D.". Then, in the rest of this chapter, we revise our model's syntactic and semantic rules to reflect what we have learned about English. These revisions will take us halfway to the system PL, leaving the second half of the journey for Chapter 8.

7.1 Predicative Form: Singular Terms and Predicates

In this section, we begin to refine our idea of form. The refinement will not be complete until Chapter 8. Our aim in this chapter is merely to introduce *some* of the notions on which the new idea of form will rest.

For a start on these new notions, consider again the Hatfield argument, which we discussed at the end of the introduction to this chapter:

All psychiatrists are M.D.s.

Hatfield is a psychiatrist.

So, Hatfield is an M.D.

As we saw, although this argument is valid, its validity does not rest on its sentential form. Nor does the argument's validity rest on its content; arguments with contents entirely different from the Hatfield argument (such as "All executives are rich; Robinson is an executive; so, Robinson is rich") are valid for precisely the same reason as the Hatfield argument. But, if the Hatfield argument's validity does not rest on either its sentential form or its content, on what *does* its validity rest?

As we will show in Chapter 8, the Hatfield argument's validity rests on the pattern made by expressions such as "Hatfield", ". . . is a psychiatrist", and ". . . is an M.D.". That is, the argument's validity does rest on its *form*. But expressions such as "Hatfield" and ". . . is a psychiatrist" aren't simple clauses, and they're not sentential operators either. So, when we say that the argument's validity rests on its form, we are not talking about sentential form. Rather, we are talking about form of another sort, which we call *predicative* form.

We will not complete the development of the idea of predicative form until Chapter 8. As we indicated in the introduction to this chapter, our aim now is just to lay some groundwork. We do this by noting that expressions such as "Hatfield" and ". . . is an executive" can be sorted into two groups. Some are singular terms, and others predicates.

We can explain *singular terms* in this way:

A **singular term** is a word or string of words that people can use to pick out one particular object, as if by pointing.

Some singular terms (such as "Hatfield," "Rover," and "Scott Hall") are *names* for real people, nonhuman animals, buildings, institutions, and so on. Others (such as "Sherlock Holmes" and "Atlantis") are names for nonexistent people or things. Still others (such as "the richest person in the world" and "the oldest college in Massachusetts") are not names at all, but *descriptive phrases*. What these expressions all have in common is that a person who uses one tries, perhaps unsuccessfully, to pick out one particular person or thing.

A singular term can be used on different occasions to pick out different things. Thus, the singular term "Bob" is used, at different times and places, to pick out thousands of different people each day. But, on any given occasion of its use, a person who uses a singular term tries to pick out one thing and no more.

When a singular term appears in a clause, it is accompanied by a *predicate:*

> A **predicate** is a word or string of words that contains one or more blanks and that becomes a clause when the blanks are filled with singular terms.

Thus, despite obvious differences among them, the phrases ". . . is a psychiatrist," "on Thursday, . . . caught the flu," and "something bumped into . . ." are all predicates.

Not all predicates have the same number of blanks. Some (such as ". . . was hit") have one blank; others (such as ". . . was hit by —") have two; others (such as ". . . was hit by — while__watched") have three; and so on. We say that predicates with one blank are *one-placed,* that those with two blanks are *two-placed,* and so on.

We also distinguish *simple* predicates from *complex* predicates:

> A predicate is **simple** just in case the result of filling its blanks with singular terms is a simple clause (that is, a clause not containing any sentential operators); a predicate is **complex** just in case the result of filling its blanks with singular terms is a complex clause (that is, a clause containing one or more sentential operators).

Thus, the predicate ". . . will be happy" is simple, while the predicate "if Bill comes to the party, . . . will be happy" is complex.

For the sake of simplicity, we limit our attention in this chapter and the next to *simple, one-placed predicates* and ignore all others. (In later chapters, we will have more to say about predicates of other sorts.)

What is the semantic job of a simple, one-placed predicate? Philosophers have argued over this question since the time of the ancient Greeks. Our view, with which readers are, of course, free to disagree, is that predicates mention *properties,* which many objects can have at the same time. Thus, we view the predicate ". . . is tall" as mentioning the property of tallness, which all tall objects share.

Together, predicates and singular terms form clauses. Consider, for example,

> many pitchers struck out Willie Mays,

a simple clause made from the predicate "many pitchers struck out . . ." and the singular term "Willie Mays". We call clauses of this sort *singular simple clauses,* or sometimes just *singular clauses:*

A clause is a **singular simple clause** just in case it can be broken up, with nothing left over, into a singular term and a (simple, one-placed) predicate.

Some simple clauses (such as "many pitchers struck out Willie Mays" and "Hatfield is a psychiatrist") are singular clauses, but others (such as "All psychiatrists are M.D.s") are not singular clauses.

In previous chapters, where our interest was in sentential form, we viewed all simple clauses as indivisible units. We now see, however, that singular simple clauses are made from singular terms and simple, one-placed predicates. This insight inspires the changes in our model of English that we will make in the next few sections.

Exercises 7.1

1. *Defend or criticize:* The expression "Hatfield" is not a simple clause or a sentential operator, and neither is the expression ". . . is a psychiatrist".

2. *Defend or criticize:* Every simple clause can be broken up into a singular term and a predicate.

3. *Defend or criticize:* If Bossy were the only cow in the world, the expression ". . . is a cow" would pick out exactly one object, and it would therefore be a singular term.

4. *Defend or criticize:* The name "Bob" is not a singular term—for, while a singular term picks out just one object, the word "Bob" picks out literally thousands of objects.

5. *Defend or criticize:* The phrase ". . . is a cow" is not a singular term—for, while a singular term picks out just one object, this phrase picks out thousands of objects.

6. *Defend or criticize:* Since every singular term picks out an object, and since there is no Santa Claus, the expression "Santa Claus" is not a singular term.

7. *Defend or criticize:* Predicates are exactly the same as sentential operators. Both look very much like clauses, both have blanks in them, and both become clauses when the blanks are filled.

8. Which of the following are singular terms? Which are simple, one-placed predicates? Which are singular clauses?

a. Dr. James C. Tsai, D.D.S.	b. Socrates
c. Sally hit Tom	d. At noon, . . . ate lunch
e. Mary is poor but honest	f. cow
g. . . . is tall	h. the tallest man here

i. some boxers feared Rocky

j. all psychiatrists are M.D.s

k. each psychiatrist is an M.D.

l. Alice is unhealthy

m. . . . will walk unless it rains

n. Sally slapped . . .

o. . . . hit —

p. Akron is famous for tires

7.2 The Syntax of Constants and Predicate Letters

In the last section, we noted that some English clauses are made from singular terms and simple, one-placed predicates. We now reflect this insight in our formal model of English.

To do this, we add *constants* and *predicate letters* to our model's vocabulary:

Constants are the lowercase letters "a" through "m". (We will save "n" through "z" for another use, which we will discuss in the next chapter.)

Predicate letters are the uppercase letters "A" through "Z".

Both syntactically and semantically, constants correspond to English singular terms, and predicate letters correspond to (simple, one-placed) English predicates.

Predicate letters look very much like sentence letters. In fact, given an uppercase letter such as "P" out of context, we can't tell whether it is the predicate letter "P" or the sentence letter "P". But this will not be a problem. Whenever an uppercase letter is used, its context will show whether it is a predicate letter or a sentence letter.

Having added constants and predicate letters to our model's vocabulary, we need to revise the model's rules of formation. As we have said, our aim is to make constants correspond to English singular terms and predicate letters to predicates. And, as we saw earlier in this chapter, the result of putting a singular term into the blank in a predicate is an English clause. Accordingly, we establish the following rule of formation for our model:

F7:   The result of writing a constant immediately to the right of a predicate letter is a symbolic sentence.

This rule allows us to form symbolic sentences, such as "Fa"* and "Fb", which are made from just predicate letters and constants. By analogy to English, we call such sentences **singular symbolic sentences,** or sometimes just *singular sentences.*

---

* In pronouncing the names of symbolic sentences or wffs, sound all letters. Thus "Fa" is pronounced "eff-ay," not "fah."

As the sentence letter "P" is a symbolic sentence by itself, so is the singular sentence "Fa". As we can put a dash in front of the sentence letter "P" to get the symbolic sentence "−P", we can put a dash in front of "Fa" to get "−Fa". As we can join the sentence letters "P" and "Q" with an ampersand to get the conjunction "(P & Q)", we can join "Fa" and "Gb" to get the conjunction "(Fa & Gb)". Indeed, from a syntactic point of view, sentence letters and singular sentences are interchangeable. Where one can go in a symbolic sentence, so can the other.

By adding singular sentences to our model, we have moved only part way from CL to the more sophisticated system PL. To complete the move, we need to make several more changes in the system's syntax. But we will not make these additional changes until Chapter 8. For the moment, we have just made two changes in our model: (1) we have added constants and predicate letters to the model's vocabulary, and (2) we have added to the model's rules of formation a new rule (F7) that allows the formation of singular sentences.

Exercises 7.2

1. *Defend or criticize:* Now that we have added rule F7 to our system, some of the sequences that used to be symbolic sentences no longer are symbolic sentences.

2. *Defend or criticize:* The capital letter "P" can be used either as a sentence letter or as a predicate letter.

3. Which of the following are symbolic sentences?

a. Fa	b. fa
c. F(a)	d. aF
e. F − a	f. −(Fa)
g. (−Fa)	h. (Fa ∨ − Gb)
i. (Af ∨ − Bg)	j. (Ax ∨ Gy)
k. (Fa ∨ Rab)	l. (aG ∨ bF)
m. (P → (Z → X))	n. (P → (Zc → Xi)
o. (P → Pa)	p. (a → Pa)
q. (P → Pp)	r. (P → p)

4. *Defend or criticize:* If we take a symbolic sentence of CL and replace all its sentence letters with singular symbolic sentences, the result is always a symbolic sentence.

5. *Defend or criticize:* If we take a symbolic sentence containing constants and predicate letters and replace all its singular sentences with sentence letters, the result is always a symbolic sentence.

6. *Defend or criticize:* Sentence letters are syntactically simple (that is, none of their parts are expressions of our system), but singular sentences are syntactically complex (that is, some of their parts *are* expressions of our system).

7.3 The Semantics of Constants and Predicate Letters

In the last section, we looked at the syntax of constants, predicate letters, and singular sentences. In this section, we examine the semantics of these new expressions. What does a valuation look like for a singular symbolic sentence such as "Fa"? And, given a valuation for a sentence containing constants and predicate letters, how can we calculate the sentence's value in the valuation?

Since Chapter 4, we have set up valuations for symbolic sentences simply by assigning the values *t* and *f* to sentence letters. Now that our model of English contains constants and predicate letters, however, we need to do more. In particular, we need to deal with groups — or *sets* — of objects. Accordingly, we prepare for the new ideas of valuation by introducing some ideas from the branch of mathematics called *set theory*. We have been using these ideas all along without much comment. (For example, the collection of CL's sentence letters is a set.) But, since the ideas of set theory will become more important to us as we go further into our study of logic, we now take the time to make these ideas explicit.

The fundamental ideas in set theory are those of *set* and *set membership:*

A **set** is a collection of distinct objects, each of which is called a **member** of the set.

Things of any sort can be members of sets — cabbages, kings, sentences, numbers, or even sets. And a given set can have any number of members. One set (namely, the empty set) has *no* members; some sets have only one member; some sets have just two members; and some sets have an infinite number of members.

To name a set, we list its members, separate the items on the list by commas, and enclose the result in curly brackets. Thus,

{1, 2, 3, 4}

names the set whose members are the numbers one, two, three, and four. Similarly,

{Washington, Adams, Jefferson}

names the set whose members are the first three presidents of the United States. (An exception to the rule for naming sets is the empty set, which we will denote with ∅.)

Sets are defined by their members. That is, set *A* is the same set as set *B* just in case *A* has exactly the same members as *B*. Thus, the set {3, 2, 1} is exactly the same set as {II, III, I} — namely, the set whose members are the numbers one, two, and three.

One final idea from set theory:

> A first set is a **subset** of a second just in case all members of the first are members of the second — or, in other words, there are no members of the first except objects that are members of the second.

The set {2, 4, 6} is a subset of the set {1, 2, 3, 4, 5, 6}, the set {2, 4, 6} is a subset of itself, and the empty set is a subset of *every* set.

With the ideas of set, member, and subset in hand, we can describe the steps to be taken in setting up a valuation for symbolic sentences containing constants and predicate letters. There are four:

> Step 1: We choose a nonempty set to serve as the valuation's **domain of discourse.**
>
> Step 2: We assign a **referent,** which must be a member of the domain of discourse, to each constant appearing in the given sentences.
>
> Step 3: We assign an **extension,** which must be a subset of the domain of discourse, to each predicate letter appearing in the given sentences.
>
> Step 4: We assign exactly one value — either *t* or *f* — to each sentence letter appearing in the given sentences.

We now explain these steps one by one.

Step 1: Identifying a Domain of Discourse

To see the need for this step, imagine that a professor, while lecturing, hears a giggle and asks who is laughing. Were someone to answer, "A Zen monk on Mount Fuji," the answer would obviously be wrong, even if there *were* a laughing monk on Fuji. In asking who was laughing, the professor's attention was plainly limited to the people in the classroom. That is, the set of people in the room was the *domain* of the professor's discourse.

In ordinary conversation, context usually makes the domain of discourse clear. In our formal model of English, however, context is not enough. When setting up a valuation for a symbolic sentence such as "(Fa & −Ga)", we need explicitly to choose a set of objects to serve as the valuation's domain. In doing this, we announce that we are strictly limiting our attention to this set's members.

Any set *except the empty set* will do as a domain. For convenience, though, we generally choose sets of whole, positive numbers. Numbers have well-known names, and there are as many of them as we will ever need.

Step 2: Assigning Referents to Constants

We want our model's constants to correspond to English singular terms, and singular terms can be used to pick out objects. Accordingly, when setting up a valuation for a group of symbolic sentences, we assign exactly one *referent* to each constant in those sentences. These referents must be members of the valuation's domain of discourse, but there are no other restrictions. There is nothing wrong, for instance, with a single object's being the referent of two or more constants (just as there is nothing logically wrong with one person's having two or more aliases).

Step 3: Assigning Extensions to Predicate Letters

As we have said, English predicates mention properties, which more than one object can have at the same time. Thus, the predicate ". . . is red" mentions the property of redness, which all red objects share.

To mirror these facts in our model of English, we assign sets—collections of objects—to predicate letters when setting up valuations. In a given valuation, the set assigned to a predicate letter is called that predicate letter's *extension*. The extensions of predicate letters in a given valuation must be *subsets* of that valuation's domain. After all, in setting up a domain, we strictly limit our attention to the domain's members. But there are no other restrictions on how we assign extensions to predicate letters. Any subset of the domain—even the empty set, or the domain itself—can serve as the extension of a given predicate letter, and two or more predicate letters can have exactly the same extension.

Step 4: Assigning Values to Sentence Letters

Symbolic sentences may contain sentence letters along with constants and predicate letters. When setting up valuations for sentences of this sort, we do with the sentence letters just what we have done in the past. That is, to each sentence letter, we assign exactly one value, either t or f.

To illustrate these four steps, we set up a valuation for the symbolic sentence "((Fa → − Gb) ∨ P)". First, we choose a domain of discourse, such as this:

domain of discourse: {1, 2, 3}

Second, we assign referents to the constants "a" and "b":

referent of "a":   1
referent of "b":   3

Third we assign extensions to the predicate letters "F" and "G", — say, like this:

extension of "F":   {1, 2, 3}
extension of "G":   ∅

Finally, we assign a value to the symbolic sentence letter "P":

value of "P": f

Having done this, we have set up a valuation for our sample symbolic sentence. For convenience, we call this valuation *v*.

Let's calculate the value of the symbolic sentence

((Fa → − Gb) ∨ P)

in valuation *v*. Being a disjunction, this symbolic sentence has the value *t* unless both of its disjuncts have the value *f*. And, since the disjunction's first disjunct is a conditional, it has the value *t* unless its antecedent has the value *t* while its consequent has the value *f*. That much follows from rules of valuation V3 and V5, which have been in our system since Chapter 4. But, by themselves, our old rules do not allow us to calculate the value of the symbolic sentence "((Fa → − Gb) ∨ P)" in valuation *v*. To complete the calculation, we need a new rule telling us how to calculate the values of the *singular* symbolic sentences "Fa" and "Gb".

The guiding thought behind the new rule is that we want such symbolic sentences to mirror the semantics of singular English clauses such as "Joe is tall." Accordingly, we now take another look at the semantics of singular clauses of English.

As we saw earlier in this chapter, each singular clause of English is made from a singular term and a (simple, one-placed) predicate. Generally, the singular term picks out some object, and the predicate mentions a property that the members of some set share. As a general rule,

> a singular clause of English is true just in case the object picked out by the clause's singular term is one of the objects having the property mentioned by the clause's predicate.

Consider, for instance, the singular clause

Joe is tall.

This clause is true just in case the object picked out by the singular term "Joe" is among the things having the property mentioned by the predicate ". . . is tall" — namely, tallness.

Since we want singular symbolic sentences to mirror singular clauses of English, we establish the following rule of valuation for our model:

V7: In a given valuation for it, a singular symbolic sentence has the value *t* just in case the referent of its constant is in the extension of its predicate letter. Otherwise, in that valuation, the singular sentence has the value *f*.

In our sample valuation *v*, the referent of the constant "a" is in the extension of the predicate letter "F". So, the symbolic sentence "Fa" has the value *t* in *v*. But, in *v*, the referent of "b" is not in the extension of "G", and the singular symbolic sentence "Gb" therefore has the value *f*.

Once we know the values of the singular symbolic sentences "Fa" and "Gb", we can easily calculate the value of the sample symbolic sentence "((Fa → − Gb) ∨ P)". Since "(Fa → − Gb)" is a conditional whose antecedent and consequent both have the value *t* in *v*, the conditional itself has the value *t* in *v* (rule V5). So, the symbolic sentence "((Fa → − Gb) ∨ P)", being a disjunction whose first disjunct has the value *t* in *v*, must itself have the value *t* in *v* (rule V4).

This example illustrates a general point. To calculate the values of symbolic sentences containing constants and predicate letters, we generally use rule V7 to calculate the values of singular symbolic sentences and then go on just as if we were using the old system CL. Once we know the values of singular symbolic sentences, we can use our old rules of valuation — V1 through V6 — to calculate the values of the negations, conjunctions, disjunctions, conditionals, and biconditionals in which those singular symbolic sentences appear.

Exercises 7.3

1. *Defend or criticize:* A set is a collection of objects, each of which is called a member of the set.

2. *Defend or criticize:* The set {Washington, Adams, Jefferson} is the same set as {Adams, Jefferson, Washington}.

3. *Defend or criticize:* Every set is a subset of itself.

4. *Defend or criticize:* The set {1, 2, 3} is a subset of the set {two, three, one}.

5. *Defend or criticize:* The empty set is a subset of every set.

6. *Defend or criticize:* Since the empty set has no members, it has no subsets.

7. *Defend or criticize:* The empty set is a member of some sets.

8. *Defend or criticize:* The empty set is a subset of itself.

9. *Defend or criticize:* There are exactly two valuations for the singular symbolic sentence "Fa": one in which it has the value *t* and one in which it has the value *f*.

10. Of the valuations for the sentence "(Fa ∨ Gb)", how many have the set {1, 2} as their domain of discourse?

11. What, if anything, goes wrong in the following attempts to construct valuations for the sentence "((Fa & Gb) ∨ Ga)"?

      a. domain of discourse: ∅

            referent of "a": 1

            referent of "b": 1

         extension of "F": ∅

      b. domain of discourse: {1, 2, 3}

            referent of "a": {1}

            referent of "b": {2}

         extension of "F": {1, 2, 3}

         extension of "G": {1, 2, 3, 4}

      c. domain of discourse: {1}

            referent of "a": 2

            referent of "b": 1

         extension of "F": {1}

         extension of "G": {1}

12. Following are some symbolic sentences and a valuation for them. Calculate the value of each symbolic sentence in the given valuation.

    a. Fa

    b. −(Fa → Gb)

    c. (Fa & −Gb)

    d. (Fb ↔ −Gb)

    e. (Fb → Gb)

    f. (Fc → Gc)

    g. −((Fb & Gb) → Hb)

    h. −((Fc & Gc) → Hc)

    i. (−(Fa & Gb) → Hc)

    j. ((Fa & Gb) → P)

    k. (P → Fa)

    domain of discourse: {1, 2, 3}

          referent of "a": 1

          referent of "b": 2

          referent of "c": 3

       extension of "F": {1, 2, 3}

       extension of "G": {1, 2}

       extension of "H": {1}

          value of "P": *f*

13. For each of the sentences listed in the previous exercise, calculate its value in the valuation described here:

    domain of discourse: {1, 2, 3}

          referent of "a": 1

referent of "b": **2**

referent of "c": **3**

extension of "F": {1}

extension of "G": {1, 3}

extension of "H": {1, 2, 3}

value of "P": *f*

7.4 Translating with Constants and Predicate Letters

Having added constants and predicate letters to our system, we can do a better job than before of translating English sentences into our model. In this section, we explain how.

What makes translation from English into our model possible is that expressions of English correspond, both syntactically and semantically, to expressions of the model. As we saw in Chapter 5, sentence letters and symbolic operators correspond, respectively, to simple clauses and sentential operators of English. Also, as we have shown in this chapter, symbolic constants and predicate letters correspond, respectively, to singular terms and (simple, one-placed) predicates of English.

The correspondences that we described in Chapter 5 are not perfect. (As we pointed out, for instance, the arrow does not perfectly capture the semantics of the sentential operator "if, then".) And the correspondences described in this chapter are not perfect either. While the constant in a singular symbolic sentence has a referent in *every* valuation for that sentence, the singular term in the sentence "Santa Claus wears a red suit" seems not to pick out any object in the real world. Also, although there is always a definite yes or no answer to questions about whether a given object is in the extension of a given predicate letter, things seem to be not as clear-cut in English. (Is the predicate "many people have heard of . . ." true of the person whose professional name was "Mark Twain" and whose given name was "Samuel Clemens"? If so, why does the sentence "Many people have heard of Samuel Clemens" seem false? If not, why does the sentence "Many people have heard of Mark Twain" seem true?)

Still, given that our system is a highly simplified model of English, we have made its expressions correspond to their English counterparts as closely as possible. In view of the correspondences, we say (as we did in Chapter 5) that, in replacing expressions of English with the corresponding expressions of the system, we *translate* English sentences into symbolic sentences.

Consider, for example, the sentence

Many people admire Willie Mays.

We can associate the singular term "Willie Mays" with a constant — say, "a" —

and the (simple, one-placed) predicate "many people admire . . ." with a predicate letter—say, "F"—in our scheme of correspondence. Replacing expressions of English with the corresponding expressions of our model, we get

      Fa

which is our translation of the original sentence.

      If we had translated the same sentence into CL using the methods of
Chapter 5, the result would have been a sentence letter, which would not have
revealed very much about the original sentence's form. In contrast, the translation "Fa" reveals that the original sentence is a singular clause, made from a
singular term and a predicate.

      Translations of singular clauses of English are always singular symbolic
sentences. Consider, for example, the sentence

      Willie Mays is a sports legend,

which begins with the singular term "Willie Mays", and the sentence

      Pitchers struck out Willie Mays often,

which has the term "Willie Mays" in its middle. We may translate either of these
sentences with "Gb", "Ha", or any other singular symbolic sentence—just as
earlier we translated the sentence "Many people admire Willie Mays" with
"Fa". To do so, we set up a scheme of correspondence that associates the singular
term in the English clause with a symbolic constant and the predicate in the
English clause with a predicate letter. Having set up such a scheme, we can move
from English into our system by replacing English expressions with the corresponding symbolic expressions, making minor adjustments so that the symbolic
constant always appears *after* the predicate letter.

      Since we can translate singular clauses, we can also translate longer,
more complex sentences in which singular clauses appear. Consider, for example, the sentence

      Jan or Stacy ate cake, while someone—either Tom or Marcie—ate ice
      cream.

The first step toward translating this sentence is to expand abbreviations,
like this:

      Jan ate cake or Stacy ate cake, and Tom ate ice cream or Marcie ate ice
      cream.

The next step is to set up a scheme of correspondence—say, like this:

      a: Jan

      b: Stacy

      c: Tom

d: Marcie

F: . . . ate cake

G: . . . ate ice cream

Here, as before, we associate singular terms with constants and (one-placed, simple) predicates with predicate letters.

Replacing the expressions in the original English sentence with their symbolic counterparts, we get the translation,

((Fa ∨ Fb) & (Gc ∨ Gd)).

(As when translating in Chapter 5, we have added parentheses to indicate grouping.)

For the sample sentence about cake and ice cream to be true, two conditions must be met: (1) either the object picked out by the singular term "Jan" or the one picked out by the singular term "Stacy" must have the property mentioned by the predicate ". . . ate cake", and (2) either the object picked out by the singular term "Tom" or the one picked out by the singular term "Marcie" must have the property mentioned by the predicate ". . . ate ice cream". Similarly, for the symbolic sentence "((Fa ∨ Fb) & (Gc ∨Gd))" to have the value *t* in a valuation, two conditions must be met: (1) either the referent of the constant "a" or that of the constant "b" must be in the extension of the predicate letter "F", and (2) either the referent of the constant "c" or that of the constant "d" must be in the extension of the predicate letter "G". Thus, the translation corresponds to the original sentence semantically as well as syntactically.

Our examples illustrate a general point about translating with constants and predicate letters. Given an English sentence, we expand abbreviations and look for *singular* clauses (that is, clauses made up just from singular terms and simple, one-placed predicates). Next, we set up a scheme of correspondence that associates the singular terms in these clauses with constants and the predicates in them with predicate letters. (An English expression should have just one symbolic expression associated with it even if the English expression appears many times in the sentence being translated, and a symbolic expression should be assigned to just one expression of English.) Once we have set up a scheme of correspondence, we replace the expressions of English with the associated symbolic expressions, making minor changes in order and supplying punctuation where necessary. In general, the resulting translation will correspond to the original English sentence both syntactically and semantically.

What about simple clauses of English other than singular clauses? How, for instance, should we translate the first premise of the Hatfield argument, "All psychiatrists are M.D.s"? The fact is that, by itself, the addition of constants and predicate letters to our system has had no effect on how we translate such clauses. Until Chapter 8, we will have no choice but to translate simple clauses other than singular clauses with sentence letters.

Exercises 7.4

1. *Defend or criticize:* Semantically, constants of our system correspond to English singular terms, predicate letters to English predicates, and singular symbolic sentences to singular clauses of English.

2. *Defend or criticize:* In setting up a scheme of correspondence, we associate singular terms of English with predicate letters and (simple, one-placed) predicates of English with constants.

3. *Defend or criticize:* The translation of an English sentence is a *singular* symbolic sentence just in case the English sentence consists of a *singular* clause.

4. *Defend or criticize:* Although the sentence "Someone is tall" contains the predicate ". . . is tall", its translation into the system developed in this chapter does not contain a predicate letter.

5. Suppose we are trying to translate the sentence "Tom has brown hair, but John is blond."

a. In setting up a scheme of correspondence, may we associate the constant "a" with the singular term "Tom" and then go on to associate the same constant with the singular term "John"?

b. In setting up a scheme of correspondence, may we associate the predicate letter "F" with the predicate "Tom has brown hair, but . . . is blond"?

c. In setting up a scheme of correspondence, may we associate the predicate letter "F" with the predicate ". . . has brown hair" and then go on to associate the same predicate letter with the predicate ". . . is blond"?

d. If we associate the constant "a" with the singular term "Tom", the constant "b" with the singular term "John", the predicate letter "F" with the predicate ". . . has brown hair", and the predicate letter "G" with the predicate ". . . is blond", may we then translate the original sentence with "(aF & bG)"?

6. Translate the following sentences, using constants and predicate letters where appropriate:

a. Alice is beautiful.
b. Alice is beautiful if Jeremy is rich.
c. Alice is beautiful if she is rich.
d. Alice is beautiful only if she is rich.
e. If Alice isn't beautiful, Jeremy is rich unless he's ill.
f. Everyone is beautiful.
g. If Alice isn't beautiful, no one is.
h. If someone is beautiful, then he/she is rich.

7.5 Overview

Noting that there are valid arguments whose validity we cannot demonstrate with the methods of CL, we began in this chapter to refine our model of English.

As we saw, some English clauses are made from singular terms and simple, one-placed predicates:

> A *singular term* is a word or string of words that people can use to pick out one particular object, as if by pointing.

> A *simple, one-placed predicate* is a word or string of words that contains exactly one blank and that becomes a simple clause when the blank is filled with a singular term.

If a clause is made from just a singular term and a simple, one-placed predicate, we call it a *singular clause*.

In an attempt to model facts about singular clauses in our system, we added constants (lowercase letters "a" through "m") and predicate letters (uppercase letters "A" through "Z") to its vocabulary. With this additional vocabulary came a new rule of formation:

> F7:   The result of writing a constant immediately to the right of a predicate letter is a symbolic sentence.

If the only rule used in the construction of a given symbolic sentence is F7, we call the given sentence a *singular symbolic sentence*.

To help us describe the semantics of singular symbolic sentences, we introduced some ideas from set theory:

> A *set* is a collection of distinct objects, each of which is called a *member* of the set.

> Set *A* is one and the same set as set *B* just in case *A* has exactly the same members as *B*.

> A first set is a *subset* of a second just in case all members of the first are members of the second.

Using these ideas, we outlined the steps involved in constructing *valuations* for symbolic sentences containing constants and predicate letters.

> Step 1:   We choose a nonempty set to serve as the valuation's *domain of discourse*.

> Step 2:   We assign a *referent*, which must be a member of the domain of discourse, to each constant appearing in the given sentences.

Step 3:   We assign an *extension,* which must be a subset of the domain of discourse, to each predicate letter appearing in the given sentences.

Step 4:   We assign exactly one value—either *t* or *f*—to each sentence letter appearing in the given sentences.

In calculating the values of symbolic sentences in valuations of this new sort, we used the following rule of valuation for singular symbolic sentences:

V7:   In a given valuation for it, a singular symbolic sentence has the value *t* just in case the referent of its constant is in the extension of its predicate letter. Otherwise, in that valuation, the singular sentence has the value *f.*

This rule ensures that singular symbolic sentences correspond semantically to singular clauses of English—for, in general, a singular clause of English is true just in case the object picked out by its singular term is among the objects having the property mentioned by its predicate.

In light of the correspondence of singular symbolic sentences to singular clauses of English, we revised our method of translation. When we find a *singular* simple clause in a sentence we are translating, we assign a constant to its singular term and a predicate letter to its predicate, making sure that no symbolic expression gets associated with two different expressions of English. Then, to complete the translation, we replace expressions of English with the corresponding expressions of the system, making minor changes in order and supplying punctuation where necessary.

The revisions we have made in our system in this chapter have taken us part way from the simple system CL to the more sophisticated system PL. In the next chapter, we will complete PL's development.

Chapter 8

Predicate Logic: Variables and Quantifiers

At the beginning of Chapter 7, we considered the Hatfield argument:

> All psychiatrists are M.D.s.
>
> Hatfield is a psychiatrist.
>
> ─────────────────────
>
> So, Hatfield is an M.D.

Translating this argument into CL, we got "P; Q; So, R", a translation that did not help us to demonstrate the argument's validity or to understand why it is valid. So, we set out to move from CL to a more refined model of English: predicate logic, or PL.

Noting that the Hatfield argument's second premise and conclusion are made from singular terms and (simple, one-placed) predicates, we began the development of PL by adding constants and predicate letters to CL's vocabulary. Using these new expressions, we can translate the Hatfield argument like this:

> P
>
> Fa
>
> ─────
>
> So, Ga

Unlike the translation "P; Q; so R", this one captures the important fact that there is a singular term that appears both in the argument's second premise and in its conclusion.

But even the translation "P; Fa; so Ga" hides facts important to the Hatfield argument's evaluation. In particular, since we are still translating the argument's first premise with a sentence letter, our translation hides the fact that there is a property (namely, the property of being a psychiatrist) mentioned in both the argument's premises. Similarly, the translation hides the fact that there is a property (namely, the property of being an M.D.) mentioned both in the argument's first premise and in its conclusion.

In this chapter, we develop methods for capturing and dealing with facts like these, thereby completing the development of our new system of logic, predicate logic (PL). The difference between PL and CL is great, and moving directly from one to the other might be confusing. So, we split the move into two steps. In the first, which we took in Chapter 7, we refined the model so that it can mirror the inner structure of *singular* clauses such as "Hatfield is a psychiatrist" and "Hatfield is an M.D.". In the second step, which we take in this chapter, we refine the model again—this time so that it can mirror the inner structure of sentences such as "All psychiatrists are M.D.s". The resulting system, PL, provides us with a method for demonstrating validity that is much more powerful than CL's.

First, we turn our attention in the next section to English clauses containing words such as "all" and "some". Studying the inner structure of these clauses will lead us to formulate definitions of *predicative form* and *predicative validity*. These definitions, in turn, will lead us to revise the model's rules of formation, valuation, and derivation. Having made these revisions, we end the chapter with an assessment of the progress made in the move from CL to PL. The assessment will show that, using PL's methods, we can demonstrate the validity of the Hatfield argument and of many other arguments whose validity rests on the use of words like "all" and "some".

8.1 Predicative Form: Pronouns and Quantifying Phrases

In this section, we sharpen our idea of the *form* of sentences and arguments. We begin by looking again at the Hatfield argument, which we used as an example in the last chapter and again in the introduction to this one:

All psychiatrists are M.D.s.

Hatfield is a psychiatrist.

So, Hatfield is an M.D.

As we have seen, the system CL is of little use in demonstrating this argument's validity. Then how can we show that the argument is valid?

We might begin by noticing that the sentences of the Hatfield argument have to do with two properties (the property of being a psychiatrist and the property of being an M.D.) and with a person (Hatfield). In any logically possible situation in which the argument's premises are true,

    a.   each thing that has the first property also has the second, and

    b.   the person (Hatfield) has the first property.

And, in any possible situation in which the argument's conclusion is false,

    c.   the person (Hatfield) does not have the second property.

But clearly there is no logically possible situation that meets all three of these conditions. Condition (a) is met just in case *everything* with the first property has the second, but conditions (b) and (c) are met only if *something* with the first property does *not* have the second. So, there is no possible situation in which the Hatfield argument's premises are true while its conclusion is false, and the argument therefore is valid.

In this demonstration of the Hatfield argument's validity, we used the fact that there is a person (namely, Hatfield) who is mentioned both in the argument's second premise and in its conclusion. This fact is reflected in the argument's form, since the singular term "Hatfield" appears both in the argument's second premise and in its conclusion. But what about the fact that there is a property (the property of being a psychiatrist) mentioned in both the argument's premises? At first, it may seem that this fact is not reflected in the argument's form. For, although the property of being a psychiatrist is mentioned in the first premise by the plural noun "psychiatrists", it is mentioned in the second premise by the predicate ". . . is a psychiatrist". Since there is no one expression that appears in both premises, it is difficult to see how we can view the fact that both mention the same property as a matter of *form*.

Or consider the fact that the Hatfield argument's first premise and its conclusion both are about the property of being an M.D. The property is mentioned in different ways in the different sentences—in the premise by the expression "M.D.s", and in the conclusion by the expression ". . . is an M.D.". So, the fact that the property of being an M.D. is mentioned both in the argument's first premise and in its conclusion, though important to the argument's validity, may seem not to be reflected in the argument's form.

But there is a way to view the validity of the Hatfield argument, and of other similar arguments, as a matter of form. The discovery of this was a leap forward in human thought made in the beginning of this century. The key was noticing the connection of sentences such as

    1.   All psychiatrists are M.D.s.

to sentences such as

2. Each thing is such that, if it is a psychiatrist, then it is an M.D.

Despite the differences in wording, these sentences say the same thing. Thus, we can view sentences like (1) as *abbreviations* of sentences like (2).

There are real advantages to viewing things in this way. Unlike sentence (1), sentence (2) does contain the predicates ". . . is a psychiatrist" and ". . . is an M.D.", which appear in the Hatfield argument's second premise and conclusion, respectively. So, if we take sentence (1) to be an abbreviation of sentence (2), we can view the connections among the sentences of the Hatfield argument as matters of form. And, if the argument's validity is a matter of form, there is some hope that our formal methods, when properly revised, will be able to demonstrate the argument's validity.

Let's take a closer look, then, at the sentence

2. Each thing is such that, if it is a psychiatrist, then it is an M.D.

In this sentence, the blanks in the predicates ". . . is a psychiatrist" and ". . . is an M.D." are filled, not by singular terms, but by the pronoun "it". Sometimes (as in "Harold's car is easy to spot because *it* is red") this pronoun picks out a particular object, just as a singular term would. But, as used in sentence (2), the pronoun "it" does *not* pick out any particular object.

To see how the pronoun "it" is used in sentence (2), notice that this pronoun is used together with the phrase "each thing is such that". By putting this phrase in front of the clause

if it is a psychiatrist, then it is an M.D.,

we say, in effect, that the clause would be true *no matter what* particular object we might think of as picked out by the pronoun "it".

We call expressions like "each thing is such that" **quantifying phrases.** There are many such phrases in English, but we will focus on just two: "each thing is such that" and "at least one thing is such that". Since the phrase "each thing is such that" helps us to say that properties are shared *universally,* it is called the **universal quantifying phrase.** On the other hand, since the phrase "at least one thing is such that" helps us to say that there *exist* things with certain properties, it is called the **existential quantifying phrase.**

Now, with quantifying phrases and pronouns in mind, let's look back at the first premise of the Hatfield argument:

All psychiatrists are M.D.s.

As we are now viewing things, this sentence abbreviates

Each thing is such that, if it is a psychiatrist, then it is an M.D.

And this expanded sentence can be broken up, with nothing left over, into the universal quantifying phrase "each thing is such that", the sentential operator "if, then", the predicate ". . . is a psychiatrist", the predicate ". . . is an M.D.", and the pronoun "it".

Having seen this, we are in position to offer a new definition of *form:*

> The **predicative form** of a sentence or argument is the way in which it has been built up from singular terms, (simple, one-placed) predicates, sentential operators, quantifying phrases, pronouns, and simple clauses that cannot be broken up into these parts.

This idea replaces the idea of sentential form, which we developed in Chapter 3.

To reveal the predicative form of a sentence or an argument that has been made explicit, we take the following steps:

1. We expand all abbreviations (taking care to replace sentences such as "All psychiatrists are M.D.s" with sentences such as "Each thing is such that, if it is a psychiatrist, then it is an M.D.").

2. Insofar as possible, we break the expanded sentence or argument down into singular terms, (simple, one-placed) predicates, sentential operators, quantifying phrases, and pronouns. (Some clauses can be broken down into these parts in more than one way. The clause "Sally slapped Bill", for example, can be viewed as made up either from the singular term "Sally" and the predicate ". . . slapped Bill" or from the singular term "Bill" and the predicate "Sally slapped . . .".)

3. If we find a simple clause (such as "it is raining"*) that cannot be broken down into singular terms, (simple, one-placed) predicates, quantifying phrases, and pronouns, we replace it with an uppercase letter (the first, wherever it occurs, with "*P*"; the second with "*Q*"; and so on).

4. We replace each (simple, one-placed) predicate with an uppercase letter (the first, wherever it occurs, with "*F*"; the second with "*G*"; and so on).

5. We replace each remaining singular term with a lowercase letter (the first, wherever it occurs, with "*a*"; the second with "*b*"; and so on).

By applying these steps to a given sentence or argument, we make it easy to see its predicative form.

Consider, for example, the sentence

Everything is red.

---

* Note that, as it is used in the sentence "It is raining", the expression ". . . is raining" is not a predicate, since it does not become a clause when its blank is filled with a singular term.

Since this sentence consists of a simple clause, we would reveal its *sentential* form by replacing the whole thing with the letter *"P"*. But, as we just explained, we are now viewing this sentence as an abbreviation for

Each thing is such that it is red.

Replacing the predicate ". . . is red" with the letter *"F"*, we reveal the sentence's *predicative* form:

Each thing is such that *F* it.

(Note that we put the pronoun "it" *after* the letter *"F"*. To keep things uniform, we view all the uppercase letters that replace predicates as having their blanks for singular terms and pronouns on their right.)

For a more complex example of revealing predicative form, consider the sentence

If many people follow the new trends, the publisher of *Fashion* magazine will be happy and someone will make a lot of money.

The predicative form of this sentence is

If *P*, then *Fa* and at least one thing is such that *G* it.

Since the clause "many people follow the new trends" cannot be broken up into singular terms, predicates, quantifying phrases, and pronouns, we have replaced it with the letter *"P"*. Since the clause "the publisher of *Fashion* magazine will be happy" is made from a singular term and a (simple, one-placed) predicate, we have replaced it with *"Fa"*. And, since the clause "someone will make a lot of money" abbreviates the clause "at least one thing is such that it will make a lot of money", we have replaced it with "at least one thing is such that *G* it".

How does the procedure for revealing predicative form apply to the sentence

Every dog hates some cat,

in which two quantifying phrases work together? Since sentences of this sort pose special problems, we will postpone our discussion of them until the next chapter. For now, we limit our attention to sentences in which quantifying phrases work independently of one another.

Among sentences of this sort are the premises and conclusion of the Hatfield argument. Applying the procedures for revealing predicative form to these sentences, we get

Each thing is such that, if *F* it, then *G* it.

Fa
———————
So, *Ga*

As we will show later in this chapter, this predicative form reveals everything that accounts for the Hatfield argument's validity. The argument is valid in virtue of having this form, and any other argument of the same predicative form is valid, too.

Accordingly, we introduce the idea of *predicative validity:*

> An argument form is **predicatively valid (P-valid)** just in case every argument of that predicative form is valid.

P-validity stands to predicative form as S-validity stands to sentential form. In particular, just as we can demonstrate an argument's validity by showing that its sentential form is S-valid, we can demonstrate an argument's validity by showing that its predicative form is P-valid.

But how, in general, can we demonstrate the P-validity of predicative forms? To answer this question, we will refine our model of English, thereby completing the move from CL to the system called predicate logic, or PL. In addition to providing us with a method for demonstrating the validity of arguments such as the Hatfield argument, PL will help us to see what it is about these arguments that accounts for their validity.

Exercises 8.1

1. *Defend or criticize:* When using the system CL, we viewed clauses such as "each thing is such that it is red" as single, indivisible units. But, in this section, we viewed clauses of this sort as made from three parts: a quantifying phrase, a pronoun, and a predicate.

2. *Defend or criticize:* In this section, we looked at two English quantifying phrases: the existential quantifying phrase "each thing is such that" and the universal quantifying phrase "at least one thing is such that".

3. *Defend or criticize:* The sentence "At least one thing is such that it is red" is true just in case one or more things has the property mentioned by the predicate ". . . is red".

4. *Defend or criticize:* The sentence "Each thing is such that it is red" is true just in case one or more things has the property mentioned by the predicate ". . . is red".

5. *Defend or criticize:* Like a singular term, the pronoun "it" can be put into the blank in a predicate to form a clause. Hence, from a semantic point of view, the pronoun "it" closely resembles a singular term.

6. *Defend or criticize:* In the sentence "Harold has a new car and it is red," the pronoun "it" picks out Harold's car, just as a singular term might. But, in the sentence "At least one thing is such that it is red," the pronoun "it" doesn't pick out any particular thing.

7. *Defend or criticize:* Syntactically, the quantifying phrase "each thing is such that . . ." is just like the predicate ". . . is red". Fill in the blank in either of these expressions, and the result is a clause.

8. For each of the following sentences, explain how it might be built from predicates, pronouns, quantifying phrases, and sentential operators.

  a. At least one thing is such that it is red.
  b. It's not the case that each thing is such that it is red.
  c. Each thing is such that, if it is red, then it is round.
  d. At least one thing is such that it's not the case that it is red.
  e. If each thing is such that it is red, then at least one thing is such that it is round.
  f. Either it's not the case that each thing is such that it is red, or at least one thing is such that it's not the case that it is round.

9. Consider the argument

  All executives are rich.

  Robinson is an executive.
  _____

  So, Robinson is rich.

  a. Review the reasoning that we used to demonstrate the Hatfield argument's validity. Then use the same reasoning to demonstrate the validity of the argument about Robinson.
  b. While the Hatfield argument is about Hatfield's being a psychiatrist, the Robinson argument is about Robinson's being an executive. Explain why it is that we can use the same reasoning to demonstrate the validity of two arguments that differ so greatly in content.

10. Using no expressions other than the quantifying phrases "each thing is such that" and "at least one thing is such that", the pronoun "it", the predicates ". . . is squishy" and ". . . lives in the sea", and the sentential operator "if, then", construct at least 18 different English sentences.

8.2 The Syntax of Variables and Quantifiers

Our aim in this section is to mirror in our model of English the syntactic facts discovered in the previous section. Accordingly, we add three new expressions to the model's vocabulary: one corresponding to the universal quantifying phrase "each thing is such that", one corresponding to the existential quantifying phrase "at least one thing is such that", and one corresponding to the pronoun "it". After adding these expressions to the system's vocabulary, we make the required changes in its rules of formation, thereby moving from CL to the new system of predicate logic, or PL.

PL's vocabulary includes all the expressions of CL's: sentence letters, symbolic operators, and parentheses. It also includes constants and predicate letters, which we introduced in Chapter 7. The only other expressions in PL's vocabulary are

the universal quantifier: [x]

the existential quantifier: [∃x]

the variable: x

Syntactically and semantically, the quantifier "[x]" corresponds to the English quantifying phrase "each thing is such that", the quantifier "[∃x]" to the quantifying phrase "at least one thing is such that", and the variable "x" to the pronoun "it".

While our symbolic quantifiers are made up of several marks, each should be viewed as a single, indivisible item of vocabulary. The several marks —for example, "[" and "]"—are not expressions of PL by themselves, just as the crossbar in the sentence letter "H" is not by itself an expression of CL.

We can combine the expressions of PL in accordance with the following rules of formation:

F1: A sentence letter is a wff as it stands.

F2: The result of writing a dash in front of a wff is itself a wff.

F3: The result of flanking an ampersand with wffs and enclosing the whole in parentheses is itself a wff.

F4: The result of flanking a vel with wffs and enclosing the whole in parentheses is itself a wff.

F5: The result of flanking an arrow with wffs and enclosing the whole in parentheses is itself a wff.

F6: The result of flanking a double arrow with wffs and enclosing the whole in parentheses is itself a wff.

These rules are exactly the same as the correspondingly numbered rules of CL except that they talk about *wffs* rather than about *symbolic sentences* (a difference that we will explain shortly).

In addition to the rules F1 through F6, we need a rule of formation telling us what to do with the variable "x". We want this variable to correspond to the English pronoun "it", which has roughly the same syntax as a singular term. And, in our system, constants correspond to singular terms. So, rather than write a new rule of formation for the variable "x", we simply rewrite rule F7 from the previous chapter:

F7:   The result of writing a constant *or a variable* immediately to the right of a predicate letter is a wff.

In PL, the place for either a variable or a constant is just to the right of a predicate letter — just as, in English, the place for either a pronoun or a singular term is in a blank space in a predicate.

We also need rules of formation telling us where we can put the symbolic quantifiers, "[x]" and "[∃x]". As we have said, we want these expressions to correspond, respectively, to the English quantifying phrases "each thing is such that" and "at least one thing is such that". And, in a sentence such as "Each thing is such that it is red," the quantifying phrase stands in front of a clause (in this case, "it is red") that contains a pronoun. Accordingly, we let the universal quantifier "[x]" stand in front of (some) wffs containing the variable "x":

F8:   If a wff contains an instance of the variable "x" but no quantifier, then the result of writing "[x]" in front of that wff is itself a wff.

And we have a similar rule for the existential quantifier "[∃x]":

F9:   If a wff contains an instance of the variable "x" but no quantifier, then the result of writing "[∃x]" in front of that wff is itself a wff.

Rules F8 and F9 do not allow us to construct the sequences "[x]Fa" or "[∃x]P", since neither the singular symbolic sentence "Fa" nor the sentence letter "P" contains the variable "x". Nor do these rules allow us to construct the sequence "[x](Fx ∨ [∃x]Gx)", since the wff "(Fx ∨ [∃x]Gx)" already contains a quantifier. But the rules do allow us to construct such wffs as "[x]Fx", "[∃x]Gx", and "[x](Fx ↔ Gx)".

A sequence of expressions is a wff of PL just in case it can be constructed in accordance with rules F1 through F9. But, while *all* of CL's wffs are symbolic sentences, only *some* of PL's wffs are. What determines whether a wff of PL is or is not a symbolic sentence?

In answering this question, it is useful to view quantifiers as having scopes. The *scope* of a quantifier is the first full formula following it. More precisely,

In a given wff, the *scope* of a given instance of a quantifier begins with the mark immediately to the quantifier's right and continues on to the right until the marks after the quantifier, taken in order, form a complete wff.

Thus, in the wff "([∃x]Fx ∨ [x](Fx ↔ Gx))", the scope of the quantifier "[∃x]" is the sequence "Fx". But, in the same formula, the scope of the quantifier "[x]" is the wff "(Fx ↔ Gx)", since "(", "(F", "(Fx", "(Fx ↔ ", "(Fx ↔ G", and "(Fx ↔ Gx" are not wffs by themselves.

Given the idea of scope, we can distinguish *bound* occurrences of the variable "x" from *free* occurrences:

On a given occurrence in a wff, a variable is **bound** just in case it falls within the scope of a quantifier; otherwise, it is **free**.

Thus, in the wff "(Fx → [x]Gx)", the variable "x" is free on its first occurrence but bound on its second.

Now, having distinguished bound variables from free variables, we can distinguish the wffs of PL that are symbolic sentences from those that are not:

A wff of PL is a *symbolic sentence* just in case it doesn't contain any free variable.

The wffs "P", "Fa", "[x](Fx → Gx)", and "([∃x]Fx ∨ [∃x]Gx)" are symbolic sentences, since all of the variables in them are bound. In contrast, the wffs "Fx", "([x]Fx → Gx)", and "(Fx & [x]Gx)" are not symbolic sentences, since on one occurrence in each the variable "x" is free.

We categorize the symbolic sentences of PL (as we did those of CL) in accordance with the *last* rule used in their formation. This categorization will be important to us when we start constructing derivations in PL. In PL, as in CL, we need to know the category to which a given symbolic sentence belongs to tell which rule of inference we may apply to that sentence.

As before, a symbolic sentence is a *conjunction* just in case the last rule used in its formation is F3, a *disjunction* just in case the last rule used in its formation is F4, a *singular sentence* just in case the last rule used in its formation is F7, and so on. Among the symbolic sentences of PL, then, are sentences in each of the following categories:

sentence letters	(1)	negations of sentence letters	(7)
conjunctions	(2)	negations of conjunctions	(8)
disjunctions	(3)	negations of disjunctions	(9)
conditionals	(4)	negations of conditionals	(10)
biconditionals	(5)	negations of biconditionals	(11)
singular sentences	(6)	negations of singular sentences	(12)
	negations of negations	(13)	

But this categorization, though exclusive, is not exhaustive. The symbolic sentences "[x]Fx" and "[∃x]Fx" don't fall into any of the thirteen categories, and neither do their negations, "−[x]Fx" and "−[∃x]Fx".

To correct this, we will add three more categories to the list of basic forms:

universally quantified sentences	(14)
existentially quantified sentences	(15)
negations of quantified sentences	(16)

A symbolic sentence is in category (14) just in case the last rule used in its formation is F8; it is in category (15) just in case the last rule used in its formation is F9; and it is in category (16) just in case it is the negation of a sentence in category (14) or (15). (We put the negations of universally and existentially quantified sentences together in a single category because there will be a single rule of inference that applies to all of them.)

With the addition of these three new categories, our categorization again becomes exclusive and exhaustive. Every symbolic sentence of PL falls into exactly one of the categories.

Exercises 8.2

1. *Defend or criticize:* The variable "x" occurs three times in the symbolic sentence "(Fx ∨ [x]Gx)".

2. *Defend or criticize:* Syntactically, the variable "x" works exactly like a constant. This is as it should be, since the syntax of English pronouns closely resembles that of English singular terms.

3. *Defend or criticize:* Syntactically, the quantifier "[x]" works exactly like the quantifier "[∃x]". This is as it should be, since the syntax of the English quantifying phrase "each thing is such that" is exactly the same as that of the English quantifying phrase "at least one thing is such that".

4. Which of the following sequences of marks are wffs of PL? Which are symbolic sentences? (Assume here that "F" and "G" are predicate letters and that "P" is a sentence letter.)

a.	Fa	b.	Fx
c.	F[x]	d.	xF[x]
e.	F(x)	f.	Fy
g.	−Fx	h.	F − x
i.	(Fx → Gx)	j.	(x → Gx)
k.	([∃x] → Gx)	l.	([∃x]x → [x]Fx)
m.	[x]P	n.	[x]Fa
o.	[x]Fx	p.	[y]Fy
q.	[∃x]Fx	r.	[x](Fx ↔ Gx)
s.	(Fx ↔ [x]Gx)	t.	[∃x](Fx ↔ [x]Gx)
u.	([∃x]Fx ↔ [x]Gx)	v.	[x](Fx ↔ [x]Gx)
w.	[x](Fx → P)	x.	([x]Fx → P)
y.	(F → [x]P)	z.	[x] − Fx
aa.	[x] − (Fx ∨ Gx)	bb.	[x](−Fx ∨−Gx)
cc.	− [x](Fx ∨ Gx)	dd.	− [x] − (− Fx ∨−Gx)
ee.	[−x] − (Fx ∨ Gx)		
ff.	([x]Gx ∨ (Fx → [∃x]Gx))		

gg. $([\exists x](Fx \lor (Gx \& Hx)) \to [x](Gx \leftrightarrow Hx))$

hh. $[\exists x](Gx \to [x](Fx \to Hx))$

ii. $([x](Fx \lor Gx) \to [\exists x](Hx \to -Fx)))$

jj. $(-[x]Fx \to ([x] - Fx \leftrightarrow -[x] - (Fx \lor Gx)))$

5. *Defend or criticize:* In the wff

$$[x]((Fx \leftrightarrow Gx) \lor (Hx \lor Gx))$$

the scope of the quantifier "[x]" extends from the very first through the very last rounded parenthesis.

6. *Defend or criticize:* A wff of PL is a symbolic sentence just in case the "x"'s in it, if any, occur within the scopes of quantifiers.

7. Which of the following wffs are symbolic sentences of PL? (Assume here that "F" and "G" are predicate letters and that "P" is a sentence letter.)

a. P
b. Fa
c. Fx
d. [x]Fx
e. $([x]Fx \lor [\exists x]Gx)$
f. $([x]Fx \lor Gx)$
g. $[x](Fx \lor Gx)$
h. $(Fx \lor [x]Gx)$
i. $([x]Fx \to Ga)$
j. $[x](Fx \to Ga)$
k. $-[x] - (Fx \to Gx)$
l. $(P \lor [x](Fx \& Gx))$

8. *Defend or criticize:* A symbolic sentence is a *universally quantified sentence* [category (14)] just in case its very first expression is the quantifier "[x]"; a symbolic sentence is an *existentially quantified sentence* [category (15)] just in case its very first expression is the quantifier "[∃x]"; and a symbolic sentence is *the negation of a quantified sentence* [category (16)] just in case the first two expressions in it are a dash and a quantifier, in that order.

9. As we have said, a sentence is a *conditional* just in case the last rule used in its formation is F5, a sentence is *universally quantified* just in case the last rule used in its formation is F8, and a sentence is *existentially quantified* just in case the last rule used in its formation is F9.

   Which of the following sentences are conditionals [category (4)]? Which are the negations of conditionals [category (10)]? Which are universally quantified sentences [category (14)]? Which are existentially quantified sentences [category (15)]? And which are negations of quantified sentences [category (16)]?

a. $(Fa \to Ga)$
b. $-[\exists x](Fx \to Gx)$
c. $([\exists x]Fx \to [x]Gx)$
d. $--[\exists x](Fx \to Gx)$
e. $-([\exists x]Fx \to [x]Gx)$
f. $[\exists x] -- (Fx \to Gx)$
g. $(-[\exists x]Fx \to [x]Gx)$
h. $[x]((Fx \to Gx) \lor Hx)$
i. $[\exists x](Fx \to Gx)$
j. $(-[\exists x](Fx \to Gx) \& [x](Gx \to Hx))$

▦ 8.3 The Semantics of Variables and Quantifiers

Having described PL's rules of vocabulary and formation in the last section, we now turn to its rules of valuation — rules that will make the quantifier "[x]" correspond semantically to the quantifying phrase "each thing is such that" and make the quantifier "[∃x]" correspond semantically to the quantifying phrase "at least one thing is such that".

When we mention *valuations* in the statement of these rules, we are talking about valuations just like those that we constructed in Chapter 7. Given a symbolic sentence of PL, we construct a valuation of this sort by

a.   choosing a (nonempty) set of objects as the valuation's domain of discourse;

b.   assigning a referent (which must be a member of the domain) to each constant appearing in the given sentences;

c.   assigning an extension (which must be a subset of the domain) to each predicate letter appearing in the given sentences; and

d.   assigning exactly one value (either t or f) to each sentence letter appearing in the given sentences.

We do not make any assignments to our three new items of vocabulary: "[x]", "[∃x]", and "x".

In PL, as in CL, a negation has the value t when and only when the negated sentence has the value f (rule V2); a conjunction has the value t when and only when both of its conjuncts have the value t (rule V3); a disjunction has the value f when and only when both of its disjuncts have the value f (rule V4), and so on. Also, as we said in Chapter 7, a singular sentence has the value t when and only when the referent of its constant is in the extension of its predicate letter (rule V7).

Still, to calculate the values of some of PL's symbolic sentences, we need some new rules of valuation — rules for universally and existentially quantified sentences. Central to these new rules is the idea that objects can *satisfy* wffs containing free variables (that is, variables not in the scopes of quantifiers).

To get some idea of what we mean by *satisfaction,* consider the English clause

it is a planet

If we suppose that the pronoun "it" in this clause is being used to pick out, say, Mars or Venus, the clause is true. But, if the pronoun "it" is being used to pick out, say, the city of Taos, New Mexico, the clause is false. We can mark this difference by saying that Mars and Venus *satisfy* the clause "it is a planet" but that Taos does not. As we are using the term "satisfies", in other words, an object satisfies the clause "it is a planet" just in case the clause would be true if the pronoun "it" picked out that object.

We can mirror this idea in our model of English. Suppose that we have a wff containing one or more free occurrences of the variable "x" and a valuation for that wff. Then,

> An object from the valuation's domain **satisfies** the wff just in case, by replacing the free occurrences of "x" in that wff with a constant referring to that object, we produce a symbolic sentence with the value *t* in the valuation.

Consider, for example, the wff

$$(Ax \rightarrow Bx)$$

and the valuation

domain of discourse:	{1, 2, 3}
referent of "a":	1
referent of "b":	2
extension of "A":	{2, 3}
extension of "B":	{1, 3}

By replacing the "x"s in the wff "(Ax → Bx)" with the constant "a", we would produce a conditional whose antecedent has the value *f* in the given valuation. And, by replacing the "x"s in the given wff with a constant referring to the number 3, we would produce a conditional whose antecedent and consequent both have the value *t* in the given valuation. (It doesn't matter that the valuation doesn't assign any constant to the number 3. What's important is that, *if* the valuation did assign a constant to the number 3, and *if* we were to replace the free "x"s in the given wff with that constant, the resulting sentence *would* have the value *t* in the given valuation.) According to the definition of satisfaction, then, both the number 1 and the number 3 satisfy the wff "(Ax → Bx)" in the given valuation. But, in the same valuation, the number 2 does *not* satisfy the wff "(Ax → Bx)". For, by replacing the free "x"s in this wff with the constant "b", we would produce a conditional whose value in the given valuation is *f*.

Now that we have defined satisfaction, we can state the rule of valuation for symbolic sentences beginning with the universal quantifier, "[x]":

> V8:   A universally quantified symbolic sentence has the value *t* in a given valuation just in case, if we were to erase its initial universal quantifier, the resulting wff would be satisfied by *each* object in the valuation's domain.

(Note that when we erase the initial quantifier from the front of a universally quantified sentence, the result is *always* a wff containing one or more free occurrences of the variable "x".)

The English sentence "Each thing is such that it is a planet" would be true just in case everything satisfied the clause "it is a planet". Similarly, the symbolic sentence "[x]Fx" has the value *t* in a valuation just in case everything in the valuation's domain satisfies the wff "Fx". Thus, rule V8 ensures that the symbolic quantifier "[x]" corresponds semantically to the English quantifying phrase "each thing is such that".

Here is the rule of valuation for symbolic sentences beginning with the existential quantifier, "[∃x]":

> V9:   An existentially quantified symbolic sentence has the value *t* in a given valuation just in case, if we were to erase its initial existential quantifier, the resulting wff would be satisfied by *at least one* object in the valuation's domain.

This rule ensures that the symbolic quantifier "[∃x]" corresponds semantically to the English quantifying phrase "at least one thing is such that". As the sentence "At least one thing is such that it is a planet" is true just in case the clause "it is a planet" is satisfied by at least one thing, the symbolic sentence "[∃x]Fx" has the value *t* in a valuation just in case, in that valuation, the wff "Fx" is satisfied by at least one thing.

For practice in using rules V8 and V9, consider the symbolic sentence

$$([x](Fx \rightarrow Gx) \rightarrow [\exists x](Gx \ \& -Hx))$$

and the valuation

> domain of discourse: {1, 2, 3, 4}
>
> extension of "F": {1, 2}
>
> extension of "G": {1, 2, 3}
>
> extension of "H": {1, 2, 3, 4}

What is the value of this symbolic sentence in this valuation?

Notice first that the sample symbolic sentence is a conditional, *not* a universally quantified sentence. Its antecedent — namely, "[x](Fx → Gx)" — has the value *t* in the given valuation, since every object in the valuation's domain satisfies the wff "(Fx → Gx)". But the conditional's consequent — namely, "[∃x](Gx & −Hx)" — has the value *f* in the given valuation, since no object in the valuation's domain statisfies the wff "(Gx & −Hx)". Hence, in the given valuation, the value of the original conditional is *f* (rule V5).

In the valuation from our last example, "[x]Fx" has the value *f* while "[∃x]Fx" has the value *t*. But what is the value of the wff "Fx" in this valuation? The question has no answer. Wffs containing free variables are not symbolic sentences and do not have values. That's why, in the previous section, we distinguished the wffs of PL that are symbolic sentences from those that are not. Although some wffs of PL do not have values, every symbolic sentence of PL has exactly one value — either *t* or *f* — in every valuation for it.

Exercises 8.3

1. *Defend or criticize:* Valuations for symbolic sentences of PL look exactly the same as the valuations that we constructed in Chapter 7, before our system contained quantifiers or variables.

2. Consider the valuation

domain of discourse:	$\{1, 2, 3, 4\}$
referent of "a":	1
extension of "F":	$\{1, 2, 3, 4\}$
extension of "G":	$\varnothing$
extension of "H":	$\{1, 3\}$
value of "P":	t

For each of the following wffs, say which objects in the sample valuation's domain satisfy it:

a. Fx   b. Gx
c. $-$Hx   d. (Fx $\rightarrow$ Gx)
e. ($-$Fa $\lor$ Gx)   f. (Ga $\rightarrow$ Hx)
g. (Gx $\rightarrow$ Hx)   h. (Hx $\leftrightarrow$ Gx)
i. (Hx $\rightarrow$ P)   j. $-$((Fx & Gx) $\rightarrow$ P)
k. ($-$Gx $\lor$ P)   l. ($-$(Fx $\rightarrow$ Gx) $\leftrightarrow$ Hx)

3. *Defend or criticize:* An object from a valuation's domain *satisfies* a given wff just in case, by replacing all occurrences of the variable "x" in that wff with a constant referring to that object, we produce a sentence whose value is *t* in the given valuation.

4. *Defend or criticize:* When we remove the initial quantifier from an existentially or universally quantified sentence, the result is always a wff containing one or more free occurrences of the variable "x".

5. *Defend or criticize:* In a given valuation, the wff "([x]Fx $\rightarrow$ Gx)" is satisfied by every object in the extension of the predicate letter "G".

6. *Defend or criticize:* Any object in the domain of any valuation for the wff "(Fx $\lor$ $-$Fx)" satisfies this wff.

7. *Defend or criticize:* The symbolic sentence "[x]Fx" has the value *t* in a given valuation for it just in case, in that valuation, the extension of the predicate letter "F" is the very same set as valuation's domain.

8. *Defend or criticize:* The symbolic sentence "[x](Fx $\rightarrow$ Gx)" has the value *t* in a given valuation for it just in case, in that valuation, the extension of the predicate letter "F" is a subset of the extension of the predicate letter "G".

9. *Defend or criticize:* The symbolic sentence "[x](Fx $\leftrightarrow$ Gx)" has the value *t* in a

given valuation for it just in case, in that valuation, the extension of the predicate letter "F" is exactly the same set as the extension of the predicate letter "G".

10. *Defend or criticize:* The symbolic sentence "'[∃x]Fx" has the value *f* in a given valuation just in case, in that valuation, the extension of the predicate letter "F" is the empty set.

11. *Defend or criticize:* The symbolic sentence "[∃x](Fx & Gx)" has the value *t* in a given valuation just in case every object in that valuation's domain is either in the extension of the predicate letter "F" or in the extension of the predicate letter "G".

12. *Defend or criticize:* The symbolic sentence "([x]Fx → P)" has the value *f* in a given valuation for it only if every object in the valuation's domain is in the extension of the predicate letter "F".

13. Consider the valuation

domain of discourse: {1, 2, 3}
referent of "a": 1
referent of "b": 2
extension of "F": {1, 2, 3}
extension of "G": {1, 3}

For each of the following symbolic sentences, calculate its value in the sample valuation:

a. [x]Fx
b. [∃x]−Gx
c. (Fa → Gb)
d. [x](Fx → Gb)
e. [x](Fa → Gx)
f. [∃x](Fx → Gb)
g. [∃x](Fa → Gx)
h. [x](Fx → Gx)
i. [∃x](Fx → Gx)
j. [∃x](Gx → Fx)

14. Consider the valuation

domain of discourse: {1, 2, 3, 4}
extension of "F": {1, 2, 3, 4}
extension of "G": {1, 2, 3}
extension of "H": {1, 2}

For each of the following symbolic sentences, calculate its value in the sample valuation:

a. [x](Fx → Gx)
b. [x](Gx → Fx)
c. −[∃x](−Fx ∨ −Gx)
d. −[x](Gx ∨ Hx)
e. [x]((Gx & Hx) → Fx)
f. [x]((Fx ∨ Hx) → Gx)
g. [x]((Gx → Fx) ∨ (Fx → Hx))
h. [x]((Gx ∨ Hx) ↔ Fx)

15. Calculate the value of each of the sentences from the previous exercise in the following valuation:

$$\begin{aligned}
\text{domain of discourse:} \quad & \{1, 2, 3, 4\} \\
\text{extension of ''F'':} \quad & \{1, 2\} \\
\text{extension of ''G'':} \quad & \{1, 2, 3\} \\
\text{extension of ''H'':} \quad & \{1, 2, 3, 4\}
\end{aligned}$$

16. For each of the following symbolic sentences, find a valuation in which it has the value *t*:

    a.   [x](Fx ∨ −Gx)
    b.   [x](Fa → Gx)
    c.   −[∃x](Fx & Gx)
    d.   (−[∃x]Fx & −[∃x]Gx)
    e.   ([∃x]Fx & [x]Gx)
    f.   [x](Fx → −Gx)
    g.   [x]((Fx & Gx) → Hx)

8.4 Derivation in PL

Having presented PL's syntactic and semantic rules in the last two sections, we devote this section to defining PL-validity and to developing a method for demonstrating the PL-validity of symbolic arguments. In later sections, we will apply what we learn about PL-validity to the evaluation of English arguments.

The definition of PL-validity is this:

> A symbolic argument of PL is **PL-valid** just in case there is no valuation in which its premises have the value *t* while its conclusion has the value *f*.

This definition follows the definition of CL-validity word for word.

But this similarity hides an important difference. While the words may be the same, the ideas behind some of those words have changed. This is true, in particular, of the idea of *valuation*. To construct a valuation of a symbolic argument of CL, we just assigned a value—either *t* or *f*—to each sentence letter appearing in that symbolic argument. In contrast, to construct valuations for symbolic arguments of PL, we need to choose a domain of discourse, assign referents to constants, and assign extensions to predicate letters. Thus, in the move from CL to PL, we have moved from one idea of valuation to another.

This difference has an important consequence regarding the number of valuations for symbolic arguments. If an argument of CL has a number, *n*, of *n* sentence letters in it, there are 2^n different valuations for that argument—no more, no less. So, given a symbolic argument of CL, we can list all the valuations for it on a truth table and go through those valuations, one by one, looking for counterexamples. For a symbolic argument of PL, however, there are an infinite number of different valuations. Some have the set {1} as their domain of discourse, some the set {2}, some the set {3}, some the set {1, 2}, some the set {1, 2, 3}, and so on. So, we can never look through all the valuations for a symbolic argument of PL to see whether any are counterexamples. No matter how many we look through without finding a counterexample, there will still be more to be examined.

Then how can we demonstrate PL-validity? Given a symbolic argument, how can we ever be sure that there is no valuation in which its premises have the value *t* while its conclusion has the value *f*? There are several such ways, but we will focus on the one that reveals most about the way people actually reason in English. Given a symbolic argument, we attempt to construct a *derivation* for it. If we succeed, we infer that the symbolic argument is PL-valid.

PL's methods of derivation are very much like CL's. In particular, PL has all of CL's rules of inference: Prem, DNI, DNE, Conj, Simp, CS, Adj, DS, DM, MP, MT, ENC, D, HS, BCI, BCE, ENB, R, SuppCD, CD, SuppID, and ID. In addition, PL's system of derivation has four new rules: the Rule of Universal Instantiation (UI), the Rule of Existential Instantiation (EI), the Rule of Quantifier Exchange (QE), and the Rule of Existential Generalization (EG).

To see why the new rules are needed, consider the (PL-valid) symbolic argument

[x](− Fx ∨ Gx)

[∃x]Fx

_____

So, [∃x]Gx

In constructing a derivation for this argument, we might list its premises and begin an indirect derivation, like this:

1.   [x](− Fx ∨ Gx)   Prem
2.   [∃x]Fx   Prem
3.   − [∃x]Gx   SuppID

Here line (1) contains a universally quantified sentence, line (2) an existentially quantified sentence, and line (3) the negation of an existentially quantified sentence. Hence, of the rules we now have, we cannot use any except DNI, Conj, Adj, or R. But using these rules will not bring us any closer to the sample argument's conclusion. Limited to our current rules of inference, we are stuck.

To correct this, we establish the **Rule of Universal Instantiation (UI)** and the **Rule of Existential Instantiation (EI)**. In effect, these rules allow us to erase quantifiers from the beginnings of sentences and to replace variables with constants. In this way, UI and EI allow us to move from quantified sentences to sentences whose forms are familiar from our study of CL: conjunctions, disjunctions, negations, and so on.

The central idea in the rules UI and EI is that of *instantiation:*

> A wff is an **instantiation** of a universally or existentially quantified sentence just in case we can produce it by erasing the quantified sentence's initial mark (which will be either "[x]" or "[∃x]"), choosing a constant, and substituting the constant for all free occurrences of the variable in the remaining wff.

Thus, "(Fa → Ga)" and "(Fb → Gb)" are both instantiations of the universally quantified sentence "[x](Fx → Gx)", while "(Fa → Gb)", "(Fx → Ga)", and "(Fx → Gx)" are not.

Using the idea of instantiation, we can state the rule UI in this way:

> UI: If a universally quantified sentence (that is, a sentence whose very first expression is "[x]") appears as a line of a derivation, we may write any instantiation of it as a subsequent line.

This rule allows us to derive the symbolic conditional "(Fh → Gh)" from the universally quantified sentence "[x](Fx → Gx)" — just as, in English, we might derive the conditional "If Hatfield is a psychiatrist, then Hatfield is an M.D." from the sentence "Each thing is such that, if it is a psychiatrist, then it is an M.D.".

As UI allows us to move from universally quantified sentences to their instantiations, EI allows us to move from existentially quantified sentences to their instantiations. But, unlike UI, EI comes with restrictions:

> EI: If an existentially quantified sentence (that is, a sentence whose very first expression is "[∃x]") appears as a line of a derivation, we may write an instantiation of that sentence as a subsequent line of the derivation — *provided that* the constant with which we replace the variable "x" has not previously appeared anywhere in the derivation or in the symbolic argument being tested for PL-validity.

This rule allows us to move in a derivation, say, from "[∃x]Gx" to "Ga" — *provided* the constant "a" is entirely new to the derivation.

While EI may seem strange at first, it actually corresponds to a move that people make in ordinary reasoning. Several years ago, when a vicious killer was on the rampage in the Los Angeles area, people began calling the killer "The Night Stalker." They didn't know *who* was committing the murders; they just knew that *someone* was. But, for convenience (and vividness in the case of the press), they started to use the phrase "The Night Stalker" to refer to the killer.

There wasn't anything wrong with this. Sometimes, if we know that one or more things have a certain property, it's convenient to have a way to refer to one of those things.

But there *would* have been something wrong if people in Los Angeles had decided to call the murderer Richard M. Nixon. Hearing a sentence such as "Richard M. Nixon killed again last night," someone might mistakenly believe that the expression "Richard M. Nixon" was being used, as usual, to refer to the 37th president of the United States. And this person might then go on to infer that the 37th president of the United States was a murderer. The speaker could easily have avoided this confusion by choosing a term — such as "The Night Stalker" — that was not already in use.

We can avoid similar confusions in our system by requiring that, when using EI, we introduce a constant not previously used in the problem at hand — one not yet present either in the derivation or in the symbolic argument being tested for PL-validity. That's why EI, unlike UI, comes with restrictions.

Now that we have the rules EI and UI, let's look back at our sample derivation. So far, we've only got this:

1. [x](− Fx ∨ Gx)   Prem
2. [∃x]Fx   Prem
3. −[∃x]Gx   SuppID

But, using EI and UI, we can go on, like this:

4. Fa   2 EI
5. (− Fa ∨ Ga)   1 UI
6. −− Fa   4 DNI
7. Ga   5,6 DS

We haven't yet reached the desired conclusion ("[∃x]Gx"), but we do seem to be making progress.

To complete the derivation, we need to use the sentence on line (3). Since this sentence does not begin with a universal or existential quantifier, we cannot apply EI or UI to it. We need a new rule, which we call the **Rule of Quantifier Exchange (QE):**

> QE: If a line of a derivation contains a sentence whose first two expressions are a dash and a universal quantifier (in that order), we may replace those expressions with an existential quantifier and a dash (in that order) and write the result as a line of the derivation. Similarly, if a line of a derivation contains a symbolic sentence whose first two expressions are a dash and an existential quanti-

fier (in that order), we may replace those expressions with a universal quantifier and a dash (in that order) and write the result as a line of the derivation.

This rule allows us to move from the negations of quantified sentences to sentences whose very first expressions are quantifiers. For example, the first part of the rule allows us to move from "− [x](Fx → Gx)" to "[∃x] − (Fx → Gx)", and the second part allows us to move from "− [∃x](Fx & Gx)" to "[x] − (Fx & Gx)".

To see what lies behind the rule QE, consider the symbolic sentences "− [x]Fx" and "[∃x] − Fx". Since each of these sentences has the value *t* in a given valuation when and only when there is something in the valuation's domain that is not in the extension of the predicate letter "F", the sentences have the same value as each other in every valuation for them. In other words, the sentences are **PL-equivalent**. Similarly, since the symbolic sentences "− [∃x]Fx" and "[x] − Fx" have the value *t* when and only when the extension of the predicate letter "F" is the empty set, these sentences are also PL-equivalent. And this point can be generalized: *Whenever* we use rule QE, we move from a symbolic sentence to another that is PL-equivalent.

Using the rule QE, we can complete the sample derivation, like this:

1.	[x](− Fx ∨ Gx)	Prem
2.	[∃x]Fx	Prem
3.	− [∃x]Gx	SuppID
4.	Fa	2 EI
5.	(− Fa ∨ Ga)	1 UI
6.	− − Fa	4 DNI
7.	Ga	5,6 DS
8.	[x] − Gx	3 QE
9.	− Ga	8 UI
10.	[∃x]Gx	3 − 9 ID

Here we follow the application of QE on line (8) with the application of UI line (9). Then, with "Ga" on line (7) and "− Ga" on line (9), we complete our indirect derivation on line (10) by using ID.

Notice that, in this derivation, we used EI *before* UI. If we had done otherwise — if, for instance, we had applied UI to the symbolic sentence on line (1) before applying EI to the one on line (2) — we would still have been able to finish the derivation, but it would have been longer and more complex. In general,

Given the choice of applying rule EI to one line of a derivation or rule UI to another, we can keep derivations shorter and simpler by using EI first.

To ignore this rule of thumb is to invite extra work.

The rules we now have will allow us to construct a derivation for *any* PL-valid argument. Still, for convenience, we will add one more rule — the **Rule of Existential Generalization (EG):**

> EG: If a symbolic sentence containing one or more constants appears in a derivation, we may choose constants of one type (the "a"s, or the "b"s, or the "c"s, and so on), replace some or all of those constants with variables, put an existential quantifier in front of what we have, and write the result as a line of the derivation.

While rules UI and EI allow us to move from quantified symbolic sentences to some of their instantiations, rule EG allows us to move from some symbolic sentences, such as "(Fa ∨ Gb)", to existentially quantified sentences of which they are instantiations, such as "[∃x](Fx ∨ Gb)".

Like UI and EI, EG mirrors a move that people make when reasoning in English. Once, the TV announcer at a UC Berkeley basketball game saw a sign that said "Nobody beats the [UC Berkeley] Golden Bears" and reasoned in this way:

> Nobody beats them? But *UCLA* has beaten them nine times in a row. So, I guess *somebody* beats them!

Here the announcer moved from the premise that *UCLA* beats the Golden Bears to the more general conclusion that *someone* beats them. Before adding EG to our system, we would have needed to use SuppID and ID to mirror this simple inference in our model of English. But now we can mirror it directly — by using EG to move from "Fa" to "[∃x]Fx".

Here is a derivation in which rule EG is used three times:

1.	(Fa → Gb)	Prem
2.	([∃x](Fx → Gb) → Gb)	Prem
3.	([∃x](Fa → Gx) → Hb)	Prem
4.	[∃x](Fx → Gb)	1 EG
5.	[∃x](Fa → Gx)	1 EG
6.	Gb	2,4 MP
7.	Hb	3,5 MP
8.	(Gb & Hb)	6,7 Conj
9.	[∃x](Gx & Hx)	8 EG

The symbolic sentence on line (1) is an instantiation both of the symbolic sentence "[∃x](Fx → Gb)" and of the symbolic sentence "[∃x](Fa → Gx)". So, by applying rule EG to this sentence twice, we produced "[∃x](Fx → Gb)" on line (4) and "[∃x](Fa → Gx)" on line (5). Later, we applied EG to the symbolic sentence on line (8) to produce the desired conclusion on line (9). We could have reached this conclusion without using EG, but the derivation would have been much longer.

As we have seen, rule EG allows us to move from instantiations of existentially quantified sentences to the existentially quantified sentences themselves. Should we also have a rule allowing us to move from instantiations of universally quantified sentences to the universally quantified sentences themselves?

Well, people sometimes do generalize from premises about one particular object to conclusions about every object of some sort. (For example, a geometer might prove that a particular triangle has a certain property, notice that the same proof can be repeated for any triangle at all, and conclude that *all* triangles have the property in question.) But generalizing from one case to all cases is very tricky. The study of one case can lead to a conclusion about all cases only if certain conditions are met. A rule of universal generalization would have to mention all of these conditions and would therefore be very hard to state and to remember. As we see it, then, introducing a rule of universal generalization would not be worth the effort — especially since such a rule would not increase the power of our method for demonstrating PL-validity.

Accordingly, we will not add a rule of universal generalization to our system of derivation. The only difference between CL's system of derivation and PL's is that PL's has four rules dealing with quantifiers: UI, EI, QE, and EG. If we can construct a derivation for a symbolic argument using PL's system of derivation, we can be sure that the argument is PL-valid.

Exercises 8.4

1. *Defend or criticize:* In this section we added just three new rules of inference to our system of derivation: UI, EI, and EG.

2. Which of the following sentences are instantiations of the sentence "[x]((Fa ∨ Gx) ↔ (Fx ↔ P))"?
   a. ((Fa ∨ Gx) ↔ (Fx ↔ P))
   b. ((Fa ∨ Ga) ↔ (Fa ↔ P))
   c. ((Fb ∨ Gb) ↔ (Fb ↔ P))
   d. ((Aa ∨ Ba) ↔ (Aa ↔ Q))
   e. ((Fa ∨ Gb) ↔ (Fb ↔ P))
   f. ((Fa ∨ Gb) ↔ (Fc ↔ P))

3. How many different instantiations does the sentence "[x](Fx ↔ P)" have?

4. *Defend or criticize:* The rule UI allows us to move in a derivation from the sentence "([x]Fx ↔ P)" to the sentence "(Fa ↔ P)".

5. Consider the following four symbolic arguments:

a. Fa
   ____
   So, [x]Fx

b. Fa
   ____
   So, [∃x]Fx

c. [x]Fx
   ____
   So, Fa

d. [∃x]Fx
   ____
   So, Fb

Which of these symbolic arguments are PL-valid? If an argument is PL-valid, demonstrate its PL-validity by constructing a derivation. If an argument is PL-invalid, demonstrate its PL-invalidity by producing a valuation in which its premises have the value *t* while its conclusion has the value *f*.

6. Consider the symbolic argument

[x](− Fx ∨ Gx)
[∃x](Fx & −Hx)

_____

So, [∃x](Gx & −Hx)

Construct a derivation for this argument using EI before using UI. Now construct a derivation for the same argument, this time using UI before EI. Which derivation do you prefer? Why?

7. *Defend or criticize:* In a given valuation, the sentences "−[x]Fx" and "[∃x] − Fx" have the value *t* just in case something in the valuation's domain is not in the extension of the predicate letter "F".

8. *Defend or criticize:* In a given valuation, the sentences "−[∃x]Fx" and "[x] − Fx" have the value *t* just in case the extension of the predicate letter "F" is the empty set.

9. *Defend or criticize:* In a given valuation, the sentences "−[x] − Fx" and "[∃x]Fx" have the value *t* just in case something in the valuation's domain is in the extension of the predicate letter "F".

10. *Defend or criticize:* In a given valuation, the sentences "−[∃x] − Fx" and "[x]Fx" have the value *t* just in case the extension of the predicate letter "F" includes the valuation's whole domain.

11. Consider the PL-valid argument

Fa
[x]Gx

_____

So, [∃x](Fx & Gx)

Construct a derivation for this argument using rule EG. Now construct a derivation for this argument without using rule EG. Which derivation do you prefer?
Why?

12. Find the mistakes, if any, in each of the following attempts at derivation:

a. 1.	$-[x]Fx$	Prem
2.	$([\exists x]Fx \rightarrow Ga)$	Prem
3.	$[\exists x] --Fx$	1 QE
4.	$[\exists x]Fx$	2 DNE
5.	Ga	2,4 MP

b. 1.	$[x]((Ax \lor Ca) \rightarrow Bx)$	Prem
2.	$(Ab \lor Ca)$	Prem
3.	$((Ab \lor Ca) \rightarrow Ba)$	1 UI
4.	Ba	2,3 MP

c. 1.	$[x]Ax$	Prem
2.	$(Aa \rightarrow -Ab)$	Prem
3.	$-Ac$	SuppID
4.	Aa	1 UI
5.	$-Ab$	2,4 MP
6.	Ab	1 UI
7.	Ac	3–6 ID

d. 1.	$[x](Fx \rightarrow Ga)$	Prem
2.	$[x]Fx$	Prem
3.	$-[\exists x]Gx$	SuppID
4.	$[x]-Gx$	3 QE
5.	$-Ga$	4 UI
6.	Ga	1,2 MP
7.	$[\exists x]Gx$	3–6 ID

e. 1.	$[\exists x]Fx$	Prem
2.	$[x](Fx \rightarrow Gx)$	Prem
3.	Fa	1 EI
4.	$(Fa \rightarrow Ga)$	2 UI
5.	Ga	3,4 MP

f. 1.	$[\exists x]Fx$	Prem
2.	$[\exists x]-Fx$	Prem
3.	Fa	1 EI
4.	$-Fa$	2 EI
5.	$(Fa \& -Fa)$	3,4 Conj
6.	$[\exists x](Fx \& -Fx)$	5 EG

g. 1. (Fa & Ga)   Prem
   2. [∃x](Fa & Gx)   1 EG
h. 1. Fa   Prem
   2. [∃x]Fx   1 EG

13. Using as few lines as possible, construct a derivation for the symbolic argument

   ([x](Ax ∨ −Bx) → −[∃x] − Cx)
   −−([x](Ax ∨ −Bx) ∨ [∃x]Bx)
   ([∃x]Bx → −[∃x] − Cx)
   —————————————————

   So, −[∃x) − Cx

14. Construct derivations for the following symbolic arguments:

a. [x](Fx & −Gx)   b. −[x] − Fx
   ——————————   ————————
   So, [∃x] − Gx   So, [∃x]Fx

c. [x]Fx   d. [x](Fx ↔ Gx)
   ——————   ——————————
   So, [∃x]Fx   So, [x](Fx → Gx)

e. [x](Fx → Gx)   f. [x](Ax → Bx)
   [∃x]Fx   [∃x](Cx & Ax)
   ——————   ——————————
   So, [∃x]Gx   So, [∃x](Cx & Bx)

g. [x](Fx → Gx)   h. −[∃x]Cx
   [x](Gx → Hx)   [x](Bx → Cx)
   ——————————   ——————————
   So, [x](Fx → Hx)   So, [x] − (Cx ∨ Bx)

i. [x](Bx ↔ Cx)   j. (Fa → Gb)
   [x]Bx   [x](Gx → Hx)
   ——————   [x](−Hb ↔ Ix)
   So, [∃x]Cx   ——————————
                                            So, (Fa → [x] − Ix)

k. [x]((Ax ∨ Bx) → (Cx & Dx))   l. [x](Fx ∨ Gx)
   ——————————————————   [x] − Gx
   So, [x](Ax → Cx)   ([x]Fx → [x](−Gx → Hx))
                                            ——————————————————
                                            So, [x]Hx

m. (Fa ∨ Ga)

([∃x]Fx → [x] − Hx)

([∃x]Gx → [x] − Hx)

So, −Ha

n. (([∃x]Bx → [x](− Cx → Bx))

[∃x](Ax & Bx)

[x](Bx → Ax)

So, [x](− Cx → Ax)

o. ([x]Fx → [∃x]Gx)

([∃x]Gx → − [x]Hx)

So, ([x]Fx → [∃x] − Hx)

p. ([x]Fx → − [x](Fx ∨ − Fx))

So, [∃x](− Fx ∨ Ga)

q. − [∃x](Fx & Gx)

[x](− Fx → Hx)

So, [x](Gx → Hx)

r. − ([∃x]Ax ∨ [∃x]Bx)

So, − [∃x](Ax ∨ Bx)

s. [x](Fx ∨ − Gx)

[x](Fx → Hx)

[x](− Gx → Hx)

So, [x]Hx

t. [x]Fx

([∃x]Fx → [x](Gx & − Hx))

So, [x] − (Gx → Hx)

u. [x]Ax

[x]Bx

([x]Ax → [x](Bx → − Cx))

((Aa & Ab) → [x](− Cx → Dx))

So, [x]Dx

v. ([∃x](Ax & Bx) → [x]Cx)

− Ca

So, [x](Ax → − Bx)

8.5 Translating from English into PL

In the rest of this chapter, we describe a method for applying our test for PL-validity to the evaluation of English arguments. In outline, the method is the same as that described in Chapters 5 and 6. That is, given a text containing an argument, we

a. make the argument explicit,

b. paraphrase it into Standard English,

c. translate the paraphrase into PL, and

d. try to construct a derivation for the translation.

If we fail to construct the derivation, we won't draw any inference at all about the validity or invalidity of the original argument. But, if we succeed, we will generally infer that the argument is valid.

Having devoted Chapter 2 to a discussion of making arguments explicit, we deal in this section with paraphrasing into Standard English and translating into PL. In the next section, we will explain the connection of PL-validity to validity in English.

When we first introduced the idea of Standard English in Chapter 5, we said that a sentence is in Standard English just in case it can be broken down into parts each of which is either a simple clause or one of the seven favored sentential operators: "it's not the case that", "and", "or", "unless", "if, then", "only if", and "if and only if". Since each of these operators corresponds to a symbolic operator of CL, translation from Standard English into CL was easy. We simply replaced sentential operators with the corresponding symbolic operators and simple clauses with sentence letters, adding parentheses where needed.

But, since first introducing the idea of Standard English, we have greatly improved our formal system's ability to mirror English syntax. No longer limited to sentence letters and symbolic operators, we can now form symbolic sentences containing constants (corresponding to English singular terms), predicate letters (corresponding to simple, one-placed English predicates), quantifiers (corresponding to English quantifying phrases), and variables (corresponding to English pronouns). So, if paraphrasing into Standard English is to remain a useful first step toward translation, we must update our idea of Standard English, bringing it into line with the refinements we have made in our system.

Our new definition of Standard English is this:

A sentence is in *Standard English* just in case it can be broken up into parts (with nothing left over) so that each part is either

a. one of the seven favored sentential operators,

b. a simple, one-placed predicate,

c. a singular term,

d. the pronoun "it", or

e. one of the two favored quantifying phrases: "each thing is such that" or "at least one thing is such that".

Consider, for example, the sentence

Everything is beautiful.

The first word of this sentence, "everything", is made from the word "every", which works like the phrase "each thing is such that", and the word "thing", which works like the pronoun "it". Hence, when we expand abbreviations, we get

Each thing is such that it is beautiful.

This sentence says the same thing as "Everything is beautiful", and it can be broken down (with nothing left over) into the quantifying phrase "Each thing is such that", the pronoun "it", and the predicate ". . . is beautiful". The sentence is therefore the Standard English paraphrase for "Everything is beautiful".

Some other sentences do not have adequate paraphrases in Standard English. Some simple clauses, such as "it is raining", can't be paraphrased into Standard English because they don't contain any predicates. Some complex clauses, such as "It's possible that Al will win the election", can't be paraphrased into Standard English because they contain sentential operators that don't correspond to any operators of Standard English. And some clauses, such as "Almost nothing is such that it is red", can't be paraphrased into Standard English because they contain quantifying phrases that don't correspond semantically to either quantifying phrase of Standard English. We call clauses like these **intractable**. To say that a clause is intractable is just to say that it cannot be adequately paraphrased into Standard English.

When we try to paraphrase a group of sentences into Standard English, we may find that some of the clauses in those sentences are intractable. The others can be broken down, with nothing left over, into singular terms, (simple, one-placed) predicates, the favored sentential operators, the favored quantifying phrases, and the pronoun "it". Accordingly, to set up a scheme of correspondence for translating the sentences into PL, we

a.   associate each singular term appearing in the sentences with its own constant of PL,

b.   associate each (simple, one-placed) predicate in the sentence with its own predicate letter of PL, and

c.   associate each intractable English clause (that is, each clause that cannot be paraphrased into Standard English) with its own sentence letter of PL.

In setting up a scheme of correspondence, we don't need to worry about English quantifying phrases, or pronouns, or sentential operators—just about singular terms, predicates, and (occasionally) intractable simple clauses.

To translate a sentence or argument from Standard English into PL, we simply replace the expressions in it, one by one, with the corresponding expressions of PL. Consider, for example, the sentence

If Biff is a dog, something is a cat.

Paraphrasing into Standard English, we get

> If Biff is a dog, then at least one thing is such that it is a cat.

We can set up a scheme of correspondence for this sentence, like this:

> b: Biff
> D: . . . is a dog
> C: . . . is a cat

Using this scheme of correspondence, we can translate the sentence into PL:

> (Db → [∃x]Cx)

Here the translation corresponds, expression by expression, to the Standard English paraphrase of the original sentence — the predicate letter "D" to the predicate ". . . is a dog", the constant "b" to the singular term "Biff", the arrow to the sentential operator "if, then", the quantifier "[∃x]" to the quantifying phrase "at least one thing is such that", the variable "x" to the pronoun "it", and the predicate letter "C" to the predicate ". . . is a cat".

For another example, suppose we want to translate the sentence

> All dogs are brown.

As a first step toward translation, we paraphrase the sentence into Standard English:

> Each thing is such that, if it is a dog, then it is brown.

Using the obvious scheme of correspondence, we can translate the paraphrase of the original sentence into PL:

> [x](Dx → Bx)

Here again, our translation corresponds closely to the Standard English paraphrase of the original sentence. The quantifier "[x]" corresponds to the quantifying phrase "each thing is such that", the predicate letter "D" to the predicate ". . . is a dog", the predicate letter "B" to the predicate ". . . is brown", the variable "x" to the pronoun "it", and the arrow to the sentential operator "if, then".

As our examples show, translation from Standard English into PL is easy. Usually, the most difficult part of translating is paraphrasing into Standard English. And even paraphrasing is generally easy for those who have mastered certain common patterns.

Using "*A*" as a stand-in for an English noun phrase (such as "beautiful thing") and "*B*" as a stand-in for another such phrase, we can display five common patterns like this:

1. "Everything is an *A*" paraphrases as "Each thing is such that it is an *A*".

2. "Something is an *A*" paraphrases as "At least one thing is such that it is an *A*".

3. "All *A*s are *B*s" paraphrases as "Each thing is such that, if it is an *A*, then it is a *B*".

4. "Some *A*s are *B*s" paraphrases as "At least one thing is such that it is an *A* and it is a *B*".

5. "No *A*s are *B*s" paraphrases as "It's not the case that at least one thing is such that it is an *A* and it is a *B*".

As patterns (3), (4), and (5) indicate, English sentences that do not seem to contain sentential operators often paraphrase into sentences of Standard English that do. For instance, in pattern (3), the sentential operator "if, then" appears in the paraphrase, although there is no hint of it in the original sentence. To those practiced in paraphrasing, this is not surprising. Often (but *not* always) a paraphrase containing the quantifying phrase "each thing is such that" will also contain the operator "if, then", and a paraphrase containing the quantifying phrase "at least one thing is such that" will contain the operator "and".

It's a good idea to memorize these five common patterns. Those who master them will find paraphrasing into Standard English much easier than those who approach each new problem from scratch.

To see why, consider the sentence

A tortilla is made either from corn or from wheat.

Although this sentence begins with the phrase "a tortilla", the sentence is not about any *one* tortilla, but about *all*. Accordingly, we can begin to paraphrase the sentence into Standard English like this:

All tortillas are either things made from corn or things made from wheat.

Since this sentence fits the form "All *A*s are *B*s", we know from pattern (3) that its Standard English paraphrase is going to look like this:

Each thing is such that, if it . . . , then it —.

Filling in the blanks, we get

Each thing is such that, if it is a tortilla, then either it is made from corn or it is made from wheat.

And, under an obvious scheme of correspondence, we can translate this sentence as

[x](Tx → (Cx ∨ Wx)).

In coming to this translation, our knowledge of common pattern (3) helped us to paraphrase the original sentence by hinting at the general structure of the finished paraphrase.

So far in our examples, we have translated *sentences* into PL. We can also translate *arguments*. To translate an argument, we simply translate all the sentences in the argument under the same scheme of correspondence.

Consider, for example, the argument

No novel is old.

The Iliad is an old book.

So, some book is not a novel.

Expanding abbreviations and paraphrasing into Standard English in accordance with common patterns (1) and (5), we get

It's not the case that at least one thing is such that it is a novel and it is old.

The Iliad is a book, and *The Iliad* is old.

So, at least one thing is such that it is a book and it is not the case that it is a novel.

Next, we establish a scheme of correspondence for the argument, like this:

N: . . . is a novel
O: . . . is old
B: . . . is a book
a: *The Iliad*

Under this scheme, we can translate the argument into PL like this:

$-[\exists x](Nx\ \&\ Ox)$

$(Ba\ \&\ Oa)$

So, $[\exists x](Bx\ \&\ -Nx)$

If anything is difficult in this translation, it is the move from the original version of the argument into Standard English. Once we have the Standard English version, translation is easy; we simply replace English expressions with corresponding expressions of PL.

Our final example has to do with the argument

Either all men are corrupt, or most men are honest.

All corrupt men are unhappy.

So, if most men aren't honest, all men are unhappy.

The result of paraphrasing this argument into Standard English is this:

Either each thing is such that, if it is a man, then it is corrupt, *or* most men are honest.

Each thing is such that, if it is a man and it is corrupt, then it's not the case that it is happy.

So, if it's not the case that most men are honest, then each thing is such that, if it is a man, then it's not the case that it is happy.

For the most part, the paraphrase is straightforward. Notice, however, that the clause "most men are honest" is intractable, since it contains the nonstandard quantifying phrase "most".

Here is a scheme of correspondence for the sample argument:

M: . . . is a man
C: . . . is corrupt
H: . . . is happy
P: most men are honest

Under this scheme, we can translate the sample argument like this:

([x](Mx → Cx) ∨ P)
[x]((Mx & Cx) → −Hx)

So, (−P → [x](Mx → −Hx))

Once again, to move from a Standard English paraphrase into PL, we simply replace English expressions with the corresponding symbolic expressions.

Having translated an English argument into PL, we may be able to demonstrate the translation's PL-validity with a derivation. And the fact that an English argument has a PL-valid symbolic translation generally indicates that the argument is valid. Hence, as we will explain in the next section, translation into PL is part of a general method for demonstrating the validity of English arguments.

Exercises 8.5

1. *Defend or criticize:* When writing papers, stories, or poems, it's always best to use Standard English.

2. *Defend or criticize:* A sentence is in Standard English just in case it doesn't contain any expressions other than (a) the seven favored sentential operators, (b) singular terms, (c) predicates, (d) the quantifying phrase "each thing is such that", and (e) the pronoun "it".

3. *Defend or criticize:* The syntax of Standard English closely resembles the syntax of the system PL.

4. *Defend or criticize:* The sentence "Something in the fire is hot" can be paraphrased into Standard English with the sentence "At least one thing is such that, if it is in the fire, then it is hot."

5. *Defend or criticize:* The sentence "It's possible that Larry is at home" cannot be paraphrased into Standard English.

6. *Defend or criticize:* The sentence "There are exactly two coins in my pocket" cannot be paraphrased into Standard English.

7. Which of the following sentences are in Standard English? If a sentence is not in Standard English, either paraphrase it into Standard English or explain why paraphrasing it is impossible.
   a. If Sally is a freshman, then Glen is a sophomore.
   b. At least one thing is such that it is a paperweight if and only if it is heavy.
   c. Most dogs are dachshunds.
   d. All dogs are dachshunds.
   e. Some dogs are dachshunds.
   f. Some dogs are not dachshunds.
   g. No dogs are dachshunds.
   h. No dogs that are in New Jersey are dachshunds.
   i. It's possible that no dogs are dachshunds.
   j. All old Croatians are tall men.
   k. It's raining outside.
   l. Either all men are honest or no men are brave.
   m. Clarence is honest unless some honest men are not brave.
   n. A dollar bill is either a silver certificate or a treasury note.
   o. Only treasury notes are dollar bills.
   p. All and only treasury notes are dollar bills.
   q. Any reporter is a journalist.
   r. If any reporters are journalists, then all are.

s. No reporters are rich men, if all publishers are stingy or stupid.

t. If something is a mammal, then it's an animal.

8. *Defend or criticize:* Once we have set up a scheme of correspondence, we can translate a Standard English sentence into PL simply by replacing Standard English expressions with the corresponding expressions of PL.

9. *Defend or criticize:* Since some English clauses cannot be paraphrased into Standard English, some English clauses cannot be translated into PL.

10. *Defend or criticize:* To set up a scheme of correspondence for a sentence in Standard English, we associate English singular terms with symbolic constants, English sentential operators with symbolic operators, English predicates with symbolic predicate letters, and intractable English clauses with symbolic sentence letters.

11. Using the methods of Chapter 2 along with those of the previous section, translate the following arguments into PL. (Remember to expand all abbreviations, to paraphrase into Standard English, and to establish a scheme of correspondence.)

a. Some apes are chimps. And all chimps are of the genus *gorilla*. So, some apes are of the genus *gorilla*.

b. Any vegetable that isn't high in vitamin C must not be green, since every green vegetable is high in vitamin C.

c. If something is a Ford or a Chevy, it's inexpensive. It follows that Fords are good buys. After all, something isn't a good buy only if it's expensive.

d. The guests were all happy if and only if there was a band. So, if there was no band, some of the guests were unhappy.

e. If something's filling, it's unhealthy. The proof is this: Anything filling or fattening is sweet, but nothing sweet is healthy.

f. All lawyers are members of the bar. So, if everyone in the Smith family is a lawyer, all of them are members of the bar.

g. Either there are some lions or there are some members of the species *felix leo*. I remember that much from my zoology class. But, as Jane has just reminded us, all members of the species *felix leo* are lions. And, clearly, all lions are ferocious. We can conclude, I guess, that there are some ferocious things.

h. Each of the libraries is full only if it is a good place to study. But the fact is that a library that's not full is always a good place to study. So, if there are any libraries, some of them are good places to study.

i. Since termites are always annoying pests, and since pests are always troublemakers, termites must be troublemakers. My Aunt Charlotte's house was infested by termites, and they nearly destroyed the whole foundation.

8.6 PL-Validity, P-Validity, and Validity

In the previous section, we discussed translation into PL, the first step of our new method for demonstrating validity. Having translated an argument from English into PL, we can complete the demonstration of its validity simply by deriving the translation's conclusion from its premises using PL's rules of inference. In this section, we explain why the method works.

For our first example, we look once again at our old friend the Hatfield argument:

All psychiatrists are M.D.s.

Hatfield is a psychiatrist.

_____

So, Hatfield is an M.D.

As we have seen, CL's methods cannot demonstrate this argument's validity. The addition in Chapter 7 of constants and predicate letters to CL's vocabulary did allow us to display the inner structure of the argument's second premise and conclusion, but even that is not enough. What we need is some way of mirroring the inner structure of the argument's *first* premise — a way of capturing the fact that the properties mentioned in the argument's first premise are the same as those mentioned in its second premise and conclusion.

PL provides such a way. Translating the argument into PL under the obvious scheme of correspondence, we get

$[x](Px \rightarrow Mx)$
Ph

_____

So, Mh

That the predicate letter "P" appears in both the translation's premises mirrors the fact that the property of being a psychiatrist is mentioned in both of the Hatfield argument's premises. Similarly, that the predicate letter "M" appears both in the translation's first premise and in its conclusion mirrors the fact that the property of being an M.D. is mentioned both in the Hatfield argument's first premise and in its conclusion.

Indeed, the translation captures everything about the Hatfield argument that accounts for its validity. So, by demonstrating the PL-validity of this translation with a derivation, we can infer that the Hatfield argument itself is valid.

As one might expect, the justification for this inference has to do with *sets* and *predicative form*. The fact that we can construct a derivation for the Hatfield argument's PL-translation entails that a certain arrangement of sets is impossible. In turn, the fact that this arrangement of sets is impossible entails that the Hatfield argument's predicative form is P-valid and, hence, that the argument itself is valid.

To understand the details of this reasoning, suppose that there is an arrangement of sets meeting these conditions:

1. Set *A* is a subset of set *B*;
2. object *O* is a member of set *A*; and
3. object *O* is not a member of set *B*.

If there were such an arrangement of sets, we could use sets *A* and *B* and object *O* to construct a valuation for the Hatfield argument's symbolic translation, like this:

domain of discourse:	a set containing all members of set *A* and all members of set *B*
referent of "h":	object *O*
extension of "P":	set *A*
extension of "M":	set *B*

In this valuation, the extension of the predicate letter "P" would be a subset of the extension of the predicate letter "M" [condition (1)], and the referent of constant "h" would be a member of the extension of "P" [condition (2)]. Accordingly, in this valuation, both premises of the Hatfield argument's PL-translation would have the value *t* (rules V7 and V8). But, since the object *O* is *not* a member of set *B* [condition (3)], the value of the translation's conclusion in the given valuation would be *f*. So, the valuation we constructed would be a counterexample to the Hatfield argument's translation.

But, once we demonstrate the translation's PL-validity with a derivation, we know that there are *no* counterexamples to it! We may therefore infer that there is no arrangement of sets of the sort just described. If there were, the Hatfield argument's PL-translation would not have been PL-valid, and we would not have been able to derive its conclusion from its premises using PL's rules of inference.

That there cannot be an arrangement of sets meeting conditions (1), (2), and (3) has an important consequence regarding the Hatfield argument's predicative form,

Each thing is such that, if *F* it, then *G* it.

Fa

So, *Ga*

In any situation in which an argument of this form has true premises and a false conclusion, there would have to be a set of things (call it *A*) having the property mentioned by the argument's first predicate, a set of things (call it *B*) having the property mentioned by the argument's second predicate, and an object (call it *O*) picked out by the argument's singular term. And, in this situation,

1. set *A* would have to be a subset of set *B*,
2. object *O* would have to be a member of set *A*, and
3. object *O* could not be a member of set *B*.

Conditions (1) and (2) would have to be met for the situation to be one in which the argument's premises are true, and condition (3) would have to be met for the situation to be one in which the argument's conclusion is false.

But, as we just saw, the fact that we can construct a derivation for the Hatfield argument's PL-translation shows that *there cannot be such an arrangement of sets.* So, in constructing a derivation for the Hatfield argument's PL-translation, we in effect demonstrate the validity of *every* argument with the same form. In other words, we demonstrate the P-validity of the argument's predicative form.

Since every argument with a P-valid predicative form is valid, it follows that the Hatfield argument itself is valid. Thus, in constructing a derivation for the Hatfield argument's PL-translation, we have demonstrated the Hatfield argument's validity.

We may generalize from this example. Typically, if we can construct a derivation for an argument's symbolic translation, we can infer that the argument is valid.

There are a few cases in which this inference seems questionable. For instance, although the argument

There are no unicorns.
_____

So, all unicorns are crocodiles.

seems invalid, we can construct a derivation for its translation, "$-[\exists x]Ux$; so $[x](Ux \rightarrow Cx)$". The problem here, which has been with us since Chapter 5, lies in the fact that our model's arrow does not correspond very well to the English operator "if, then". As we have indicated, however, the proper response to this problem is not to abandon formal methods for demonstrating validity, but rather to apply those methods with caution — especially when an arrow appears in the translation of an argument's conclusion. If we observe this caution, we can confidently use our formal methods to demonstrate the validity of arguments in English.

In addition to providing us with these methods, PL shows us what it is about certain arguments that accounts for their validity. When we translate an argument from English into PL, we lose much of what is going on in its premises and conclusion. Indeed, *all* that we capture in the argument's PL-translation are some facts about the pattern of the expressions in it and some facts about the semantics of its sentential operators and quantifying phrases. Yet, as we have seen, we can sometimes demonstrate an argument's validity simply by constructing a derivation for its PL-translation. We would not be able to do so unless, in translating the argument into PL, we captured *everything* that accounts for its validity. Accordingly, if an argument is one whose validity we can demonstrate with PL's methods, its validity must be due entirely to the pattern of its sentential operators, singular terms, predicates, quantifying phrases, and pronouns and to those facts about the semantics of its sentential operators and quantifying phrases reflected in PL's rules of valuation. In short, if we can demonstrate an argument's validity with the methods of PL, its validity must be due entirely to its predicative form.

Let's apply this insight to the evaluation of an argument of historical interest. The argument comes from Bishop George Berkeley's *Principles of Human Knowledge* (1711), a work that challenges our ordinary assumptions about the world around us. At one point, Berkeley argues:

> But, [if] it were possible that solid, figured, movable substances may exist [outside] the mind . . . , yet how is it possible for us to know this? Either we must know it by sense or by reason. As for our senses, by them we have the knowledge only of our sensations, [or] ideas. . . . It remains therefore that if we have any knowledge at all of external things, it must be by reason, inferring their existence from [our sensations]. But what reason can [cause] us to believe the existence of bodies [outside] the mind from what we perceive, since the very patrons of Matter do not pretend there is any necessary connection between [these bodies] and our [sensations]? I say it is granted on all hands (and what happens in dreams, frenzies, and the like puts it beyond dispute) that it is possible we might be affected with all the [sensations] we have now, though there were no bodies existing [outside the mind].

(Since we are here interested in the passage as logicians rather than as historians of philosophy, we have taken the liberty of editing it extensively.)

Berkeley's conclusion concerns the existence of what we will call *mind-independent material objects* — objects that Berkeley calls "solid, figured, movable substances . . . [outside] the mind," "external things," "bodies [outside] the mind," or "Matter." The conclusion is this:

> We (human beings) do not know that mind-independent material objects exist.

Berkeley does not state this conclusion explicitly, but the rhetorical question with which the passage begins makes the conclusion apparent.

Two of Berkeley's premises are explicit:

1. If we know that something exists, we know either by sense or by reason that it exists.

2. Anything we know to exist by sense is a sensation.

Another premise seems to be this:

3. Mind-independent material objects are not sensations.

Although premise (3) is not stated, it's something that Berkeley would take for granted, and the argument looks much better with it than without it.

The argument also has a fourth premise, which is stated. To establish this fourth premise, Berkeley offers a subargument. In view of what happens in dreams and "frenzies" (that is, hallucinations), Berkeley contends that there are possible situations in which all our sensations are just as they are now even though there are no mind-independent material objects. From this, he infers that any argument from premises describing our sensations to the conclusion that material objects exist must be invalid. But Berkeley apparently believes that there is no chance of our knowing by reason that mind-independent material objects exist unless we can find a valid argument leading from premises about our sensations to a conclusion about mind-independent material objects. Accordingly, Berkeley maintains that

4. We do not know by reason that mind-independent material objects exist.

(It is perhaps worth noticing that, in support of this premise, Berkeley subscribes to the view that the only *acceptable* arguments are *valid* arguments, thereby rejecting the idea that there are acceptable *inductive* arguments. Compare what we said about induction near the end of Chapter 1.)

Having now identified Berkeley's premises and conclusion, we can make his main argument explicit, like this:

1. If we know that something exists, we know either by sense or by reason that it exists.
2. Anything we know to exist by sense is a sensation.
3. Mind-independent material objects are not sensations.
4. We do not know by reason that mind-independent material objects exist.

---

5. So, we do not know that mind-independent material objects exist.

Translating the argument into PL under an obvious scheme of correspondence, we get this:

1. $[x](Kx \rightarrow (Sx \lor Rx))$
2. $[x](Sx \rightarrow Ix)$
3. $-[\exists x](Mx \mathbin{\&} Ix)$
4. $-[\exists x](Mx \mathbin{\&} Rx)$

---

5. So, $-[\exists x](Mx \mathbin{\&} Kx)$

This symbolic argument is PL-valid, as we can show with a derivation. Accordingly, we may infer that Berkeley's argument itself is valid.

This does not mean, of course, that we ought to accept the argument's conclusion. As we pointed out in Chapter 1, the conclusions of valid arguments are not always true. Still, the knowledge that Berkeley's argument is valid does have important consequences. Since valid arguments never lead from true premises to false conclusions, a valid argument with a false conclusion must have one or more false premises. So, after we see that Berkeley's argument is valid, we are no longer free to accept its premises while rejecting its conclusion. We can reject its conclusion only if we are prepared to reject one or more of its premises.

But each of Berkeley's premises seems true — or, at least, plausible. So, there is a problem here. If we reject Berkeley's weird-sounding conclusion, which of his premises should we reject? This problem is what makes Berkeley's argument so disturbing and so interesting to philosophers. To reject the argument's seemingly false conclusion, we must reject one of its seemingly true premises. Something has got to go, but what?

By themselves, the methods of PL do not provide an answer to this question. Still, our knowledge of the argument's validity is what prevents us from rejecting the argument's conclusion while accepting its premises. Thus, by allowing us to demonstrate the validity of Berkeley's argument, PL's methods help us to see clearly the interesting philosophical questions the argument raises.

The methods also show us what it is about the argument that accounts for its validity. To those not trained in logic, it might seem that the argument's validity rests on the meaning of the terms "knowledge", "sense", "reason", and "material object". Yet, as we have seen, these meanings have very little to do with the argument's logical evaluation. What accounts for the argument's validity are the facts captured in its PL-translation: facts about patterns of expressions and about the semantics of quantifying phrases and sentential operators — in other words, facts about predicative form.

Exercises 8.6

1. *Defend or criticize:* Any argument with a PL-valid translation is valid.

2. *Defend or criticize:* Generally, if we find that an argument in English has a PL-invalid translation, we may infer that the argument itself is invalid.

3. *Defend or criticize:* If we can demonstrate that a given argument is valid using PL's methods, we can be certain that *every* argument with the same predicative form as the given argument is valid, too.

4. *Defend or criticize:* Whether the English sentence "All psychiatrists are M.D.s" is true in a possible situation has something to do with *sets*. Similarly, whether the symbolic sentence "[x](Px → Mx)" has the value *t* in a valuation has something to do with sets.

5. In the last chapter and again in this one, we considered the Hatfield argument:

All psychiatrists are M.D.s.

Hatfield is a psychiatrist.

So, Hatfield is an M.D.

Translate this argument into PL and demonstrate the translation's PL-validity with a derivation. What can you conclude about the validity of the original argument? Why?

6. In the previous section, we considered the following translation of an argument from Berkeley's *Principles:*

[x](Kx → (Sx ∨ Rx))

[x](Sx → Ix)

−[∃x](Mx & Ix)

−[∃x](Mx & Rx)

So, −[∃x](Mx & Kx)

Using a derivation, demonstrate this symbolic argument's PL-validity. What (if anything) does the derivation show about the argument that it translates?

7. Make the arguments in the following passages explicit. Then, using the method described in this chapter, demonstrate the arguments' validity.

a. All dogs are canines, and all canines are mammals. Hence, Biff is a dog only if he's a mammal.

b. Oranges are always citrus fruits. So, there are no seedless oranges. For every citrus fruit has seeds.

c. Although there are no computer chips in our last shipment to you, everything that you ordered is in the shipment. But, if none of the things you ordered were computer chips, only warehouse workers saw your letter. It seems to me, then, that no one saw your letter but warehouse workers.

d. There is some dispute as to whether Pluto should be counted as a planet, but it's plain to me that it should be. And, if Pluto is a planet, some planet is very cold. But, as Prof. Higgenbothem's theory tells us, no cold planet has rings. So, some planet doesn't have rings.

e. If only virtuous people were witnesses at the trial, all of the witnesses testified honestly. For either all of the witnesses testified honestly or some lied. And no one virtuous ever lies.

f. If there are any sages, all yogis are sages. And, if there are any adepts, all sages are adepts. So, if any sages are adepts, all yogis are adepts.

g. Every airplane has either a propeller or a jet engine. I know for a fact, however, that no airplane made by Hillsquick Industries has a propeller. Hence, it seems to me that, if everything made by Hillsquick is an airplane, everything made by them has a jet engine.

h. All hard gems are useful, and whatever is useful is valuable. But, if there is something that's inexpensive but valuable, no gem is valuable. So, if some useful thing is inexpensive, no gem is hard.

8. Using the methods described in this chapter, demonstrate the validity of the arguments in Exercise 8.5.11.

8.7 Overview

As we said near the beginning of this chapter, the *predicative form* of a sentence or argument is the way in which it is built up from

simple, one-placed predicates

singular terms,

quantifying phrases,

pronouns,

sentential operators, and

simple clauses that don't contain predicates.

To reveal the predicative form of a sentence or argument, we expand abbreviations, break the expanded sentence or argument down into expressions of the sort just listed, replace predicates with uppercase letters such as "*F*" and "*G*", replace remaining singular terms with lowercase letters such as "*a*" and "*b*", and replace simple clauses that don't contain predicates with uppercase letters such as "*P*" and "*Q*".

Some arguments — like our example, the Hatfield argument — are valid just because of their predicative form. Accordingly, we introduced the idea of P-validity:

A predicative form is *P-valid* just in case every argument of that form is valid.

In this chapter, we have refined our model of English so that it can mirror facts about predicative form. Our aim has been to develop a reliable and efficient method for demonstrating the P-validity of predicative forms and, hence, for demonstrating the validity of particular arguments in English.

The refinements that we made in our model took us from CL to predicate logic (PL). PL's vocabulary contains:

a. sentence letters, symbolic operators, and parentheses,
b. the expressions introduced in Chapter 7: constants and predicate letters, and
c. three new expressions: the variable "x", the universal quantifier "[x]", and the existential quantifier "[∃x]".

Syntactically, the variable "x" works just as a constant does:

> The result of writing a variable immediately to the right of a predicate letter is a wff of PL (rule F7).

And quantifiers can stand out in front of (some) wffs containing variables:

> If a wff of PL contains one or more instances of the variable "x" but no quantifiers, then the result of writing a universal or existential quantifier in front of that wff is itself a wff (rules F8 and F9).

Sentence letters, symbolic operators, parentheses, constants, and predicate letters work syntactically just as they have in previous chapters.

While all of CL's wffs were symbolic sentences, only *some* of PL's wffs are symbolic sentences. In particular, a wff of PL is a symbolic sentence just in case every variable in it is bound (or, in other words, is within the scope of a quantifier).

Valuations for symbolic sentences of PL look exactly like those discussed in Chapter 7. After specifying a domain of discourse, these valuations assign referents to constants, extensions to predicate letters, and values to sentence letters.

In valuations of this sort, objects *satisfy* (or fail to satisfy) wffs containing free variables:

> An object from a valuation's domain *satisfies* a wff containing a free variable just in case, by replacing the free variables in that wff with a constant referring to that object, we produce a symbolic sentence having the value *t* in that valuation.

This idea of satisfaction plays an important role in the rules of valuation for quantified sentences:

> In a given valuation, a sentence whose first mark is a universal quantifier has the value *t* just in case, if we erase the sentence's initial quantifier, the resulting wff is satisfied by *each* object in the valuation's domain (rule V8). And a sentence whose first mark is an existential quantifier has the value *t* in a valuation just in case, if we erase the sentence's initial quantifier, the resulting wff is satisfied by *at least one object* in the valuation's domain (rule V9).

These rules ensure that the quantifier "[x]" corresponds to the English phrase "each thing is such that" and that the quantifier "[∃x]" corresponds to the phrase "at least one thing is such that".

After adding quantified sentences to our system, we modified its system of derivation. One new rule, QE, allows us to deal with the negations of quantified sentences. The other new rules rest on the idea of instantiation:

> A wff is an *instantiation* of a (universally or existentially) quantified sentence just in case we can produce the wff by erasing the quantified sentence's initial mark (which will be either "[x]" or "[∃x]"), choosing a constant, and substituting the constant for all free variables in the remaining wff.

Using this idea, we introduced the rules UI, EI, and EG. If a universally quantified sentence appears in a derivation, UI allows us to write any of its instantiations. If an existentially quantified sentence appears in a derivation, EI allows us to write any of its instantiations *provided that* the constant we introduce is entirely new to the derivation. And, if an instantiation of an existentially quantified sentence appears in a derivation, EG allows us to write that existentially quantified sentence.

PL's system of derivation is a part of a powerful method for demonstrating the validity of arguments in English. The method has four steps:

1. We make the argument explicit.
2. We expand all abbreviations and, insofar as possible, paraphrase into Standard English.
3. We translate into PL.
4. Using PL's system of derivation, we try to demonstrate the PL-validity of the symbolic translation.

The first of these steps has remained unchanged since Chapter 2. And the only change in the second step is that we have refined our idea of Standard English. As we are now looking at things, a sentence is in Standard English just in case each of the expressions in it is either

a. one of the seven favored sentential operators ("it's not the case that", "and", "or", "unless", "if, then", "only if", and "if and only if"),
b. a simple, one-placed predicate,
c. a singular term,
d. the pronoun "it", or
e. one of the two favored quantifying phrases: "each thing is such that" and "at least one thing is such that".

If a clause cannot be adequately paraphrased into Standard English, we leave it as is and treat it as an indivisible unit.

The third step, translation, begins with our setting up a scheme of correspondence. Now that we have moved from CL to PL, our schemes of correspondence associate constants with singular terms, predicate letters with (simple, one-placed) predicates, and sentence letters with intractable clauses. Once we have such a scheme, we complete a translation by replacing expressions of Standard English with the corresponding expressions of PL, adding parentheses, and making small changes in word order where necessary.

If we succeed in constructing a derivation for an argument's PL-translation, we can be confident that the predicative form of the original argument is P-valid and, hence, that the argument itself is valid.

Chapter 9

Relation Logic: Many-Placed Predicate Letters and Multiple Quantification

In Chapter 8, we developed the system PL, which models facts about predicative form and provides us with a sophisticated method for demonstrating the validity of English arguments. In the effort to streamline the development of PL, however, we left two loose ends. First, having noted that some English predicates (such as ". . . struck out—") contain more than one blank, we proceeded to ignore them, restricting ourselves, in the interest of simplicity, to predicates containing only one blank. Second, having noted that there are clauses (such as "everybody loves somebody") in which two or more quantifying phrases work together, we ignored these clauses, again in the interest of simplicity.

But what we have ignored sometimes has a bearing on the evaluation of arguments. Consider, for example, the argument

Abelard loved Heloise.

_____

So, somebody loved somebody.

Letting the constant "a" correspond to the singular term "Abelard", the predicate letter "H" to the predicate ". . . loved Heloise", and the predicate letter "L" to the predicate ". . . loved somebody", we can translate the argument into PL like this:

Ha

_____

So, [∃x]Lx

Alternatively, letting "h" correspond to "Heloise", "A" to "Abelard loved . . .", and "S" to "somebody loved . . .", we can translate the argument like this:

Ah
———————
So, [∃x]Sx

But, whichever of these equally correct ways of translating we choose, our translation is clearly PL-invalid. In fact, the result is a PL-invalid argument no matter how we translate the Abelard argument into PL. So, the Abelard argument, though valid in virtue of its form, cannot be shown to be valid by PL's methods.

One source of the problem is that, while PL's predicate letters have just one blank after them for constants, the predicate ". . . loved—" contains two places for singular terms. Because of this difference, the Abelard argument's PL-translation cannot capture the important fact that the predicate ". . . loved —" appears both in the argument's premise and in its conclusion.

Another source of the problem is that the Abelard argument's conclusion, "Somebody loved somebody", contains two quantifying phrases that work together. Since PL's rules of formation prohibit the formation of symbolic sentences that have one quantifier inside the scope of another, the PL-translation of the Abelard argument's conclusion cannot capture important facts about that sentence's structure.

In this chapter, then, we look at predicates with more than one blank and at quantifying phrases that work together with others. Our investigations will sharpen our ideas about form and validity and will lead us to formulate definitions of *relational form* and *relational validity*. In light of these definitions, we will refine our model of English, moving from PL to the even more sophisticated system, *relation logic*, or RL. After stating RL's rules of formation and valuation, we will define RL-validity and develop a test for it. Finally, near the end of the chapter, we will study the relation of RL to English and evaluate the progress made in moving from PL to RL.

9.1 Relational Form: Many-Placed Predicates and Multiple Quantification in English

In this section, we refine our ideas about the form of English sentences and arguments. The refined ideas take account of many-placed predicates and of quantifying phrases that work together with other quantifying phrases.

Our first example is the Abelard argument, which we considered briefly in the introduction to this chapter:

Abelard loved Heloise.

So, somebody loved somebody.

What is the best way to view this argument's *form?*

Notice first that, when we take the singular terms "Abelard" and "Heloise" out of the premise "Abelard loved Heloise", we are left with ". . . loved — ". This expression clearly is a predicate, since it becomes a clause when its blanks are filled with singular terms. But, unlike the predicates we have been dealing with so far, this one contains two blanks.

As we have said, if a predicate has a certain number, *n*, of blanks in it, we say that it is *n-placed*. So, for example, the phrase ". . . is red" is a *one-placed* predicate, the phrase ". . . is the same color as — " is a *two-placed* predicate, the phrase ". . . is closer to — than to __" is a *three-placed* predicate, and so on.

One-placed predicates mention properties of objects. The predicate ". . . is tall", for instance, mentions the property of tallness. Similarly, many-placed predicates mention *relations* between or among objects. For instance, the predicate ". . . is taller than — " mentions the relation of being-taller-than, and the predicate ". . . is between — and __" mentions the relation of being-in-between.

Let's apply this thought to the sentence "Abelard loved Heloise". What this sentence says, in effect, is that one *person* (Abelard) bears a certain *relation* (that of having-loved) to another *person* (Heloise). Accordingly, to grasp the structure of the sentence accurately, we should view it as made from three expressions: the singular term "Abelard", the *two*-placed predicate ". . . loved — ", and the singular term "Heloise". The singular terms pick out the people Abelard and Heloise, and the predicate mentions the relation of having-loved.

Consider now the Abelard argument's conclusion, "Somebody loved somebody". In the previous chapter, we saw that it is often useful to expand clauses containing words like "somebody" into clauses containing quantifying phrases like "at least one thing is such that" and "each thing is such that". But there is a problem with expanding the sentence "Somebody loved somebody" in this way. If we just plow straight ahead, as we did in the previous chapter, we end up with

at least one thing is such that at least one thing is such that it loves it.

But, in this clause, we cannot tell which occurrence of the pronoun "it" goes with which quantifying phrase.

Fortunately, a simple trick can solve this problem. When expanding abbreviations in clauses such as "somebody loved somebody", we deal with quantifying phrases one at a time, *using a different typeface each time.* For example, in dealing with the clause

somebody loved somebody,

we begin by making its first quantifying phrase explicit, like this:

at least one thing is such that it loved somebody.

Then, when making its second quantifying phrase explicit, we introduce a new typeface, like this:

at least one thing is such that *at least one thing is such that* it loves *it*.

Here, the fact that one quantifying phrase and one instance of the pronoun "it" are in italics makes it plain that the two are linked to one another.

Once we expand the sample sentence in this way, we can see that it is made from five expressions: two instances of the existential quantifying phrase "at least one thing is such that", two instances of the pronoun "it", and one instance of the (two-placed) predicate ". . . loved —".

Since we cannot discover this important fact by examining the sentence's *predicative* form, we move to a new idea of form — that of *relational* form:

> The **relational form** of an English sentence or argument is the way it is made from singular terms, predicates (including *many*-placed predicates), sentential operators, quantifying phrases, pronouns, and simple clauses that can't be broken up into these parts.

To reveal the relational form of an English sentence or of an argument that has been made explicit, we

a. expand all abbreviations in it, using different typefaces where necessary to keep track of the links between quantifying phrases and pronouns,

b. replace each simple clause that cannot be broken up into quantifying phrases, predicates, singular terms, and pronouns with an uppercase letter (the first such clause, wherever it occurs, with "*P*", the second with "*Q*", and so on),

c. replace each singlar term with a lowercase letter (the first, wherever it occurs, with "*a*", the second with "*b*", and so on), and

d. replace each remaining predicate with an uppercase letter (the first predicate, wherever it occurs, with "*F*", the second with "*G*", and so on).

This procedure for revealing relational form is similar to that for revealing predicative form (Chapter 8), but there are two differences. First, unlike the old procedure, the new one allows us to keep track of the links between quantifying phrases and pronouns by using different typefaces. Second, unlike the old procedure, the new one requires that we replace the singular terms in a sentence or argument with lowercase letters *before* dealing with predicates. The effect is that we can no longer use capital letters to replace predicates, such as ". . . loved Heloise", which contain singular terms.

Applying our new procedure for revealing relational form to our example, the Abelard argument, we get the argument's relational form:

Fab

_____

So, at least one thing is such that *at least one thing is such that F* it *it*.

After expanding abbreviations, we merely replace both of the argument's singular terms with lowercase letters and the argument's predicate ". . . loved —" with the letter "*F*", in both the premise and the conclusion.

Unlike the argument's predicative form, its relational form reveals the important fact that the argument's premise contains the same two-placed predicate as its conclusion. Indeed, the argument's relational form reveals all the features of the argument that bear on its validity. As we will show later in this chapter, the Abelard argument is valid just because it has this form, and any other argument with the same relational form is valid, too.

Accordingly, we introduce the idea of *relational validity:*

An argument form is **relationally valid (R-valid)** just in case every argument having the same relational form is valid.

Clearly, R-validity stands to relational form as P-validity stands to predicative form.

Our aim in the remainder of this chapter is to capture in our model of English those features of relational form that bear on R-validity. The result will be the system **relation logic** (RL), which is more powerful than any system we have developed so far in this book. Using RL, we can demonstrate the validity of many arguments (such as the one about Abelard) that we cannot show to be valid when limited to the methods of PL. And RL will also provide some insight into what it is about these arguments that accounts for their validity.

Exercises 9.1

1. *Defend or criticize:* When revealing the predicative and relational forms of the sentence "Cleveland is north of Akron", we have three choices. We can view it (a) as made from the singular term "Cleveland" and the (one-placed) predicate ". . . is north of Akron", (b) as made from the singular term "Akron" and the (one-placed) predicate "Cleveland is north of . . . ", or (c) as made up of the singular terms "Cleveland" and "Akron" and the (two-placed) predicate ". . . is north of —".

2. Consider these three arguments:

a.   Cleveland is north of Akron.

_____

Therefore, Cleveland is north of something.

    b. Cleveland is north of Akron.

          ————————————————————

       Therefore, something is north of Akron.

    c. Cleveland is north of Akron.

          ————————————————————————————————

       Therefore, Cleveland is north of something, and something is north of Akron.

Translate these arguments into CL, and test the resulting symbolic arguments for CL-validity. Then translate the arguments into PL, and test the resulting symbolic arguments for PL-validity. Are PL's methods more powerful than CL's? Is there a need for an even more powerful system?

3. Which of the following expressions are English predicates?
    a. . . . is tall—
    b. Tom hit . . .
    c. . . . hit Allan
    d. Tom hit Allan, and . . .
    e. If Tom hit Allan, then Allan hit . . .
    f. probably,—
    g. Tom is between . . . and Allan.
    h. . . . is between—and __.
    i. at least one thing is such that . . . , and everything is such that—
    j. Tom . . .

4. Explain how each of the following sentences can be built up from the predicate ". . . is smarter than—" along with other English expressions.
    a. Blair is smarter than Heather.
    b. Blair is smarter than anyone.
    c. It's not the case that everyone is smarter than someone.
    d. Someone is smarter than someone.
    e. If someone is smarter than someone, everyone is smarter than Blair.

5. *Defend or criticize:* In the system PL, we can never put a quantifier in front of an expression that already contains a quantifier. This is one respect in which PL differs from English.

6. Display the relational forms of the following sentences:
    a. Albert kissed Bette.
    b. Albert kissed someone.
    c. Albert kissed someone unless everybody hates him.
    d. Someone didn't kiss Bette.
    e. Someone sued someone.
    f. There is someone who hasn't sued anyone.
    g. Everyone has sued someone or other.

7. *Defend or criticize:* The Abelard argument (discussed in the text) has a P-invalid predicative form, but an R-valid relational form.

▥ 9.2 The Syntax of Many-Placed Predicate Letters and Multiple Quantification

In the last section, we suggested that the Abelard argument ("Abelard loved Heloise; so, somebody loved somebody") owes its validity to its relational form. And, as we saw, the relational form of the argument has to do with facts about the use of a many-placed predicate and with the way in which two quantifying phrases work together. Since we cannot capture these facts when translating the argument into PL, we cannot use PL's methods to demonstrate the Abelard argument's validity.

To correct this, we add many-placed predicate letters to our model's vocabulary and eliminate some of the restrictions on the use of quantifiers. The result of these changes will be the new system, **relation logic** (or **RL**), with which we will be able to demonstrate the validity of the Abelard argument and of other arguments like it.

The vocabulary of RL contains all the expressions of PL: sentence letters, symbolic operators, parentheses, constants, variables, quantifiers, and predicate letters. In fact, RL's vocabulary differs from PL's in only three ways — one having to do with variables, one with quantifiers, and one with predicate letters:

1. While PL's vocabulary contains only one variable, "x", RL's contains many — the lowercase letters "n" through "z".

2. While PL's only quantifiers are "[x]" and "[∃x]", RL has a universal and an existential quantifier associated with each of its variables. Associated with the variable "x" are the universal quantifier "[x]" and the existential quantifier "[∃x]", associated with "y" are "[y]" and "[∃y]", and so on.

3. While each of PL's predicate letters has (exactly) one place after it for a constant or variable, RL's predicate letters may have more than one blank after them. Predicate letters will still be uppercase letters "A" through "Z", but in RL each of these letters can be a one-placed predicate letter, a two-placed predicate letter, a three-placed predicate letter, and so on. (On any given occasion, the context will make it clear how a letter is being used.)

Except for these three differences, RL's vocabulary is exactly the same as PL's.

In view of the changes in our system's vocabulary, we need to make a few changes in its rules of formation. One has to do with F7, the rule about singular sentences. In PL, this rule said that, whenever we write a constant or variable immediately to the right of a predicate letter, the result is a wff. But now that we have many-placed predicate letters in our system, the rule will be this:

> F7:   For any number *n*, the result of writing a string of *n* constants or variables immediately to the right of an *n*-placed predicate letter is a wff.

Suppose, for example, that "F" is a one-placed predicate letter, "G" a two-placed predicate letter, and "H" a three-placed predicate letter. Then "Fx", "Fa", "Gxx", "Gxy", "Gax", "Hxxx", "Hxay", and "Haaa" are all wffs of RL, but "Fxy", "xGx", and "Hxx" are not.

Having revised rule F7, we also need to revise our idea of a *singular sentence*. In PL, whose predicate letters are all one-placed, a singular sentence consists of a (one-placed) predicate letter followed by a constant. But, now that our system contains many-placed predicate letters,

> a wff is a *singular sentence* just in case its first expression is an *n*-placed predicate letter and the rest is a string of *n* constants.

Thus, if "F" is a three-placed predicate letter, "Faaa", "Faba", and "Fabc" are all singular sentences.

Having explained the syntax of many-placed predicate letters, let's shift our attention to RL's stock of quantifiers. To see why RL needs more than two quantifiers, think about the sequence

$$[x][\exists x](Fx \rightarrow Gx).$$

Is the variable after the predicate letter "F" linked to the quantifier "[x]" or to the quantifier "[∃x]"? What about the variable after the "G"? By applying the rule UI to this sequence, can we get "[∃x](Fa → Ga)", or "[∃x](Fa → Gx)", or "[∃x](Fx → Ga)"?

When developing PL in the previous chapter, we avoided questions of this sort by prohibiting the formation of wffs in which a variable appears within the scope of two or more quantifiers. But in RL it's much easier to keep track of which variables are linked to which quantifiers than in PL. For, unlike PL, RL has variables of many different sorts, each with its own two quantifiers.

Consider, for example, the sequence

$$[x][\exists y](Fy \rightarrow Gx).$$

In this sequence, the shape of the quantifiers reveals the linkage of quantifiers with variables. Clearly, the variable "x" is linked to the quantifier "[x]", and the variable "y" to the quantifier "[∃y]".

Since we now have an easy way to keep track of the links between quantifiers and variables, we can do away with some of the restrictions built into PL's rules of formation. When using PL's rules, we can put a quantifier in front of a wff just in case the wff contains a variable but no quantifier. But the formation rules of the new system RL say this:

F8:   If a wff contains a variable but neither of *that* variable's quantifiers, then the result of writing that variable's universal quantifier in front of the wff is itself a wff.

F9:   If a wff contains a variable but neither of *that* variable's quantifiers, then the result of writing that variable's existential quantifier in front of the wff is itself a wff.

As with the rules of PL, these new rules prohibit our constructing sequences such as "[x][∃x](Fx → Gx)" in which a variable appears in the scope of *both* of its own quantifiers. But, unlike PL's rules, the new rules do sometimes allow us to put quantifiers in front of wffs that already contain quantifiers.

For example, using the new rules of formation, we may construct the symbolic sentence

[∃x][∃y]Fxy.

First, we write the variables "x" and "y" after the two-placed predicate letter "F" to form the wff "Fxy" (rule F7). Next, since "Fxy" contains the variable "y" but neither of that variable's quantifiers, we can put the quantifier "[∃y]" in front of it to form the wff "[∃y]Fxy" (rule F9). Finally, since the wff "[∃y]Fxy" contains the variable "x" but neither of that variable's quantifiers, we can put the quantifier "[∃x]" in front of it to form the symbolic sentence "[∃x][∃y]Fxy" (rule F9).

With wffs of this sort in our system, we need to make small changes in the definitions of *bondage* and *freedom*. When discussing the system PL in the previous chapter, we called the variable "x" *bound* on a given occurrence just in case the occurrence fell within the scope of some quantifier or other, and we called "x" *free* on a given occurrence just in case on that occurrence it was not bound. Now, however, we will say this:

On a given occurrence, a variable is *bound* just in case it occurs within the scope of one of that variable's own quantifiers, and *free* otherwise.

In the wff "[y]Fxy" the variable "y" is bound, since it occurs within the scope of the quantifier "[y]". But in the same formula, the variable "x" is free. Though appearing within the scope of the quantifier "[y]", it does not appear within the scope of one of its own quantifiers, "[x]" or "[∃x]".

Given this new understanding of bondage and freedom, we can say which wffs of RL are symbolic sentences:

A wff of RL is a *symbolic sentence* of RL just in case it does not contain any free variables.

Thus, the wffs "[x][∃y]Fxy" and "[x](Hx → [y]Iyyx)" are symbolic sentences of RL, but the wffs "[x]Fxy" and "(Hx → [y]Iyyx)" are not. The difference is that, in the wffs that are symbolic sentences, each variable is linked to one, and to *only* one, quantifier.

Exercises 9.2

1. *Defend or criticize:* Every symbolic sentence of PL is a symbolic sentence of RL, and every symbolic sentence of RL is a symbolic sentence of PL.

2. *Defend or criticize:* We can tell just by looking at it that the expression "F" is a one-placed predicate letter.

3. Which of the following sequences are symbolic sentences of RL? Which of the symbolic sentences are singular symbolic sentences of RL? (Assume here that "M" is a sentence letter, "N" a one-placed predicate letter, "O" a two-placed predicate letter, and "P" a three-placed predicate letter.)

a.	M	b.	Na
c.	Nx	d.	Oxx
e.	(Oaa ∨ −M)	f.	(Oaa ∨ x)
g.	−(Paba)	h.	Pxxa
i.	(M → −Oa)	j.	(−Pabc → (M ∨ −Oax))

4. *Defend or criticize:* If there is one occurrence of the variable "x" in a symbolic sentence, one of the variable "y", and none of the other variables, then that sentence must contain *two* quantifiers — no more, no less.

5. Which of the following sequences are wffs of RL? Which are symbolic sentences? (Assume that "P" is a sentence letter, "F" a one-placed predicate letter, "R" a two-placed predicate letter, and "S" a three-placed predicate letter.)

a. [x]P
b. [∃x]Rax
c. [∃x][∃y]Rxy
d. [∃x][a]Rax
e. [x](P → −[∃y]Rxy)
f. [y](Fy → −Saxy)
g. [x](Fx → [∃y]Rax)
h. (Fx → [∃y]Sax)
i. [x](Fx → [∃x]Rax)
j. ([x]Fx → [∃x]Rxy)
k. −[x][y](−Ray → Rxa)
l. ([x][y]Rxy → [x]Fx)
m. [x][y](Rxy → [∃w]Swww)

n.   [x] − [y] − [z] − (−Sxyz ∨ −P)
o.   [x][y][z](Rxy → Ryx)

6. *Defend or criticize:* The symbolic sentence "− ([x]Fx → [y]Gy)" is the negation of a quantified sentence since its first expression is a dash while its second expression is a quantifier.

7. Identify the basic form of each of the following symbolic sentences:
   a.   Rab
   b.   [x][y]Rxy
   c.   [x] − [y]Rxy
   d.   [∃x][∃y]Rxy
   e.   −[∃x] − [y]Rxy
   f.   ([x]Rxx ↔ [∃y]Ryy)
   g.   [x](Rxx ↔ [∃y]Rxy)
   h.   − ([x]Rxx ↔ − [z]Fz)
   i.   − (([x][y]Rxy ∨ [x]Rxx) → [∃x][∃y]Rxy)
   j.   (− ([x][y]Rxy ∨ [x]Rxx) → [∃x][∃y]Ryx)

9.3 The Semantics of Singular Sentences

In the previous section, we added many-placed predicate letters to our model of English, and we changed the system's rules of formation to allow the construction of wffs in which one quantifier appears within the scope of another. In this section and the next, we revise our model's semantics accordingly. In this one, we look at the semantics of singular sentences and, in the next, at the semantics of sentences containing quantifiers.

The first order of business is to revise our idea of valuation. To set up a valuation for a group of symbolic sentences of PL, we identified a domain of discourse, assigned referents to constants, assigned extensions to one-placed predicate letters, and assigned values to sentence letters. Now that we have moved from PL to RL, there will be just one difference: In addition to assigning extensions to one-placed predicate letters, we will also assign them to many-placed predicate letters.

How? If the extension of a one-placed predicate letter is a set of objects, what should we take as the extension of a many-placed predicate letter? Our guiding thought here is that we want RL's many-placed predicate letters to mirror many-placed predicates of English. For the moment, then, let's shift our attention from the model back to English itself. An example from English will help us to understand the semantics of many-placed predicates and, hence, to see how to deal with many-placed predicate letters of RL.

Imagine, then, that one day during a college's intramural tennis tournament the PE Department posts the following announcement:

Matches played today. (Winners' names on left.)

Kobayashi, Jones

Stein, Ackrill

Taylor, Lioni

Just by looking at this list, we can tell that the sentence "Kobayashi won a match today against Jones" is true, that the sentence "Ackrill won a match today against Stein" is false (since Stein beat Ackrill), and that the sentence "Papadopolos won a match today against Taylor" is false (since Papadopolos did not even play). Indeed, if we assume that no one in the tournament has more than one last name and that the list reports all the matches played, the list tells us all we need to know to figure out the value (truth or falsity) of *any* sentence that we can construct by putting names into the blanks in the predicate ". . . won a match today against —".

This example suggests a way of dealing with the semantics of RL's many-placed predicate letters. Since we want these predicate letters to correspond to many-placed English predicates such as ". . . won a match today against —", we construct lists for them that correspond to the list on the PE Department's announcement. So, for example, when setting up a valuation for a symbolic sentence containing the two-placed predicate letter "F", we associate with "F" a list of *pairs* — say, like this:

2, 1

3, 5

4, 4

Which item comes first in a pair is important here, just as it was in the case of the PE Department's announcement.

To make these ideas more precise, we borrow another idea from set theory: the idea of an *ordered set*. With sets of the sort we have talked about so far, the order in which members are listed doesn't make any difference. So, for example, "{1, 2, 3}", "{3, 2, 1}", and "{2, 1, 3}" all name exactly the same set — the one whose members are the first three positive, whole numbers. But with *ordered* sets, whose names we form with the pointed brackets "⟨" and "⟩", order does make a difference. Thus, "⟨1, 2⟩" names the ordered set whose first member is the number 1 and whose second member is the number 2, but "⟨2, 1⟩" names the different ordered set whose first member is the number 2 and whose second member is the number 1.

If an ordered set has exactly two members, we call it an ordered *pair* (even if both of the set's members are the same object). Similarly, we call ordered sets with three members ordered *triples*, and those with four members ordered *quadruples*. And, in general, we call an ordered set an ordered *n-tuple*, where n is the number of the set's members. Thus, $\langle 4, 2, 1, 3, 1, 4 \rangle$ is an ordered *six-tuple* (even though its third and fifth members are both the number 1).

Using the idea of ordered sets, we can precisely define the idea of valuation for the system RL. To set up a valuation for a given group of symbolic sentences of RL, we

1. identify a (nonempty) set of objects to serve as the valuation's domain of discourse,
2. assign a referent (which must be a member of the domain) to each constant appearing in the group of sentences,
3. assign an extension (which must be a subset of the domain) to each one-placed predicate letter appearing in the group of symbolic sentences, and
4. assign a value — either t or f — to each sentence letter appearing in the group of symbolic sentences.

In addition, if the sentences contain n-placed predicate letters, where n is greater than 1, we

5. assign an extension (which must be a collection of ordered n-tuples) to each n-placed predicate letter appearing in the group of symbolic sentences.

Thus, in a given valuation, the extension of a two-placed predicate letter is a collection of ordered pairs, the extension of a three-placed predicate letter is a collection of ordered triples, and so on. The only restriction on how we assign these extensions is that, in a given valuation, the members of the ordered n-tuples in the extensions of many-placed predicate letters must all be members of that valuation's domain of discourse.

Given, say, the symbolic sentence

[x](Fxa → [∃y]Gbcy),

we can construct a valuation for it, in this way:

domain of discourse:	{1, 2, 3}
referent of "a":	1
referent of "b":	2
referent of "c":	3
extension of "F":	$\langle 1, 2 \rangle$, $\langle 2, 2 \rangle$, $\langle 3, 1 \rangle$, $\langle 3, 2 \rangle$, $\langle 3, 3 \rangle$
extension of "G":	$\langle 1, 3, 2 \rangle$, $\langle 1, 1, 2 \rangle$, $\langle 2, 3, 3 \rangle$, $\langle 1, 2, 3 \rangle$

Since "F" is used as a two-placed predicate in the sample symbolic sentence, we assign it a collection of ordered pairs as an extension. But, since "G" is used as a three-placed predicate in the sample symbolic sentence, its extension in the sample valuation is a collection of ordered triples.

To calculate the values of symbolic sentences of RL in given valuations, we need a rule telling us how to evaluate singular symbolic sentences such as "Fab" and "Gbca" — symbolic sentences consisting of an *n*-placed predicate letter followed by a string of *n* constants. Here again, our inspiration comes from English. In our example about the tennis tournament, the sentence "Kobayashi won a match today against Jones" is true just in case "Kobayashi, Jones" appears as one line of the list on the PE Department's announcement. More generally, in our example, a sentence of the form "*a* won a match today against *b*" is true just in case the PE Department's list contains a pair whose first member is the referent of the sentence's first singular term and whose second member is the referent of its second singular term. Similarly, the singular symbolic sentence "Fab" will have the value *t* when and only when the extension of the (two-placed) predicate letter "F" contains an ordered pair whose first member is the referent of the constant "a" and whose second member is the referent of the constant "b".

The precise statement of the rule is this:

> In a given valuation, a singular symbolic sentence containing a many-placed predicate letter has the value *t* just in case the extension of that predicate letter contains an ordered *n*-tuple whose first member is the referent of the symbolic sentence's first constant, whose second member is the referent of its second constant, whose third member is the referent of its third constant, and so on. Otherwise, in that valuation, the symbolic sentence has the value *f*.

Rather than give this rule a new number, we will view it as an addition to V7, the rule of valuation for singular symbolic sentences.

To see how the new rule works, consider the singular symbolic sentences "Fab" and "Gbca" and the valuation that we described earlier:

domain of discourse: {1, 2, 3}
referent of "a":   1
referent of "b":   2
referent of "c":   3
extension of "F":   ⟨1, 2⟩, ⟨2, 2⟩, ⟨3, 1⟩, ⟨3, 2⟩, ⟨3, 3⟩
extension of "G":   ⟨1, 3, 2⟩, ⟨1, 1, 2⟩, ⟨2, 3, 3⟩, ⟨1, 2, 3⟩

In this valuation, the referent of "a" is the number 1, the referent of "b" is the number 2, and the extension of "F" contains the ordered pair ⟨1, 2⟩. So, in the given valuation, the value of "Fab" is *t* (rule V7). However, in the sample valuation, the ordered triple ⟨2, 3, 1⟩ is *not* in the extension of the predicate letter "G", and the value of "Gbca" is therefore *f*.

With the introduction of rule V7, then, we have gone some way toward explaining the semantics of the system RL. Indeed, rule V7 allows us to calculate the value of any singular symbolic sentence of RL in any valuation for it.

But what about symbolic sentences, such as "[x][y]Rxy" and "[x][∃y]Sxay", in which one quantifier appears within the scope of another? How can we calculate the values of these sentences in given valuations? We will answer these questions in the next section. Our only aim in this one has been to describe the semantics of many-placed predicate letters and of the singular symbolic sentences in which they appear.

Exercises 9.3

1. *Defend or criticize:* The extensions of one-placed predicate letters are sets of objects, but the extensions of many-placed predicate letters are collections of ordered sets.

2. *Defend or criticize:* When we know the collection of pairs of which a two-placed English predicate is true, we know all there is to know about the semantics of that predicate.

3. How many different ordered pairs are there whose members include no objects except the numbers 1 and 2?

4. What is the collection of pairs of which the two-placed English predicate ". . . is both younger and older than—" is true?

5. Consider the four-placed English predicate

> . . . is a number twice as big as—, three times as big as __, and four times as big as · · · .

The ordered quadruple ⟨12, 6, 4, 3⟩ is such that, if a name for its first member were put into the predicate's first blank, a name for its second member into the second blank, a name for its third member into the third blank, and a name for its fourth member into the fourth blank, the result would be a true sentence. Find three other ordered quadruples that have this property. How many more are there?

6. What errors are there in the following attempt to set up a valuation for the symbolic sentence "((Rab → Saac) ↔ Pa)"?

domain of discourse: {1, 2, 3, 5}
extension of "a": 1
extension of "b": 1
extension of "c": 5
extension of "R": ⟨1, 2⟩, ⟨5, 3⟩, ⟨4, 1⟩
extension of "S": ⟨1, 2⟩, ⟨5, 3⟩, ⟨1, 1⟩
value of "P": *t*

7. *Defend or criticize:* If a symbolic sentence contains four different constants —
say, "a", "b", "c", and "d" — then any valuation in which that sentence has the
value *t* must have at least four different objects in its domain of discourse.

8. For each of the following symbolic sentences, construct a valuation in which
it has the value *t*:
a. (P → Q)
b. (Fa → Ga)
c. (Fa → Rab)
d. (P → (Rab ∨ −Sabcd))
e. (Rab & Rba)

9. Consider the valuation

domain of discourse: {1, 2, 3}
referent of "a": 1
referent of "b": 2
referent of "c": 3
extension of "R": ⟨1, 2⟩, ⟨2, 1⟩, ⟨3, 1⟩, ⟨2, 2⟩

Calculate the value of each of the following symbolic sentences in the given
valuation:
a. Raa
b. Rab
c. Rba
d. Rbb
e. Rbc
f. −Rcb
g. (−Rcc → Rca)
h. −(Rcb ↔ Rbc)
i. (Raa ∨ (−Rbb → Rca))

10. Consider the valuation

> domain of discourse: {1, 2, 3, 4}
> referent of "a": 1
> referent of "b": 2
> referent of "c": 3
> referent of "d": 4
> referent of "e": 4
> extension of "F": ⟨1, 4⟩, ⟨4, 1⟩
> extension of "G": ⟨1, 1, 2⟩, ⟨1, 2, 3⟩, ⟨4, 4, 4⟩, ⟨4, 2, 1⟩
> value of "H": t

Calculate the value of each of the following symbolic sentences in the given valuation:

   a.   (Fae → H)
   b.   (Fac → (−H ∨ Gabc))
   c.   −(Gdcd ↔ Gaba)
   d.   (Gded → Geba)
   e.   −(−Gaac → (Feb → −Gaab))

9.4 The Semantics of Multiple Quantification

In RL, unlike PL, symbolic sentences may contain quantifiers within the scope of other quantifiers. Having explained the semantics of many-placed predicate letters in the previous section, we turn in this one to the semantics of these multiply quantified sentences. Given a sentence like "[x][y]Rxy" and a valuation for it, how can we calculate the value of the sentence in the valuation?

To prepare for answering this question, we take another look at the idea of *satisfaction*. In Chapter 8, when we introduced this idea, our system had only one variable, "x". In view of the fact that it now has many different variables, we will restate the definition of *satisfaction*, like this:

> *If all of the free variables in a wff are of one type* (for example, if all are "x"s or all are "y"s or all are "z"s), an object from a given valuation's domain of discourse *satisfies* the wff just in case, by replacing all the wff's free variables with a constant referring to that object, we produce a sentence whose value in the given valuation is *t*.

Except for the italicized phrase at its beginning, this definition is exactly the same as the old one.

The new definition doesn't tell us how to apply the idea of satisfaction to wffs, such as "[x]Sxyz", that contain free variables of two or more different types. But, for our purposes, this won't matter. When we apply the idea of satisfaction, it will generally be to wffs that we get by erasing quantifiers from the beginnings of symbolic sentences, and, in such wffs, all of the free variables are of *one* sort.

With this in mind, we can state RL's versions of rules V8 and V9 using the same words as in Chapter 8:

V8:   A universally quantified symbolic sentence has the value *t* in a given valuation just in case, by erasing the universal quantifier from the sentence's beginning, we produce a wff that is satisfied by every object in the valuation's domain of discourse. Otherwise, the sentence has the value *f*.

V9:   An existentially quantified symbolic sentence has the value *t* in a given valuation just in case, by erasing the existential quantifier from the sentence's beginning, we produce a wff that is satisfied by at least one object in the valuation's domain of discourse. Otherwise, the sentence has the value *f*.

As before, a universally quantified sentence has the value *t* when and only when *everything* satisfies the wff following the sentence's initial quantifier, and an existentially quantified sentence has the value *t* when and only when *something* satisfies the wff following the sentence's initial quantifier.

To see how rules V8 and V9 apply to sentences of RL, consider the sentence "[x]Rax" and the valuation

domain of discourse: {1, 2, 3}

referent of "a":   1

extension of "R":   ⟨1, 1⟩, ⟨2, 1⟩, ⟨1, 2⟩, ⟨1, 3⟩, ⟨3, 3⟩

According to rule V8, "[x]Rax" has the value *t* in the given valuation just in case every object in the valuation's domain of discourse satisfies the wff "Rax". And every object in the valuation's domain *does* satisfy this wff. (The number 1 satisfies it, since ⟨1, 1⟩ is in the extension of "R"; the number 2 satisfies it, since ⟨1, 2⟩ is in the extension of "R"; and the number 3 satisfies it, since ⟨1, 3⟩ is in the extension of "R".) So, in the given valuation, the value of "[x]Rax" is *t*.

What about sentences in which one quantifier appears within the scope of another? Think, for example, about the sentence

[∃x][∃y]Rxy

and the valuation

domain of discourse: {1, 2}
    referent of "a": 1
    referent of "b": 2
    extension of "R": ⟨1, 2⟩, ⟨2, 2⟩

What is the value of the given sentence in the sample valuation?

Well, if we erase the initial quantifier from the sentence "[∃x][∃y]Rxy", the result is "[∃y]Rxy". In the given valuation, the number 1 satisfies this wff, since "[∃y]Ray" has the value *t*. And, according to rule V9, an existentially quantified sentence has the value *t* in a given valuation whenever one or more objects in the valuation's domain satisfies the wff following the sentence's initial quantifier. Accordingly, in the given valuation, "[∃x][∃y]Rxy" has the value *t*.

Now consider the sentence "[x][y]Rxy". According to rule V8, this sentence has the value *t* in a valuation just in case every object in the valuation's domain satisfies the wff "[y]Rxy". In the sample valuation, the number 1 does not satisfy this wff, since the pair ⟨1, 1⟩ is not in the extension of "R". So, in the given valuation, the value of "[x][y]Rxy" is *f*.

As our examples suggest, RL's rules of valuation allow us to calculate the value of any sentence of RL in any valuation for it. But, as the examples also suggest, calculations in RL are not always as mechanical or straightforward as they were in PL.

For our final example in this section, we look at a tricky case — one in which our first instincts may lead us astray. The case has to do with the idea of *RL-equivalence:*

> Two symbolic sentences of RL are **RL-equivalent** just in case they have the same value as one another in every valuation for them.

With this definition in mind, consider the symbolic sentences "[x][∃y]Rxy" and "[∃y][x]Rxy". Are these sentences RL-equivalent, or is there valuation in which one has the value *t* while the other has the value *f*?

Well, "[x][y]Rxy" is RL-equivalent to "[y][x]Rxy", and "[∃x][∃y]Rxy" is RL-equivalent to "[∃y][∃x]Rxy". So, it may seem that the order of the quantifiers in a symbolic sentence doesn't make much difference. Besides, in both "[x][∃y]Rxy" and "[∃y][x]Rxy", the quantifier "[x]" is linked to the variable "x", and the quantifier "[∃y]" to the variable "y". So what semantic difference can it make that the quantifiers appear in different orders in the two sentences?

Plenty! To see this, consider the valuation

domain of discourse: {1, 2, 3}
    referent of "a": 1
    referent of "b": 2
    referent of "c": 3
    extension of "R": ⟨1, 2⟩, ⟨2, 3⟩, ⟨3, 1⟩

All three objects in this valuation's domain satisfy the wff "[∃y]Rxy", since each of these objects appears as the first member of an ordered pair in the extension of the predicate letter "R". According to rule V9, then, the value of "[x][∃y]Rxy" in the given valuation is *t*. But, for an object in the given valuation's domain to satisfy the wff "[x]Rxy", it would have to be the second member of three ordered pairs in the extension of "R"—one whose first member is 1, one whose first member is 2, and one whose first member is 3. Since there is no such object, none of the objects in the valuation's domain satisfies the wff "[x]Rxy", and (according to rule V9) the value of the sentence "[∃y][x]Rxy" in the given valuation is *f*.

The sentences "[x][∃y]Rxy" and "[∃y][x]Rxy" therefore are *not* RL-equivalent! There are valuations, like the one we just considered, in which the first has the value *t* while the second has the value *f*.

In this respect, the system RL does not differ from English. To see this, compare the sentence

1.   Everybody loves at least one person.

to the sentence

2.   There is at least one person whom everybody loves.

Sentence (1) is true if Mary loves Bill, Tom loves Mary, Steve loves himself, and so on. But sentence (2) is true only if Mary, Tom, Bill, and Steve all love the *same* person. So, in English as in RL, the order in which two quantifiers appear in a sentence can make an important semantic difference—especially if one of the quantifiers is universal and the other existential.

Exercises 9.4

1. *Defend or criticize:* If all the free variables in a wff are of one type (e.g., if all are "x"s or all are "y"s or all are "z"s), an object from a given valuation's domain of discourse *satisfies* the wff just in case, by replacing all the wff's free variables with a constant, we produce a sentence with the value *t* in the given valuation.

2. Consider the valuation

domain of discourse: {1, 2, 3}
referent of "a":   1
referent of "b":   2
referent of "c":   3
extension of "P":   {1, 2}
extension of "R":   ⟨1, 1⟩, ⟨1, 2⟩, ⟨1, 3⟩, ⟨2, 1⟩, ⟨2, 3⟩, ⟨3, 1⟩, ⟨3, 2⟩
extension of "S":   ⟨1, 2, 2⟩, ⟨1, 2, 3⟩, ⟨1, 2, 1⟩, ⟨2, 2, 2⟩

For each of the following wffs, say which objects in the given valuation's domain satisfy it:

    a. Px
    b. [x]Rxy
    c. [x]Ryx
    d. [∃y]Rxy
    e. [y]Rxy
    f. (Pa → [∃y]Rxy)
    g. (Px & [∃y]Rxy)
    h. (Px → [∃y]Rxy)
    i. [∃y](Px & Rxy)
    j. [∃y](−Px & Rxy)
    k. ([∃y](Py & Rxy) & [∃z](−Pz & Rxz))
    l. [∃z]Szxa
    m. (Pz & [∃x][∃y]Sxyz)

3. *Defend or criticize:* In the valuation given in the previous exercise, the number 1 satisfies the wff "Rxy".

4. Consider the valuation

    domain of discourse: {1, 2}
        referent of "a":   1
        referent of "b":   2
        extension of "F":   {1}
        extension of "G":   ∅
        extension of "H":   ⟨1, 1⟩, ⟨1, 2⟩
        extension of "I":   ⟨1, 1⟩, ⟨1, 2⟩, ⟨2, 1⟩, ⟨2, 2⟩

Calculate the value of each of the following sentences in the given valuation:

    a. [x]Hxa   b. [x]Hax
    c. [x]Hxb   d. [y]Hby
    e. [∃x][∃y]Hxy   f. [x][y]Hxy
    g. [∃x][y]Hxy   h. [x][∃y]Hxy
    i. [∃x]Hxx   j. [y]Hyy
    k. [x][y]Ixy   l. [x][∃y]Ixy
    m. [∃y][x]Ixy   n. [∃x][∃y] − Ixy
    o. [x](Gx → [∃y]Hxy)   p. [x](Fx → [∃y]Hxy)
    q. [x](− Gx → [∃y]Hxy)   r. [x]((Fx ∨ Gx) ↔ Hxx)
    s. [y](Fy → ([∃z]Hxz ∨ [w]Hwx))

5. *Defend or criticize:* The sentences "[∃x][∃y]Rxy" and "[∃y][∃x]Rxy" are RL-equivalent.

6. *Defend or criticize:* The sentences "[x][y]Rxy" and "[y][x]Rxy" are RL-equivalent.

7. *Defend or criticize:* The sentences "[x][∃y]Rxy" and "[∃y][x]Rxy" are RL-equivalent.

8. Consider these two English sentences:

> Every dog hates some cat or other.
> Some cat is such that every dog hates it.

Describe a possible situation in which the first of these sentences is true and the second false. Can you also describe a possible situation in which the first is false and the second true? If not, why not?

9.5 Derivation in RL

As some symbolic arguments of PL are PL-valid, some arguments of RL are RL-valid:

> A symbolic argument is **RL-valid** just in case there is no valuation in which its premises have the value *t* while its conclusion has the value *f*.

And, as we use derivations to demonstrate PL-validity, we can also use them to demonstrate RL-validity. In fact, if a symbolic argument is RL-valid, we can (in theory) derive its conclusion from its premises using just the rules we now have; no new rules of inference are needed.

For an example of derivation in RL, consider the argument

[x](Ax → [y](By → −Cxy))
[x][y]Cxy
_____

So, [x][y](−Ax ∨ −By)

We begin a derivation for this argument by writing its premises and using SuppID, like this:

1.	[x](Ax → [y](By → −Cxy))	Prem
2.	[x][y]Cxy	Prem
3.	−[x][y](−Ax ∨ −By)	SuppID

To continue, we apply QE to the sentence on line (3) and EI to the result:

4. $[\exists x] - [y](-Ax \lor -By)$ 3 QE
5. $-[y](-Aa \lor -By)$ 4 EI

To move from the sentence on line (3) to the one on line (4), we simply replaced "$-[x]$" with "$[\exists x]-$". And, to move from the sentence on line (4) to the one on line (5), we simply erased the initial quantifier "$[\exists x]$" and replaced the free "x"s in the remaining wff with a constant new to the derivation. So here the rules QE and EI work exactly as they did in PL.

As rule QE allows us to move from a sentence beginning with "$-[x]$" to one beginning with "$[\exists x]-$", it also allows us to move from a sentence beginning with "$-[y]$" to one beginning with "$[\exists y]-$". Accordingly, we can apply QE to the sentence on line (5) of the sample derivation to get this:

6. $[\exists y] - (-Aa \lor -By)$ 5 QE

Notice, however, that QE does *not* allow us to move from the sentence on line (5) to "$[\exists x] - (-Aa \lor -By)$" or to "$[\exists z] - (-Aa \lor -By)$". Whenever we apply QE, we move from a sentence containing one quantifier for a certain variable to the other quantifier for that *same* variable.

To continue the sample derivation, we apply EI to the sentence on line (6):

7. $-(-Aa \lor -Bb)$ 6 EI

Although the quantifier in the sentence on line (6) is "$[\exists y]$" rather than "$[\exists x]$", this is a straightforward application of EI. We simply erased the quantifier from the beginning of an existentially quantified sentence, chose a constant new to the derivation, and replaced all free variables with that constant.

Now, by applying UI to the sentence on line (1), we can get this:

8. $(Aa \rightarrow [y](By \rightarrow -Cay))$ 1 UI

Here again, we have simply erased a quantifier from the beginning of a sentence and replaced the free variables with a constant. (We didn't replace the "y"s in the wff "$(Ax \rightarrow [y](By \rightarrow -Cay))$" with "a", since the variable "y" was bound on all occurrences.

From line (8), we can easily reach the desired conclusion. The complete derivation is this:

1.	[x](Ax → [y](By → −Cxy))	Prem
2.	[x][y]Cxy	Prem
3.	−[x][y](−Ax ∨ −By)	SuppID
4.	[∃x] − [y](−Ax ∨ −By)	3 QE
5.	−[y](−Aa ∨ −By)	4 EI
6.	[∃y] − (−Aa ∨ −By)	5 QE
7.	−(−Aa ∨ −Bb)	6 EI
8.	(Aa → [y](By → −Cay))	1 UI
9.	−−Aa	7 DM
10.	Aa	9 DNE
11.	[y](By → −Cay)	8,10 MP
12.	(Bb → −Cab)	11 UI
13.	−−Bb	7 DM
14.	Bb	13 DNE
15.	−Cab	12,14 MP
16.	[y]Cay	2 UI
17.	Cab	16 UI
18.	[x][y](−Ax ∨ −By)	3−17 ID

Having completed this derivation, we can be sure that the sample argument is RL-valid.

The only tricky points in the derivation came when we applied UI at lines (12), (16), and (17). How did we know which constants to introduce on these lines? How did we know, for example, to write "(Bb → −Cab)" on line (12) rather than "(Ba → −Caa)" or "(Bc → −Cac)"? The answer is that we looked ahead. Since we noticed that we could get "Bb" from the sentence on line (7), we produced the conditional "(Bb → −Cab)" on line (12), knowing that we would then be able to apply MP. As it happened, this strategy worked. If it hadn't, we could have gone back and applied UI again to the sentence on line (11), using a different constant.

As our example indicates, RL's rules of inference are almost exactly the same as PL's. But, as the example also indicates, it is harder to keep track of what is going on with variables and constants in RL that it was in PL. This is, of course, to be expected. The difficulty we face in using RL's system of derivation is the price we pay for the increased subtlety and sophistication of our model of English.

Exercises 9.5

1. *Defend or criticize:* RL's system of derivation has only one more rule of inference than PL's.

2. *Defend or criticize:* In RL, the rule UI works in exactly the same way as it does in PL.

3. Find the errors, if any, in the following attempts at derivation:

    a. 1. (Fa → Rab)   Prem
       2. [∃x](Fx → Rab)   1 EG
       3. [∃y][∃x](Fx → Ray)   2 EG
       4. [∃z][∃y][∃x](Fx → Rzy)   3 EG
       5. [∃y][∃x](Fa → Rzy)   4 EI
       6. [∃x](Fa → Rzc)   5 EI
       7. (Fa → Rdc)   6 EI
    b. 1. (Fa → Rab)   Prem
       2. [∃y](Fy → Ryb)   1 EG
       3. [∃y](Fy → [∃z]Ryz)   2 EG
    c. 1. −[x][y]Sxyx   Prem
       2. [∃y] − [y]Sxyx   1 QE
       3. − [y]Sxax   2 EI
       4. [∃x] − Sxax   3 QE
       5. − Sbab   4 EI

4. Using derivations, demonstrate the RL-validity of each of the following symbolic arguments:

    a. [x][y]Rxy
         ─────────
       So, [∃x][y]Rxy

    b. [x][y]Rxy
         ─────────
       So, [∃x][∃y]Rxy

    c. [∃x](Ax & Bx)
       [x](Ax → Cxx)
         ─────────────
       So, [∃x][∃y]Cxy

    d. [x](Fx → [∃y](Gy & Hyx))
       − [∃x][∃y]Hxy
         ────────────────────
       So, − [∃x]Fx

e. [∃x][y][z]Axzy
   ――――――――――
   So, [∃x]Axxx

f. [x](Ax → − [∃y](By & Cxy))
   [y](By & Cay)
   ――――――――――――――
   So, − Aa

g. [x](Ax → [∃y]Bxy)
   ――――――――――――
   So, − [∃x](Ax & [y] − Bxy)

h. [x](Ax → Bx)
   − [∃x](Bx & Cxx)
   ――――――――――――
   So, − [∃x](Ax & [y]Cyx)

i. [x](Ax → Bx)
   [∃x][∃y](Ax & Cxy)
   [x][y](Cxy → Dyx)
   ――――――――――――
   So, [∃x](Bx & [∃y]Dyx)

j. [x][y]((Ax & − By) → Cxy)
   [∃x](− Bx & Dx)
   ――――――――――――――
   So, [x](Ax → [∃y](Dy & Cxy))

k. [∃x](Ax & [y](By → Cxy))
   ([∃x]Ax → [∃y]By)
   ――――――――――――
   So, [∃x][∃y]Cxy

l. − [∃x](− Gx ∨ − [∃y]Fy)
   ――――――――――――――
   So, [∃z]Fz

m. [x][y]((Fx & Gy) → Hxy)
   [∃x][∃y]((Fx & Iy) & − Hxy)
   ――――――――――――――
   So, [∃x](Ix & − Gx)

n. [x][∃y]Ayx
   [x][y](Ayx → Bxy)
   ――――――――――――
   So, [x][∃y]Bxy

o. [∃x](Ax & [y](By → Cxy))
  − [∃x](Ax & [∃y](Dy & Cxy))
  _____
  So, − [∃x](Bx & Dx)

p. − [∃x]Txx
  _____
  So, [∃x]([y](Tay → Txy) & − Txa)

q. [x](Fx → ([∃y]Gxy → [∃z]Gzx))
  [x]([∃z]Gzx → Gxx)
  − [∃x]Gxx
  _____
  So, [x](Fx → [y] − Gxy)

r. [x]([∃y]Rxy → [z]Rzx)
  _____
  So, ([∃x][∃y]Rxy → [x][y]Rxy)

s. ([x][∃y]Axy → [x][∃y]Bxy)
  [∃x][y] − Bxy
  _____
  So, [∃x][∃y] − Axy

9.6 Translating from English into RL

In the previous section, we developed a system of derivation for RL. Now we describe a method for applying this system to the evaluation of arguments in English. In outline, the method is the same as the one we followed in Chapter 8. That is, given an argument in English, we translate it into a symbolic argument of RL and attempt to demonstrate the translation's RL-validity with a derivation. Generally, if we succeed, we may infer that the original argument is valid.

In this section and the next, we will examine the details of this method. In this section, we look at translation from English into RL and, in the next, at the relation of RL-validity to the validity of arguments in English.

For the most part, the steps for translating a sentence or argument that has been made explicit from English into RL are the same as those for translating from English into the old system PL:

a. We expand all abbreviations in the sentence or argument.

b. Insofar as possible, we paraphrase the sentence or argument into Standard English—that is, into English whose only quantifying phrases are "each thing is such that" and "at least one thing is such that'', whose only pronoun is ''it'', and whose only sentential operators are ''it's not the case that'', ''and'', ''or'', ''unless'', ''if, then'', ''only if'', and ''if and only if''.

c.   We set up a scheme of correspondence, which associates predicate letters with English predicates, constants with English singular terms, and sentence letters with intractable English clauses.

d.   We replace English expressions with the corresponding expressions of RL, leaving the sentence's syntax unchanged.

The result of this process is a symbolic sentence or argument that corresponds, both syntactically and semantically, to the English original.

The major difference between translation into PL and translation into RL has to do with the *order* in which we perform the steps just outlined. When translating into PL, we finished paraphrasing into Standard English before setting up a scheme of correspondence, and we finished setting up a scheme of correspondence before replacing any expressions of English with their symbolic counterparts. If we tried to follow this order in translating into RL, though, we would often get lost in a maze of quantifying phrases. Accordingly, we translate into RL in stages. That is, we set up certain parts of our schemes of correspondence before we finish paraphrasing into Standard English, and we replace some English expressions with their symbolic counterparts before we finish setting up our schemes of correspondence.

For example, as a first step toward translating the sentence

1.   There is a man who likes all women,

we paraphrase it with

2.   At least one thing is such that it is a man and it likes all women.

Sentence (2) is not yet in Standard English, since it contains the quantifying phrase ''all''. Still, (2) indicates quite a lot about how our final translation is going to look. We know that the phrase ''at least one thing is such that'' corresponds to an existential quantifier, that the pronoun ''it'' corresponds to a variable, and that the sentential operator ''and'' corresponds to the ampersand: These correspondences are built into the rules of our system. Accordingly, we know that the final translation of sentence (2) into RL will look something like this:

3.   [∃x](x is a man & x likes all women)

String (3) isn't in English, and it isn't a wff of RL either. But mixed strings of this sort are often useful to us as we move step by step from English sentences to their RL-translations.

To complete the translation of sentence (1), we need to find a symbolic replacement for the sequence ''x is a man''. This is easy. Letting the (one-placed) predicate letter "M" correspond to the English predicate ". . . is a man", we can translate "x is a man" with "Mx".

Now what we need is a symbolic replacement for the sequence

   4.   x likes all women.

In finding this replacement, it will be useful to forget (just for the moment) that the mark "x" is a variable of RL and to pretend that it is an English singular term. If "x" were a singular term, how would we translate sequence (4)?

As we noted in the last chapter, when presented with an English clause having an unfamiliar form, we can make things easier for ourselves by paraphrasing it into one whose form is familiar. Accordingly, we paraphrase sequence (4) with the sequence

   5.   All women are liked by x,

which has the familiar form "All *As* are *Bs*". As we showed in Chapter 8, sentences of this form can be paraphrased into sentences of the form "Each thing is such that, if *F* it, then *G* it". Accordingly, we paraphrase sequence (4) into Standard English like this:

   6.   Each thing is such that, if it is a woman, then x likes it.

(Another, equally good paraphrase of (5) is "Each thing is such that, if it is a woman, then it is liked by x".)

To translate sequence (6) into RL, we need to make some additions to our scheme of correspondence. In particular, we need to associate a one-placed predicate letter with the predicate ". . . is a woman" and a two-placed predicate letter with the two-placed predicate ". . . likes —":

   W*x*:   *x* is a woman

   L*xy*:   *x* likes *y*

Here, the italicized "*x*"s and "*y*"s (which should not be confused with the variables "x" and "y") serve to show how the blanks in predicate letters match up with the blanks in the corresponding English predicates. They show, for example, that the predicate letter "L" has two blanks after it, that the first of these blanks corresponds to the first blank in the predicate ". . . likes —" and that the second blank corresponds to the second blank in ". . . likes —".

With the new additions to our scheme of correspondence, we can translate sequence (6) in this way:

   7.   [y](Wy → Lxy)

Since we have already used the quantifier "[∃x]" and the variable "x" in our translation, we avoid confusion here by replacing the phrase "each thing is such that" with the quantifier "[y]" and the pronoun "it" with the variable "y".

We can now complete the translation of the original English sentence "Some man likes all women". For some time now, we have known that the entire translation would look like this:

3.   [∃x](x is a man & x likes all women)

Now we know that, under our scheme of correspondence,

"x is a man" translates as "Mx", and

"x likes all women" translates as "[y](Wy → Lxy)".

Replacing the English phrases in sequence (3) with their translations, we get

[∃x](Mx & [y](Wy → Lxy)),

which is the RL-translation of the original sentence "Some man likes all women".

For another example of translation, consider the sentence

Any movie that wins an Academy Award is produced by a major studio.

Paraphrasing this sentence into the familiar "All *As* are *Bs*" form, we get

All movies that win Academy Awards are produced by a major studio.

Next, moving toward Standard English, we get this:

Each thing is such that, if it is a movie that wins an Academy Award, then it is produced by a major studio.

Clearly, the translation of this last sentence will look something like this:

[x](x is a movie that wins an Academy Award → x is produced by a major studio)

All we need to do to complete the translation is to find symbolic replacements for the two sequences that remain in English: "x is a movie that wins an Academy award" and "x is produced by a major studio".

In paraphrasing the first of these sequences into Standard English, we use the favored sentential operator ". . . and —" to get rid of the word "that":

x is a movie *and* x wins an Academy Award

Eventually, the clause "x is a movie" will be replaced by the wff "Mx", and the operator ". . . and —" will be replaced by an ampersand. But how should we translate "x wins an Academy Award"?

Here, the tiny word "an" does the work of the word "some", which corresponds to the Standard English quantifying phrase "at least one thing is such that". We can therefore paraphrase the sequence "x wins an Academy Award" with the Standard English sequence

at least one thing is such that it is an Academy Award and x wins it, which translates into RL like this:

[∃y](Ay & Wxy)

(We use the quantifier "[∃y]" and the variable "y" here since we used "[x]" and "x" earlier in the translation.)

Having found a symbolic replacement for "x wins an Academy award", we now turn to the sequence

x is produced by a major studio.

Recognizing that the word "a" here does the work of an existential quantifying phrase, we can paraphrase this sequence into Standard English like this:

at least one thing is such that it is a major studio and it produced x.

And, under the obvious scheme of correspondence, we can translate this sequence with

[∃z](Sz & Pzx).

(Here again, to prevent confusion, we choose a quantifier and variable new to the translation.)

Putting what we have together, we get

[x]((Mx & [∃y](Ay & Wxy)) → [∃z](Sz & Pzx)),

which is our translation of the English sentence "Any movie that wins an Academy Award is produced by a major studio."

This example shows how far we have come since Chapter 5. Back then, when we were dealing with the simple system CL, we would have had no choice but to translate our sample sentence about movies with a sentence letter, and our translation therefore would not have revealed anything at all about the sentence's inner structure. Later, when we were dealing with PL, we could not have done any better at translating the sample sentence than "[x](Ax → Px)". But, now that we've stepped up to the system RL, we can translate the same English sentence as

[x]((Mx & [∃y](Ay & Wxy)) → [∃z](Gz & Pzx)).

Unlike the sentence's translations into CL and PL, this one reveals that the sentence contains three quantifying phrases: one expressed by the word "any", another hidden in the small word "an", and a third hidden in the tiny word "a".

The placement of these quantifying phrases affects the relational form of the sentence. And, as we will show, the relational form of a sentence bears on the validity of arguments in which that sentence occurs. Accordingly, the method for demonstrating validity described in the next section will be more powerful than either CL's or PL's.

Exercises 9.6

1. *Defend or criticize:* The sentence "At least one thing is such that every person likes it" is in Standard English.

2. *Defend or criticize:* In setting up a scheme of correspondence for translating into RL, we associate predicate letters with predicates. We might, for example, associate the letter "F" with the one-placed English predicate ". . . has a dog" and the predicate letter "G" with the one-placed predicate ". . . has a dog if Dave has a cat".

3. *Defend or criticize:* In translating a sentence of Standard English into PL or RL, we first translate it into Standard English and then replace English expressions with the corresponding expressions of PL or RL, leaving the sentence's syntax unchanged.

4. Translate the following sentences step by step from English into RL:
   a. There is a teacher who admires a student.
   b. All students admire all teachers.
   c. Some teacher admires all students.
   d. Every student admires some teacher or other.
   e. There is a teacher whom every student admires.
   f. Everyone doubts something or other.
   g. Anyone who doubts something is certain of at least one thing.
   h. Each person who is certain of something or other either doubts something or is certain of everything.
   i. Every head of a mouse is a head of an animal.
   j. All who draw circles draw figures.
   k. Anyone who beats his wife beats his spouse.
   l. Every head of a brown horse is the head of an animal with fleas.
   m. There is a salesman from whom every consumer has bought an appliance.
   n. Anybody who buys an appliance from someone is a consumer.
   o. Any consumer who buys an appliance from himself is a salesperson.
   p. No one is a salesperson if she hasn't sold an appliance to anyone.
   q. If someone sells an appliance to a consumer, then the consumer buys an appliance from someone.

9.7 RL-Validity, R-Validity, and Validity

Once we have translated an argument from English into RL, we can try to demonstrate the translation's RL-validity with a derivation. If we succeed, we can usually infer that the original argument is valid.

Why? What is the connection between an argument's having an RL-valid symbolic translation and its being valid? In this section, we sketch answers to these questions.

Our first example for study is the Abelard argument, which we discussed earlier in this chapter:

Abelard loved Heloise.
_____

So, somebody loved somebody.

We can translate this argument into RL like this:

Lah
_____

So, [∃x][∃y]Lxy

And, using the system of derivation described earlier in this chapter, we can easily demonstrate this symbolic argument's RL-validity. But what justifies our going on to infer that the Abelard argument itself is valid?

Well, consider the Abelard argument's relational form:

Fab
_____

So, at least one thing is such that *at least one thing is such that F it it.*

Suppose, for the moment, that we have before us a sample argument of this form and a situation S in which the sample argument's premises are true while its conclusion is false.

In S, there must be an object (call it O_1) picked out by the argument's first singular term, an object (call it O_2) picked out by the argument's second singular term, and a relation (call it R) mentioned by the argument's (two-placed) predicate. And, in S, it must be the case that

(a)   object O_1 stands in relation R to object O_2, but

(b)   nothing bears relation R to itself or anything else.

Condition (a) must be met for the sample argument's premise to be true in S, and condition (b) must be met for its conclusion to be false.

Now, using objects O_1 and O_2 and the relation R, we can construct a valuation for the Abelard argument's RL-translation, like this:

domain of discourse:	the set of things that exist in situation S, including O_1 and O_2
referent of "a":	object O_1
referent of "b":	object O_2
extension of "L":	the collection of ordered pairs whose first members bear relation R to their second members in situation S

Since object O_1 bears relation R to object O_2 in situation S [condition (a)], "Lah" has the value t in this valuation (rule V7). And, since nothing bears relation R to anything in situation S [condition (b)], "$[\exists x][\exists y]Lxy$" has the value f in this valuation (rule V8). Accordingly, the sample valuation is a counterexample to the Abelard argument's symbolic translation.

Having demonstrated the translation's RL-validity with a derivation, however, we know that there isn't any counterexample to it! It follows that there is no valuation like the one we tried to describe. From this it follows that there is no possible situation S meeting conditions (a) and (b) and, hence, that *no argument with the same relational form as the Abelard argument is invalid.* So, having constructed a derivation for the Abelard argument's RL-translation, we may infer that the Abelard argument's relational form is R-valid.

However, to say that an argument has an R-valid relational form is just to say that *every* argument of that form is valid. So, from the fact that the Abelard argument's relational form is R-valid, it follows that the Abelard argument itself is valid.

We can summarize our reasoning in this way: The fact that we can construct a derivation for the Abelard argument's RL-translation shows that the translation is RL-valid and, hence, that there is no valuation of the sort we tried to set up. In turn, the fact that there is no such valuation shows that the Abelard argument's relational form is R-valid and, hence, that the argument itself is valid. So, having constructed a derivation for the Abelard argument's RL-translation, we may infer that the argument itself is valid.

This illustrates a general point. Typically, if we find that an argument has an RL-valid translation, we may infer that the argument's relational form is R-valid and, hence, that the argument itself is valid.

For our final example in this section, we apply this point to the argument

All Californians are Americans.

So, every spouse of a Californian is the spouse of an American.

This argument is clearly valid; in any possible situation in which Californians are Americans, the spouses of Californians are the spouses of Americans. But what is it about the argument that accounts for its validity?

To see, let's put the argument through RL's test for validity. Translating the argument into RL under an obvious scheme of correspondence, we get

$[x](Cx \rightarrow Ax)$

So, $[x]([\exists y](Cy \mathbin{\&} Sxy) \rightarrow [\exists z](Az \mathbin{\&} Sxz))$

Since we can demonstrate this translation's RL-validity with a derivation, we can infer that the sample argument is valid.

Of course, we already knew that the sample argument is valid. Our problem was to figure out *why* it's valid. And our derivation helps us see this. We would not have been able to demonstrate the sample argument's validity with RL's methods unless its RL-translation captured everything about the argument that accounts for its validity. But the translation did not capture any facts about the meanings of terms such as "spouse" or "of". Indeed, all that it captured were some facts about the patterns of the argument's expressions and some facts about the semantics of quantifiers, variables, and sentential operators. So, these must be the facts that account for the argument's validity. That is, the sample argument must be valid in virtue of its relational form.

This may be surprising; at first glance, the sample argument's relational form may seem uncomplicated and uninteresting. Looking closer, however, we find that the argument's conclusion contains the word "every", which indicates a universal quantifying phrase, and the words "a" and "an", which indicate existential quantifying phrases. These small words are easy to ignore. Yet, as we have seen in our studies of PL and RL, the presence of such quantifying words can have an important bearing on whether an argument is valid. Indeed, in our example, we must notice where these words appear in order to account for the argument's validity.

Exercises 9.7

1. Demonstrate the validity of the Abelard argument discussed in this section.

2. *Defend or criticize:* If we can demonstrate an English argument's validity with the methods of PL, we can also demonstrate its validity with the methods of RL.

3. *Defend or criticize:* If we can demonstrate an English argument's validity with the methods of RL, we can also demonstrate its validity with the methods of PL.

4. *Defend or criticize:* Every English argument with an R-valid relational form is valid.

5. *Defend or criticize:* Every English argument with the same relational form as the Abelard argument is valid.

6. *Defend or criticize:* If we demonstrate an English argument's validity with the methods of RL, we know that the argument has an R-valid relational form.

7. Using derivations, demonstrate the validity of the following arguments:
   a. There is something to which everything is connected. So, everything is connected to something or other.
   b. All dogs hate all cats. There is a cat. So, something is hated by all dogs.
   c. If one thing touches a second, then the second touches the first. My pen touches my pencil. If my pencil touches my pen, something is on the desk. So, something is on the desk.

d. Every man in town owns a red car. But Jim owns no car, and Jim is a man. Hence, there is a man who is not in town.

e. Each thing at the art show is a masterpiece. And any woman who produces a masterpiece is a genius. But Carrie, who is a woman, produced one of the things in the show. So, Carrie is a genius.

f. If one person is indebted to a second, the second is not indebted to the first. It follows that people are never indebted to themselves.

g. If one sentence entails a second, then the second confirms the first. If one sentence confirms a second, then it also confirms any sentence that the second entails. But, for any two sentences, there is a sentence that entails them both. Therefore, any sentence confirms every sentence.

8. Demonstrate the validity of the argument discussed in this section about the spouses of Californians.

9.8 Overview

In this chapter, we developed ways of dealing with many-placed predicates and with quantifying phrases that work together with others.

We began by defining relational form, like this:

The *relational form* of an English sentence or argument is the way in which it has been made up from singular terms, predicates (including many-placed predicates), sentential operators, quantifying phrases, pronouns, and simple clauses that can't be broken up into these parts.

To reveal the relational form of an English sentence or argument that has been made explicit, we

a. expand all abbreviations (using different typefaces to indicate links between quantifying phrases and pronouns);

b. replace simple clauses that don't contain singular terms or pronouns with uppercase letters (the first, wherever it occurs, with "*P*", the second with "*Q*", and so on);

c. replace singular terms with lowercase letters (the first, wherever it occurs, with "*a*", the second with "*b*", and so on); and

d. replace remaining predicates, regardless of the number of blanks in them, with uppercase letters (the first, wherever it occurs, with "*F*,", the second with "*G*", and so on).

The main differences between this procedure and the one for revealing predicative form are that step (a) allows us to use different typefaces and that step (d) allows us to replace many-placed predicates with letters.

Since there are arguments that are valid in virtue of their relational form, we defined the notion of relational validity:

An argument's relational form is *relationally valid* (R-valid) just in case every argument having that relational form is valid.

Our aim in this chapter was to reflect facts about relational validity in our formal model of English.

To do so, we began by adding several new variables and quantifiers to our model's vocabulary. Then we modified rules of formation F7, F8, and F9 in this way:

F7:   For any number *n*, the result of writing a string of *n* constants or variables immediately to the right of an *n*-placed predicate letter is a wff.

F8:   If a wff contains a variable but neither of that variable's quantifiers, the result of writing that variable's universal quantifier in front of that wff is itself a wff.

F9:   If a wff contains a variable but neither of that variable's quantifiers, the result of writing that variable's existential quantifier in front of that wff is itself a wff.

Except for these changes, RL's syntactic rules are the same as PL's.

To reflect the semantics of many-placed predicates in our model, we added something to our definition of valuation:

When setting up a valuation for sentences of RL, we assign to each many-placed predicate letter appearing in those sentences an extension, which must be a collection of ordered sets. The extension of a two-placed predicate letter must be a collection of ordered pairs; the extension of a three-placed predicate letter, a collection of ordered triples; and so on.

As before, valuations assign referents (objects) to constants, extensions (sets of objects) to one-placed predicate letters, and values (*t* or *f*) to sentence letters.

Next, we rephrased our definition of satisfaction:

If all free variables in a wff are of one type (for example, if all are "x"s, or all are "y"s, or all are "x_1"s), an object from a given valuation's domain of discourse *satisfies* the wff just in case, by replacing all the wff's free variables with a constant referring to that object, we produce a sentence whose value in the given valuation is *t*.

With this definition in hand, we were able to state RL's rules of valuation using the same words as PL's:

V8:   A universally quantified symbolic sentence has the value *t* in a given valuation just in case, by erasing the universal quantifier from the sentence's beginning, we produce a wff that is satisfied by every object in the valuation's domain of discourse. Otherwise, the sentence has the value *f*.

V9:   An existentially quantified symbolic sentence has the value *t* in a given valuation just in case, by erasing the existential quantifier from the sentence's beginning, we produce a wff that is satisfied by at least one object in the valuation's domain of discourse. Otherwise, the sentence has the value *f*.

As in PL, a universally quantified sentence has the value *t* when and only when *everything* satisfies the wff following its initial quantifier, and an existentially quantified sentence has the value *t* when and only when *something* satisfies the wff following its initial quantifier.

The definition of RL-validity was no surprise:

A symbolic argument is *RL-valid* just in case there is no valuation in which its premises have the value *t* while its conclusion has the value *f*.

To demonstrate the RL-validity of a symbolic argument, we need only derive its conclusion from its premises using the rules of inference RL inherited from PL. Here again, no new rules were necessary.

Because of RL's relation to English, our system of derivation figured into a method for demonstrating the validity of arguments in English. Given an argument that has been made explicit, we can translate it into RL and try to construct a derivation for its translation. If we succeed, we may generally infer that the argument itself is valid.

While translating into RL is similar to translating into PL, there are two important differences. First, when setting up a scheme of correspondence, we can now associate *many*-placed predicate letters with *many*-placed English predicates. Second, as we showed in our examples, it's a good idea to translate into RL step by step. In the first step, we might translate some English expressions into RL while leaving others in English; in the next step, we might translate more English expressions, and so on.

An argument's RL-translation captures so much of the argument's relational form that, in demonstrating the translation's RL-validity, we demonstrate the R-validity of the argument's relational form. But any argument with an R-valid form is itself valid. Thus, in addition to providing us with a powerful method for demonstrating validity, RL shows us *why* certain arguments are valid. If we can demonstrate an argument's validity with RL's methods, we can be sure that the argument owes its validity to facts about the arrangement of its parts (predicates, singular terms, sentential operators, and so on) and facts about the semantics of its quantifiers and sentential operators. That is, if we can demonstrate an argument's validity with RL's methods, we can be sure that the argument is valid in virtue of its relational form.

Chapter 10

Relation Logic with Identity

As we saw in Chapter 9, if we can construct a derivation for an argument's RL-translation, we may infer that the argument's relational form is R-valid and, hence, that the argument itself is valid. The system RL therefore provides us with a powerful and efficient method for demonstrating validity.

Still, there are valid arguments we cannot show to be valid using RL's methods. An example is the simple argument

>Zorro is Don Diego.
>Zorro is brave.
>
>———————————
>
>So, Don Diego is brave.

The best we can do at translating this argument into RL is the RL-*in*valid symbolic argument

>Iab
>
>Ba
>
>———
>
>So, Bb

Since we cannot derive this symbolic argument's conclusion from its premises, we cannot demonstrate the Zorro argument's validity with the methods of RL.

To correct this, we will make one small refinement to our model of English. The refinement, which we describe in the first few sections of this chapter, involves adding the identity sign "=" to the model's vocabulary and doing some minor tinkering with its rules of formation, valuation, and derivation. The changes will be so small that, rather than coin a completely new name for the resulting system, we call it *relation logic with identity,* or *RL$_i$*.

In preparation for presenting this system, we will devote the first section of this chapter to one more look at the idea of form. Next, we will revise RL's rules of vocabulary, formation, valuation, and derivation. Having thus made RL into RL$_i$, we will then discuss our new model's relation to English, paying special attention to the translation of sentences about number and sentences containing the word "the". Finally, at the end of the chapter, we will offer some last thoughts on the value of our formal system as a model of English.

10.1 A Final Look at Form

To prepare for the changes we will make in our model of English, we devote this section to a final look at the idea of form.

Our idea of form has changed several times as we have gone along in this book: We examined *sentential* form in Chapter 3, *predicative* form in Chapter 8, and *relational* form in Chapter 9. But, no matter which idea of form we were using, our aims were the same. After examining some sample arguments, we tried to capture in our idea of form just those features of the arguments that accounted for their validity.

For an example of this point, think back to a sample argument from Chapter 9:

Abelard loved Heloise.
_____

So, somebody loved somebody.

To account for the validity of this argument, we had to talk about the placement of the expressions "Abelard" and "Heloise" in the blanks in the expression ". . . loved—", but not about what these terms say or mean. Accordingly, we replaced these expressions with letters when revealing the Abelard argument's (relational) form. But, since the meaning of the quantifying word "somebody" did have a bearing on the Abelard argument's validity, we did not replace this word with a letter. Rather, for reasons that we explained in Chapter 8, we expanded the word "somebody" into the longer English phrase "at least one thing is such that". The resulting form,

Fab
_____

So, *at least one thing is such that* at least one thing is such that *F*, it *it*,

captured just those facts about the argument that account for its validity.

With this in mind, consider the argument

Russia borders on China.

─────────────────

So, China borders on Russia.

This argument is clearly valid; one thing could not possibly border on a second unless the second bordered on the first. Yet the argument has the R-*in*valid relational form "*Rba*; so, *Rab*".* So, this argument's relational form does *not* capture everything that accounts for its validity.

The Russia/China argument therefore differs from the Abelard argument considered earlier. We can replace the predicate ". . . loved—" in the Abelard argument with any other predicate without making the argument invalid—for the meaning of the predicate ". . . loved—" has no bearing on the Abelard argument's validity. In contrast, if we replace the predicate ". . . borders on—" in the Russia/China argument with, say, ". . . is north of—", the result would *not* be valid. The meaning of the predicate ". . . borders on—" *does* have a bearing on the validity of the Russia/China argument.

So far, when we have found that an argument's validity depends on the meaning of some expression, we have generally left expressions of that sort in English when revealing form. We did this, for instance, with sentential operators in Chapter 3 and again with quantifying phrases in Chapter 8. Should we do the same with predicates? Having noticed that the validity of the Russia/China argument rests on the meaning of the predicate ". . . borders on—", should we leave *predicates* in English when revealing the forms of sentences and arguments?

We could do this, but we won't. If we did, our procedure for revealing form would turn out to be little more than a way of moving from one English version of an argument to another, and we would lose the contrast between form and content that has been important to us throughout this book. So, in spite of the problem that the Russia/China argument raises, we will generally continue to replace predicates with letters when revealing form.

Yet we will make *one exception* to this general rule. The exception has to do with the predicate

. . . is identical to —†

─────────────────

* Many are tempted to say that the sample argument rests on the *unstated* premise "If one thing borders on a second, then the second borders on the first." If it did, the argument's relational form would be R-valid, and we could easily demonstrate the argument's validity with the methods of RL. But the sample argument is valid *as it stands;* we can't imagine a possible situation in which its premise is true while its conclusion is false. And the principle of fidelity (Chapter 2) leads us to say that, if an argument's stated premises validly entail its conclusion, we shouldn't look for unstated premises.

† Sometimes this predicate means ". . . is one and the same thing as —", but sometimes it means ". . . is completely similar to —". Here, and in the rest of the book, we use it in the *first* of these senses.

Unlike ". . . borders on—" or ". . . is twice as large as—" or most other predicates we might think of, ". . . is identical to—" applies to *any* objects that we might be talking about. And the study of the predicate ". . . is identical to—" leads to especially interesting results about number, which we will discuss later in this chapter. Accordingly, when revealing the form of English arguments we will leave this one predicate in English.

The decision to do this takes us from the idea of relational form to the new idea of *i-relational* form:

> The **i-relational form** of an English sentence or argument is the way it has been made from sentential operators, singular terms, quantifying phrases, pronouns, the predicate ". . . is identical to—", other (one-placed and many-placed) predicates, and simple clauses that can't be broken down into these parts.

To reveal the i-relational form of a sentence or an argument that has been made explicit, we

  a. expand all abbreviations,

  b. replace each simple clause that can't be broken down into quantifying phrases, predicates, singular terms, and pronouns with an uppercase letter (the first, wherever it occurs, with "*P*", the second with "*Q*", and so on),

  c. replace each remaining singular term with a lowercase letter (the first, wherever it occurs, with "*a*", the second with "*b*", and so on), and

  d. replace each remaining predicate *other than* ". . . is identical to—" with an uppercase letter (the first, wherever it occurs, with "*F*", the second with "*G*", and so on).

In many cases, the result of applying this procedure to a sentence or argument will be exactly the same as that of applying the procedure described in Chapter 9 for revealing relational form. A difference will show up, though, if the argument or sentence whose form we are revealing contains the predicate ". . . is identical to—". When we apply our procedures for revealing relational form, we replace this predicate with a letter; when we apply the procedures for revealing i-relational form, we do not.

To see the importance of this seemingly small difference, compare the argument we mentioned at the beginning of this chapter,

> Zorro is Don Diego.
>
> Zorro is brave.
>
> _____
>
> So, Don Diego is brave.

to the argument

> The planet Mercury is smaller than the planet Pluto.
>
> The planet Mercury is hot.
> _____
>
> So, the planet Pluto is hot.

Both of these arguments have the *relational* form

> *Fab*
>
> *Ga*
> _____
>
> So, *Gb*

But the first argument is valid, while the second is not. So, if we think of form as we did in Chapter 9, we must say that the first argument owes its validity to something other than its form, and we must therefore abandon all hope of demonstrating the first argument's validity with formal methods of the sort we have been discussing in this book.

But, when we switch to the idea of i-relational form, things are different. While the Zorro argument has the i-relational form

> *a* is identical to *b*
>
> *Fa*
> _____
>
> So, *Fb*

the argument about the planet Pluto has the *different* i-relational form

> *Fab*
>
> *Ga*
> _____
>
> So, *Gb*

So, from the fact that the Pluto argument is invalid, nothing at all follows about whether the Zorro argument owes its validity to its form. The Zorro argument and the Pluto argument have different i-relational forms.

In fact, as we will demonstrate later in this chapter, the Zorro argument *does* owe its validity to its i-relational form. The argument is valid precisely because it has this form, and any other argument with the same i-relational form is valid, too.

Accordingly, we define *i-relational validity* as follows:

> An argument form is **i-relationally valid (IR-valid)** just in case every argument of that i-relational form is valid.

Our aim in the rest of this chapter will be to mirror the idea of IR-validity in our model of English. In the next section, we will modify the model by adding the expression "=", which corresponds both syntactically and semantically to the English predicate ". . . is identical to —". As we said at the beginning of the chapter, the result will be the system RL_i—a system whose methods for demonstrating validity are even more powerful than RL's.

Exercises 10.1

1. The predicate ". . . is identical to —" has two different senses. Sometimes (as in the sentence "Your car is identical to mine") it means ". . . is completely similar to—". Other times (as in "Ohio is identical to The Buckeye State") it means ". . . is one and the same thing as —". In which sense have we been using the predicate ". . . is identical to —" in this chapter?

2. *Defend or criticize:* The expressions ". . . borders on —" and ". . . is identical to —" are both two-placed predicates, for each becomes a simple clause when we fill its blanks with singular terms. Hence, the sentence "Russia borders on China" has the same form as the sentence "Russia is identical to China."

3. *Defend or criticize:* Whether we say that the argument

> Alice is identical to Mrs. Jones.
>
> Alice is tall.
>
> _____
>
> So, Mrs. Jones is tall.

is valid in virtue of its form depends on our definition of form.

4. Consider the argument

> Texas is big.
>
> _____
>
> So, at least one thing is such that it is big.

Replace the singular term "Texas" in this argument with some other singular term. Is the resulting argument valid?

Next, replace both occurrences of the predicate ". . . is big" in the argument with some other predicate. Is the resulting argument valid?

Finally, replace the quantifying phrase "at least one thing is such that" with the quantifying phrase "more than one thing is such that". Is the resulting argument still valid?

5. *Defend or criticize:* Every English argument with an R-valid relational form also has an IR-valid i-relational form, and every argument with an IR-valid i-relational form also has an R-valid relational form.

6. In revealing the i-relational form of sentences, we replace some, but not all, of the expressions in them with letters. Which expressions do we replace with letters and which do we leave in English?

7. Reveal the i-relational forms of the following sentences:
   a. Linda knows Mrs. Jones.
   b. Linda is Mrs. Jones.
   c. Either Linda knows Mrs. Jones, or Linda is Mrs. Jones.
   d. If Linda doesn't know Mrs. Jones, then she isn't Mrs. Jones.
   e. Linda, who is the same person as Mrs. Jones, hates Carl.
   f. If Carl and Harry are the same person, then Linda hates him unless it's raining.
   g. Everything is identical to something.
   h. Everything golden is identical to something valuable.
   i. There is something golden, and each valuable thing is identical to it.
   j. Nothing is identical to everything.

10.2 RL$_i$'s Syntactic and Semantic Rules

As we noted in the previous section, the meaning of the predicate ". . . is identical to —" has a bearing on the validity of certain arguments. To improve our model's ability to deal with such arguments, we introduce a new expression, "=", into the model's vocabulary. The result will be the system RL$_i$, whose syntactic and semantic rules we state in this section.

The only difference between RL$_i$'s vocabulary and RL's is that RL$_i$'s contains the expression "=". Because this expression corresponds to the English predicate ". . . is identical to —", we call it the **identity sign**.

Along with the identity sign comes a new rule of formation:

F10: If we flank the identity sign with two variables, or two constants, or one constant and one variable, the result is a wff of RL$_i$.

This rule ensures that the syntax of the expression "=" is almost exactly the same as that of a two-placed predicate letter. As "Faa", "Fab", "Fax", and "Fxy" are well-formed formulae, so are "a=a", "a=b", "x=a", and "y=x". As we can put a dash in front of "Fab" to form "−Fab", we can put a dash in front of "a=b" to form "−a=b". As we can flank the arrow with "Fxa" and "Gyb" to form "(Fxa → Gyb)", we can flank the arrow with "x=a" and "y=b" to form "(x=a → y=b)". As we can put "[x]" in front of "(Fxy ↔ Gyx)" to form "[x](Fxy ↔ Gyx)", we can put "[x]" in front of "(x=y ↔ y=x)" to form "[x](x=y ↔ y=x)". Indeed, the *only* syntactic respect in which the identity sign differs from a two-placed predicate letter is that one of the identity sign's blanks is on its right while the other is on its left, whereas all of a predicate letter's blanks are on its right.

Because the syntax of the identify sign so closely resembles that of a two-placed predicate letter, the addition of rule F10 to our system does not force us to change its other syntactic rules. In particular, we continue to use the definition of *symbolic sentence* developed in Chapter 8:

> A wff is a *symbolic sentence* just in case it does not contain any free variables.

Thus, the wffs "a=b", "−a=a", "[x](a=x)", and "[x][∃y](x=a → −y=a)" are symbolic sentences of RL_i, while the wffs "x=a", and "[∃y](x=a → −y=a)" are not.

What is the basic form of, say, "a=b"? We could group sentences of this sort with singular sentences like "Fab", but it is more convenient to put them into a group of their own. Accordingly, if the only rule used in the construction of a symbolic sentence is F10 (that is, if the sentence consists of an identity sign flanked by two constants), we call that sentence an **identify sentence**. And, as you might guess, we will call sentences like "−a=b" the **negations of identity sentences**.

Notice that, despite appearances, the syntax of the sentence "−a=b" is quite different from that of the symbolic sentence "(−P → Q)" and from that of familiar mathematical sentences such as "−x = 2". In "(−P → Q)" the scope of the dash goes no farther than the sentence letter "P", and in "−x = 2" the scope of the minus sign (which should not be confused with our system's dash!) is just the expression "x". But in "−a=b" the scope of the dash is the whole identity statement "a=b". Thus, the syntax of "−a=b" is like that of "−Fab": Both are the negations of symbolic sentences containing constants.

Having described the syntax of sentences containing identity signs, let's turn now to their semantics.

When setting up a valuation for an identity sentence or any other sentence of RL_i, we simply follow the steps outlined in the previous chapter. That is, we

a. specify a domain of discourse,
b. assign referents to constants,
c. assign extensions (sets of objects) to one-placed predicate letters,
d. assign extensions (collections of ordered *n*-tuples) to *n*-placed predicate letters where *n* is greater than one, and
e. assign values (*t* or *f*) to sentence letters.

Although the identity sign's syntax is like that of a two-placed predicate letter, we do not assign any extension to it.

The only new rule of valuation in RL$_i$ is

V10: In a given valuation, an identity sentence has the value t just in case its first constant has one and the same referent as its second; otherwise, in that valuation, the sentence has the value f.

Consider, for example, the valuation

domain of discourse: {1, 2, 3}
referent of "a": 1
referent of "b": 1
referent of "c": 3

Here, the constant "a" has the same referent as the constant "b", and the sentence "a=b" therefore has the value t. In contrast, since the constant "a" does not have the same referent as the constant "c", "a=c" has the value f.

For a somewhat more complex and interesting example of the use of rule V10, consider the sentence

1. $[\exists y][x](Fx \rightarrow x=y)$

and the valuation

domain of discourse: {1, 2, 3}
referent of "a": 1
referent of "b": 2
referent of "c": 3
extension of "F": {1, 2}

Which value does sentence (1) have in this valuation?

Since (1) begins with an existential quantifier, it has the value t just in case at least one object in the valuation's domain satisfies the wff "$[x](Fx \rightarrow x=y)$" (rule V8). So, in the given valuation, sentence (1) has the value t just in case one or more of the sentences

2. $[x](Fx \rightarrow x=a)$
3. $[x](Fx \rightarrow x=b)$
4. $[x](Fx \rightarrow x=c)$

has the value t.

For the moment, let's focus on sentence (2). Being a universally quantified sentence, (2) has the value t in the given valuation just in case every object in the valuation's domain satisfies the wff "$(Fx \rightarrow x=a)$" (rule V9). But, in the given valuation, the number 2 does not satisfy this wff. So, in the given valuation, sentence (2) has the value f.

Similar reasoning shows that sentences (3) and (4) also have the value *f* in the given valuation. But, as we have said, sentence (1) has the value *t* in the given valuation only if sentence (2) or sentence (3) or sentence (4) has the value *t*. It follows that, in the given valuation, sentence (1) has the value *f*.

Reasoning in this way, we can calculate the value of any sentence containing the identity sign in any valuation for it. And we have therefore completed our description of RL_i's basic syntactic and semantic rules. In the next section, we will describe RL_i's rules of derivation.

Exercises 10.2

1. *Defend or criticize:* Syntactically, the identity sign closely resembles a two-placed predicate letter.

2. Which of the following strings are wffs of RL_i? Which are symbolic sentences?

a.	(a=b)	b.	a=b
c.	−a=b	d.	−(a=b)
e.	a=−b	f.	a −=b
g.	(a → a=b)	h.	(a → b)
i.	(a=b → c=c)	j.	x=x
k.	x=y	l.	(Fx → −a=b)
m.	[y][x]x=x	n.	[x](x=x)
o.	[x][y](x=y → y=x)		
p.	[x][y][z]((x=y & y=z) → x=z)		

3. *Defend or criticize:* An identity sentence consists of exactly three expressions. The first and third are constants, and the second is the identity sign.

4. *Defend or criticize:* When setting up a valuation for a symbolic sentence containing the identity sign, we treat the identity sign just like a two-placed predicate and assign a collection of ordered pairs to it as its extension.

5. Consider the valuation

domain of discourse:	{1, 2, 3, 4}
referent of "a":	1
referent of "b":	1
referent of "c":	3
referent of "d":	4
extension of "F":	{1}
extension of "G":	∅
extension of "R":	⟨1, 1⟩, ⟨2, 2⟩, ⟨3, 3⟩

For each of the following symbolic sentences, calculate its value in the given valuation.

a. a=b
b. b=c
c. −c=d
d. [∃x](Fx & x=a)
e. [x](x=a → Fx)
f. (a=d ↔ [∃x]Gx)
g. [x][y](Rxy → x=y)
h. [∃x](Fx & [y](Fy → x=y))
i. [∃x][∃y]((Rxx & Ryy) & −x=y)

6. *Defend or criticize:* The symbolic sentence "a=a" has the value *t* in every valuation for it, and so does the sentence "[∃x]x=a".

7. *Defend or criticize:* The symbolic sentences

a. [x]x=x
b. [x][y](x=y → y=x)
c. [x][y][z]((x=y & y=z) → x=z)

have the value *t* in every valuation for them.

8. For each of the following symbolic sentences, construct a valuation in which the sentence has the value *t*:

a. −a=b
b. −([∃x]Fx → −a=b)
c. [∃x]((Fx & Gx) & x=a)
d. [∃x][∃y]((Fx & Fy) & −x=y)
e. [x](x=a → Rxx)
f. [x](x=x ↔ Rxx)
g. [x](x=x ↔ [y]Rxy)
h. [x](Fa ↔ a=x)
i. [x](Fx ↔ a=x)
j. [∃x](Fx & [y](Fy → y=x))

9. In the previous section, we said that the symbolic sentences "[x](Fx → x= b)" and "[x](Fx → x=c)" have the value *f* in the valuation

domain of discourse: {1, 2, 3}
referent of "a": 1
referent of "b": 2
referent of "c": 3
extension of "F": {1, 2}

Show that we were right by calculating the values of these sentences in this valuation.

10.3 Derivation in RL_i

In the last section, we established a rule of formation (F10) and a rule of valuation (V10) for sentences containing the identity sign. In this section, we define RL_i-validity and modify our system of derivation so that we can demonstrate arguments' RL_i-validity.

The definition of RL_i-validity is hardly surprising:

A symbolic argument of RL_i is **RL_i-valid** just in case there is no valuation in which its premises have the value *t* while its conclusion has the value *f*.

To demonstrate the RL_i-validity of particular symbolic arguments, we construct derivations in much the same way as we did in the last chapter.

We do, however, need some new rules of inference. To see why, consider the symbolic argument

(Fa ↔ Ga)

b＝a

So, [∃x]((Fx ↔ Gx) & x＝b)

As we show later in this section, this argument is RL_i-valid; there is no valuation in which its premises have the value *t* while its conclusion has the value *f*. Yet, limited to the rules of inference that RL_i has inherited from RL, we cannot derive this argument's conclusion from its premises. Accordingly, we establish two new rules of inference: the *Rule of Reflexivity* (Refl) and the *Rule of Substitution* (Sub).

The **Rule of Reflexivity (Refl)** is this:

If both constants in an identity sentence are of the same type (for instance, if both are "a"s, or both "b"s, or both "c"s), we can write that identity sentence as a line of a derivation, whenever we want.

As we have seen (Exercise 10.2.6), sentences like "a＝a" and "b＝b" have the value *t* in every valuation for them, and they therefore follow RL_i-validly from any sentences that we may have in a derivation. The rule Refl helps us to use this fact by allowing us to enter sentences like "a＝a" into derivations.

Our second new rule of inference is the **Rule of Substitution (Sub)**:

If an identity sentence appears as a line of a derivation, we can substitute either of its constants for the other, one or more times, in any (unboxed) sentence of the derivation and write the result as a line of the derivation.

Using this rule, we can move, say, from "a=b" and "(Fa → Ga)" to "(Fa → Gb)", or "(Fb → Ga)", or "(Fb → Gb)".

The rule Sub corresponds to a move that people make in English. From the sentences "Zorro is Don Diego" and "Zorro is brave," we can naturally and validly infer the sentence "Don Diego is brave." After all, if Zorro has a certain property and Don Diego *is* Zorro, then Don Diego must also have that property. Similarly, if the referent of a certain constant is in the extension of a certain predicate letter and a second constant has the same referent, then the referent of the second constant must also be in the extension of the predicate letter. Accordingly, the rule Sub allows us to move, say, from "Fa" and "a=b" to "Fb".

Let's use the new rules Refl and Sub to construct a derivation for the argument we considered earlier in this section:

> (Fa ↔ Ga)
>
> b=a
>
> ———————————
>
> So, [∃x]((Fx ↔ Gx) & x=b)

As we have said, we cannot derive this argument's conclusion from its premises when limited to RL's rules of derivation. But, now that we have the new rules Refl and Sub, we can construct the derivation, like this:

1.	(Fa ↔ Ga)	Prem
2.	b=a	Prem
3.	− [∃x]((Fx ↔ Gx) & x=b)	SuppID
4.	[x] − ((Fx ↔ Gx) & x=b)	3 QE
5.	− ((Fb ↔ Gb) & b=b)	4 UI
6.	(Fb ↔ Gb)	1,2 Sub
7.	b=b	Refl
8.	((Fb ↔ Gb) & b=b)	6,7 Conj
9.	[∃x]((Fx ↔ Gx) & x=b)	3–8 ID

Since the sentence on line (5) is the negation of a conjunction, we try on subsequent lines to derive the conjunction itself and so to complete the indirect derivation started on line (3). We derive one of these conjuncts on line (6) using Sub, and the other on line (7) using Refl. We then complete the derivation using Conj and ID on lines (8) and (9).

The only difference between RL$_i$'s system of derivation and RL's is that RL$_i$'s has rules Refl and Sub, and all inferences constructed in accordance with these rules are RL$_i$-valid. Accordingly, having derived the sample argument's conclusion from its premises, we can be certain that the argument is RL$_i$-valid.

Exercises 10.3

1. *Defend or criticize:* Since the sentence "a=a" has the value *t* in every valuation for it, this sentence RL_i-validly follows from any other sentence.

2. *Defend or criticize:* Since "[∃x]x=x" has the value *t* in every valuation for it, and since every valuation is a valuation for it, "[∃x]x=x" has the value *t* in every valuation.

3. *Defend or criticize:* The rule Sub tells us that, whenever a sentence containing a constant appears as an (unboxed) line of a derivation, we can replace the constant with another and write the result as a line of the derivation.

4. Using the rules Refl and Sub, along with rules such as SuppID and ID, derive each of the following sentences without using the rule Prem:
   a. [x]x=x
   b. [x][y](x=y → y=x)
   c. [x][y][z]((x=y & y=z) → x=z)

5. For each of the following arguments, demonstrate its RL_i-validity by constructing a derivation:

   a. Fa
   _____
   So, [∃x](Fx & x=a)

   b. Rab
   _____
   So, [∃x][∃y]((x=a & y=b) & Rxy)

   c. Rab
   _____
   So, [x][y]((x=a & y=b) → Rxy)

   d. Rab
   a=c
   [x][y](Rxy → Ryx)
   _____
   So, Rbc

   e. [x][y](Rxy → −x=y)
   _____
   So, −[∃x]Rxx

   f. [∃x][∃y] − x=y
   [x](Fx ↔ x=a)
   _____
   So, [∃x] − Fx

g. [x](Fx → (Gx & Hx))

[∃y][x](Gx ↔ x=y)
_____

So, −[∃x][∃y]((Fx & Fy) & −x=y)

h. [x][y](Rxy → x=y)
_____

So, ((Fa & −Fb) → −Rab)

10.4 Connections between RL$_I$ and English

Since Chapter 6, we have been demonstrating validity by making arguments explicit, translating them into symbolic arguments, and constructing derivations for the translations. When we have succeeded in constructing a derivation for a given argument's translation, we have generally inferred that the argument itself was valid.

We will continue to use this method in much the same way as we did in Chapter 9. There are, in fact, only two differences: (1) we now translate the predicate ". . . is identical to—" with the identity sign rather than with a two-placed predicate letter, and (2) we now can use rules Refl and Sub when constructing derivations.

Let's apply the method to the Zorro argument mentioned at the beginning of this chapter:

Zorro is Don Diego.

Zorro is brave.
_____

So, Don Diego is brave.

Since this argument does not have an R-valid relational form, the methods of Chapter 9 are unable to demonstrate its validity. But, having added the identity sign to our system's vocabulary, we can translate the argument in this way:

a=b

Ba
_____

So, Bb

Using the new rule Sub, we can easily derive this translation's conclusion from its premises. And, having thus demonstrated the translation's RL$_I$-validity, we may infer that the original argument is valid.

To see why this inference is justified, consider the i-relational form of the original argument:

> *a* is identical to *b*
>
> *Fa*
>
> ───────────
>
> So, *Fb*

And suppose that we have before us a sample argument of this form that is invalid.

On this supposition, there must be a situation *S* in which the sample argument's premises are true while its conclusion is false. In *S*, there must be an object (call it O_1) picked out by the argument's first singular term, an object (O_2) picked out by its second singular term, and a property (*P*) mentioned by its one-placed predicate. Also, since *S* is supposed to be a situation in which the sample argument's premises are true while its conclusion is false, it must be the case that in *S*

(a) O_1 is one and the same thing as O_2.

(b) O_1 has property *P*, and

(c) O_2 does not have property *P*.

Conditions (a) and (b) must be met for the sample argument's premises to be true, and condition (c) must be met for its conclusion to be false.

If there were a situation *S* meeting these conditions, we could set up a valuation for the translation of the Zorro argument ("a=b; Ba; so, Bb"), in this way:

> domain of discourse: the set of things in situation *S*
>
> referent of "a": O_1
>
> referent of "b": O_2
>
> extension of "B":   the set of things having property *P* in situation *S*

In this valuation, the translation's first premise ("a=b") would have the value *t* [rule V10 and condition (a)], its second premise ("Ba") would have the value *t* [rule V7 and condition (b)], and its conclusion would have the value *f* [rule V7 and condition (c)]. Accordingly, the valuation would be a counterexample to the Zorro argument's translation, and the translation would be RL_i-invalid.

But, having constructed a derivation for this translation, we know that it is RL_i-valid and, hence, that there is *no* counterexample to it. It follows that there is no valuation like the one we tried to construct. This means that there is no logically possible situation *S* meeting conditions (a), (b), and (c) and, hence, that there is no invalid argument with the same i-relational form as the Zorro argument. So, from the fact that we can construct a derivation for the Zorro argument's translation, it follows that the argument's i-relational form is IR-valid.

That an argument has an IR-valid form entails, of course, that the argument itself is valid. Accordingly, having constructed a derivation for the Zorro argument's translation, we may infer that the argument itself is valid.

The example illustrates a general point: If we find that an argument has an RL_i-valid translation, we may confidently infer that the argument's i-relational form is IR-valid and, hence, that the argument itself is valid.

Exercises 10.4

1. *Defend or criticize:* RL_i's method for demonstrating the validity of arguments in English is better than RL's.

2. *Defend or criticize:* From the fact that a given argument has an RL_i-valid translation, it generally follows that every argument having the same i-relational form as the given argument is valid.

3. *Defend or criticize:* From the fact that a given argument does not have an RL_i-valid translation, it generally follows that every argument having the same i-relational form is invalid.

4. *Defend or criticize:* To determine the validity of an English argument using RL_i, we follow roughly the same steps as we did when using the old system RL.

5. Using the methods described in the last section, demonstrate the validity of the following English arguments:

    a. Either Paul is in class, or Mr. Cool is eating lunch.

       Paul is Mr. Cool.

       ―――――――――――――――――――――――――

       So, Mr. Cool is in class unless Paul is eating lunch.

    b. Alice and Ms. Baker are the same person.

       Alice is the very same person as Carol.

       ―――――――――――――――――――――――――

       So, Carol is identical to Ms. Baker.

    c. If a first thing is in the same place as a second, then the things are identical to one another.

       The World Trade Center is in the same place as the tallest building in New York.

       ―――――――――――――――――――――――――

       So, the World Trade Center is the tallest building in New York.

    d. Every dog hates some cat or other.

       Spot is a dog, and Spot is Fido.

       If a first thing hates a second, then the second hates the first.

       ―――――――――――――――――――――――――

       So, some cat hates Fido.

e. If there is something that's identical to itself, then something is due east of Athens.

So, something identical to Athens has something due east of it.

10.5 Translating Sentences about Number

So far, we have used the identity sign to translate the English predicate ". . . is identical to —". In this section and the next, we will use it to translate certain sentences that do not contain this, or any similar, predicate.

Our focus in this section is on sentences about *number*, such as "No more that *three* people can ride in that car," "At least *two* people are late," and "Exactly *four* chickens got out of the coop." To apply our formal methods for demonstrating validity to arguments containing sentences of this sort, we must translate the sentences into RL$_i$. But how should we do this?

Often, the translation of such sentences hinges on the fact that symbolic existential quantifiers correspond to the English phrase "at least one thing is such that". Given, say, the sentence

One or more things are red,

we might paraphrase it into Standard English as

At least one thing is such that it is red,

and translate it like this:

[∃x]Rx.

Here we translate an English sentence about number, using just the methods described in the last chapter.

But things do not go quite as smoothly when we try to translate a sentence about *minimum* number, such as

At least two things are red.

It may seem, at first, that we can translate this sentence with

[∃x][∃y](Rx & Ry).

To see that this translation is inaccurate, however, imagine a valuation *v* in which the referent of the constant "a" is in the extension of the predicate letter "R". In *v*, the referent of "a" satisfies the wff "(Ra & Ry)", and "[∃y](Ra & Ry)" therefore has the value *t* (rule V8). But, if "[∃y](Ra & Ry)" has the value *t* in *v*, so does "[∃x][∃y](Rx & Ry)" (rule V8). Accordingly, "[∃x][∃y](Rx & Ry)" has the value *t* in any valuation in which the referent of the constant "a" is in the extension of the predicate letter "R" — even if that thing is the *one and only* member of that extension. Despite its two quantifiers, then, the sentence "[∃x][∃y](Rx & Ry)" is a better translation for "At least *one* thing is red" than for "At least *two* things are red."

A much better translation for "At least two things are red" is:

[∃x][∃y]((Rx & Ry) & −x=y).

Since this sentence has the value *t* when and only when there are at least two different things in the extension of the predicate letter "R", it corresponds semantically to the English sentence "At least two things are red."

Of course, the syntax of this symbolic sentence is not at all like that of the English sentence "At least two things are red." For instance, although the symbolic sentence contains two ampersands, the English sentence does not contain a single "and" or "but". And, in the past, we have tried to make our translations correspond syntactically as well as semantically to the sentences that they translate. Should we, then, settle for

[∃x][∃y]((Rx & Ry) & −x=y)

as our translation of

At least two things are red,

or should we continue to develop our system in the hope of coming up with something better?

It's possible to refine our model of English further than we have, and the authors of some other texts do so. But RL_i is already fairly complex, and it provides us with a very powerful method for demonstrating validity. Accordingly, many logicians and philosophers suggest that, when we have problems using RL_i to demonstrate validity, we ought instead to try tactics that don't involve changing the system itself.

Following this suggestion in the case at hand, we regard the symbolic sentence "[∃x][∃y]((Rx & Ry) & −x=y)" as an acceptable translation of the English sentence "At least two things are red." Similarly, on the basis of semantic considerations, we regard other symbolic sentences as translations of English sentences about minimum number — even if they do not correspond to those English sentences syntactically (see Exercise 10.5.2).

Since we can translate sentences about minimum number, we can also translate sentences about *maximum* number. Consider, for example, the sentence

1. At most one thing is red.

In effect, this sentence is the denial of the sentence

2. At least two things are red.

Accordingly, we can translate sentence (1) simply by placing a dash in front of our translation of sentence (2), like this:

$$-[\exists x][\exists y]((Rx \mathbin{\&} Ry) \mathbin{\&} -x{=}y).$$

Although this symbolic sentence does not capture the syntax of sentence (1), the translation is still a good one. Sentence (1) is true when and only when there are fewer than two things having the property mentioned by the predicate ". . . is red", and "$-[\exists x][\exists y]((Rx \mathbin{\&} Ry) \mathbin{\&} -x{=}y)$" has the value *t* when and only when there are fewer than two things in the extension of the predicate letter "R".

Having come up with ways to translate sentences about maximum number and sentences about minimum number, we can also translate sentences about *exact* number. Consider, for example, the sentence

3.   Exactly one thing is red.

The key to translating this sentence is to paraphrase it with the conjunction:

4.   At least one thing is red, *and* at most one thing is red.

As we said earlier in this section, we can translate the first conjunct of sentence (4) with

$[\exists x]Rx$

and the second conjunct with

$$-[\exists x][\exists y]((Rx \mathbin{\&} Ry) \mathbin{\&} -x{=}y).$$

Joining these two symbolic sentences with an ampersand, we get

5. $([\exists x]Rx \mathbin{\&} -[\exists x][\exists y]((Rx \mathbin{\&} Ry) \mathbin{\&} -x{=}y)),$

which we can view as a translation of sentence (3), "Exactly one thing is red." Sentence (3) is true when and only when exactly one thing has the property mentioned by the predicate ". . . is red", and symbolic sentence (5) has the value *t* when and only when exactly one thing is in the extension of the predicate letter "R".

Other symbolic sentences translate sentence (3) just as well as sentence (5). Among them are the shorter and prettier sentences

$[\exists x](Rx \mathbin{\&} [y](Ry \rightarrow x{=}y))$

and

$[\exists y][x](Rx \leftrightarrow x{=}y).$

Like (5), these sentences have the value *t* when and only when there is exactly one thing in the extension of the predicate letter "R".

Since we can translate sentence (3), we can translate other sentences about exact number as well. For instance, we can translate

Exactly two things are red.

with

$[\exists x][\exists y](((Rx \ \& \ Ry) \ \& \ -x=y) \ \& \ [z](Rz \rightarrow (z=x \lor z=y)))$.

The complexity of an English sentence's translation increases as the numbers mentioned in that sentence become larger, but, as long as the numbers are positive and whole, translation is possible.

Translation of this sort helps us demonstrate the validity of arguments in English. Consider, for instance, the argument

The club has at least two members.

The club has exactly one officer.

So, not all members of the club are officers.

Letting "M" correspond to the predicate ". . . is a member of—", "O" to the predicate ". . . is an officer of —", and "c" to the singular term "the club", we can translate the argument like this:

$[\exists x][\exists y]((Mxc \ \& \ Myc) \ \& \ -x=y)$

$[\exists x](Oxc \ \& \ [y](Oyc \rightarrow x=y))$

So, $-[x](Mxc \rightarrow Oxc)$

To demonstrate the original argument's validity, we need to demonstrate the RL_i-validity of this symbolic argument with a derivation (Exercise 10.5.8).

There is something surprising here. The original English argument seems to contain names for the numbers one and two, and the validity of the argument seems to rest on the arithmetic truth that two is greater than one. Yet we demonstrated the argument's validity without taking any of this into account. In making the argument explicit, we did not regard it as resting on any unstated premises about numbers, and, in translating into RL_i, we did not associate the words "one" and "two" with constants. Indeed, in demonstrating the validity of this argument about number, we did not do *anything* that looked like the arithmetic we learned in elementary school.

Observations of this sort have led some logicians—including the founders of modern logic, Gottlob Frege and Bertrand Russell—to suspect that the language of arithmetic is just a system like RL_i in disguise. And, since the semantic rules of RL_i have to do with sets, some have gone on to say that there is a deep and important connection between arithmetic and set theory. But discussions of these issues would carry us beyond the scope of this book. For our purposes, what's important is that, using RL_i in the way we have described, we can demonstrate the validity of many English arguments about number.

Exercises 10.5

1. Consider the valuation,

domain of discourse: {1}

extension of "R": {1}

and these two sentences:

  i. [∃x]Rx
  ii. [∃x][∃y](Rx & Ry)

  a. Using a derivation, show that sentence (i) entails sentence (ii).
  b. Find the value of the sentence (i) in the given valuation.
  c. Using what you said in parts (a) and (b) of this exercise, show that the value of sentence (ii) in the given valuation is *t*.
  d. Referring to what you said in part (c), show that sentence (ii) is not a good translation of the English sentence "At least two things are red."
  e. Show with a derivation that sentence (ii) entails sentence (i).
  f. Citing the derivations that you constructed in parts (a) and (e), show that sentences (i) and (ii) are RL_i-equivalent — or, in other words, that there is no valuation in which one has the value *t* while the other has the value *f*.

2. Translate the following sentences into RL_i:
  a. At least one thing is big.
  b. At least two things are big.
  c. More than one thing is big.
  d. No less than one thing is big.
  e. At least three things are big.
  f. At least two big things are sitting on the table.
  g. Every table has more than one big thing sitting on it.

3. *Defend or criticize:* In previous chapters, we generally viewed a symbolic sentence as a translation of an English sentence only if it mirrored the syntax of that English sentence. But in this chapter, we sometimes view symbolic sentences as translations of English sentences on the basis of purely *semantic* resemblances.

4. *Defend or criticize:* The sentence

Each thing is such that it is red only if everything red is identical to it.

is true just in case at most one thing is red.

5. Construct a valuation for the sentence

[x](Rx → [y](Ry → y=x))

in which two or more things are in the extension of the predicate letter "R", and show that the value of the sentence in this valuation is *f*.

6. Translate the following sentences into RL$_i$:
   a. At most one thing is cold.
   b. At most two things are cold.
   c. No more than two things are cold.
   d. Fewer than three things are big.
   e. No more than one of the things on the table is cold.
   f. If there is a table in the kitchen, there is at most one noncold thing on it.

7. Consider the sentences

$$[\exists x](Rx \ \& \ [y](Ry \rightarrow x=y))$$

and

$$[\exists y][x](Rx \leftrightarrow x=y).$$

By deriving the first sentence from the second and then the second from the first, show that the sentences are RL$_i$-equivalent.

8. Near the end of the previous section, we considered the symbolic argument

   1. $[\exists x][\exists y]((Mxc \ \& \ Myc) \ \& \ -x=y)$
   2. $[\exists x](Oxc \ \& \ [y](Oyc \rightarrow x=y))$
   _____
   3. So, $-[x](Mxc \rightarrow Oxc)$

Demonstrate this argument's RL$_i$-validity with a derivation.

9. Using the methods described in this section, demonstrate the validity of the following English arguments:
   a. There are at least two crackers in the box. So, there is at least one cracker in the box.
   b. Some, but not all, Panamanians are happy. Hence, there are at least two Panamanians.
   c. Since Harold has exactly one car, he has no more than one car.
   d. There is exactly one cold thing. It follows, then, that no more than one thing is both cold and old.
   e. There is one student in the class—no more, no less. But at least one student in the class has red hair. So, all of the students in the class have red hair.

10.6 Translating Sentences Containing Definite Descriptions

As we showed in the last section, the symbolic translations of sentences about number may contain identity signs even if the sentences themselves do not contain the predicate "... is identical to —". In this section, we show that sentences may be about number even if they do not contain words like "one", "two", and "three". Having shown this, we will be able to use the identity sign in the translation of some sentences that do not at first seem to have anything to do with either identity or number.

The sentences on which we focus in this section contain expressions called *definite descriptions:*

A **definite description** is an English phrase that begins with the word "the" and has the syntax of a singular term.

Examples of definite descriptions are "the man who came to dinner," "the first woman astronaut," and "the potato under the refrigerator."

According to our definition, definite descriptions have the same syntax as singular terms: All fit into the blanks in predicates to form clauses. But definite descriptions are sometimes put to the same semantic use as singular terms, and sometimes to another use.

Suppose, for example, that as a meeting is about to begin Dave asks Sara who is going to take notes. Suppose that, glancing toward Fumio, who has just been elected club president, Sara replies

1.   The new president will take notes.

What exactly has Sara said?

Well, Sara might have been saying *about Fumio* that *he* will take the notes. If so, she could just as well have said

2.   The new president — namely, *Fumio* — will take notes.

In sentence (2), the definite description "the new president" picks out a certain individual, exactly as the singular term "Fumio" does.

On the other hand, Sara might not even know that Fumio has been elected president. It might be that, in using sentence (1), she is just reminding Dave of a rule of the club requiring a new president to take notes. The people who wrote the rule did not have Fumio (or anyone else) in mind when they wrote it. So, if Sara is merely reciting the rule when she asserts sentence (1), she is saying

3.   The new president *(whoever that may be)* will take notes.

In this sentence, the definite description "the new president" does *not* function as a singular term — for it is not used to pick out any particular person.

If a definite description is used as a singular term [as in sentence (2)], we call it a **referential definite description**. In contrast, if a definite description is used in some other way [as in sentence (3)], we call it a **nonreferential definite description.**

When translating from English into RL_i, it's important to distinguish definite descriptions that are referential from those that are not. Think back, for example, to Sara's original statement:

1. The new president will take notes.

If the definite description "the new president" is used referentially in this sentence, we can let it correspond to a symbolic constant such as "a" and translate the sentence with, say,

Na.

On the other hand, if the definite description in sentence (1) is used nonreferentially, we should paraphrase sentence (1) in this way:

Exactly one thing is such that it was just elected president, and it will take notes.

This sentence is about *number*, and, in accordance with what we said in the previous section, we can translate it with

$[\exists x]((Px \ \& \ [y](Py \rightarrow x=y)) \ \& \ Nx)$

(where "P" corresponds to ". . . was just elected president" and "N" to ". . . will take notes").

How can sentence (1) have two translations that differ so dramatically from one another? The answer is that there are two, very different ways of viewing its *form*. If the function of the definite description in sentence (1) is just to pick out a certain person, we can view (1) as a singular sentence made from a singular term and a (simple, one-placed) predicate. However, if we view sentence (1) as saying that exactly one (perhaps unidentified) object has a certain collection of properties, we should view it as made from predicates and quantifying phrases, but no singular terms.

In our example, which way we interpreted the definite description "the new president" depended on what we understood Sara to mean. When a definite description appears in an argument, however, the argument's structure may provide us with a reason for viewing the description in one way rather than another.

To see this, consider the argument

The new toaster is broken.

_____

So, something new is broken.

This argument seems to be valid. How could the new toaster be broken unless something new is broken? But, if we take the phrase "the new toaster" to be a *referential* definite description, we must translate the argument in this way:

Ba
_____

So, [∃x](Nx & Bx)

Since this translation is RL₁-*invalid,* our formal methods seem unable to demonstrate the validity of the original argument about the toaster.

In contrast, if we view "the new toaster" as a *nonreferential* definite description, we can translate the argument in this way:

[∃x](((Nx & Tx) & [∃y]((Ny & Ty)) → x=y) & Bx)
_____

So, [∃x](Nx & Bx)

Unlike our first translation, this one is RL₁-*valid.* So, other things being equal, we should take the definite description "the new toaster" to be nonreferential in the sample argument. By doing so, we do justice to the fact that the original English argument seems to be valid in virtue of its form.

Exercises 10.6

1. At one point in the previous section, we translated the argument

The new toaster is broken.
_____

So, something is broken.

with

[∃x](((Nx & Tx) & [∃y]((Ny & Ty)) → x=y) & Bx)
_____

So, [∃x](Nx & Bx)

Demonstrate this symbolic argument's RL₁-validity with a derivation. What can you conclude about the original argument's i-relational form?

2. Which of the following phrases are definite descriptions?
   a. the highest
   b. . . . is the highest mountain
   c. the highest mountain in the U.S.
   d. the elf who
   e. the man over there

f. the greatest golfer this side of . . .

g. a great golfer in Nebraska

3. *Defend or criticize:* Every definite description has the syntax of a singular term.

4. *Defend or criticize:* Like the singular term "George Washington", the definite description "the first president of the United States" picks out a certain individual whenever we use it.

5. Translate the following sentences into RL_i. (Do not translate the parts in parentheses; they are there only to indicate how the sentences are to be interpreted.)

a. Exactly one person is a winner, and he or she will get the prize money.

b. John will get the prize money.

c. The winner (namely, John) will get the prize money.

d. The winner (whoever that may turn out to be) will get the prize money.

6. Consider the argument

Every Californian is either male or female.

The Californian who can fly is not male.

So, the Californian who can fly is female.

Assume that the definite description "the Californian who can fly" is used referentially in this argument, and translate the argument into RL_i. If the translation is RL_i-valid, demonstrate its RL_i-validity with a derivation. Otherwise, produce a valuation in which its premises have the value t while its conclusion has the value f.

Now, assume that the definite description "the Californian who can fly" is used nonreferentially in the argument, and translate the argument into RL_i. If the translation is RL_i-valid, demonstrate its RL-validity with a derivation. Otherwise, produce a valuation in which its premises have the value t while its conclusion has the value f.

10.7 Overview

In this chapter, we moved from the system RL to the more refined system RL_i.

We began by moving from the idea of relational form to that of i-relational form:

The *i-relational form* of an English sentence or argument is the way it has been made from singular terms, sentential operators, quantifying phrases, pronouns, the predicate ". . . is identical to —", other predicates, and simple clauses that can't be broken down into these parts.

The procedure for revealing i-relational form is exactly the same as that for revealing relational form except that we leave the predicate ". . . is identical to —" in English.

The new definition of form led to a new definition of validity:

An argument form is *i-relationally valid* (IR-valid) just in case every argument of that i-relational form is valid.

Our aim in this chapter has been to reflect facts about IR-validity in our model of English and thus to refine our formal methods for demonstrating the validity of arguments in English.

We began by adding the *identity sign* "=" to our model's vocabulary and by setting up a new syntactic rule:

F10: If we flank the identity sign with two variables, or two constants, or one constant and one variable, the result is a wff of RL_i.

When we use F10 to make a symbolic sentence out of two constants and the identity sign, we call the result an *identity sentence*.

The only way in which RL_i's semantics differs from RL's is that RL_i has rule V10:

V10: In a given valuation, an identity sentence has the value *t* just in case the referent of its first constant is one and the same object as the referent of its second constant. Otherwise, in that valuation, the identity sentence has the value *f*.

This rule ensures that the identity sign corresponds semantically to the English predicate ". . . is identical to —".

The definition of RL_i-validity was this:

A symbolic argument of RL_i is *RL_i-valid* just in case there is no valuation in which its premises have the value *t* while its conclusion has the value *f*.

To demonstrate RL_i-validity, we use RL's system of derivation, strengthened with two new rules of inference. Rule Refl says that we can write identity sentences, such as "a=a", whose constants are both of the same type, whenever we want in a derivation. And rule Sub says that, if an identity sentence appears as a line of a derivation, we can substitute either of its constants for the other, one or more times, in any (unboxed) sentence in the derivation.

To translate arguments from English into RL_i, we generally follow the same methods as when translating into RL. There are, however, three important differences: (1) we now translate the predicate ". . . is identical to —" with the identity sign "=" rather than with a two-placed predicate letter, (2) we now use the identity sign in translating sentences about (minimum, maximum, and exact) number, and (3) we now use the identity sign in the translation of *nonreferential* definite descriptions (phrases of the form "the so-and-so" that do not work semantically as singular terms).

After translating an argument from English into RL_i, we can attempt to demonstrate the translation's RL_i-validity with a derivation. If we succeed, we may confidently infer that the i-relational form of the original argument is IR-valid and, hence, that the argument itself is valid.

Appendix

Trees

In Section 5.5, we tested symbolic arguments for CL-validity using truth tables. As we said, we can always construct a truth table for symbolic arguments of CL, and we can always tell from an argument's table whether the argument is CL-valid. But truth table construction can be very tedious, and it doesn't correspond to anything people do when reasoning in English. So, in Chapter 6, we developed another method for demonstrating CL-validity: the method of derivation. Derivations for symbolic arguments tend to be shorter and more elegant than the arguments' truth tables. And, as we pointed out, the process of constructing derivations *does* correspond to a process people go through when reasoning in English. Still, the method of derivation had a disadvantage: When we tried to construct a derivation for a given symbolic argument and failed, it was hard to tell whether the failure was due to the argument's CL-invalidity or to our own lack of ingenuity and perseverance.

The method of *trees,* which we develop in this appendix, is an alternative to the method of derivation. Like truth tables, trees for symbolic arguments of CL can be constructed without much thought, and they always show us whether the symbolic arguments for which they were constructed are CL-valid. Also, like derivations, trees for symbolic arguments of CL are generally shorter, more elegant, and less tedious than the arguments' truth tables. In addition, it's much easier to demonstrate the reliability of the tree method as a test for CL-validity than to demonstrate the reliability of the method of derivation.

Then why didn't we discuss trees instead of derivations in Chapter 6? Well, in this book, we view systems of logic as models of English. And, unlike the study of derivation, the study of trees doesn't shed much light on the ways people reason in English. So, we have put the discussion of trees in an appendix.

This appendix is divided into three sections. In the first, we state CL's rules for tree construction. In the second, we explain how trees can be used to test symbolic arguments for CL-validity and CL-invalidity. And, in the third, we extend the method of trees so that it can be applied to symbolic arguments of PL and RL, the systems described in Chapters 7, 8, and 9.

A. CL's Tree Rules

In this section, we present rules for the construction of trees in the system CL, illustrating the rules with a sample tree.

The first step in constructing a tree is to list one or more symbolic sentences as the tree's *initial sentences*. Our sample tree has the initial sentences

$$(A \mathbin{\&} B)$$
$$(A \rightarrow (-B \lor (D \lor E)))$$
$$--((A \rightarrow E) \rightarrow -(D \lor E))$$

(In the next section, when we discuss the uses of trees, it will become clear how to choose initial sentences.)

To continue the tree, we apply *rules of inference*, which tell us what we can write beneath the tree's initial sentences. CL's tree system has nine such rules:

T1: If a conjunction appears in a tree, list its conjuncts.

T2: If a disjunction appears in a tree, draw downward branching lines, write one disjunct at the end of one branch, and write the other disjunct at the end of the other branch.

T3: If a conditional appears in a tree, draw downward branching lines, write the negation of its antecedent at the end of one branch, and write its consequent at the end of the other branch.

T4: If a biconditional appears in a tree, draw downward branching lines, list its sides at the end of one branch, and list the negations of its sides at the end of the other branch.

T5: If the negation of a conjunction appears in a tree, draw downward branching lines, write the negation of one conjunct at the end of one branch, and write the negation of the other conjunct at the end of the other branch.

T6: If the negation of a disjunction appears in a tree, list the negations of the disjuncts.

T7: If the negation of a conditional appears as a sentence in a tree, list the conditional's antecedent and the negation of its consequent.

T8: If the negation of a biconditional appears as a sentence in a tree, draw downward branching lines. At the end of one branch list the biconditional's right side and the negation of its left side. At the end of the other branch list the biconditional's left side and the negation of the biconditional's right side.

T9: If the negation of the negation of a symbolic sentence appears as a sentence in a tree, write that symbolic sentence.

(These rules are based on those in *Formal Logic: Its Scope and Limits* by R. Jeffrey, who credits the rules' development to R. Smullyan, E. Beth, and J. Hintikka.)

Instead of struggling to remember the verbal statements of these rules, one can memorize these simple applications of the rules:

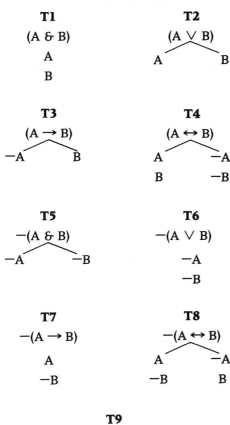

These simple applications of the rules display patterns that become less obvious as the sentences to which the rules are applied become more complex.

Consider, for example, the symbolic sentence

$$-((P \mathrel{\&} Q) \vee (-P \vee Q)).$$

Since this is the negation of a disjunction, the rule that applies to it is T6. So, if this symbolic sentence were to appear in a tree, part of the tree might look like this:

$$-((P \mathrel{\&} Q) \vee (-P \vee Q))$$
$$-(P \mathrel{\&} Q)$$
$$-(-P \vee Q)$$

Although it may not be immediately obvious, this is a simple application of rule T6: Beneath the negation of a disjunction, we have listed the negations of its disjuncts.

Unless a symbolic sentence of CL is a sentence letter or the negation of a sentence letter, exactly one of our rules of inference applies to it. To tell which rule, we need only identify the symbolic sentence's basic form. If the sentence is a conjunction, rule T1 applies to it; if it's a disjunction, rule T2; if it's the negation of a biconditional, rule T8; and so on.

With this in mind, let's return to the tree we began earlier in this section. So far, we have simply listed the tree's initial sentences:

$$(A \mathrel{\&} B)$$
$$(A \rightarrow (-B \vee (D \vee E)))$$
$$--((A \rightarrow E) \rightarrow -(D \vee E))$$

To continue the tree, we pick one of these sentences and apply the appropriate rule of inference to it. If, say, we pick the conjunction "(A & B)", rule T1 tells us to write the conjuncts "A" and "B".

But here a question arises. Rule T1 tells us to write the results "A" and "B" *beneath* "(A & B)", but this symbolic sentence already has things written beneath it. Where, then, do we write the results?

The answer is that we write the results at the end of the tree's one and only open path:

> A *path* in a tree is a constantly descending sequence of symbolic sentences that begins at the top of the list of initial sentences and continues all the way through the tree.

At the outset, a tree has just one path, which is made up of the tree's initial sentences. But, as a tree grows, it may branch into several different paths.

If we apply rule T1 to the conjunction "(A & B)" and write the result at the end of the tree's path, we get this:

$$✓(A \ \& \ B)$$
$$(A \rightarrow (-B \lor (D \lor E)))$$
$$--((A \rightarrow E) \rightarrow -(D \lor E))$$
$$A$$
$$B$$

(The check mark in front of "(A & B)" reminds us as we go along in the tree's construction that we have already applied the appropriate rule to this symbolic sentence. In general, we check a sentence after we apply a rule to it, and then we don't apply any additional rules to that sentence.)

To continue the tree, we simply pick another sentence and apply the appropriate rule to it. It does no good to pick "A" or "B", since our system does not have a rule we can apply to sentence letters. And we can't pick "(A & B)" since it's already been checked. So, we pick "(A → (−B ∨ (D ∨ E)))".

Applying rule T3 to this conditional, and writing our results at the end of the tree's one path, we get this:

$$✓(A \ \& \ B)$$
$$✓(A \rightarrow (-B \lor (D \lor E)))$$
$$--((A \rightarrow E) \rightarrow -(D \lor E))$$
$$A$$
$$B$$

$$-A \qquad\qquad (-B \lor (D \lor E))$$
$$\otimes$$

The tree now has *two* paths in it: one running from "(A & B)" through "−A" and one running from "(A & B)" through "(−B ∨ (D ∨ E))".

The first of these paths has the mark ⊗ at its end. We write this mark at the end of a path just in case one symbolic sentence in the path is the negation of another symbolic sentence in that path. We write this mark at the end of the path down our sample tree's left side, for instance, because that path passes through both "A" and "−A". In writing this mark, we *close* the path. A path that is not closed (such as the one running down the sample tree's right side) is said to be *open*.

Now that we have distinguished open paths from closed paths, we can give a general answer to our question about where to write the results we get by applying rules of inference:

> When we apply a rule of inference to a symbolic sentence in a tree, we must write the results at the end of every open path in which that symbolic sentence appears (and nowhere else).

According to this rule, we should never write results at the ends of closed paths. And, according to this rule, when we apply a rule of inference to a sentence that appears in more than one open path, we should write our results down more than once.

The distinction between open paths and closed paths also allows us to say precisely which symbolic sentences may have rules applied to them:

> We may apply a rule of inference to any unchecked symbolic sentence, regardless of its place in a tree, provided that it is neither a sentence letter nor the negation of a sentence letter, and provided that it appears in at least one open path.

We may not apply rules to sentences that appear only in closed paths, since there is nowhere to write the results. We can't apply rules of inference to checked sentences, since they have already been "used up." And we can't apply rules to sentence letters or the negations of sentence letters, since none of our rules applies to sentences of these sorts.

With this in mind, let's look back at our sample tree:

$$✓(A \ \& \ B)$$
$$✓(A \rightarrow (-B \lor (D \lor E)))$$
$$- -((A \rightarrow E) \rightarrow - (D \lor E))$$
$$A$$
$$B$$

$$-A \qquad\qquad (-B \lor (D \lor E))$$
$$\otimes$$

When we reach this point in the tree's construction, there are just two sentences to which we may apply rules of inference:

$$- -((A \rightarrow E) \rightarrow - (D \lor E))$$

and

$$(-B \lor (D \lor E)).$$

Applying rule T9 to the first of these symbolic sentences and rule T3 to the result, we continue the sample tree:

✓(A & B)
✓(A → (−B ∨ (D ∨ E)))
✓−−((A → E) → −(D ∨ E))
A
B
$\diagup$
−A   (−B ∨ (D ∨ E))
⊗   ✓((A → E) → −(D ∨ E))
−(A → E)   −(D ∨ E)

(Notice that, although the symbolic sentence to which we applied rule T9 appears in two paths, we only wrote our results in one of them. The reason, of course, is that the path down the left side of the tree is closed.)

Next, we apply rule T2 to the disjunction "(−B ∨ (D ∨ E))":

✓(A & B)
✓(A → (−B ∨ (D ∨ E)))
✓−−((A → E) → −(D ∨ E))
A
B
$\diagup$
−A   ✓(−B ∨ (D ∨ E))
⊗   ✓((A → E) → −(D ∨ E))
−(A → E)   −(D ∨ E)
−B   (D ∨ E)   −B   (D ∨ E)
⊗   ⊗   ⊗

Since the sentence to which we apply the rule appears in two open paths, we have to write the results twice, producing four paths. But, of these paths, three close immediately. (We close the path down the right side of the tree because it contains both "(D ∨ E)" and "−(D ∨ E)". As this path illustrates, we can close any path containing a symbolic sentence and its negation—even if the symbolic sentence is *not* a sentence letter.)

If we continue the sample tree, we get this:

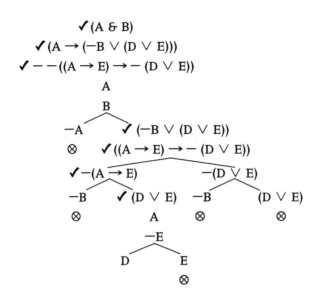

Now the only unchecked symbolic sentences in open paths are sentence letters and the negations of sentence letters. So, the tree is finished; there is nothing more we may do to it.

The construction of our sample tree illustrates the general instructions for tree construction:

1. List the tree's initial sentences.

2. Scan the tree for a symbolic sentence to which to apply a rule of inference. (As we have said, any unchecked symbolic sentence will do, provided it's not a sentence letter or the negation of a sentence letter, and provided it appears in at least one open path.)

3. If there is no symbolic sentence to which you may apply a rule of inference, stop; the tree is finished.

4. If you find a symbolic sentence to which to apply a rule, apply the rule, writing the results at the end of every open path in which the symbolic sentence appears (and nowhere else).

5. If any path contains a symbolic sentence and the negation of that sentence, close the path.

6. Return to instruction (2).

By following this "program," we can construct a finished tree for any symbolic sentences of CL.

All trees constructed in accordance with the "program" are well-formed. But some well-formed trees are messy and ugly, while others are trim elegant. How can we keep our trees elegant?

Here it's important to notice that, while some of our rules of inference (T1, T6, T7, and T9) produce simple lists, the others (T2, T3, T4, T5, and T8) cause branching. We never increase the number of open paths in a tree by applying a listing rule. But, by applying a branching rule, we may increase the number of paths, and we may then need to write some of our results more than once. So, whenever possible, it's a good idea to *use listing rules before branching rules* (see Exercise Appendix A.1).

A second tactic for ensuring elegance is to *keep an eye out for ways to use branching rules without increasing the number of open paths.* If, for example, a path contains both a conditional and that conditional's antecedent, we can apply rule T3 to the conditional, knowing that at least one of the paths we create will close immediately (see Exercise Appendix A.2).

That's all there is to know about constructing trees for symbolic sentences of CL. Following the rules stated in this section will ensure that your trees are well-formed, and following our tactical hints will ensure that the trees are as elegant and compact as possible.

Exercises Appendix A

1. Using rule T1 *before* rule T2, construct a tree whose initial sentences are "(P & Q)" and "(P ∨ Q)". Now, using rule T2 *before* rule T1, construct a tree with the same initial sentences. Which tree do you prefer? Why?

2. Using rules T2, T8, and T3 *in that order,* construct a tree whose initial sentences are "(P ∨ Q)", "−(R ↔ −S)", and "((P ∨ Q) → (R ↔ −S))". Now, using rule T3 *first,* construct a tree with the same initial sentences. Which tree do you prefer? Why?

3. *Defend or criticize:* If a tree contains an unchecked conditional, the tree isn't finished. There is still a rule of inference that we must apply.

4. *Defend or criticize:* When a tree is finished, every symbolic sentence in every path of the tree is checked.

5. *Defend or criticize:* When we apply a rule of inference to a symbolic sentence that's in more than one open path, we must write our results down several times—once at the end of each open path in which the symbolic sentence appears.

6. Below are four lists of symbolic sentences. For each list, construct a finished tree using the sentences on the list as the tree's initial sentences. (A caution for those who may have been reading ahead: In this exercise, view the lists simply as lists, *not* as symbolic arguments.)

a. $-A$

(B $\lor$ C)

$(-A \rightarrow -B)$

$--(C \rightarrow A)$

b. $(-(A \lor B) \lor (C \leftrightarrow -D))$

$-(C \leftrightarrow -D)$

$(-(-A \, \& \, -B) \rightarrow C)$

c. $((A \rightarrow B) \, \& \, (B \rightarrow A))$

$(B \rightarrow (C \lor D))$

$(A \, \& \, -(C \lor D))$

d. $(A \leftrightarrow B)$

$-(-A \lor -B)$

$-(A \, \& \, -(B \, \& \, C))$

B. The Uses of Trees

At the outset of this appendix, we said that trees provide us with a way to test symbolic arguments for CL-validity. In this section, we explain how.

The test itself is simple. To apply it to a given symbolic argument of CL, we construct a tree whose initial sentences are the argument's premises and the *negation* of the argument's conclusion. If we find that all paths in the finished tree close, we can conclude that the symbolic argument is CL-valid. If one or more of the tree's paths stay open, we can conclude that the symbolic argument is CL-invalid. To apply the test, that's all one needs to know.

To understand why the test works, however, one needs to know this important fact:

1. A finished tree has an open path through it if and only if there is a valuation in which the tree's initial sentences all have the value *t* together.

As we have said, a tree for a given symbolic argument has as its initial sentences the argument's premises and the negation of the argument's conclusion. And, obviously, the negation of a conclusion has the value *t* just in case the conclusion itself has the value *f*. So, a tree for a symbolic argument has an open path through it just in case there is a valuation in which the argument's premises have the value *t* while its conclusion has the value *f*. But, according to the definition of CL-validity, there is such a valuation just in case the argument is CL-invalid. So, given sentence (1), we can derive this result: *A finished tree for a symbolic argument of CL has an open path through it just in case the symbolic argument is CL-invalid.*

But what *proof* is there that sentence (1) is true? In the remainder of this section, we will sketch an answer to this question.

In developing the answer, it will be useful to think of open paths as *describing* valuations. To find the valuation (or valuations) that an open path describes, we simply

a. assign the value *t* to each sentence letter that appears as a sentence in the path,

b.   assign the value *f* to each sentence letter whose negation appears as a sentence in the path, and

c.   assign whichever value we want to other sentence letters that may appear in the tree.

Clearly, every open path through a finished tree describes at least one valuation, and some describe more than one.

Consider, for example, this tree:

$$\checkmark(-(R \mathbin{\&} S) \rightarrow (-R \mathbin{\&} Q))$$
$$\checkmark -((R \mathbin{\&} S) \rightarrow P)$$
$$\checkmark(R \mathbin{\&} S)$$
$$-P$$
$$R$$
$$S$$

$\checkmark - -(R \mathbin{\&} S)$	$\checkmark(-R \mathbin{\&} Q)$
$\checkmark(R \mathbin{\&} S)$	$-R$
R	Q
S	$\otimes$

The only open path here runs from the top of the tree down the tree's left side to the sentence letter "S". To find the valuations that this path describes, we

a.   assign the value *t* to both "R" and "S", since both of these sentence letters appear as sentences in the path,

b.   assign the value *f* to "P", since "−P" appears as a sentence in the path, and

c.   assign either value we want to "Q", since neither "Q" nor "−Q" appears as a sentence in the path.

Our sample path therefore describes two valuations: one in which "R", "S", and "Q" have the value *t* while "P" has the value *f*, and one in which "R" and "S" have the value *t* while "P" and "Q" have the value *f*.

What values do the sentences in the path have in the valuations the open path describes? That "−P", "R", and "S" (the unchecked sentences in the path) have the value *t* in these valuations follows directly from the definition of *valuation described by an open path*. But what about the checked sentences in the path? What values do these more complex sentences have in the valuations that the open path describes?

We could, of course, calculate the values one by one, but we don't really need to do so. All of the sentences in the open path, including the tree's initial sentences, must have the value *t* in every valuation the path describes.

To see why, notice this about the tree system's nine rules of inference (T1 through T9):

> If we apply a rule to a symbolic sentence, and if all the sentences in one list of results have the value *t* in some valuation, then the symbolic sentence to which we applied the rule must also have the value *t* in that valuation.

We express this fact by saying that rules T1 through T9 *transmit the value t upward.*

When we apply rule T2 to a disjunction, for example, we get two lists of results: one consisting of the disjunction's left disjunct and one of its right disjunct. And a disjunction has the value *t* when either of its disjuncts has the value *t*. So, if we apply rule T2 to a symbolic sentence, and if all the sentences in one list of results have the value *t* in some valuation, the symbolic sentence to which we applied the rule must also have the value *t* in that valuation. In other words, rule T2 (like all the other rules of inference for the tree system) transmits the value *t* upward.

With this in mind, think once again about our sample tree:

$$\checkmark (-(R \mathrel{\&} S) \rightarrow (-R \mathrel{\&} Q))$$
$$\checkmark -((R \mathrel{\&} S) \rightarrow P)$$
$$\checkmark (R \mathrel{\&} S)$$
$$-P$$
$$R$$
$$S$$

$\checkmark --(R \mathrel{\&} S)$	$\checkmark (-R \mathrel{\&} Q)$
$\checkmark (R \mathrel{\&} S)$	$-R$
R	Q
S	$\otimes$

As we saw earlier in this section, the unchecked sentences in this tree's open path all have the value *t* in the valuations that the path describes. Having shown that our rules transmit the value *t* upward, we now know, in addition, that the sentences from which the unchecked sentences come must also have the value *t* in these valuations. (For example, since "R" and "S" both have the value *t* in the valuations the open path describes, so must "(R & S)".) And, since these more complex sentences have the value *t* in the valuations the open path describes, so must the sentences from which *they* came. [Since "(R & S)" has the value *t* in the valuations the open path describes, so must "−−(R & S)", and, since "−−(R & S)" has the value *t* in these valuations, so must the sentence "(−(R & S) → (−R & Q))".] Indeed, since all our rules transmit the value *t* upward, *every* sentence in the open path must have the value *t* in every valuation that the open path describes.

But a tree's initial sentences are in each of the tree's paths, and each open path describes at least one valuation. We may therefore conclude that

2.   If there is an open path through a finished tree, there is a valuation in which the tree's initial sentences all have the value *t* together.

That's why, when we find an open path through the finished tree for a symbolic argument of CL, we may infer that the argument is CL-invalid. (*Remember:* The initial sentences of a tree for a symbolic argument include the argument's premises and the *negation* of the argument's conclusion.)

It's also the case that

3.   If there is a valuation in which a tree's initial sentences all have the value *t* together, there is at least one open path through the finished tree.

But this statement is distinct from (2) (see Exercise Appendix B.8), and it therefore requires a proof of its own.

For this proof, the important fact about our rules of inference is this:

When we apply one of our tree system's rules of inference to a sentence that has the value *t* in a given valuation, then at least one list of results consists of sentences each of which has the value *t* in that valuation.

We express this fact by saying that the tree system's rules of inference *transmit the value t downward*.

Consider, for example, rule T3, which allows us to move from a conditional to two lists of results: one consisting of the negation of the conditional's antecedent, and the other consisting of the conditional's consequent. When a conditional has the value *t*, either its consequent has the value *t* or its antecedent has the value *f*. That is, when a conditional has the value *t*, either its consequent or the negation of its antecedent has the value *t*. Accordingly, when we apply rule T3 to a sentence that has the value *t* in a given valuation, we get at least one list of results that consists of sentences having the value *t* in that valuation. In other words, rule T3 (like all the other of the tree system's rules of inference) transmits the value *t* downward.

Keeping this fact in mind, suppose that you have before you a finished tree and that you have found a valuation—call it *v*—in which all of the tree's initial sentences have the value *t* together. Put your finger at the top of the tree and move it down the list of initial sentences. Clearly, all the sentences you have touched so far have the value *t* in valuation *v*.

If the tree goes on beyond this, it must go on to results obtained by applying a rule of inference to one of the sentences you have already touched. Maybe the tree branches at this point, and there is more than one list of results. Still, the tree's initial sentences all have the value *t* in valuation *v*, and the rules of inference all transmit the value *t* downward. So, it must be possible for you to move your finger down the tree to a list of results, each sentence of which also has the value *t* in *v*. Do so. Then repeat the process as long as you can. Eventually, you will come to the end of a path. You will have touched all the sentences in the path, and every sentence that you touched will have had the value *t* in valuation *v*.

The path you traced did not include a symbolic sentence and that sentence's negation; if it had, there could not have been a valuation *v* in which all the sentences in the path had the value *t* together. So, the path that you traced must be *open*. We can therefore conclude, as noted before, that

3. If there is a valuation in which the initial sentences of a finished tree all have the value *t* together, there is an open path through that tree.

That's why, when we find that all paths through the finished tree for a symbolic argument close, we can infer that the argument is CL-valid.

We now have sketched proofs of sentences (2) and (3). Together, these sentences entail that

1. There is an open path through a finished tree if and only if there is a valuation in which the tree's initial sentences have the value *t* together.

And this is exactly what we set out to prove earlier in the section. As we explained, it is the truth of (1) that ensures the reliability of the tree test for CL-validity.

Exercises Appendix B

1. *Defend or criticize:* The initial sentences of a tree for a symbolic argument are the argument's premises and its conclusion.

2. *Defend or criticize:* A symbolic argument is CL-valid just in case all paths of a tree for that argument close.

3. Using trees, test the following symbolic arguments for CL-validity:

a. $(-A \lor B)$
   $-(B \& C)$
   _____
   So, $(-C \rightarrow -A)$

b. $(A \& B)$
   $(-D \rightarrow (-A \& -C))$
   _____
   So, $(A \& D)$

c. $(A \lor (B \& C))$
   $(D \rightarrow -C)$
   $-(A \& B)$
   _____
   So, $(-D \lor -B)$

d. $(A \rightarrow (B \lor D))$
   $(-B \lor A)$
   $-(A \leftrightarrow D)$
   _____
   So, $(A \leftrightarrow B)$

e. $(A \rightarrow B)$
$(-C \rightarrow (D \rightarrow E))$
$(C \lor (A \lor D))$
$-C$
_____
So, $(B \lor E)$

f. $((A \& B) \rightarrow C)$
$-(A \rightarrow D)$
$(D \lor (-E \rightarrow -B))$
_____
So, C

4. As we said in this section, there is an open path through a finished tree if and only if there is a valuation in which the tree's initial sentences have the value *t* together. With this in mind, describe how trees might be used

   a. to tell whether a symbolic sentence of CL is a CL-contradiction,
   b. to tell whether a symbolic sentence of CL is a CL-tautology,
   c. to tell whether a symbolic sentence of CL is a CL-contingency,
   d. to tell whether two symbolic sentences of CL are CL-equivalent,
   e. to tell whether a set of symbolic sentences of CL is CL-consistent.

5. Construct a tree with the initial sentences

   $-A$
$(B \rightarrow A)$
$(C \lor B)$

Does the tree have an open path through it? If so, what valuations do the open paths describe? What are the values of the tree's initial sentences in the valuations that the open paths describe? (Check what you say here with a truth table.)

6. *Defend or criticize:* It would be impossible to invent a rule of inference that transmitted the value *t* upward but not downward, and it would be impossible to invent a rule of inference that transmitted the value *t* downward but not upward.

7. Consider the following rule of inference (which is *not* one of CL's):

   If a sentence is a disjunction, draw three downward branching lines. At the end of the first branch, list the disjunction's disjuncts; at the end of the second branch, list the disjunction's right disjunct and the negation of its left disjunct; and, at the end of the third branch, list the disjunction's left disjunct and the negation of its right disjunct.

Does this rule transmit the value *t* upward? Does it transmit the value *t* downward? If we were to use this rule instead of our rule T2, would trees still provide a reliable test for CL-validity? Why do you suppose we chose rule T2 for our system instead of this rule?

8. Consider the following two sentences:
   a. If there is an open path through a finished tree, there is a valuation in which the tree's initial sentences all have the value *t* together.

　　　　b. If there is a valuation in which the tree's initial sentences all have the
　　　　value *t* together, there is an open path through the tree.

Say which of these sentences is true of our tree system for CL. Now imagine a tree system exactly like CL's except that its rules allow us to close any path with a "Q" in it. Which of the sentences above would be true of this system? Next, imagine a tree system exactly like CL's except that it forbids our closing any path with a "Q" in it. Which of the above sentences is true of this system?

C. Trees for PL and RL

　　　　In the first two sections of this appendix, we developed a method for using trees in demonstrating CL-validity. Given a symbolic argument of CL, we can construct a tree whose initial sentences are the argument's premises and the negation of its conclusion. As we showed, all of the paths of the tree will close just in case the symbolic argument is CL-valid.

　　　　In this section, we add three rules of inference to our tree system, thereby changing CL's tree system into a system for the more sophisticated systems PL (Chapters 7 and 8) and RL (Chapter 9).

　　　　For our first example, let's take a symbolic argument of PL:

　　　　$([x](Ax \rightarrow Bx)$ & $[x]Dx)$
　　　　$[x]((Bx$ & $Dx) \rightarrow Cx)$

　　　　————————————

　　　　So, $[x](Ax \rightarrow Cx)$

How can we demonstrate this symbolic argument's PL-validity with a tree?

　　　　In outline, the method is the same as that described in the last section. That is, to demonstrate the symbolic argument's PL-validity, we construct a tree whose initial sentences are the symbolic argument's premises and the negation of the argument's conclusion. Since all paths in our tree will close, the tree will demonstrate the symbolic argument's PL-validity.

　　　　As you might guess, the beginning of the tree looks like this:

　　　　$\checkmark([x](Ax \rightarrow Bx)$ & $[x]Dx)$
　　　　　　$[x]((Bx$ & $Dx) \rightarrow Cx)$
　　　　　　　$-[x](Ax \rightarrow Cx)$
　　　　　　　$[x](Ax \rightarrow Bx)$
　　　　　　　　$[x]Dx$

The first two sentences in this tree (counting from the top) are the sample argument's premises, the third is the negation of the argument's conclusion, and the next two are results we got by applying rule T1 (the rule for conjunctions) to the tree's first sentence.

At this point in the tree's construction, we face a problem. While rules T1 through T9 tell us what to do with conjunctions, disjunctions, and the like, they do *not* tell us what to do with universally quantified sentences (symbolic sentences whose very first marks are universal quantifiers), existentially quantified sentences (symbolic sentences whose very first marks are existential quantifiers), or the negations of quantified sentences. To deal with symbolic sentences of these sorts, we need new rules of inference.

The rule we apply to the negations of quantified sentences is this:

> T10:   If a path of a tree contains a symbolic sentence whose first two expressions are a dash and a universal quantifier (in that order), we can replace those expressions with an existential quantifier and a dash (in that order) and write the result at the end of every open path in which the symbolic sentence appears. Similarly, if a path in a tree contains a symbolic sentence whose first two expressions are a dash and an existential quantifier (in that order), we can replace those expressions with a universal quantifier and a dash (in that order) and write the result at the end of every open path in which the symbolic sentence appears.

This rule allows us to move from the negations of quantified sentences to sentences whose very first expressions are quantifiers. So, for example, the first part of the rule allows us to move from "— [x]Fx" to "[∃x] — Fx", and the second part allows us to move from "— [∃x]Fx" to "[x] — Fx".

(Rule T10 closely resembles the Rule of Quantifier Exchange (QE), which we discuss at length in Chapter 8. For a more complete explanation of T10, readers should read our explanation of that rule in Section 8.4.)

Applying rule T10 to the third sentence in our sample tree, we can continue the tree:

$$✓([x](Ax → Bx) \ \& \ [x]Dx)$$
$$[x]((Bx \ \& \ Dx) → Cx)$$
$$✓ - [x](Ax → Cx)$$
$$[x](Ax → Bx)$$
$$[x]Dx$$
$$[∃x] - (Ax → Cx)$$

Now all of the unchecked sentences in the tree begin with an existential or a universal quantifier.

If we could somehow strip the quantifiers from these unchecked sentences (and get rid of the variables), we might be able to finish the tree using the old rules T1 through T9. And, indeed, our tree system *will* have two rules for stripping quantifiers from the beginnings of sentences.

Central to the statement of both these rules is the idea of instantiation:

> A wff is an *instantiation* of a universally or existentially quantified sentence just in case we can produce that wff by erasing the quantified sentence's initial mark (which will be either a universal or an existential quantifier), choosing a constant, and substituting the constant for all free occurrences of the variable in the remaining wff.

On this definition, "(Fa ↔ Ga)" and "(Fb ↔ Gb)" are both instantiations of the universally quantified sentence "[x](Fx ↔ Gx)", while "(Fa ↔ Gb)", "(Fx ↔ Ga)", and "(Fx ↔ Gx)" are not. (For practice with the idea of instantiation, see Exercise 8.4.2.)

Using the idea of instantiation, we can state the rule for applying to existentially quantified sentences:

> T11:   If a sentence whose very first expression is an existential quantifier appears in a tree, we may write any instantiation of that sentence as a subsequent line of the tree—*provided that* the constant with which we replace the variable(s) has not previously appeared anywhere in the tree.

This rule would allow us to write down "(Fa ∨ Ga)", for example, if "[∃x](Fx ∨ Gx)" appears unchecked in a tree—provided, of course, that the constant "a" has not yet appeared anywhere in the tree.

(Rule T11 closely resembles the Rule of Existential Instantiation (EI), which we discuss at length in Chapter 8. For a more complete explanation of T11, readers should turn to Section 8.4.)

We can use rule T11 to continue our sample tree:

$$✓([x](Ax \rightarrow Bx) \mathrel{\&} [x]Dx)$$
$$[x]((Bx \mathrel{\&} Dx) \rightarrow Cx)$$
$$✓ - [x](Ax \rightarrow Cx)$$
$$[x](Ax \rightarrow Bx)$$
$$[x]Dx$$
$$✓[∃x] - (Ax \rightarrow Cx)$$
$$✓ - (Aa \rightarrow Ca)$$
$$Aa$$
$$-Ca$$

Here we have simply applied T11 to "[∃x] − (Ax → Cx)" and T7—the rule for negations of conditionals—to the result.

To complete the tree, we need only one more rule — a rule that we can apply to sentences whose very first mark is a universal quantifier:

> T12: If a universally quantified sentence appears in a tree, we may write any instantiation of that sentence at the end of any path in which the sentence occurs.

As rule T11 allows us to move from existentially quantified sentences to their instantiations, rule T12 allows us to move from universally quantified sentences to *their* instantiations. But there are two important differences between these rules. First, while we must choose a constant new to the tree when applying T11, we can choose *any constant we want* when applying T12. Second, while we check a sentence after applying T11 to it, we *do not* check a sentence after applying T11. This means that, if we want, we can apply T12 to the same sentence over and over again, instantiating with a different constant each time. Indeed, to complete some trees for symbolic arguments of RL, we will *need* to apply T12 to a sentence several times.

(Rule T12 closely resembles a rule discussed in Chapter 8: the Rule of Universal Instantiation (UI). For a more complete explanation of T12, see Section 8.4.)

Using T12, we can complete our sample tree:

$$\checkmark ([x] (Ax \rightarrow Bx) \,\&\, [x]Dx)$$
$$[x] ((Bx \,\&\, Dx) \rightarrow Cx)$$
$$\checkmark - [x] (Ax \rightarrow Cx)$$
$$[x] (Ax \rightarrow Bx)$$
$$[x]Dx$$
$$\checkmark [\exists x] - (Ax \rightarrow Cx)$$
$$\checkmark - (Aa \rightarrow Ca)$$
$$Aa$$
$$-Ca$$
$$\checkmark (Aa \rightarrow Ba)$$

The pattern here is a common one. Having used rule T10 (together with the old rules) to produce sentences whose first marks are quantifiers, we stripped off the quantifiers using T11 and T12. Then, treating singular symbolic sentences (such as "Aa" and "Ba") just like sentence letters, we completed the tree using the rules from CL's tree system, T1 through T9.

Notice that, when constructing the sample tree, we used T11 (the rule for existentially quantified sentences) *before* T12 (the rule for universally quantified sentences). We still would have been able to complete the tree if we had used T12 before T11, but it would have been longer and more complex. When given the choice of applying T11 to one sentence or T12 to another, it's generally a good idea to use T11 first.

Since all the paths in the sample tree closed, the tree shows that the sample symbolic argument is PL-valid. Indeed, whenever all paths in a symbolic argument's tree close, the tree shows that the argument is PL-valid. (The proof of this, however, would take us far beyond the scope of this appendix.)

If we work on a tree for a symbolic argument and find that one or more of its paths stay open, can we conclude that the argument is PL-invalid? No. For a variety of reasons, demonstrating PL-invalidity with trees is much trickier than demonstrating CL-invalidity. So, in general, if we work on a tree for a symbolic argument of PL and find that one or more of its paths stay open, we do not conclude anything at all about the argument's PL-validity or PL-invalidity.

The tree system for the system RL is just like that for PL. Given a symbolic argument of RL, we construct a tree for it using the rules we now have (T1 through T12). If one or more of the paths in the tree stay open, the tree shows nothing at all about the given argument's RL-validity or RL-invalidity. On the other hand, if all paths in the tree close, the tree shows that the argument is RL-valid.

Consider, for example, the symbolic argument

[∃x][y]Rxy

So, [y][∃x]Rxy

A tree for this argument of RL might start off like this:

[∃x][y]Rxy
✓ − [y][∃x]Rxy
[∃y] − [∃x]Rxy
✓ − [∃x]Rxa
[x] − Rxa

We begin the tree, of course, by listing the sample argument's premise and the negation its conclusion. Then we apply T10 to the negation of the argument's conclusion, T11 to the result "[∃y] − [∃x]Rxy", and T10 to the result "−[∃x]Rxa".

Having reached this point in the tree, we can either apply rule T12 to "[x] − Rxa" or apply rule T11 to "[∃x][y]Rxy", the tree's very first sentence. As we said earlier, it's generally best to use T11 before T12. And, applying the rules in that order, we can easily finish the sample tree:

✓[∃x][y]Rxy
✓ − [y][∃x]Rxy
✓[∃y] − [∃x]Rxy
✓ − [∃x]Rxa
[x] − Rxa
[y]Rby
Rba
−Rba
⊗

Since "−Rba" is the negation of "Rba", the tree's one and only path has closed. And, since all the tree's paths have closed, we can be sure that the sample argument is RL-valid.

Exercises Appendix C

1. Find the errors, if any, in the following attempts at tree construction. Don't stop after you have found one error in a tree; there may be more. (In each case, the first three symbolic sentences in the tree are its initial sentences.)

a.　　　✓ [x] [∃y] Rxy
　　✓([x]−Rxx ∨ −[∃z]Gz)
　　　　　Gb
　　　　／‾‾‾‾‾＼
[x]−Rxx　　　✓ −[∃z]Gz
[x]Rxa　　　　−Gb
Raa
−Raa
⊗

b. ✓ ([∃ x]Fx → [x] (Fx → Gxa))
           ✓ [∃x]Fx
        ✓ −[∃x]Gxx

−[∃x]Fx   ✓ [x](Fx → Gxa)
[x]−Fx   Fa
  ⊗   ✓ (Fa → Gaa)

           −Fa   Gaa
            ⊗   [x]−Gxx
                     −Gaa
                     ⊗

c. [x] [y] [z] ((−Rxy & −Ryz) → Rxz)
          [x]Rxx
     ✓ −[x] [y] (Rxy → −Ryx)
     ✓ [∃x] −[y] (Rxy → −Ryx)
      ✓ −[y] (Ray → −Rya)
      ✓ [∃ y]−(Ray → −Rya)
       ✓ −(Rab → −Rba)
         −Rab
         −Rba
  [y] [z] ((−Ray & −Ryz) → Raz)
   [z] ((−Rab & −Rbz) → Raz)
   ✓ ((−Rab & −Rba) → Rab)

✓ −(−Rab & −Rba)   Rab
−−Rab   −−Rba   ⊗
 ⊗   ⊗

2. In Exercise 9.5.4, we presented nineteen symbolic arguments of RL. Using trees, demonstrate the validity of each of these symbolic arguments.

Solutions to Selected Exercises

 Chapter 1

Exercises 1.1

1. This is correct, except that the word *argument* has been misspelled. Because the word *argue* ends with an *e*, people often mistakenly write *arguement*. Why not take this opportunity to fix the right spelling in your mind?

2.b The premises of this argument are that *all mice are animals,* that *all animals die,* and that *Herman is a mouse.* The conclusion is that *Herman will die.*

2.d The argument's conclusion, which is expressed by the passage's first two sentences, is that *Watergate demonstrated the value of the American political system.* One of the argument's premises seems to be that *blame for the Watergate incident should fall on individuals rather than on the system,* and another seems to be that *the system brought the facts to light and will bring the guilty to justice.* Other premises, if any, are difficult to detect.

3. Yes. Every sentence of an argument is either a premise or a conclusion, and every argument has exactly one conclusion.

5. No. An argument can have any number of premises.

7. No. The reasoning of an argument leads *from* the premises *to* the conclusion, not the other way around.

Exercises 1.2

1. Suppose two people discuss their disagreement about who is the best candidate for president. The *dispute* is the interaction in which the people are engaged, while the *arguments* are the lines of reasoning the people in the dispute use to persuade one another.

3. Yes. In typical cases, an arguer's audience accepts the argument's premises from the outset. The arguer tries to show the audience that, *because* they accept the argument's premises, they should accept its conclusion, too.

4.b Yes. The word *so* marks the conclusion.

4.d No. This passage contains a *description* of practices at Willowberry School, not an argument.

4.f No. This passage contains a description, an offer, and a request — but no argument.

5. The conclusion is that *the balloons burst*. The premises are that *John brought the balloons from the house to the garage,* that *the house was warmer than the garage,* that *air expands when moved from a cooler to a warmer place,* and that *when the air in balloons expands, the balloons burst.*

7. For several purposes. Perhaps the most common is to *deceive* — to persuade others of what the arguers believe to be false.

Exercises 1.3

1.   Gerry missed class this morning.

     Gerry never misses class unless he is sick.

     _____

     So, Gerry is sick today.

3. This passage does not contain an argument.

5.   Tom is an idiot or he doesn't care.

     Tom does care.

     _____

     So, Tom is a fool.

7.   Many conversations in the White House are about the weak spots in our nation's defense.

     Conversations about the weak spots in our nation's defense should not be made public.

     _____

     So, some of what is said in the White House should be kept secret.

Exercises 1.4

1.a Yes. There are arguments in all four groups.

1.c There are valid arguments in groups (1), (3), and (4), but there are no valid arguments in group (2).

1.e All sound arguments are in group (1).

3. Yes. This follows directly from the definition of soundness.

5. No. The following argument has a false premise and so is unsound:

> If San Francisco is in Oregon then it is in the United States.
>
> San Francisco is not in the United States.
> _____
>
> So, San Francisco is not in Oregon.

But it has a true conclusion.

7. No. The following valid argument has a false premise but a true conclusion:

> San Francisco is a city in Russia.
> _____
>
> So, San Francisco is a city.

9. No. Both premises of the following invalid argument are true:

> Cleveland either is in Ohio or in Utah.
>
> Cleveland is in Ohio.
> _____
>
> So, Cleveland is in Utah.

11. Not quite. If an argument is sound, it is valid, and its premises therefore *imply* its conclusion. *Inferring* is something done by the people to whom the argument is presented. An arguer (or an arguer's premises) *implies*; an audience *infers*.

Exercises 1.5

1.a Yes. We can imagine what it would be like for Young to be a registered resident of Maryland.

1.c Yes. While we all know that there is no such man, we can imagine what it would be like for there to be one.

3. Yes. An argument is valid just in case there is *no* logically possible situation in which its premises are true while its conclusion is false. So, an argument is *in*valid just in case there *is* such a situation.

5.   Yes. If an argument's conclusion is true in every logically possible situation in which its premises are true, there is no logically possible situation in which its premises are true while its conclusion is false and, hence, the argument is valid. On the other hand, if an argument is valid, there is no logically possible situation in which its premises are true while its conclusion is false. So, its conclusion is true in every possible situation in which its premises are true.

7.   No. Consider the argument "Some dogs are brown; so, some pizzas have pepperoni on them." We can easily imagine a situation in which the argument's premise and conclusion are both true — the real world is such a situation. Yet the argument is *in*valid, since we can imagine a situation in which its premise is true while its conclusion is false.

9.a   Imagine a situation in which Miller is a tall, wise woman.

9.c   Imagine a situation in which Young is a resident of California, but not of Maryland or Ohio.

Chapter 2

Exercises 2.1

1.a   The conclusion is that *Alice is smarter than anyone I know.*

1.c   The conclusion is that *if you can block Nick Buoniconti, you can beat the Dolphins.*

1.e   The conclusion is that *it's not the case that, to save money, we should eat more fish.*

1.g   The conclusion is that *we should regulate pornography.*

Exercises 2.2

1.   All sound arguments have true conclusions, but Brutus's and Antony's conclusions can't both be true. So, at least one of the two arguments must be unsound. As we made these arguments explicit in the previous section, however, both are valid. It follows that one or the other must have a false premise. Since the arguments' stated premises are true, one of their *unstated* premises must be false. As we (the authors of this book) see it, Brutus's unstated premise — namely, that *Caesar would not have refused the crown with reluctance unless he were ambitious* — expresses a subtler understanding of human motives than Antony's unstated premise — namely, that *Caesar would not have refused the crown if he had been ambitious.* Accordingly, it's our view that, other things being equal, the crowd should have accepted Brutus's

unstated premise and, hence, Brutus's conclusion. Whether Caesar's being ambitious gave Brutus a good reason to kill him is, of course, another question.

3. No. On the contrary, if a premise is one that an arguer's audience regards as obvious, it may be an error to *state* it. The audience might wonder why the arguer had bothered to say something that obvious, and they might therefore be distracted from the arguer's main line of thought.

5. No. Sometimes, when making an argument explicit, we should identify premises that the arguer did not state. But, in these cases, we should think of the premises as already parts of the argument. After all, our aim in making arguments explicit is to reveal the arguments with which we have been presented, not to repair arguments or to make up arguments of our own.

7.a Marcia was an avid Lakers fan and supporter.

If Marcia was an avid Lakers fan and supporter, she hoped that the Lakers would make it to the play-offs.

So, Marcia hoped that the Lakers would make it to the play-offs.

7.c All dogs love Burger Munchies.

Spot is a dog.

So, Spot will love Burger Munchies.

Exercises 2.3

1. No. As we showed in the discussion of the newspaper column about Miami and Orlando, we are sometimes justified in saying that an argument has an unstated premise that the arguer is *not* taking for granted.

3. No. This was the point of our discussion of the police officer's argument at the end of the previous section. If an arguer's stated premises do not entail the conclusion, if the arguer is not relying on something that we can expect the audience to be taking for granted, and if there is no hint of an unstated premise in what the arguer actually said or wrote, we should *not* say that the argument rests on an unstated premise. Sometimes, when we can't be both faithful and charitable, we should be *faithful*.

5.a   Claremont Graduate School does not offer a Ph.D. in physics.
Malcolm's degree is a Ph.D.
Malcolm's degree is from Claremont Graduate School.

———————————————

So, Malcolm's degree is not in physics.

5.c   An American won the Nobel prize for literature last year.

If an American won the Nobel prize for literature last year, Norman Mailer won't win it this year.

———————————————

So, Norman Mailer won't win the Nobel prize for literature this year.

5.e   If you like the taste of gas, you'll hate the taste of Spark cigarettes.

You hate the taste of gas.

———————————————

So, you'll love the taste of Spark cigarettes.

This argument is invalid. Nonetheless, the arguer seems plainly to be relying on the audience's taking the second premise for granted.

6.b   People with beards don't look like real Americans.

People who don't look like real Americans shouldn't be allowed to vote.

———————————————

So, people with beards shouldn't be allowed to vote.

6.d   I'm only taking courses on things I'm interested in.
I'm only interested in things that teach me something new.
Logic doesn't teach me anything new.

———————————————

So, I'm not taking a course on logic.

6.e   There is no point to trying to save money by eating fish, unless fish is cheaper than meat.
Meat is cheaper than fish.

———————————————

So, there is no point trying to save money by eating fish.

6.g   We should do whatever we can to preserve our society.

Upholding moral standards will help preserve our society.

To regulate pornography and other similar activities of consenting adults is to uphold moral standards.

So, we should regulate the conduct of consenting adults.

Exercises 2.4

1.   No one under 35 can be president of the United States.

Jefferson became president in 1801, and he died in 1826.

So, Jefferson was more than 57 when he died.

The statement about the founding fathers is a side remark.

3.   The temperature in San Diego was over 100° yesterday.

If the temperature in San Diego was over 100° yesterday, people in San Diego were uncomfortable.

So, people in San Diego were uncomfortable.

The sentence about the *Times* is a supporting assertion whose function is to provide evidence for the truth of argument's first premise.

5.   One way to make the argument explicit is this:

There's no life on Mars.

If there is no life on Mars, there are no canals on Mars.

So, there are no canals on Mars.

And another way is this:

There is life on Mars only if its surface temperature is as warm as Earth's.

Mars's surface is cooler than Earth's.

If there is no life on Mars, there are no canals on Mars.

So, there are no canals on Mars.

On the first reading of the passage, the sentences about Mars's surface temperature are supporting assertions whose function is to demonstrate the truth of the premise that there is no life on Mars. On the second reading, the sentence "So, there is no life on Mars" is a connecting link.

7.   Of the several different ways to make the argument in this complex passage explicit, one is this:

> I cannot be faithful.
>
> If I cannot be faithful, I cannot stay married.
>
> If I cannot stay married, I cannot get married.
> _____
>
> So, I cannot get married.

On this reading of the passage, the statements about looking and thinking are supporting assertions whose function is to provide evidence for the argument's first premise.

Exercises 2.5

1.a   The other applicants for the job are going to withdraw.

> If the other applicants withdraw, I will be the only applicant.
>
> If I am the only applicant, I will get the job.
> _____
>
> So, I will get the job.

1.c   If the next card dealt to me is a face card, I'll win.

> The next card dealt to me will be a face card.
> _____
>
> So, I'm going to win.

1.e   If Al makes an effort, he'll do well in the course.

> Al will make an effort.
> _____
>
> So, Al will do well in the course.

Exercises 2.6

1.   Everyone who has just gotten a divorce is unhappy.

> Prof. Treadmill just got a divorce.
> _____
>
> So, Prof. Treadmill is unhappy.

3.   There is no argument in this passage.

5.   I could order anything, and I always order pizza when I can.
             It's not the case that I could order both pizza and steak.

             So, I ordered pizza.

Chapter 3

Exercises 3.1

1.   As we are using the term *clause,* strings (a), (d), (e), and (f) are clauses, and the others are not. Although strings (c) and (h) are grammatical sentences, they cannot be used to make *statements.*

3.a   Put the simple clauses *John comes to the party* and *Mary will be happy* into the blanks in the sentential operator "if . . . , then —".

3.c   Put the simple clauses *John will come to the party* and *Mary will be happy* into the blanks in the sentential operator ". . . , or else —".

3.e   Put the simple clauses *John will bring his wife to the party* and *he will come alone* into the blanks in the operator ". . . or —". Put the result into the first blank in the operator ". . . , and —" and the simple clause *he'll have a good time* into the second.

3.g   Put the simple clause *Bill was invited to the party* into the blank in the operator "it's not the case that . . . ". Put the result into the first blank in the operator "although . . . , —" and the simple clause *he refuses to stay home* into the second.

5.   It's not the case that golf is fun.
      It's not the case that skiing is expensive.
      If golf is fun, then golf is fun.
      If skiing is expensive, then skiing is expensive.
      If golf is fun, then skiing is expensive.
      If skiing is expensive, then golf is fun.
      If it's not the case that golf is fun, then skiing is expensive.
      If golf is fun, then it's not the case that skiing is expensive.
      If it's not the case that golf is fun, then it's not the case that skiing is expensive.
      If it's not the case that skiing is expensive, then it's not the case that golf is fun.

7.   No. Consider the argument "Either it's raining or it's snowing; it's not raining; so, it's snowing." This argument does not have the same content as the McCoy argument, but it *does* have the same form.

Exercises 3.2

1. No. Between making the argument explicit and replacing simple clauses with letters, there is another, very important step: expanding all abbreviations.

2.b Alice didn't go to the store.

2.d Larry bought the book, ran home, and read it.

3. Sentences (b), (c), (e), (f), and (g) contain abbreviations of complex clauses; the others do not. [Note the *il-* in sentence (e).]

5.a P just in case Q.

5.c P.

5.e If P, Q unless R.

5.g P.

6.b P unless it's not the case that Q.

   Q.
   _____

   So, P.

6.d P and Q, or (it's not the case that P) and (it's not the case that Q).

   Q just in case R.
   _____

   So, Q and P, if R.

Exercises 3.3

1. Yes. Since we demonstrated the validity of the Miller argument without mentioning its content, we can use the same reasoning to demonstrate the validity of any argument with the same sentential form. Hence, any argument with that form is valid (that is, the form is S-valid).

3. No. The McCoy argument is valid but not S-valid. The term *S-validity* applies to argument *forms,* not to particular arguments.

5. Yes. According to the definition of sentential validity, an argument has an S-*valid* sentential form just in case *every* argument of that form is valid. It follows that an argument has an S-*in*valid form just in case *some* argument of that form is invalid.

7. Yes. Suppose that we have found an argument with the form in question and that we can imagine a situation in which its premises are true while its conclusion is false. The fact that we can imagine this situation shows that the argument is invalid. And the fact that the argument is invalid shows that its sentential form is S-invalid.

8.b Consider the argument "Jones can run for president only if she's over 35; she's over 35; so, she can run for president." Imagine a situation just like the real world except that Jones is over 35, but she is not a native American. In this possible situation, the argument's premises are true (for only people over 35 can run for president, and Jones is over 35) while its conclusion is false (for only native Americans can run for President). It follows that the argument is invalid and, hence, that its sentential form is S-invalid.

8.d Consider the argument "Fido is a dog only if Fido is a mammal; Fido is a mammal only if Fido is an animal; so, Fido is a dog only if Fido is an animal." Imagine that Fido is a cat, not a dog. In this possible situation, the argument's premises are true while its conclusion is false. It follows that the argument is invalid and, hence, that its sentential form is S-invalid.

8.f Consider the argument "The cookies are good only if they are sweet; the cookies are sweet only if they have sugar in them; so, the cookies are good if they have sugar in them." Imagine a situation in which (i) the cookies have to be sweet to be good, (ii) they have to have sugar in them to be sweet, (iii) they do have sugar in them, but (iv) they have been burned and are inedible. In this possible situation, the argument's premises are true while its conclusion is false. It follows that the argument is invalid and, hence, that its sentential form is S-invalid.

8.h Consider the argument "It's not the case that the flag is both red and green; so, it's not the case that the flag is red or green." Imagine a situation in which the flag is red but not green. In this possible situation, the argument's premises are true while its conclusion is false. It follows that the argument is invalid and, hence, that its sentential form is S-invalid.

Exercises 3.4

1. Yes. If a given argument has an S-valid form, then every argument of that form — including the given argument — is valid.

2.b This argument has the S-valid form *modus ponens*, and it is therefore valid.

2.d This argument has the S-valid form *modus tollens*, and it is therefore valid.

2.f This argument has the S-valid form of the disjunctive syllogism, and it is therefore valid.

2.h This argument has the S-valid form of the constructive dilemma, and it is therefore valid.

3.a   See the answer to Exercise 3.3.8.b

5.   If one takes an S-valid sentential form containing the operator "if, then" and replaces the "if, then" with "only if" (leaving everything else the same) the result is always an S-valid form. Similarly, if one takes an S-valid form containing the operator "or" and replaces the "or" with "unless" (leaving everything else the same) the result is always an S-valid form.

6.b   This S-invalid form resembles the fallacy of denying the antecedent.

6.d   This S-valid form resembles *modus ponens.*

6.f   This S-valid form resembles *modus ponens.*

Chapter 4

Exercises 4.1

1.   Yes. Monopoly is a simplified representation of the business of real estate: As people buy property with money and get deeds, Monopoly players play-buy play-property with play-money and get pieces of paper that look like deeds.

3.   Yes. Since the idea of S-validity has to do with the validity of arguments, and since validity is defined in terms of the *values* of sentences in possible situations, the idea of S-validity is a semantic idea. In contrast, since the idea of sentential form has to do with the ways that sentences are built up from smaller parts, it is a syntactic idea.

5.   This code is a model of English since it can be viewed as a system governed by rules of vocabulary, formation, and valuation. Here is the code's rule of vocabulary:

> E1:   The expressions of the code are coughs, sneezes, and claps.

Here are its rules of formation:

> F1:   A cough is a wff by itself.
>
> F2:   A sneeze is a wff by itself.
>
> F3:   A clap followed by a cough is a wff.
>
> F4:   A clap followed by a sneeze is a wff.

Finally, here are its rules of valuation:

> V1:   A wff consisting of just a cough is true when and only when it's raining.

V2: A wff consisting of just a sneeze is true when and only when it's snowing.

V3: A wff consisting of a clap followed by a cough is true when and only when it's not raining.

V4: A wff consisting of a clap followed by a sneeze is true when and only when it's not snowing.

Exercises 4.2

1. There are an infinite number of symbolic sentences of CL that don't contain any expressions but the sentence letter "P" and the dash: "P", "−P", "−−P", "−−−P", and so on. But there is only one symbolic sentence of CL (namely, "P") that does not contain any expressions but "P" and the vel—for, according to rule F4, every sentence that contains a vel also contains two parentheses.

2.b This sentence letter is a symbolic sentence as it stands (rule F1).

2.d This string isn't a symbolic sentence. Since it does not contain an ampersand, vel, arrow, or double arrow, rules F3, F4, F5, and F6 have not been used in its formation. So, if it were a symbolic sentence, it would not contain any parentheses.

2.f Since "P" is a symbolic sentence (rule F1), so is "−P" (rule F2). And, since "−P" and "Q" are both sentences, so is "(−P & Q)".

2.h A symbolic sentence containing two vels and an ampersand must contain three pairs of parentheses, but this string contains just two.

2.j A symbolic sentence containing a double arrow, a vel, and an arrow must contain three pairs of parentheses, but this string contains just two.

2.l Since "R" and "P" are both symbolic sentences, so is "(R ∨ P)". Since "Q" and "(R ∨ P)" are both symbolic sentences, so is "(Q → (R ∨ P))". And, since "P" and "(Q → (R ∨ P))" are both symbolic sentences, so is "(P ↔ (Q → (R ∨ P)))".

2.n Neither the string "(P ∨ Q)P" nor the string "Q(P ∨ Q)" is a symbolic sentence. So, when we flank an ampersand with these strings and enclose the whole in parentheses, the result is not a symbolic sentence.

2.p If a symbolic sentence contains any parentheses at all, it contains an even number—one left parenthesis for each right parenthesis. But this string contains five parentheses.

3.a This is the negation of a negation.

3.c This is a conjunction.

3.e   This is a conditional.

3.g   This is a biconditional.

3.i   This is the negation of a conjunction.

4.b $-(P \rightarrow Q)$

4.d $((P \mathbin{\&} Q) \mathbin{\&} (-P \mathbin{\&} -Q))$

5.   Yes. To say that a sentence is a conditional is just to say that the last rule used in its construction was F5. Hence, to say that a sentence is a conditional is to describe how it has been put together in accordance with rules of vocabulary and formation.

7.   Yes. When we have identified a symbolic sentence's principal operator, we know where the sentence falls in our eleven-way grouping. And to know where a sentence falls in this grouping is to know its basic form.

Exercises 4.3

1.   In the given valuation, sentences (a), (c), and (e) all have the value *t*.

3.   Yes. For a conjunction to have the value *t*, both of its conjuncts must have the value *t* (rule V3).

5.   No. The other disjunct might have the value *t*, in which case the whole disjunction would have the value *t* (rule V4).

7.   Yes. A conditional has the value *t* whenever its antecedent has the value *f*.

Exercises 4.4

1.   If a symbolic sentence consists of two sentences flanking a "|" (downstroke), that sentence has the value *t* when and only when both the sentences flanking the "|" have the value *f*. If a symbolic sentence consists of two sentences flanking a "↓" (down-arrow), that sentence has the value *t* when and only when at least one of the sentences flanking the "↓" has the value *f*.

3.   Yes. A column in a table has one value on each of the table's lines.

5.a

P	Q	$-$P	$(-P \vee Q)$	$(P \vee (-P \vee Q))$
t	*t*	*f*	*t*	*t*
t	*f*	*f*	*f*	*t*
f	*t*	*t*	*t*	*t*
f	*f*	*t*	*t*	*t*

5.c

P	Q	$(((P \rightarrow Q) \rightarrow Q) \rightarrow Q)$
t	t	t
t	f	f
f	t	t
f	f	t

5.e

P	Q	R	$(P \& -P)$	$(Q \& -R)$	$((P \& -P) \rightarrow (Q \& -R))$
t	t	t	f	f	t
t	t	f	f	t	t
t	f	t	f	f	t
t	f	f	f	f	t
f	t	t	f	f	t
f	t	f	f	t	t
f	f	t	f	f	t
f	f	f	f	f	t

5.g

P	Q	R	$((Q \vee R) \rightarrow -P)$	$(P \& ((Q \vee R) \rightarrow -P))$
t	t	t	f	f
t	t	f	f	f
t	f	t	f	f
t	f	f	t	t
f	t	t	t	f
f	t	f	t	f
f	f	t	t	f
f	f	f	t	f

5.i

P	Q	R	$((P \vee (Q \leftrightarrow R)) \rightarrow -(R \& P))$
t	t	t	f
t	t	f	t
t	f	t	f
t	f	f	t
f	t	t	t
f	t	f	t
f	f	t	t
f	f	f	t

Exercises 4.5

1. Yes. Since a CL-tautology has the value *t* in every valuation for it, its negation has the value *f* in every valuation for it and is therefore a CL-contradiction. Conversely, since a CL-contradiction has the value *f* in every valuation for it, its negation is a CL-tautology. Finally, since a CL-contingency has the value *t* in at least one valuation and the value *f* in at least one valuation, its negation has the value *f* in at least one valuation and the value *t* in at least one valuation and is therefore a CL-contingency.

3. No. The symbolic sentence "(P & −P)" is a CL-contradiction, but it is not the negation of anything.

4.b The symbolic sentence "(P & Q)" is CL-equivalent to the sentence "((P ∨ Q) & (P ↔ Q))".

4.d

P	Q	(P ∨ Q)	−(−P & −Q)	(P & Q)	−(−P ∨ −Q)
t	*t*	*t*	*t*	*t*	*t*
t	*f*	*t*	*t*	*f*	*f*
f	*t*	*t*	*t*	*f*	*f*
f	*f*	*f*	*f*	*f*	*f*

6.b

P	Q	(P ∨ Q)
t	*t*	*t*
t	*f*	*t*
f	*t*	*t*
f	*f*	*f*

Since all three of the sentences in the set have the value *t* on the first line of the table, the set is CL-consistent.

7. No. Consider the set containing the sentences "P", "−Q", and "(P → Q)". Although each sentence in the set is a CL-contingency, there is no valuation in which they have the value *t* together, and the set is therefore CL-inconsistent.

Exercises 4.6

1. Yes. There cannot be a counterexample to a valid argument, since a counterexample to an argument is a valuation in which its premises have the value *t* while its conclusion has the value *f*.

3. It doesn't make sense to say of a symbolic argument that it is CL-valid in some valuations but CL-invalid in others. If there is *any* valuation in which its premises have the value *t* while its conclusion has the value *f*, the argument is CL-invalid, and that's all there is to it. There is such a valuation for the sample argument, and the argument is therefore CL-invalid.

4.b

P	Q	R	−P	(P → (Q ∨ R))
t	*t*	*t*	*f*	*t*
t	*t*	*f*	*f*	*t*
t	*f*	*t*	*f*	*t*
t	*f*	*f*	*f*	*f*
f	*t*	*t*	*t*	*t*
f	*t*	*f*	*t*	*t*
f	*f*	*t*	*t*	*t*
f	*f*	*f*	*t*	*t*

The table shows that the argument is CL-valid. There is only one line on which the conclusion has the value *f* and, on that line, the premise has the value *f*.

4.d

P	Q	R	(P → −(Q → R))	−Q	(−P → R)
t	*t*	*t*	*f*	*f*	*t*
t	*t*	*f*	*t*	*f*	*t*
t	*f*	*t*	*f*	*t*	*t*
t	*f*	*f*	*f*	*t*	*t*
f	*t*	*t*	*t*	*f*	*t*
f	*t*	*f*	*t*	*f*	*f*
f	*f*	*t*	*t*	*t*	*t*
f	*f*	*f*	*t*	*t*	*f*

The table shows that the argument is CL-valid.

4.f

P	Q	−(P → Q)	(P ↔ Q)	(Q & −Q)
t	*t*	*f*	*t*	*f*
t	*f*	*t*	*f*	*f*
f	*t*	*f*	*f*	*f*
f	*f*	*f*	*t*	*f*

As the table shows, the argument's premises are inconsistent; there is no line on which both have the value *t*. Hence—even though the argument's conclusion is a CL-contradiction—there is no counter-example to the argument and it is CL-valid.

5.   Yes. If the conclusion of a symbolic argument is a CL-tautology, there is no valuation in which it has the value *f*. Accordingly, there is no counterexample to the argument, and it is therefore CL-valid.

7.   Yes. If the argument is CL-valid, there is no valuation in which the conjunction of its premises has the value *t* while its conclusion has the value *f* and, hence, the conditional mentioned in the problem is a CL-tautology (rule V5). On the other hand, if this conditional is a CL-tautology, there is no valuation in which the conjunction of the argument's premises has the value *t* while its conclusion has the value *f* and, hence, the argument is CL-valid.

Exercises 4.7

1.a   False. 2 is a number, not a name.

1.c   True. "Two" is a name for the number 2.

1.e   False. "Two" is a name for the number 2, not for the name "2".

1.g   False. " "Two" " is the name of the name "Two", not the name of a number.

1.i   False. The name named by " "Two" " does name the same number as the name named by " "2" ", but " "two" " names one name for this number while " "2" " names another.

3.   Premise (2) should say that the numerator of "1/2" is "1", and conclusion (3) should say that the numerator of "2/4" is "2". It is numerals, not numbers, that have numerators and denominators.

Chapter 5

Exercises 5.1

1.   Yes. We *could* say that the value *t* corresponds to falsity and the value *f* to truth. But then we would have to abandon our conclusions about which of CL's symbolic operators corresponds to which sentential operator of English. For instance, if *t* corresponded to falsity rather than truth, the ampersand would not correspond semantically to "and".

3. No. The sentence "The radio is worthless because it's broken" is true only if the radio is both worthless and broken. But on the last line of the truth table for the biconditional "(P ↔ Q)", where "P" and "Q" both have the value *f*, the biconditional itself has the value *t*. So, "because" does not correspond to the double arrow. Of CL's operators, "because" corresponds most closely to the ampersand. But, as we have been viewing it, "because" typically serves, as does "since", to indicate one of an argument's premises.

5. No. In fact, the *syntax* of the arrow is exactly the same as that of the vel: When either appears in a symbolic sentence it is flanked by two other sentences. So, aside from the obvious difference in shape, the only difference between these two symbolic operators is semantic.

7. Yes. Choose any sound argument of the form

>   If *P*, then *Q*
>
>   *P*
>   ―――――
>   So, *Q*

Being sound, the argument has true premises and a true conclusion. So, its first premise must be a conditional whose antecedent and consequent are both true.

9. Yes. Consider an invalid argument of the form

>   If *P*, then *Q*
>
>   Not *P*
>   ―――――
>   So, not *Q*

Being invalid, the argument can have true premises and a false conclusion. If it does, its first premise is a conditional whose antecedent is false and whose consequent is true.

11. Yes. Both of the following sentential forms are S-valid:

> | *P* only if *Q* | *P* or *Q* |
> |---|---|
> | *Q* only if *R* | *P* only if *R* |
> | ――――――― | *Q* only if *R* |
> | So, *P* only if *R* | ――――――― |
> | | So, *R* |

Exercises 5.2

1.   No. While a scheme of correspondence associates sentence letters with simple clauses of English, the sentence letters do not become abbreviations of those clauses, since they do not take on the clauses' meanings. Being expressions of CL rather than of English, sentence letters don't really have meanings.

3.a   This sentence is not in Standard English, since it contains "not" rather than "it's not the case that".

3.c   This sentence is in Standard English, and it can be translated with "(A ∨ B)".

3.e   This sentence is in Standard English, and it can be translated with "(R ∨ (W & D))".

3.g   This sentence is in Standard English, and it can be translated with "(K → −L)".

3.i   This sentence is not in Standard English. The "if" isn't followed by a "then", and neither "otherwise" nor "n't" are operators of Standard English.

3.k   The operator ". . . if —" is not in Standard English.

Exercises 5.3

1.   No. Standard English has seven sentential operators. In addition to "it's not the case that", "and", "or", "if, then", and "if and only if", Standard English also has "unless" and "only if".

3.a   As odd as it may sound, this sentence can be paraphrased with "The patient will die, or we will operate", which translates as "(D ∨ O)".

3.c   This sentence can be paraphrased with "If it's not the case that we operate, then the patient will die", which translates as "(−O → D)".

3.e   This sentence can be paraphrased with "Tom is a politician, and Dick is a politician, and Harry is a politician", which we can translate with "(T & (D & H))" or with the CL-equivalent sentence "((T & D) & H))".

3.g   This sentence can be paraphrased with "Jack went up the hill and Jill went up the hill, and it's not the case that Mary's little lamb was far behind", which we can translate with "((J & I) & −L)".

3.i   This sentence can be paraphrased with "This woman is mad, or this woman is drunk", which translates as "(M ∨ D)".

3.k This sentence can be paraphrased with "Romance is the province of the rich, and it's not the case that romance is the profession of the unemployed", which we can translate with "(R & −U)".

3.m This sentence can be paraphrased with "Sunlight stimulates the mind, and sunlight cures diarrhea", which we can translate with "(M & D)".

3.o This sentence can be paraphrased with " 'And' has three letters in it, and 'or' has two letters in it", which we can translate with "(A & O)".

3.q This sentence can be paraphrased with "Tom keeps calling Mary, and Mary refuses to talk to Tom", which we can translate with "(T & M)".

3.s This sentence can be paraphrased with "If you have a copy of our new book, then you can save a lot of money on food", which we can translate with "(B → F)".

5. The sentence expands to "Jack went up the hill if Jill went up the hill, and Jack went up the hill only if Jill went up the hill", which paraphrases into Standard English as "If Jill went up the hill, then Jack went up the hill, *and* Jack went up the hill only if Jill went up the hill". We can translate this with "((K → L) & (L → K))"—a sentence CL-equivalent to "(K ↔ L)".

Exercises 5.4

1.a This sentence can be paraphrased with "If you stand on your head, then I'll punch you in the stomach", which translates as "(H → S)".

1.c This sentence can be paraphrased with "If you forget about the incident, then I will forget about the incident", which translates as "(Y → I)".

1.e This sentence can be paraphrased with "Truth is beauty, and beauty is truth", which translates as "(T & B)".

1.g This sentence can be paraphrased with "It's not the case that John will come to the party", which translates as "−J". The original sentence is not really about eating hats. The phrase "if . . . , I'll eat my hat" is a sentential operator that works, both syntactically and semantically, like "it's not the case that".

1.i This sentence can be paraphrased with "I think that I have enough money, and I'll take my Visa card", which translates as "(M & V)". The sentential operator "I think that" is intractable, and "just in case" does not here have its usual meaning.

1.k This sentence can be paraphrased with "If you stand on your head, then I'll punch you in the stomach" and translated as "(H → P)". The sentential operator "and" does not here have its usual meaning.

Exercises 5.5

1.   Yes. If an argument has a CL-valid translation, we may confidently infer that the argument has an S-valid form and, hence, that the argument is valid.

3.   No. Some arguments — such as "All dogs are brown; Spot is a dog; so, Spot is brown" — are valid even though they do not have CL-valid translations.

4.b   Under an obvious scheme of correspondence, the argument can be translated like this:

$(H \rightarrow N)$

$-N$

_____

So, $-H$

And the truth table for this symbolic argument is this:

H	N	$(H \rightarrow N)$	$-N$	$-H$
t	*t*	*t*	*f*	*f*
t	*f*	*f*	*t*	*f*
f	*t*	*t*	*f*	*t*
f	*f*	*t*	*t*	*t*

This table shows that the symbolic argument is CL-valid. We may infer that the original English argument has an S-valid sentential form and, hence, that it is valid.

4.d   Under an obvious scheme of correspondence, the argument can be translated like this:

$(N \& -H)$

$(-F \lor H)$

_____

So, $(H \lor F)$

And the truth table for this symbolic argument is this:

N	H	F	(N & −H)	(−F ∨ H)	(H ∨ F)
t	t	t	f	t	t
t	t	f	f	t	t
t	f	t	t	f	t
t	f	f	t	t	f
f	t	t	f	t	t
f	t	f	f	t	t
f	f	t	f	f	t
f	f	f	f	t	f

Since this table shows that the symbolic argument is CL-invalid, we may not infer anything about the validity of the original English argument or about the S-validity of its sentential form.

4.g   Under an obvious scheme of correspondence, the argument can be translated like this:

(N ∨ H)

(H → −F)
_____

So, (F → (H ↔ N))

And the truth table for this symbolic argument is this:

N	H	F	(N ∨ H)	(H → −F)	(F → (H ↔ N))
t	t	t	t	f	t
t	t	f	t	t	t
t	f	t	t	t	f
t	f	f	t	t	t
f	t	t	t	f	f
f	t	f	t	t	t
f	f	t	f	t	t
f	f	f	f	t	t

Since this table shows that the symbolic argument is CL-invalid, we may not infer anything about the validity of the original English argument or about the S-validity of its sentential form.

5.a   We can make the argument explicit like this:

> If it's raining, the ground is wet.
>
> It's raining.
>
> _____
>
> So, the ground is wet.

Paraphrasing into Standard English, we get

> If it's raining, then the ground is wet.
>
> It's raining.
>
> _____
>
> So, the ground is wet.

Translating into CL under an obvious scheme of correspondence, we get

> $(R \rightarrow W)$
>
> R
>
> _____
>
> So, W

The truth table for this argument is this:

R	W	$(R \rightarrow W)$
t	*t*	*t*
t	*f*	*f*
f	*t*	*t*
f	*f*	*t*

Since this table shows that the translation of the sample argument is CL-valid, we may infer that the original English argument has an S-valid form and, hence, that the argument is valid.

5.c   We can make the argument explicit and paraphrase it into Standard English like this:

> (It's not the case that Sara likes the pizza) unless (the pizza has pepperoni on it).
>
> It's not the case that the pizza has pepperoni on it.
>
> _____
>
> So, it's not the case that Sara likes the pizza.

Translating into CL under an obvious scheme of correspondence, we get

$(-L \lor P)$

$-P$

———————

So, $-L$

The truth table for this argument is this:

L	P	$-P$	$-L$	$(-L \lor P)$
t	*t*	*f*	*f*	*t*
t	*f*	*t*	*f*	*f*
f	*t*	*f*	*t*	*t*
f	*f*	*t*	*t*	*t*

Since this table shows that the translation of the sample argument is CL-valid, we may conclude that the original English argument has an S-valid form and, hence, that it is valid.

5.e We can make the argument explicit and paraphrase it into Standard English like this:

> You will stay up late or get up early, and it's not the case that (you will stay up late and you will get up early).
>
> You will stay up late.
>
> ————————————————————————
>
> So, it's not the case that you will get up early.

Translating into CL under an obvious scheme of correspondence, we get

$((E \lor L) \lor -(E \And L))$

L

———————

So, $-E$

The truth table for this argument is this:

E	L	$((E \lor L) \And -(E \And L))$	$-E$
t	*t*	*f*	*f*
t	*f*	*t*	*f*
f	*t*	*t*	*t*
f	*f*	*f*	*t*

Since this table shows that the translation of the sample argument is CL-valid, we may infer that the original English argument has an S-valid form and, hence, that it is valid.

5.g   We can make the argument explicit and paraphrase it into Standard English like this:

> If Mike goes to the party, then Mike will take Sara to the party, *and*, if Mike takes Sara to the party, then Mike will have a good time.
>
> ―――――――――――――――――――――――
>
> So, if Mike goes to the party, Mike will have a good time.

Translating into CL under an obvious scheme of correspondence, we get

$$((P \rightarrow S) \mathbin{\&} (S \rightarrow G))$$
―――――――――――――
So, $(P \rightarrow G)$

The truth table for this argument is this:

P	S	G	$((P \rightarrow S) \mathbin{\&} (S \rightarrow G))$	$(P \rightarrow G)$
t	*t*	*t*	*t*	*t*
t	*t*	*f*	*f*	*f*
t	*f*	*t*	*f*	*t*
t	*f*	*f*	*f*	*f*
f	*t*	*t*	*t*	*t*
f	*t*	*f*	*f*	*t*
f	*f*	*t*	*t*	*t*
f	*f*	*f*	*t*	*t*

Since this table shows that the translation of the sample argument is CL-valid, we may infer that the original English argument has an S-valid form and, hence, that it is valid.

5.i   We can make the argument explicit and paraphrase it into Standard English like this:

> Mr. Badmouth knew what was going on and Mr. Badmouth is a liar, or Mr. Badmouth is a fool.
>
> It's not the case that Mr. Badmouth is a fool.
>
> ―――――――――――――――――――――――
>
> So, Mr. Badmouth is a liar.

Translating into CL under an obvious scheme of correspondence, we get

((K & L) ∨ F)

−F

_____

So, L

The truth table for this argument is this:

K	L	F	((K & L) ∨ F)	−F
t	t	t	t	f
t	t	f	t	t
t	f	t	t	f
t	f	f	f	t
f	t	t	t	f
f	t	f	f	t
f	f	t	t	f
f	f	f	f	t

Since this table shows that the translation of the sample argument is CL-valid, we may infer that the original English argument has an S-valid form and, hence, that it is valid.

Chapter 6

Exercises 6.1

	N	R	A	(N → R)	−R	(A → N)	−A
1.	t	t	t	t	f	t	f
	t	t	f	t	f	t	t
	t	f	t	f	t	t	f
	t	f	f	f	t	t	t
	f	t	t	t	f	f	f
	f	t	f	t	f	t	t
	f	f	t	t	t	f	f
	f	f	f	t	t	t	t

Since the table shows that the argument's translation is CL-valid, we may infer that the argument has an S-valid sentential form and, hence, that it is valid.

3. No. An argument consists only of premises and a conclusion, but a derivation may contain connecting links.

5. No. Consider, for example, the following derivation:

   1. If the light was on, the door was open.
   2. The door was not open.
   3. So, the light was on.
   4. The light was on if the window was locked.
   5. So, the window was not locked.

Here sentences (1), (2), and (4) are the argument's premises, sentence (5) is its conclusion, and sentence (3) is a connecting link. The inference from (1) and (2) to (3) is invalid, and so is the inference from (3) and (4) to (5). Yet, as we could show with a truth table, conclusion (5) *does* follow from premises (1), (2), and (4). So, from the fact that there are invalid steps in the derivation, it does not follow that the argument itself is invalid.

7.a There is a derivation here. One of its inferences has the form of *modus ponens:*

> If the spring rains were heavy, the scrub grows tall.
>
> The spring rains were heavy.
>
> _____
>
> So, the scrub grows tall.

And the other inference has a form resembling *modus tollens:*

> The scrub grows tall.
>
> There are no mudslides when the scrub grows tall.
>
> _____
>
> So, there will be no mudslides.

7.c There is a derivation here. One inference has a form resembling *modus ponens:*

> If Sally has the day off, either she went to the beach or she went to the park.
>
> Sally does have the day off.
>
> _____
>
> So, either she went to the beach or she went to the park.

And the other inference in the derivation has the form of the constructive dilemma:

> Either she went to the beach or she went to the park.
>
> If she went to the beach, she's having a great time.
>
> If she went to the park, she's having a great time.
> _____
>
> So, she's having a great time.

8.b If the class is meeting, the teacher is present, and the class is meeting. So, the teacher is present [by *modus ponens*]. But, if the teacher is present, homework has been assigned. So, homework has been assigned [by *modus ponens*].

8.d If the party was loud, Mr. Murphy called the police unless it ended before 10:00 P.M. The party was loud. So, Mr. Murphy called the police unless it ended before 10:00 P.M. [by a form like *modus ponens*]. Since it didn't end before 10:00 P.M., Mr. Murphy called the police [disjunctive syllogism]. But it's not the case that both Mr. Murphy and Mrs. McNaughty called the police. Therefore, Mrs. McNaughty didn't call the police [conjunctive syllogism].

Exercises 6.2

1. No. The rule DNE applies only to the negations of negations — sentences whose *first* two marks are dashes. The symbolic sentence "(A & − −B)" is a conjunction.

3. Yes. As we showed in the previous section, if we can move from a symbolic argument's premises to its conclusion using our nine rules of inference, the argument is CL-valid.

5.a

1.	(A & (B & C))	Prem
2.	A	1 Simp
3.	(B & C)	1 Simp
4.	B	3 Simp
5.	C	3 Simp
6.	(A & B)	2,4 Conj
7.	((A & B) & C)	5,6 Conj

5.c

1.	−(A & B)	Prem
2.	(C ∨ A)	Prem
3.	−C	Prem

	4.	A	2,3 DS
	5.	−B	1,4 CS
5.e	1.	A	Prem
	2.	(−(A ∨ B) ∨ A)	1 Adj
	3.	((−(A ∨ B) ∨ A) ∨ C)	2 Adj
5.g	1.	−(−A ∨ B)	Prem
	2.	−((A ∨ C) & D)	Prem
	3.	(−(−D ∨ A) ∨ C)	Prem
	4.	−−A	1 DM
	5.	A	4 DNE
	6.	(A ∨ C)	5 Adj
	7.	−D	2,6 CS
	8.	(−D ∨ A)	7 Adj
	9.	−−(−D ∨ A)	8 DNI
	10.	C	9,3 DS
5.i	1.	A	Prem
	2.	−A	Prem
	3.	(A ∨ B)	1 Adj
	4.	B	2,3 DS

Exercises 6.3

1. Just about. MP corresponds to *modus ponens,* MT to *modus tollens,* CS to the conjunctive syllogism, DS to the disjunctive syllogism, HS to the hypothetical syllogism, and D to the form of the (constructive) dilemma. But none of CL's rules of inference corresponds to the destructive dilemma.

3. Yes. The proof, which is like that given at the end of the previous section, rests on the fact that every inference constructed in accordance with our rules of inference is CL-valid.

5.

A	B	−(A → B)	(A & −B)	(−A → B)	−(A ↔ B)	(−A ↔ B)
t	*t*	*f*	*f*	*t*	*f*	*f*
t	*f*	*t*	*t*	*t*	*t*	*t*
f	*t*	*f*	*f*	*t*	*t*	*t*
f	*f*	*f*	*f*	*f*	*f*	*f*

6.b
1. $((A \lor B) \to C)$ Prem
2. $(-B \leftrightarrow -C)$ Prem
3. $(A \lor D)$ Prem
4. $-D$ Prem
5. A   3,4 DS
6. $(A \lor B)$ 5 Adj
7. C   1,6 MP
8. $--C$ 7 DNI
9. $(-B \to -C)$ 2 BCE
10. $--B$ 8,9 MT
11. B   10 DNE

6.d
1. $(A \,\&\, (B \lor C))$ Prem
2. $(A \to (B \to -D))$ Prem
3. $(-(C \to -D) \to -A)$ Prem
4. A   1 Simp
5. $--A$ 4 DNI
6. $--(C \to -D)$ 5,3 MT
7. $(C \to -D)$ 6 DNE
8. $(B \to -D)$ 2,4 MP
9. $(B \lor C)$ 1 Simp
10. $-D$ 7,8,9 D

6.f
1. $(A \lor (B \lor C))$ Prem
2. $((A \to D) \,\&\, -D)$ Prem
3. $(-D \leftrightarrow -B)$ Prem
4. $-D$ 2 Simp
5. $(A \to D)$ 2 Simp
6. $-A$ 4,5 MT
7. $(B \lor C)$ 1,6 DS
8. $(-D \to -B)$ 3 BCE
9. $-B$ 4,8 MP
10. C   7,9 DS

6.h
1. $-(A \to B)$ Prem
2. $-(-C \to -D)$ Prem

3.	(A & −B)	1 ENC
4.	(−C & −−D)	2 ENC
5.	A	3 Simp
6.	−−D	4 Simp
7.	D	6 DNE
8.	(A & D)	5,7 Conj

6.j

1.	−(A ↔ −B)	Prem
2.	−(B ↔ −C)	Prem
3.	(−A ↔ −B)	1 ENB
4.	(−B ↔ −C)	3 ENB
5.	(−A → −B)	3 BCE
6.	(−B → −C)	4 BCE
7.	(−A → −C)	5,6 HS

Exercises 6.4

1. No. In this attempt to state the rule CD, the terms "consequent" and "antecedent" have been switched around.

3.a Line (3) cannot be cited in the annotation to line (5). When CD was used on line (4), a box should have been drawn around lines (2) and (3). And this box prevents the citation of line (3) in the annotation to line (5).

3.c Though correct as far as it goes, this derivation is not complete: The use of SuppCD on line (4) requires a corresponding use of CD later in the derivation.

4.b

1.	A	Prem
2.	(−A ∨ −B)	SuppCD
3.	−−A	1 DNI
4.	−B	2,3 DS
5.	(A & −B)	1,4 Conj
6.	((−A ∨ −B) → (A & −B))	2−5 CD

4.d

1.	(A → (B ∨ C))	Prem
2.	(−A → −D)	Prem

3.	D	SuppCD
4.	$-$B	SuppCD
5.	$--$D	3 DNI
6.	$--$A	2,5 MT
7.	A	6 DNE
8.	$(B \lor C)$	1,7 MP
9.	C	4,8 DS
10.	$(-B \rightarrow C)$	4–9 CD
11.	$(D \rightarrow (-B \rightarrow C))$	3–10 CD

4.f

1.	$(A \rightarrow (B \rightarrow C))$	Prem
2.	$((B \rightarrow C) \rightarrow (A \ \& \ D))$	Prem
3.	A	SuppCD
4.	$(B \rightarrow C)$	1,3 MP
5.	$(A \ \& \ D)$	2,4 MP
6.	D	5 Simp
7.	$(A \rightarrow D)$	3–6 CD

4.h

1.	$(A \leftrightarrow B)$	Prem
2.	$(A \rightarrow B)$	1 BCE
3.	$(B \rightarrow A)$	1 BCE
4.	$(A \leftrightarrow C)$	SuppCD
5.	$(A \rightarrow C)$	4 BCE
6.	$(B \rightarrow C)$	3,5 HS
7.	$(C \rightarrow A)$	4 BCE
8.	$(C \rightarrow B)$	7,2 HS
9.	$(B \leftrightarrow C)$	6,8 BCI
10.	$((A \leftrightarrow C) \leftrightarrow (B \leftrightarrow C))$	4–9 CD
11.	$(B \leftrightarrow C)$	SuppCD
12.	$(B \rightarrow C)$	11 BCE
13.	$(A \rightarrow C)$	2,12 HS
14.	$(C \rightarrow B)$	11 BCE
15.	$(C \rightarrow A)$	14,3 HS
16.	$(A \leftrightarrow C)$	13,15 BCI
17.	$((B \leftrightarrow C) \rightarrow (A \leftrightarrow C))$	11–16 CD
18.	$((A \leftrightarrow C) \leftrightarrow (B \leftrightarrow C))$	10,17 BCI

4.j

1.	(A → (B ∨ C))	Prem
2.	−(−(B → D) ∨ E)	Prem
3.	−(−(C → D) & −E)	Prem
4.	A	SuppCD
5.	(B ∨ C)	1,4 MP
6.	−E	2 DM
7.	−−(C → D)	3,6 CS
8.	(C → D)	7 DNE
9.	−−(B → D)	2 DM
10.	(B → D)	9 DNE
11.	D	5,8,10 D
12.	(A → D)	4–11 CD

5.a

1.	(L ↔ J)	Prem
2.	−L	SuppCD
3.	(J → L)	1 BCE
4.	−J	2,3 MT
5.	(−L → −J)	2–4 CD
6.	−J	SuppCD
7.	(L → J)	1 BCE
8.	−L	6,7 MT
9.	(−J → −L)	6–8 CD
10.	(−L ↔ −J)	5,9 BCI

6. Yes, it does; yes, it does.

Exercises 6.5

1. Yes. The only sentences that SuppID allows us to write are negations.

3. Yes. Let *S* be the set of symbolic sentences containing a symbolic argument's premises and the negation of its conclusion. The argument is CL-valid just in case there is no valuation in which its premises have the value *t* while its conclusion has the value *f*—or, in other words, just in case there is no valuation in which the sentences in *S* all have the value *t* together. So, the argument is CL-valid just in case the set *S* is CL-inconsistent.

5.   Yes. There is nothing in the rules to prevent conditional derivations and indirect derivations appearing together — provided, of course, that boxes don't overlap.

6.b   There is nothing wrong with this derivation.

6.d   There is nothing wrong with this derivation.

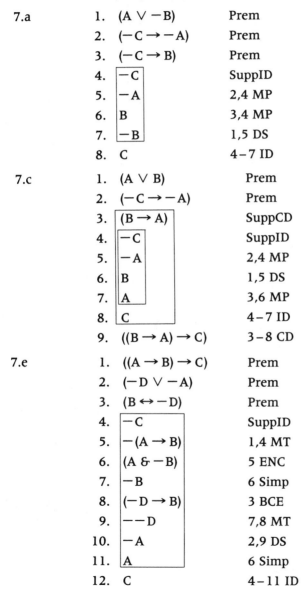

7.a

1.	$(A \lor -B)$	Prem
2.	$(-C \rightarrow -A)$	Prem
3.	$(-C \rightarrow B)$	Prem
4.	$-C$	SuppID
5.	$-A$	2,4 MP
6.	B	3,4 MP
7.	$-B$	1,5 DS
8.	C	4–7 ID

7.c

1.	$(A \lor B)$	Prem
2.	$(-C \rightarrow -A)$	Prem
3.	$(B \rightarrow A)$	SuppCD
4.	$-C$	SuppID
5.	$-A$	2,4 MP
6.	B	1,5 DS
7.	A	3,6 MP
8.	C	4–7 ID
9.	$((B \rightarrow A) \rightarrow C)$	3–8 CD

7.e

1.	$((A \rightarrow B) \rightarrow C)$	Prem
2.	$(-D \lor -A)$	Prem
3.	$(B \leftrightarrow -D)$	Prem
4.	$-C$	SuppID
5.	$-(A \rightarrow B)$	1,4 MT
6.	$(A \mathbin{\&} -B)$	5 ENC
7.	$-B$	6 Simp
8.	$(-D \rightarrow B)$	3 BCE
9.	$--D$	7,8 MT
10.	$-A$	2,9 DS
11.	A	6 Simp
12.	C	4–11 ID

7.g

1.	$((A \rightarrow B) \rightarrow C)$	Prem
2.	$(D \rightarrow (-B \rightarrow E))$	Prem
3.	$(C \vee -E)$	SuppCD
4.	D	SuppCD
5.	$-C$	SuppID
6.	$-E$	3,5 DS
7.	$-(A \rightarrow B)$	1,5 MT
8.	$(A \,\&\, -B)$	7 ENC
9.	$-B$	8 Simp
10.	$(-B \rightarrow E)$	4,2 MP
11.	E	9,10 MP
12.	C	5–11 ID
13.	$(D \rightarrow C)$	4–12 CD
14.	$((C \vee -E) \rightarrow (D \rightarrow C))$	3–13 CD

7.i

1.	$(A \rightarrow B)$	Prem
2.	$(C \rightarrow D)$	Prem
3.	$((B \vee D) \rightarrow E)$	Prem
4.	$-E$	Prem
5.	$--(A \vee C)$	SuppID
6.	$(A \vee C)$	5 DNE
7.	$-(B \vee D)$	4,3 MT
8.	$-B$	7 DM
9.	$-D$	7 DM
10.	$-C$	2,9 MT
11.	$-A$	1,8 MT
12.	A	6,10 DS
13.	$-(A \vee C)$	5–12 ID

7.k

1.	$((-A \vee B) \vee C)$	Prem
2.	$-(B \leftrightarrow -C)$	Prem

3.	$-(C \lor -A)$	SuppID
4.	$-C$	3 DM
5.	$--A$	3 DM
6.	$(-B \leftrightarrow -C)$	2 ENB
7.	$(-C \rightarrow -B)$	6 BCE
8.	$-B$	4,7 MP
9.	$(-A \lor B)$	4,1 DS
10.	$-A$	8,9 DS
11.	$(C \lor -A)$	3–10 ID

Exercises 6.6

1. Yes. As we said in the previous section, we can derive a symbolic argument's conclusion from its premises just in case the premises entail that conclusion.

2.b

1.	$(P \rightarrow -E)$	Prem
2.	$(-P \rightarrow -N)$	Prem
3.	$(-N \rightarrow -S)$	Prem
4.	$-(-E \lor -S)$	SuppID
5.	$--E$	4 DM
6.	$-P$	5,1 MT
7.	$-N$	2,6 MP
8.	$-S$	3,7 MP
9.	$--S$	4 DM
10.	$(-E \lor -S)$	4–9 ID

Since the derivation shows that the translation of the original English argument is CL-valid, we may infer that the English argument has an S-invalid sentential form and, hence, that it is valid.

2.d

1.	$((H \rightarrow S) \,\&\, (W \rightarrow N))$	Prem
2.	$((H \rightarrow -N) \,\&\, (W \rightarrow -S))$	Prem
3.	$(W \lor H)$	Prem
4.	$(W \rightarrow -S)$	2 Simp

5.	$-S$	SuppCD
6.	$(H \rightarrow S)$	1 Simp
7.	$-H$	5,6 MT
8.	W	3,7 DS
9.	$(-S \rightarrow W)$	5–8 CD
10.	$(W \leftrightarrow -S)$	4,9 BCI

Since the derivation shows that the translation of the original English argument is CL-valid, we may infer that the English argument has an S-valid sentential form and, hence, that it is valid.

3.   Yes. Because the terms used in the statement of Simp—"conjunction" and "conjunct"—are syntactic, Simp is a syntactic rule.

5.   No. As we said in the previous section, while the adequacy of CL's system of derivation can be rigorously demonstrated, the adequacy of the system of derivation in English cannot.

Chapter 7

Exercises 7.1

1.   Right. Since neither the expression "Hatfield" nor the expression "... is a logician" can stand by itself as a sentence, neither is a clause. But these expressions are not sentential operators either. There are *no* blanks in the expression "Hatfield", and the result of filling the blank in the expression "... is a logician" with a clause would not itself be a clause.

3.   No. Even if Bossy were the only cow in the world, the expression "... is a cow" would not be a singular term. A person who used this expression would not pick out Bossy as if by pointing. Rather the person would mention the property of being a cow—a property that only Bossy would happen to have.

5.   Not quite. The expression "... is a cow" is not a singular term since it does not refer to one particular thing. But, as we are using the term "pick out", this expression doesn't pick out thousands of things either. Rather it mentions the property of being a cow, which many things can share.

7.   No. Sentential operators are *similar* to predicates in that both become clauses when their blanks are properly filled. But, although we produce a clause from a sentential operator by filling its blanks with

clauses, we produce a clause from a predicate by filling its blanks with singular terms.

8. Expressions (a), (b), and (h) are singular terms. Expressions (g), (d), and (n) are simple, one-placed predicates. Expressions (c), (i), and (p) are singular clauses. [Notice that (c) can be viewed either as made from the singular term "Sally" and the predicate ". . . hit Tom" or as made from the singular term "Tom" and the predicate "Sally hit. . .".] The other expressions fall into various different categories: (e) and (l) are complex clauses; (j) and (k) are simple clauses but not singular clauses; (m) is a complex predicate; (o) is a two-placed predicate; and (f) is just a word that sometimes appears in predicates.

Exercises 7.2

1. No. Every sequence that used to be a symbolic sentence of our system still is. We haven't taken anything away from the system's vocabulary, and we haven't taken back or changed any of its rules of formation. We have just added a rule.

3. Strings (a), (h), (i), (m), and (o) are symbolic sentences. The others are not.

5. Yes. As we pointed out, singular sentences work syntactically just as sentence letters do.

Exercises 7.3

1. Yes, by definition. We should note, however, that one of the things we are calling a collection of objects — namely, the empty set — is a collection with nothing in it.

3. Yes. If A is the same set as B, every member of A is a member of B. But A is a subset of B if every member of A is also a member of B. Hence, if A is the same set as B, A is a subset of B. That is, every set is a subset of itself.

5. Yes. Whatever set A we choose, we will be unable to find a member of the empty set that is not a member of A (because we will be unable to find *any* member of the empty set!). So, according to our definition of *subset*, the empty set is a subset of *every* set.

7. Yes. Consider, for example, the set $\{\{1,2\}, \varnothing\}$, which has the set $\{1, 2\}$ as one of its members and the empty set as another.

9. No. There are two *kinds* of valuations for "Fa": those in which it has the value t and those in which it has the value f. But each of these kinds has an *infinite number* of different valuations in it — some with the domain $\{1\}$, some with the domain $\{1, 2\}$, some with the domain $\{2, 3, 5\}$, and so on.

11.a The empty set cannot be a domain of discourse, and the referents of "a" and "b" are not in the valuation's domain. Also, to be a valuation *for* the given sentence, the valuation would need to assign an extension to the predicate letter "G".

11.c The referent of the constant "a" must be in the domain of discourse.

12.b ſ

12.d ſ

12.f ſ

12.h ſ

12.j ſ

13.a *t*

13.c *t*

13.e *t*

13.g ſ

13.i *t*

13.k *t*

Exercises 7.4

1. Yes. As English singular terms generally pick out objects, constants have referents. As (simple, one-placed) English predicates generally mention properties shared by the members of some set, predicate letters have extensions. As English singular terms and (simple, one-placed) predicates go together to form singular clauses, constants and predicate letters go together to form singular symbolic sentences. As singular clauses of English generally are true when and only when the objects picked out by their singular terms have the properties mentioned by their predicates, singular symbolic sentences have the value *t* when and only when the referents of their constants are in the extensions of their predicate letters.

3. Yes. That every singular clause of English can be translated with a simple symbolic sentence follows directly from our method of translation. And, since a scheme of correspondence must associate constants with singular terms and predicate letters with (simple, one-placed) predicates, we can translate an English sentence with a singular symbolic sentence *only* if the English sentence consists of a singular clause.

5.a No. When setting up a scheme of correspondence, we may not associate any expression of our system with more than one expression of English.

5.c No, for the reason explained in our answer to Exercise 7.4.5.a.

6.b   (Rj → Ba)

6.d   (Ba → Ra)

6.f   P

6.h   P

Chapter 8

Exercises 8.1

1. Yes. In fact, the recognition of the inner structure of such clauses is what distinguished the idea of *predicative form* from the ideas of form developed in previous chapters.

3. Yes. The sentence "At least one thing is such that it is red" is true when and only when something or other has the property of redness.

5. Not quite. That the pronoun "it" can be put into the blanks in predicates to form clauses, shows that this pronoun resembles singular terms *syntactically*, not *semantically*.

7   No. It's true that we can produce clauses by filling the blanks in the quantifying phrase "at least one thing is such that . . ." and in the predicate ". . . is red". But we get a clause from the quantifying phrase only if we fill its blank with a *clause*, while we get a clause from the predicate only if we fill its blank with a *singular term* or *pronoun*.

8.b   Put the pronoun "it" into the blank in the predicate ". . . is red" to produce the clause "it is red". Produce the clause "each thing is such that it is red" by adding the quantifying phrase "each thing is such that". Finally, put this whole clause into the blank in the sentential operator "it's not the case that. . .".

8.d   Put the pronoun "it" into the blank in the predicate ". . . is red"; put the clause "it is red" into the blank in the sentential operator "it's not the case that . . .", and put the quantifying phrase "at least one thing is such that . . ." in front of the result.

8.f   Produce the long clause "it's not the case that each thing is such that it is red" as in Exercise 8.1.8.b. Produce the long clause "at least one thing is such that it is round" following steps similar to those in Exercise 8.1.8.a. Finally, put the first long clause into the first blank in the sentential operator "Either . . . or—" and the second into the second.

9.a   The first premise of the Robinson argument is true only if everything with a certain property (namely, the property of being an executive) has a second property (namely, the property of being rich). The other premise is true only if a certain thing (Robinson) has the first property. The conclusion is false only if that thing lacks the second property. Clearly, these conditions cannot be met at once. So, the argument is valid.

Exercises 8.2

1. No, it occurs only twice, after the predicate letters "F" and "G". The expression "[x]", being a single item of PL's vocabulary, does not really contain the variable "x". Besides, the wff "(Fx ∨ [x]Gx)" is not a symbolic sentence, since the variable after "F" is free.

3. Yes. As the English quantifying phrase "each thing is such that" has exactly the same syntax as the English quantifying phrase "at least one thing is such that", so the symbolic quantifier "[x]" has exactly the same syntax as the symbolic quantifier "[∃x]".

5. Yes. If we begin to the right of the quantifier and move to the right expression by expression, the marks that we pass over do not make a complete wff until we get to the last rounded parenthesis.

7. All of these wffs are symbolic sentences except (c), (f), and (h).

9. Sentences (a), (c), and (g) are conditionals; (e) is the negation of a conditional; (h) is a universally quantified sentence; (f) and (i) are existentially quantified sentences; and (b) is the negation of a quanti-fied sentence. [Sentence (d) is the negation of a negation, and (j) is a conjunction.]

Exercises 8.3

1. Yes. To construct a valuation for a sentence of PL, we identify a domain of discourse, assign referents to constants, assign extensions to predicate letters, and assign values to sentence letters — exactly as we did in Chapter 7.

2.b none

2.d none

2.f 1, 2, 3, and 4

2.h 2 and 4

2.j none

2.l 1 and 3

3. Not quite. The phrase "all occurrences of the variable 'x' " should read "all *free* occurrences of the variable 'x' ". Suppose, for example, that we have before us a valuation that assigns extensions to the predicate

letters "F", "G", and "H" and that assigns the constant "a" to the number 1. In this valuation, the number 1 satisfies the wff "([∃x](Fx & Gx) & Hx)" just in case the symbolic sentence "([∃x](Fx & Gx) & Ha)" has the value *t*. It need *not* be the case that, in this valuation, either "([∃x](Fa & Gx) & Ha)" or "([∃x](Fx & Ga) & Ha)" has the value *t*.

5.   Yes. Suppose that an object satisfies the wff "Gx" in a given valuation. Then the result of replacing the free "x" in "([x]Fx → Gx)" with a constant referring to that object would be a conditional whose consequent has the value *t*. And a conditional has the value *t* whenever its consequent has the value *t*.

7.   Yes. This follows directly from the rule of valuation for universally quantified sentences, V8.

9.   Yes. The sentence "[x](Fx ↔ Gx)" has the value *t* in a valuation just in case every object in the valuation's domain satisfies the wff "(Fx ↔ Gx)" (rule V8), and every object in a valuation's domain satisfies this wff just in case the predicate letter "F" has exactly the same extension as the predicate letter "G" (from the definition of satisfaction, rule V7, and rule V6).

11.   No. All that has to be the case for "[∃x](Fx & Gx)" to have the value *t* in a given valuation is that *some* object in the valuation's domain is both in the extension of the predicate letter "F" and in the extension of the predicate letter "G".

13.a   *t*

13.c   *f*

13.e   *f*

13.g   *t*

13.i   *t*

14.b   *t*

14.d   *t*

14.f   *f*

14.h   *f*

15.a   *t*

15.c   *f*

15.e   *f*

15.g   *t*

16.b   Any valuation in which the referent of "a" is not in the extension of "F" will do, as will any in which the extension of "G" is the whole of the domain.

16.d Any valuation in which the predicate letters "F" and "G" both have the empty set as their extensions will do.

16.f Consider any valuation in which nothing in the extension of the predicate letter "F" is in the extension of "G".

Exercises 8.4

1. No. We have added *four* new rules: UI, EI, EG, *and QE.*

3. There are an infinite number of instantiations of this sentence. Each time we put a new constant in for "x" we produce a new instantiation, and PL has an endless supply of different constants.

5. Arguments (a) and (d) are both PL-invalid, as is shown by the following valuation:

domain of discourse:	{1, 2, 3}
referent of "a":	1
referent of "b":	2
extension of "F":	{1, 3}

Arguments (b) and (c) are PL-valid, as is shown by the following derivations:

1.	[x]Fx	Prem	1.	Fa	Prem
2.	Fa	1 UI	2.	[∃x]Fx	1 EG

7. Yes. In a given valuation "−[x]Fx" has the value *t* just in case not everything in the valuation's domain is in the extension of "F", and "[∃x] − Fx" has the value *t* just in case something in the domain is not in the extension of "F".

9. Yes. The sentence "[x]−Fx" has the value *t* when and only when the extension of "F" is the empty set. So, "−[x]−Fx" has the value *t* when and only when the extension of "F" has something in it. But "[∃x]Fx" also has the value *t* when and only when the extension of "F" has something in it.

11.

1.	Fa	Prem
2.	[x]Gx	Prem
3.	Ga	2 UI
4.	(Fa & Ga)	1,3 Conj
5.	[∃x](Fx & Gx)	4 EG

1.	Fa	Prem
2.	[x]Gx	Prem

3.	$-[\exists x](Fx \,\&\, Gx)$	SuppID
4.	$[x]-(Fx \,\&\, Gx)$	3 QE
5.	$-(Fa \,\&\, Ga)$	4 UI
6.	Ga	2 UI
7.	$(Fa \,\&\, Ga)$	1,6 Conj
8.	$[\exists x](Fx \,\&\, Gx)$	3 – 7 ID

Clearly the first derivation, which uses EG, is shorter and easier to follow than the second, which does not.

12.b UI has been misused on line (3).

12.d There is an error on line (6); rule MP cannot be applied to the sentences on lines (1) and (2) since neither is a conditional.

12.f There is an error on line (4); rule EI requires that, when we move from an existentially quantified sentence to one of its instantiations, we introduce a constant *new* to the derivation.

12.h There is nothing wrong with this derivation.

13.			
	1.	$([x](Ax \lor -Bx) \to -[\exists x]-Cx)$	Prem
	2.	$--([x](Ax \lor -Bx) \lor [\exists x]Bx)$	Prem
	3.	$([\exists x]Bx \to -[\exists x]-Cx)$	Prem
	4.	$([x](Ax \lor -Bx) \lor [\exists x]Bx)$	2 DNE
	5.	$-[\exists x]-Cx$	1,3,4 D

14.b			
	1.	$-[x]-Fx$	Prem
	2.	$[\exists x]--Fx$	1 QE
	3.	$--Fa$	2 EI
	4.	Fa	3 DNE
	5.	$[\exists x]Fx$	4 EG

14.d			
	1.	$[x](Fx \leftrightarrow Gx)$	Prem
	2.	$-[x](Fx \to Gx)$	SuppID
	3.	$[\exists x]-(Fx \to Gx)$	2 QE
	4.	$-(Fa \to Ga)$	3 EI
	5.	$(Fa \leftrightarrow Ga)$	1 UI
	6.	$(Fa \to Ga)$	5 BCE
	7.	$[x](Fx \to Gx)$	2 – 6 ID

14.f			
	1.	$[x](Ax \to Bx)$	Prem
	2.	$[\exists x](Cx \,\&\, Ax)$	Prem

3.	(Ca & Aa)	2 EI
4.	(Aa → Ba)	1 UI
5.	Aa	3 Simp
6.	Ba	5,4 MP
7.	Ca	3 Simp
8.	(Ca & Ba)	6,7 Conj
9.	[∃x](Cx & Bx)	8 EG

14.h

1.	− [∃x]Cx	Prem
2.	[x](Bx → Cx)	Prem
3.	− [x] − (Cx ∨ Bx)	SuppID
4.	[∃x] − − (Cx ∨ Bx)	3 QE
5.	− − (Ca ∨ Ba)	4 EI
6.	(Ca ∨ Ba)	5 DNE
7.	[x] − Cx	1 QE
8.	− Ca	7 UI
9.	Ba	6,8 DS
10.	(Ba → Ca)	2 UI
11.	Ca	9,10 MP
12.	[x] − (Cx ∨ Bx)	3 – 11 ID

14.j

1.	(Fa → Gb)	Prem
2.	[x](Gx → Hx)	Prem
3.	[x](−Hb ↔ Ix)	Prem
4.	Fa	SuppCD
5.	− [x] − Ix	SuppID
6.	[∃x] − − Ix	5 QE
7.	− − Ic	6 EI
8.	Ic	7 DNE
9.	(−Hb ↔ Ic)	3 UI
10.	(Ic → −Hb)	9 BCE
11.	−Hb	8,10 MP
12.	(Gb → Hb)	2 UI
13.	−Gb	11,12 MT
14.	−Fa	1,13 MT
15.	Fa	4 R
16.	[x] − Ix	5 – 15 ID

	17.	$(Fa \rightarrow [x] - Ix)$	4–16 CD
14.1	1.	$[x](Fx \lor Gx)$	Prem
	2.	$[x] - Gx$	Prem
	3.	$([x]Fx \rightarrow [x](-Gx \rightarrow Hx))$	Prem
	4.	$-[x]Hx$	SuppID
	5.	$[\exists x] - Hx$	4 QE
	6.	$-Ha$	5 EI
	7.	$-[x]Fx$	SuppID
	8.	$[\exists x] - Fx$	7 QE
	9.	$-Fb$	8 EI
	10.	$(Fb \lor Gb)$	1 UI
	11.	Gb	9,10 DS
	12.	$-Gb$	2 UI
	13.	$[x]Fx$	7–12 ID
	14.	$[x](-Gx \rightarrow Hx)$	3,13 MP
	15.	$(-Ga \rightarrow Ha)$	14 UI
	16.	$-Ga$	2 UI
	17.	Ha	15,16 MP
	18.	$[x]Hx$	4–17 ID
14.n	1.	$([\exists x]Bx \rightarrow [x](-Cx \rightarrow Bx))$	Prem
	2.	$[\exists x](Ax \,\&\, Bx)$	Prem
	3.	$[x](Bx \rightarrow Ax)$	Prem
	4.	$-[x](-Cx \rightarrow Ax)$	SuppID
	5.	$[\exists x] - (-Cx \rightarrow Ax)$	4 QE
	6.	$-(-Ca \rightarrow Aa)$	5 EI
	7.	$(Ab \,\&\, Bb)$	2 EI
	8.	Bb	7 Simp
	9.	$[\exists x]Bx$	8 EG
	10.	$[x](-Cx \rightarrow Bx)$	1,9 MP
	11.	$(-Ca \rightarrow Ba)$	10 UI
	12.	$(Ba \rightarrow Aa)$	3 UI
	13.	$(-Ca \rightarrow Aa)$	11,12 HS
	14.	$[x](-Cx \rightarrow Ax)$	4–13 ID
14.p	1.	$([x]Fx \rightarrow -[x](Fx \lor -Fx))$	Prem

	2.	— [x](Fx ∨ —Fx)	SuppID
	3.	[∃x] — (Fx ∨ —Fx)	2 QE
	4.	— (Fb ∨ —Fb)	3 EI
	5.	— Fb	4 DM
	6.	— —Fb	4 DM
	7.	[x](Fx ∨ —Fx)	2–6 ID
	8.	— —[x](Fx ∨ —Fx)	7 DNI
	9.	— [x]Fx	1,8 MT
	10.	[∃x] — Fx	9 QE
	11.	— Fc	10 EI
	12.	(—Fc ∨ Ga)	11 Adj
	13.	[∃x](—Fx ∨ Ga)	12 EG
14.r	1.	— ([∃x]Ax ∨ [∃x]Bx)	Prem
	2.	— [∃x]Ax	1 DM
	3.	— [∃x]Bx	1 DM
	4.	[x] — Ax	2 QE
	5.	[x] — Bx	3 QE
	6.	— —[∃x](Ax ∨ Bx)	SuppID
	7.	[∃x](Ax ∨ Bx)	6 DNE
	8.	(Aa ∨ Ba)	7 EI
	9.	—Aa	4 UI
	10.	Ba	8,9 DS
	11.	—Ba	5 UI
	12.	— [∃x](Ax ∨ Bx)	6–11 ID
14.t	1.	[x]Fx	Prem
	2.	([∃x]Fx → [x](Gx & —Hx))	Prem
	3.	— [x] — (Gx → Hx)	SuppID
	4.	[∃x] — — (Gx → Hx)	3 QE
	5.	— —(Ga → Ha)	4 EI
	6.	(Ga → Ha)	5 DNE
	7.	Fa	1 UI
	8.	[∃x]Fx	7 EG
	9.	[x](Gx & —Hx)	2,8 MP
	10.	(Ga & —Ha)	9 UI

11.	Ga	10 Simp
12.	Ha	6,11 MP
13.	—Ha	10 Simp
14.	[x] — (Gx → Hx)	3–13 ID

14.v

1.	([∃x](Ax & Bx) → [x]Cx)	Prem
2.	—Ca	Prem
3.	——[x]Cx	SuppID
4.	[x]Cx	3 DNE
5.	Ca	4 UI
6.	—Ca	2 R
7.	—[x]Cx	3,6 ID
8.	—[∃x](Ax ∨ Bx)	1,7 MT
9.	[x] — (Ax & Bx)	8 QE
10.	—[x](Ax → —Bx)	SuppID
11.	[∃x] — (Ax → —Bx)	10 QE
12.	—(Ab → —Bb)	11 EI
13.	(Ab & ——Bb)	12 ENC
14.	Ab	13 Simp
15.	——Bb	13 Simp
16.	Bb	15 DNE
17.	(Ab & Bb)	14,16 Conj
18.	—(Ab & Bb)	9 UI
19.	[x](Ax → —Bx)	10,18 ID

Exercises 8.5

1. No. Standard English is clumsy, ugly, limited, and difficult to understand. Its *only* function is to help us translate from English into our formal model.

3. Yes. That's why paraphrasing into Standard English is a useful first step in translation into PL.

5. That's right. As we pointed out in Chapter 5, no sentential operator of Standard English corresponds to "it's possible that . . .".

7.a This sentence is in Standard English.

7.c This sentence cannot be paraphrased into Standard English, since it contains the nonstandard quantifying expression "most".

7.e This sentence's Standard English paraphrase is "At least one thing is such that it is a dog and it is a dachshund."

7.g This sentence's Standard English paraphrase is "It's not the case that at least one thing is such that it is a dog and it is a dachshund."

7.i This sentence cannot be paraphrased into Standard English since it contains the intractable sentential operator "it's possible that . . .".

7.k This sentence cannot be paraphrased into Standard English since it does not contain a predicate.

7.m One of this sentence's Standard English paraphrases is "Clarence is honest unless at least one thing is such that it is honest, and it is a man, and it's not the case that it is brave."

7.o This sentence's Standard English paraphrase is "Each thing is such that, if it is a dollar bill, then it is a treasury note."

7.q This sentence's Standard English paraphrase is "Each thing is such that, if it is a reporter, then it is a journalist."

7.s One of this sentence's Standard English paraphrases is "*If* (each thing is such that, if it is a publisher, then it is stingy or it is stupid), *then* (it's not the case that at least one thing is such that it is a reporter and it is rich and it is man)."

9. No. If a sentence cannot be paraphrased into Standard English (say, because it contains an intractable sentential operator) it can still be translated into PL with a sentence letter.

11.a
$$[\exists x](Ax \,\&\, Cx)$$
$$[x](Cx \rightarrow Gx)$$
$$\overline{}$$
$$\text{So, } [\exists x](Ax \,\&\, Gx)$$

11.c
$$[x]((Fx \,\&\, Cx) \rightarrow -Ex)$$
$$[x](-Gx \rightarrow Ex)$$
$$\overline{}$$
$$\text{So, } [x](Fx \rightarrow Gx)$$

11.e
$$[x]((Fx \lor Ax) \rightarrow Sx)$$
$$-[\exists x](Sx \,\&\, Hx)$$
$$\overline{}$$
$$\text{So, } [x]((Fx \rightarrow -Hx)$$

11.g   ([∃x]Lx ∨ [∃x]Sx)

            [x](Sx → Lx)

            [x](Lx → Fx)

            _____

            So, [∃x]Fx

11.i   [x](Tx → (Ax & Px))

            [x](Px & Mx)

            _____

            So, [x](Tx → Mx)

Exercises 8.6

1.   Generally, yes. If an English argument has a PL-valid translation, we may generally infer that it has a P-valid form. And, if the given argument has a P-valid form, it follows that every argument of that form is valid — including the given argument.

3.   Yes. As we saw in the previous section, in constructing a derivation for an argument's PL-translation, we demonstrate the P-validity of that argument's predicative form. And every argument with a P-valid predicative form is valid.

5.

1.	[x](Px → Mx)	Prem
2.	Ph	Prem
3.	(Ph → Mh)	1 UI
4.	Mh	2,3 MP

The fact that this argument has a PL-valid translation shows that its predicative form is P-valid and, hence, that the argument itself is valid.

7.a

1.	[x](Dx → Cx)	Prem
2.	[x](Cx → Mx)	Prem
3.	Db	SuppCD
4.	(Db → Cb)	1 UI
5.	Cb	3,4 MP
6.	(Cb → Mb)	2 UI
7.	Mb	5,6 MP
8.	(Db → Mb)	3–7 CD

7.c

1.	(−[∃x](Cx & Sx) & [x](Ox → Sx))	Prem
2.	(−[∃x](Ox & Cx) → [x](Lx → Wx))	Prem

3.	$-[\exists x](Cx \mathbin{\&} Sx)$	1 Simp
4.	$[x](Ox \rightarrow Sx)$	1 Simp
5.	$--[\exists x](Ox \mathbin{\&} Cx)$	SuppID
6.	$[\exists x](Ox \mathbin{\&} Cx)$	5 DNE
7.	$(Oa \mathbin{\&} Ca)$	6 EI
8.	Oa	7 Simp
9.	$(Oa \rightarrow Sa)$	4 UI
10.	Sa	8,9 MP
11.	Ca	7 Simp
12.	$(Ca \mathbin{\&} Sa)$	9,10 Conj
13.	$[\exists x](Cx \mathbin{\&} Sx)$	12 EG
14.	$-[\exists x](Cx \mathbin{\&} Sx)$	3 R
15.	$-[\exists x](Ox \mathbin{\&} Cx)$	5–14 ID
16.	$[x](Lx \rightarrow Wx)$	2,15 MP

7.e

1.	$([x](Wx \rightarrow Hx) \lor [\exists x](Wx \mathbin{\&} Lx))$	Prem
2.	$-[\exists x](Vx \mathbin{\&} Lx)$	Prem
3.	$[x](Wx \rightarrow Vx)$	SuppCD
4.	$-[x](Wx \rightarrow Hx)$	SuppID
5.	$[\exists x](Wx \mathbin{\&} Lx)$	1,4 DS
6.	$(Wa \mathbin{\&} La)$	5 EI
7.	La	6 Simp
8.	$[x] - (Vx \mathbin{\&} Lx)$	2 QE
9.	$-(Va \mathbin{\&} La)$	8 UI
10.	$-Va$	7,9 CS
11.	$(Wa \rightarrow Va)$	3 UI
12.	$-Wa$	10,11 MT
13.	Wa	6 Simp
14.	$[x](Wx \rightarrow Hx)$	4–13 ID
15.	$([x](Wx \rightarrow Vx) \rightarrow [x](Wx \rightarrow Hx))$	3–14 CD

7.g

1.	$[x](Ax \rightarrow (Px \lor Jx))$	Prem
2.	$-[\exists x]((Ax \mathbin{\&} Hx) \mathbin{\&} Px)$	Prem

3.	[x](Hx → Ax)	SuppCD
4.	− [x](Hx → Jx)	SuppID
5.	[∃x] − (Hx → Jx)	4 QE
6.	− (Ha → Ja)	5 EI
7.	(Ha & − Ja)	6 ENC
8.	Ha	7 Simp
9.	(Ha → Aa)	3 UI
10.	Aa	8,9 MP
11.	[x] − ((Ax & Hx) & Px)	2 QE
12.	− ((Aa & Ha) & Pa)	11 UI
13.	(Aa & Ha)	8,10 Conj
14.	− Pa	12,13 CS
15.	(Aa → (Pa ∨ Ja))	1 UI
16.	(Pa ∨ Ja)	10,15 MP
17.	Ja	14,16 DS
18.	− Ja	7 Simp
19.	[x](Hx → Jx)	4 − 18 ID
20.	([x](Hx → Ax) → [x](Hx → Jx))	3 − 19 CD

8.b

1.	[x]((Gx & Vx) → Cx)	Prem
2.	− [x]((Vx & − Cx) → − Gx)	SuppID
3.	[∃x] − ((Vx & − Cx) → − Gx)	2 QE
4.	− ((Va & − Ca) → − Ga)	3 EI
5.	((Va & − Ca) & − − Ga)	4 ENC
6.	(Va & − Ca)	5 Simp
7.	Va	6 Simp
8.	− − Ga	5 Simp
9.	Ga	8 DNE
10.	(Ga & Va)	7,9 Conj
11.	((Ga & Va) → Ca)	1 UI
12.	Ca	10,11 MP
13.	− Ca	6 Simp
14.	[x]((Vx & − Cx) → − Gx)	2 − 13 ID

8.d

1.	([x](Gx → Hx) ↔ B)	Prem
2.	−B	SuppCD
3.	([x](Gx → Hx) → B)	1 BCE
4.	−[x](Gx → Hx)	2,3 MT
5.	[∃x] − (Gx → Hx)	4 QE
6.	−(Ga → Ha)	4 EI
7.	(Ga & −Ha)	6 ENC
8.	[∃x](Gx & −Hx)	7 UI
9.	(−B → [∃x](Gx & −Hx))	2−8 CD

8.f

1.	[x](Lx → Bx)	Prem
2.	[x](Sx → Lx)	SuppCD
3.	−[x](Sx → Bx)	SuppID
4.	[∃x] − (Sx → Bx)	3 QE
5.	−(Sa → Ba)	4 EI
6.	(Sa & −Ba)	5 ENC
7.	Sa	6 Simp
8.	(Sa → La)	2 UI
9.	(La → Ba)	1 UI
10.	(Sa → Ba)	8,9 HS
11.	Ba	7,10 MP
12.	−Ba	6 Simp
13.	[x](Sx → Bx)	3−12 ID
14.	([x](Sx → Lx) → [x](Sx → Bx))	2−13 CD

8.h

1.	[x](Lx → (Fx → Gx))	Prem
2.	[x]((Lx & −Fx) → Gx)	Prem
3.	[∃x]Lx	SuppCD
4.	−[∃x](Lx & Gx)	SuppID
5.	[x] − (Lx & Gx)	4 QE
6.	La	3 EI
7.	−(La & Ga)	5 UI
8.	−Ga	6,7 CS
9.	(La → (Fa → Ga))	1 UI
10.	(Fa → Ga)	6,9 MP

11.	$\|$ $-$ Fa	8,10 MT
12.	$\|$ (La & $-$ Fa)	6,11 Conj
13.	$\|$ ((La & $-$ Fa) $\rightarrow$ Ga)	2 UI
14.	$\|$ Ga	12,13 MP
15.	$\|$ [∃x](Lx & Gx)	4 – 14 ID
16.	([∃x]Lx $\rightarrow$ [∃x](Lx & Gx))	3 – 15 CD

Chapter 9

Exercises 9.1

1. No. When revealing the predicative form of the sentence "Cleveland is north of Akron", we can view the sentence either in way (a) or in way (b). But when revealing this sentence's *relational* form, we have no choice but to view the sentence in way (c).

3. Expressions (a), (b), (c), (g) and (h) are simple predicates, while (e) is a complex predicate. Expressions (d), (f), (i), and (k) are not predicates.

4.b Put the singular term "Blair" into the first blank in the two-placed predicate ". . . is smarter than —" to form the one-placed predicate "Blair is smarter than . . .". Put the pronoun "it" into this predicate's blank and the quantifying phrase "each thing is such that" in front of the result to form the clause "each thing is such that Blair is smarter than it". Then abbreviate to "Blair is smarter than anyone".

4.d Put the pronoun "it" into the first blank in the predicate ". . . is smarter than —" and the quantifying phrase "at least one thing is such that" in front of the result to form the predicate "at least one thing is such that it is smarter than . . .". Put the pronoun *"it"* into this expression's blank and the quantifying phrase *"at least one thing is such that"* in front of the result to form the clause *"at least one thing is such that* at least one thing is such that it is smarter than *it"*. Then abbreviate to "someone is smarter than someone".

5. Yes. In English, we can form sentences in which two or more quantifying expressions work together. (See, for example, Exercise 9.1.4.d.) But PL's rules of formation allow us to put a quantifier in front of a wff only if that wff does not already contain a quantifier.

6.b At least one thing is such that *Fa* it.

6.d At least one thing is such that it's not the case that *F* it *a*.

6.f   At least one thing is such that *each thing is such that* it's not the case that *F* it *it*.

7.   Yes. The Abelard argument's predicative form, "*Fa*; so, at least one thing is such that *G* it", is P-invalid. (To see this, consider the argument "Spot is a dog; so there is a cat".) But, as we show in this chapter, the Abelard argument's relational form is R-valid.

Exercises 9.2

1.   No. While every symbolic sentence of PL is a sentence of RL, some sentences of RL—such as "[x][y]Rxy"—are not symbolic sentences of PL.

3.   Only sequences (a), (b), and (e) are symbolic sentences of RL, and only (b) is a singular sentence. [Sequences (c), (d), (h), and (i) are wffs of RL, but not symbolic sentences.]

5.   Only sequences (b), (c), (e), (f), (j), (k), (l), (m), and (n) are wffs of RL. Of these, all but (f) and (j) are symbolic sentences.

7.   Sentence (a) is a singular sentence; (c) a universally quantified sentence; (e) the negation of a quantified sentence; (g) a universally quantified sentence; and (i) the negation of a conditional.

Exercises 9.3

1.   Yes. In a valuation, the extension of a one-placed predicate letter is a set of objects, but the extension of an *n*-placed predicate letter ($n > 1$) is a collection of ordered *n*-tuples.

3.   There are four such sets: $\langle 1, 1 \rangle$, $\langle 1, 2 \rangle$, $\langle 2, 1 \rangle$, and $\langle 2, 2 \rangle$.

5.   Three such ordered quadruples are $\langle 12, 6, 4, 3 \rangle$, $\langle 24, 12, 8, 6 \rangle$, and $\langle 36, 18, 12, 9 \rangle$; there are infinitely many more.

7.   No. While each constant must have a referent, the referent of all four constants might be the same object.

8.b   domain of discourse: {1, 2, 3}

   referent of "a":   1

   extension of "F":   {2, 3}

   extension of "G":   {1}

8.d   Consider any valuation for this sentence in which the sentence letter "P" has the value *f*.

9.a   *f*

9.c   *t*

9.e   *f*

9.g   *t*

9.i   *t*

10.b *t*

10.d *t*

Exercises 9.4

1.   Not quite. The constant must be one that refers to the object.

2.b   1

2.d   1, 2, and 3

2.f   1, 2, and 3

2.h   1, 2, and 3

2.j   1 and 2

2.l   2

3.   No. The definition of *satisfaction* does not apply to "Rxy" since this wff contains free variables of two different types.

4.b   *t*

4.d   *f*

4.f   *f*

4.h   *f*

4.j   *f*

4.l   *t*

4.n   *f*

4.p   *t*

4.r   *t*

5.   Yes. In a given valuation, the sentence "[∃x][∃y]Rxy" has the value *t* just in case something satisfies the wff "[∃y]Rxy"—or, in other words, just in case there is at least one ordered pair in the extension of the predicate letter "R". Similarly, "[∃y][∃x]Rxy" has the value *t* just in case something satisfies the wff "[∃x]Rxy"—or, in other words, just in case there is at least one ordered pair in the extension of the predicate letter "R".

7.   No. In the text, we actually produce a valuation in which "[x][∃y]Rxy" has the value *t* while "[∃y][x]Rxy" has the value *f*.

Exercises 9.5

1. No. RL's system of derivation has the same rules of inference as PL's.

3.a The rule EI is misused on line (5), since the constant "a" is not new to the derivation.

3.c The result of applying rule QE to the sentence in line (1) should be "[∃x] − [y]Sxyx", *not* the sequence on line (2). And QE is similarly misused on line (4).

4.b

1.	[x][y]Rxy	Prem
2.	[y]Ray	1 UI
3.	Rab	2 UI
4.	[∃y]Ray	3 EG
5.	[∃x][∃y]Rxy	4 EG

4.d

1.	[x](Fx → [∃y](Gy & Hyx))	Prem
2.	−[∃x][∃y]Hxy	Prem
3.	−−[∃x]Fx	SuppID
4.	[∃x]Fx	3 DNE
5.	Fa	4 EI
6.	(Fa → [∃y](Gy & Hya))	1 UI
7.	[∃x](Gy & Hya)	5,6 MP
8.	(Gb & Hba)	7 EI
9.	Hba	8 Simp
10.	[x] − [∃y]Hxy	2 QE
11.	−[∃y]Hby	10 UI
12.	[y] − Hby	11 QE
13.	−Hba	12 UI
14.	−[∃x]Fx	3−13 ID

4.f

1.	[x](Ax → −[∃y](By & Cya))	Prem
2.	[y](By & Cay)	Prem
3.	(Aa → −[∃y](By & Cya))	1 UI
4.	(Ba & Caa)	2 UI
5.	[∃y](By & Cya)	4 EG
6.	−−[∃y](By & Cya)	5 DNE
7.	−Aa	3,6 MT

4.h			
	1.	[x](Ax → Bx)	Prem
	2.	−[∃x](Bx & Cxx)	Prem
	3.	−−[∃x](Ax & [y]Cyx)	SuppID
	4.	[∃x](Ax & [y]Cyx)	3 DNE
	5.	(Aa & [y]Cya)	4 EI
	6.	Aa	5 Simp
	7.	(Aa → Ba)	1 UI
	8.	Ba	6,7 MP
	9.	[x] − (Bx & Cxx)	2 QE
	10.	−(Ba & Caa)	9 UI
	11.	[y]Cya	5 Simp
	12.	Caa	11 UI
	13.	(Ba & Caa)	8,12 Conj
	14.	−[∃x](Ax & [y]Cyx)	3–13 ID

4.j			
	1.	[x][y]((Ax & −Bx) → Cxy)	Prem
	2.	[∃x](−Bx & Dx)	Prem
	3.	(−Ba & Da)	2 EI
	4.	−[x](Ax → [∃y](Dy & Cxy))	SuppID
	5.	[∃x] − (Ax → [∃y](Dy & Cxy))	4 QE
	6.	−(Ab → [∃y](Dy & Cby))	5 EI
	7.	(Ab & −[∃y](Dy & Cby))	6 ENC
	8.	Ab	7 Simp
	9.	−[∃y](Dy & Cby)	7 Simp
	10.	[y] − (Dy & Cby)	9 QE
	11.	−(Da & Cba)	10 UI
	12.	Da	3 Simp
	13.	−Cba	11,12 CS
	14.	[y]((Ab & −By) → Cby)	1 UI
	15.	((Ab & −Ba) → Cba)	14 UI
	16.	−Ba	3 Simp
	17.	(Ab & −Ba)	8,16 Conj
	18.	Cba	17,15 MP
	19.	[x](Ax → [∃y](Dy & Cxy))	4–18 ID

4.l
1. $-[\exists x](-Gx \lor -[\exists y]Fy)$ Prem
2. $[x] - (-Gx \lor -[\exists y]Fy)$ 1 QE
3. $-(-Ga \lor -[\exists y]Fy)$ 2 UI
4. $--[\exists y]Fy$ 3 DM
5. $[\exists y]Fy$ 4 DNE
6. Fb 5 EI
7. $[\exists z]Fz$ 6 EG

4.n
1. $[x][\exists y]Ayx$ Prem
2. $[x][y](Axy \rightarrow Bxy)$ Prem
3. $-[x][\exists y]Bxy$ SuppID
4. $[\exists x] - [\exists y]Bxy$ 3 QE
5. $-[\exists y]Bay$ 4 EI
6. $[y] - Bay$ 5 QE
7. $[\exists y]Aya$ 1 UI
8. Aba 7 EI
9. $[y](Aby \rightarrow Bay)$ 2 UI
10. $(Aba \rightarrow Bab)$ 9 UI
11. Bab 8,10 MP
12. $-Bab$ 6 UI
13. $[x][\exists y]Bxy$ 3-12 ID

4.p
1. $-[\exists x]Txx$ Prem
2. $-[\exists x]([y](Tay \rightarrow Txy) \ \& -Txa)$ SuppID
3. $[x] - ([y](Tay \rightarrow Txy) \ \& -Txa)$ 2 QE
4. $-([y](Tay \rightarrow Tay) \ \& -Taa)$ 3 UI
5. $[x] - Txx$ 1 QE
6. $-Taa$ 5 UI
7. $-[y](Tay \rightarrow Tay)$ 6,4 CS
8. $[\exists y] - (Tay \rightarrow Tay)$ 7 QE
9. $-(Tab \rightarrow Tab)$ 8 EI
10. $(Tab \ \& -Tab)$ 9 ENC
11. Tab 10 Simp
12. $-Tab$ 10 Simp
13. $[\exists x]([y](Tay \rightarrow Txy) \ \& -Txa)$ 2-12 ID

4.r

1.	[x]([∃y]Rxy → [z]Rzx)	Prem
2.	[∃x][∃y]Rxy	SuppCD
3.	[∃y]Ray	2 EI
4.	Rab	3 EI
5.	−[x][y]Rxy	SuppID
6.	[∃x] − [y]Rxy	7 QE
7.	−[y]Rcy	8 EI
8.	[∃y] − Rcy	9 QE
9.	−Rcd	10 EI
10.	([∃y]Ray → [z]Rza)	1 UI
11.	[∃y]Ray	4 EG
12.	[z]Rza	10,11 MP
13.	Rda	12 UI
14.	([∃y]Rdy → [z]Rzd)	1 UI
15.	[∃y]Rdy	13 EG
16.	[z]Rzd	14,15 MP
17.	Rcd	16 UI
18.	[x][y]Rxy	5−17 ID
19.	([∃x][∃y]Rxy → [x][y]Rxy)	2−18 CD

Exercises 9.6

1. No. This sentence contains the quantifying word "every", which is not in Standard English.

3. No. Although this is the procedure for translating into PL, if we used it in translating into RL, we would quickly get lost in a maze of quantifying phrases. Accordingly, we translate into RL in stages.

4.b [x](Sx → [y](Ty → Axy))

4.d [x](Sx → [∃y](Ty & Axy))

4.f [x](Px → [∃y]Dxy)

4.h [x]((Px & [∃y]Cxy) → ([∃z]Dxz ∨ [w]Cxw))

4.j [x]([∃y](Cy & Dxy) → [∃z](Fz & Dxy))

4.l [x]([∃y]((By & Hy) & Exy) → [∃z]((Az & Fz) & Exz))

4.n [x]([∃y][∃z](Ay & Bxyz) → Cx)

4.p −[∃x](−[∃y][∃z](Ay & Sxyz) & Lx)

Exercises 9.7

1.
1.	Lah	Prem
2.	[∃y]Lay	1 EG
3.	[∃x][∃y]Lxy	2 EG

3. No. Although we cannot demonstrate the Abelard argument's validity with the methods of PL, we can demonstrate its validity with the methods of RL.

5. Yes. From the fact that Abelard argument's translation is RL-valid, we may infer that the argument has an R-valid relational form and, hence, that every argument with the same relational form is valid.

7.a
1.	[∃x][y]Cyx	Prem
2.	− [x][∃y]Cxy	SuppID
3.	[y]Cya	1 EI
4.	[∃x] − [∃y]Cxy	2 QE
5.	− [∃y]Cby	4 EI
6.	[y] − Cby	5 QE
7.	− Cba	6 UI
8.	Cba	3 UI
9.	[x][∃y]Cxy	2 − 8 ID

7.c
1.	[x][y](Txy → Tyx)	Prem
2.	Tab	Prem
3.	(Tba → [∃x]Oxd)	Prem
4.	[y](Tay → Tya)	1 UI
5.	(Tab → Tba)	4 UI
6.	Tba	2,5 MP
7.	[∃x]Oxd	3,6 MP

7.e
1.	[x](Ax → Mx)	Prem
2.	[x]((Wx & [∃y](My & Pxy)) → Gx)	Prem
3.	(Wc & [∃x](Ax & Pcx))	Prem
4.	Wc	3 Simp
5.	[∃x](Ax & Pcx)	3 Simp
6.	(Aa & Pca)	5 EI
7.	Aa	6 Simp
8.	(Aa → Ma)	1 UI

	9.	Ma	7,8 MP
	10.	Pca	6 Simp
	11.	(Ma & Pca)	9,10 Conj
	12.	[∃y](My & Pcy)	11 EG
	13.	(Wc & [∃y](My & Pcy))	4,12 Conj
	14.	((Wc & [∃y](My & Pcy)) → Gc)	2 UI
	15.	Gc	13,14 MP

7.g	1.	[x][y](((Sx & Sy) & Exy) → Cyx)	Prem
	2.	[x][y](((Sx & Sy) & Cxy) → [z]((Sz & Eyz) → Cxz))	Prem
	3.	[x][y]((Sx & Sy) → [∃z](Sz & (Ezx & Ezy)))	Prem
	4.	− [x][y]((Sx & Sy) → Cxy)	SuppID
	5.	[∃x] − [y]((Sx & Sy) → Cxy)	4 QE
	6.	− [y]((Sa & Sy) → Cay)	5 EI
	7.	[∃y] − ((Sa & Sy) → Cay)	6 QE
	8.	− ((Sa & Sb) → Cab)	7 EI
	9.	((Sa & Sb) & − Cab)	8 ENC
	10.	(Sa & Sb)	9 Simp
	11.	[y]((Sa & Sy) → [∃z](Sz & (Eza & Ezy)))	2 UI
	12.	((Sa & Sb) → [∃z](Sz & (Eza & Ezb)))	11 UI
	13.	[∃z](Sz & (Eza & Ezb))	10,12 MP
	14.	(Sc & (Eca & Ecb))	13 EI
	15.	Sc	14 Simp
	16.	(Eca & Ecb)	14 Simp
	17.	Eca	16 Simp
	18.	Sa	10 Simp
	19.	(Sc & Sa)	15,18 Conj
	20.	((Sc & Sa) & Eca)	19,17 Conj
	21.	[y](((Sc & Sy) & Ecy) → Cyc)	1 UI
	22.	(((Sc & Sa) & Eca) → Cac)	21 UI
	23.	Cac	20,22 MP
	24.	[y](((Sa & Sy) & Cay) → [z]((Sz & Eyz) → Caz))	2 UI
	25.	(((Sa & Sc) & Cac) → [z]((Sz & Ecz) → Caz))	24 UI

26.	(Sa & Sc)	15,18 Conj
27.	((Sa & Sc) & Cac)	23,26 Conj
28.	[z]((Sz & Ecz) → Caz)	25,27 MP
29.	((Sb & Ecb) → Cab)	28 UI
30.	Ecb	16 Simp
31.	Sb	10 Simp
32.	(Sb & Ecb)	30,31 Conj
33.	Cab	29,32 MP
34.	—Cab	9 Simp
35.	[x][y]((Sx & Sy) → Cxy)	4–34 ID

Chapter 10

Exercises 10.1

1. Whenever we have used the predicate ". . . is identical to —", we have meant ". . . is one and the same thing as —". So, for example, we took the sentence "Zorro is Don Diego" to mean "Zorro is one and the same person as Don Diego," *not* "Zorro completely resembles Don Diego."

3. Yes. The sample argument has the R-*invalid* relational form "*Fab; Ga;* so, *Gb*", but the RI$_i$-*valid* i-relational form "*a* is identical to *b; Ga;* so, *Gb*". The argument is therefore valid in virtue of its i-relational form, but not in virtue of its relational form.

5. No. Although it's true that every argument with an R-valid relational form also has an IR-valid i-relational form, an argument (such as the example in Exercise 10.1.3) can have an IR-valid i-relational form while having an R-invalid relational form. As we have said, the Zorro argument is such an argument.

7.a *Fab.*

7.c *Fa,* or *a* is identical to *b.*

7.e *a* is identical to *b,* and *Fac.*

7.g Each thing is such that *at least one thing is such that* it is identical to *it.*

7.i At least one thing is such that (*F* it, and *each thing is such that,* if *G* it, then *it* is identical to it).

Exercises 10.2

1. Yes. The only *syntactic* difference is that, while a two-placed predicate letter has both blanks on its right, the identity sign has one blank on either side.

3. Yes. This follows from the definition of *identity sentence.*

5. In the given valuation, all of the sample sentences have the value *t* except sentence (b), which has the value *f.*

7. Yes. Sentence (a) always has the value *t* since every object in every domain is identical to itself. Sentence (b) has the value *t*—for a first object is identical to a second only if the second is identical to the first. And sentence (c) also has the value *t*—for, whenever a first object is identical to a second and the second to a third, the first must be identical to the third.

8.b Consider any valuation in which the constants "a" and "b" have the same referent and the predicate letter "F" has something in its extension.

8.d Consider any valuation in which the extension of the predicate letter "F" has two or more members.

8.f   domain: {1, 2, 3}

extension of "R": $\langle 1, 1 \rangle$, $\langle 2, 2 \rangle$, $\langle 3, 3 \rangle$

8.h Consider any valuation whose domain's one and only member is in the extension of the predicate letter "F".

8.j Consider any valuation in which the extension of the predicate letter "F" has exactly one member.

9. In this valuation "[x](Fx $\rightarrow$ x=b)" has the value *f* since the number 1 does not satisfy the wff "(Fx $\rightarrow$ x=b)", and "[x](Fx $\rightarrow$ x=c)" has the value *f*, since the number 1 also does not satisfy the wff "(Fx $\rightarrow$ x=c)".

Exercises 10.3

1. Yes. Since every object in every domain is identical to itself, "a=a" has the value *t* in every valuation for it (rule V10). Accordingly, there will never be a valuation in which some sentences have the value *t* while "a=a" has the value *f*, and "a=a" therefore follows RL_i-validly from any sentences whatever.

3. No. The rule Sub allows us to substitute one constant for another *only when* an (unboxed) sentence of the derivation is an identity statement that contains both constants.

5.a
1.	Fa	Prem
2.	a=a	Refl
3.	(Fa & a=a)	1,2 Conj
4.	[∃x](Fx & x=a)	3 EG

5.c
1.	Rab	Prem
2.	─ [x][y]((x=a & y=b) → Rxy)	SuppID
3.	[∃x] ─ [y]((x=a & y=b) → Rxy)	2 QE
4.	─ [y]((c=a & y=b) → Rcy)	3 EI
5.	[∃y] ─ ((c=a & y=b) → Rcy)	4 QE
6.	─ ((c=a & d=b) → Rcd)	5 EI
7.	((c=a & d=b) & ─ Rcd)	6 ENC
8.	(c=a & d=b)	7 Simp
9.	c=a	8 Simp
10.	d=b	8 Simp
11.	Rcb	1,9 Sub
12.	Rcd	10,11 Sub
13.	─ Rcd	7 Simp
14.	[x][y]((x=a & y=b) → Rxy)	2–13 ID

5.e
1.	[x][y](Rxy → ─ x=y)	Prem
2.	─ ─ [∃x]Rxx	SuppID
3.	[∃x]Rxx	2 DNE
4.	Raa	3 EI
5.	[y](Ray → ─ a=y)	1 UI
6.	(Raa → ─ a=a)	5 UI
7.	─ a=a	4,6 MP
8.	a=a	Refl
9.	─ [∃x]Rxx	2–8 ID

5.g
1.	[x](Fx → (Gx & Hx)	Prem
2.	[∃y][x](Gx ↔ x=y)	Prem
3.	─ ─ [∃x][∃y]((Fx & Fy) & ─ x=y)	SuppID
4.	[∃x][∃y]((Fx & Fy) & ─ x=y)	3 DNE
5.	[∃y]((Fa & Fy) & ─ a=y)	4 EI

6.	((Fa & Fb) & −a=b)	5 EI
7.	(Fa & Fb)	6 Simp
8.	Fa	7 Simp
9.	(Fa → (Ga & Ha))	1 UI
10.	(Ga & Ha)	8,9 MP
11.	Ga	10 Simp
12.	[x](Gx ↔ x=c)	2 EI
13.	(Ga ↔ a=c)	12 UI
14.	(Ga → a=c)	13 BCE
15.	a=c	11,14 MP
16.	Fb	7 Simp
17.	(Fb → (Gb & Hb))	1 UI
18.	(Gb & Hb)	16,17 MP
19.	Gb	18 Simp
20.	(Gb ↔ b=c)	12 UI
21.	(Gb → b=c)	20 BCE
22.	b=c	19,21 MP
23.	a=b	15,22 Sub
24.	−a=b	6 Simp
25.	−[∃x][∃y]((Fx & Fy) & −x=y)	3–24 ID

Exercises 10.4

1. Yes. If we can demonstrate an argument's validity with RL's methods, we can do so with RL$_i$'s. Yet there are some arguments (such as the Zorro argument, discussed in this chapter) whose validity we can demonstrate with RL$_i$'s methods but not RL's.

3. No. An argument with an RL$_i$-invalid translation may still be valid. (Consider, for example, the argument "John is a bachelor; so, John is unmarried".)

5.a

1.	(Ca ∨ Lb)	Prem
2.	a=b	Prem
3.	(Cb ∨ Lb)	1,2 Sub
4.	(Cb ∨ La)	2,3 Sub

5.c

1.	[x][y](Sxy → x=y)	Prem
2.	Sab	Prem

	3.	[y](Say → a=y)	1 UI
	4.	(Sab → a=b)	3 UI
	5.	a=b	2,4 MP
5.e	1.	([∃x]x=x → [∃y]Eya)	Prem
	2.	a=a	Refl
	3.	[∃x]x=x	2 EG
	4.	[∃y]Eya	3,1 MP
	5.	(a=a & [∃y]Eya)	2,4 Conj
	6.	[∃x](x=a & [∃y]Eyx)	5 EG

Exercises 10.5

1.a	1.	[∃x]Rx	Prem
	2.	Ra	1 EI
	3.	(Ra & Ra)	2,2 Conj
	4.	[∃y](Ra & Ry)	3 EG
	5.	[∃x][∃y](Rx & Ry)	4 EG

1.c Since sentence (i) RL$_i$-validly entails sentence (ii), (ii) must have the value *t* in every valuation in which (i) does—including the given valuation.

1.e	1.	[∃x][∃y](Rx & Ry)	Prem
	2.	[∃y](Ra & Ry)	1 EI
	3.	(Ra & Rb)	2 EI
	4.	Ra	3 Simp
	5.	[∃x]Rx	4 EG

2.b [∃x][∃y]((Bx & By) & −x=y)

2.d [∃x]Bx

2.f [∃x][∃y](((Bx & By) & −x=y) & (Sax & Say))

3. Yes. On the basis of a purely semantic resemblance, we viewed "[x](Rx & [y](Ry → x=y))" as a translation of "Exactly one thing is red", despite the syntactic differences.

5.   domain: {1, 2}
              referent of "a":   1
       extension of "R":   {1, 2}

In this valuation, the number 1 satisfies "Rx" but not "[y](Ry → y=x)". It follows that, in this valuation, the number 1 does not satisfy "(Rx → [y](Ry → y=x))" and, hence, that "[x](Rx → [y](Ry → y=x))" has the value *f*.

6.b   −[∃x][∃y][∃z](((Cx & Cy) & Cz) & ((−x=y & −x=z) & −y=z))

6.d   −[∃x][∃y][∃z](((Cx & Cy) & Cz) & ((−x=y & −x=z) & −y=z))

6.f   [x]((Tx & Kx) → −[∃y][∃z](((−Cy & −Cz) & −y=z) & Oyx))

7.

1.	[∃x](Rx & [y](Ry → x=y))	Prem
2.	(Ra & [y](Ry → a=y))	1 EI
3.	Ra	2 Simp
4.	[y](Ry → a=y)	2 Simp
5.	−[∃y][x](Rx ↔ x=y)	SuppID
6.	[y] − [x](Rx ↔ x=y)	5 QE
7.	−[x](Rx ↔ x=a)	6 UI
8.	[∃x] − (Rx ↔ x=a)	7 QE
9.	−(Rb ↔ b=a)	8 EI
10.	(Rb → a=b)	4 UI
11.	a=b	SuppCD
12.	Rb	11,3 Sub
13.	(a=b → Rb)	11,12 CD
14.	(Rb ↔ a=b)	10,13 BCI
15.	[∃y][x](Rx ↔ x=y)	5–14 ID

1.	[∃y][x](Rx ↔ x=y)	Prem
2.	[x](Rx ↔ x=a)	1 EI
3.	(Ra ↔ a=a)	2 UI
4.	(a=a → Ra)	3 BCE
5.	a=a	Refl
6.	Ra	4,5 MP

7.	$-[\exists x](Rx \,\&\, [y](Ry \rightarrow x{=}y))$	SuppID
8.	$[x] - (Rx \,\&\, [y](Ry \rightarrow x{=}y))$	7 QE
9.	$-(Ra \,\&\, [y](Ry \rightarrow a{=}y))$	8 UI
10.	$-[y](Ry \rightarrow a{=}y)$	6,9 CS
11.	$[\exists y] - (Ry \rightarrow a{=}y)$	10 QE
12.	$-(Rb \rightarrow a{=}b)$	11 EI
13.	$(Rb \,\&\, -a{=}b)$	12 ENC
14.	Rb	13 Simp
15.	$(Rb \leftrightarrow b{=}a)$	2 UI
16.	$(Rb \rightarrow b{=}a)$	15 BCE
17.	$b{=}a$	14,16 MP
18.	$-a{=}b$	13 Simp
19.	$-b{=}b$	17,18 Sub
20.	$b{=}b$	Refl
21.	$[\exists x](Rx \,\&\, [y](Ry \rightarrow x{=}y))$	7–20 ID

9.a

1.	$[\exists x][\exists y](((Cx \,\&\, Cy) \,\&\, (Ixa \,\&\, Iya)) \,\&\, -x{=}y)$	Prem
2.	$[\exists y](((Cb \,\&\, Cy) \,\&\, (Iba \,\&\, Iya)) \,\&\, -b{=}y)$	1 EI
3.	$(((Cb \,\&\, Cc) \,\&\, (Iba \,\&\, Ica)) \,\&\, -b{=}c)$	2 EI
4.	$((Cb \,\&\, Cc) \,\&\, (Iba \,\&\, Ica))$	3 Simp
5.	$(Cb \,\&\, Cc)$	4 Simp
6.	Cb	5 Simp
7.	$(Iba \,\&\, Ica)$	4 Simp
8.	Iba	7 Simp
9.	$(Cb \,\&\, Iba)$	6,8 Conj
10.	$[\exists x](Cx \,\&\, Ixa)$	9 EG

9.c

1.	$[\exists x](Hxa \,\&\, [y](Hya \rightarrow y{=}x)$	Prem
2.	$(Hba \,\&\, [y](Hya \rightarrow y{=}b))$	1 EI
3.	$[y](Hya \rightarrow y{=}b)$	2 Simp
4.	$--[\exists x][\exists y]((Hxa \,\&\, Hya) \,\&\, -x{=}y)$	SuppID
5.	$[\exists x][\exists y]((Hxa \,\&\, Hya) \,\&\, -x{=}y)$	4 DNE
6.	$[\exists y]((Hca \,\&\, Hya) \,\&\, -c{=}y)$	5 EI
7.	$((Hca \,\&\, Hda) \,\&\, -c{=}d)$	6 EI
8.	$(Hca \,\&\, Hda)$	7 Simp

9.	Hca	5 Simp
10.	(Hca → c=b)	3 UI
11.	c=b	9,10 MP
12.	Hda	8 Simp
13.	(Hda → d=b)	3 UI
14.	d=b	12,13 MP
15.	c=d	11,14 Sub
16.	−c=d	7 Simp
17.	−[∃x][∃y]((Hxa & Hya) & −x=y)	4–16 ID

9.e

1.	[∃x](Sx & [y](Sx → x=y))	Prem
2.	[∃x](Sx & Rx)	Prem
3.	−[x](Sx → Rx)	SuppID
4.	[∃x] − (Sx → Rx)	3 QE
5.	−(Sa → Ra)	4 QE
6.	(Sa & −Ra)	5 ENC
7.	(Sb & [y](Sx → x=b))	1 EI
8.	[y](Sx → y=b)	7 Simp
9.	Sa	6 Simp
10.	(Sa → a=b)	8 UI
11.	a=b	9,10 MP
12.	(Sc & Rc)	2 EI
13.	Sc	12 Simp
14.	(Sc → c=b)	8 UI
15.	c=b	13,14 MP
16.	c=a	11,15 Sub
17.	Rc	12 Simp
18.	Ra	16,17 Sub
19.	−Ra	6 Simp
20.	[x](Sx → Rx)	3–19 ID

Exercises 10.6

1.

1.	[∃x]((Nx & Tx) & ([y]((Ny & Ty) → x=y) & Bx))	Prem
2.	((Na & Ta) & ([y]((Ny & Ty) → a=y) & Ba))	1 EI
3.	(Na & Ta)	2 Simp

4.	Na	3 Simp
5.	([y]((Ny & Ty) → a=y) & Ba)	2 Simp
6.	Ba	5 Simp
7.	(Na & Ba)	4,6 Conj
8.	[∃x](Nx & Bx)	6 EG

The derivation shows that the original argument has an IR-valid i-relational form.

3. Yes. This follows immediately from the definition of *definite description*.

5.a [∃x](((Px & Wx) & [y]((Py & Wy) → y=x)) & Mx)

5.c Ma

Appendix

Exercises Appendix A

1.

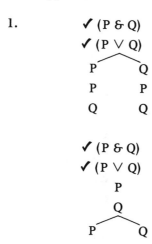

The second tree is more elegant than the first since we only had to write the results from "(P & Q)" once.

3. Not necessarily. If an unchecked conditional isn't in an *open* path, we can't apply a rule to it since there's nowhere to write our results. So, there can be a finished tree with an unchecked conditional in it.

5. This is true. The results that we get by applying a rule of inference to a symbolic sentence must go at the end of *every* open path in which the sentence appears.

6.b

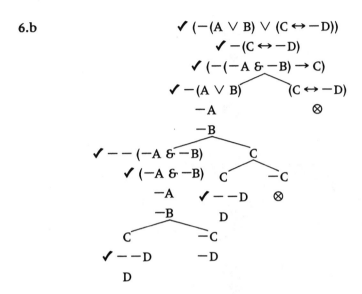

6.d

✔ (A ↔ B)
✔ −(−A ∨ −B)
✔ −(A & −(B & C))
✔ − −A
✔ − − B
A
B
A   −A
B   ⊗
−A ✔ − −(B & C)
⊗   ✔ (B & C)
B
C

Exercises Appendix B

1. No. The initial sentences of a tree for a symbolic argument are the argument's premises and the *negation* of the argument's conclusion.

3.a

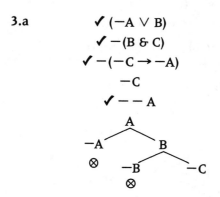

       ✓ (−A ∨ B)
       ✓ −(B & C)
      ✓ −(−C → −A)
         −C
        ✓ − − A
          A
     −A   B
     ⊗   −B   −C
          ⊗

3.c

      ✓ (A ∨ (B & C))
      ✓ (D → − C)
      ✓ −(A & B)
      ✓ − (−D ∨ −B)
       ✓ − − D
       ✓ − − B
         D
         B
   −D   −C
   ⊗
       −A   −B
    −A ✓ (B & C) ⊗
    ⊗   B
         C
         ⊗

3.e

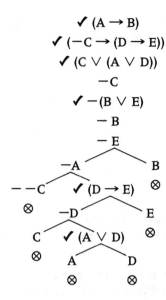

4.b If we construct a tree with only one initial sentence, all paths in the tree close just in case the sentence is a CL-contradiction (Exercise Appendix B.4.a.) But a sentence is a CL-tautology just in case its negation is a CL-contradiction. So, to see whether a given symbolic sentence is a CL-tautology, we can construct a tree whose only initial sentence is the given sentence's negation. If all paths in the tree close, the given sentence is a CL-tautology; otherwise, it's not.

4.d Two symbolic sentences are CL-equivalent just in case the argument from each to the other is CL-valid. And, in this section, we described a way to use trees to determine whether symbolic arguments are CL-valid.

5.

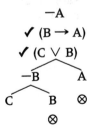

The open path through the tree describes the valuation in which "C" has the value t while "A" and "B" have the value f. And, in this valuation, all the tree's initial sentences have the value t.

A	B	C	−A	(B → A)	(C ∨ B)
t	*t*	*t*	*f*	*t*	*t*
t	*t*	*f*	*f*	*t*	*t*
t	*f*	*t*	*f*	*t*	*t*
t	*f*	*f*	*f*	*t*	*f*
f	*t*	*t*	*t*	*f*	*t*
f	*t*	*f*	*t*	*f*	*t*
f	*f*	*t*	*t*	*t*	*t*
f	*f*	*f*	*t*	*t*	*f*

The seventh line of the truth table represents the valuation described by the tree's open path, and, on this line, all the tree's initial sentences have the value *t*.

7. Since the rule transmits the value *t* upward and downward, trees would still provide a reliable test for CL-validity if this rule were to replace T2. But trees constructed with this rule would tend to be bushier and less elegant. Why branch three ways when two will do?

Exercises Appendix C

1.a (a) The tree's first sentence should not be checked; universally quantified sentences *never* get checked. (b) The symbolic sentence "[x]Rxa" should not have been written in the tree since it cannot be inferred from anything above it. (c) The path down the tree's right side should be closed, since it contains both "Gb" and "−Gb".

1.c (a) Presumably, "−Rab" and "−Rba" are supposed to be the results of applying a rule of inference to "−(Rab → Rba)", but they are not. (b) the sentence "((−Rab & −Rba) → Rab)" may not be inferred from "[z]((−Rab & −Rbz) → Raz)" since it is not an instance of that symbolic sentence.

2.a

      [x][y]Rxy

    ✓−[∃x][y]Rxy

     [x] − [y]Rxy

    ✓−[y]Ray

    ✓[∃y] − Ray

      −Rab

      [y]Ray

       Rab

       ⊗

2.c
        ✓ [∃x] (Ax & Bx)
          [x] (Ax → Cxx)
        ✓ − [∃x] [∃y] Cxy
           ✓ (Aa & Ba)
             Aa
             Ba
          ✓ (Aa → Caa)
        −Aa   Caa
        ⊗   [x] − [∃y] Cxy
               ✓ − [∃y] Cay
               [y] −Cay
                  −Caa
                   ⊗

2.e
        ✓[∃x][y][z]Axyz
        ✓−[∃x]Axxx
         [y][z]Aazy
          [z]Aaza
          Aaaa
        [x] − Axxx
         −Aaaa
           ⊗

2.g
        [x] (Ax → [∃y]Bxy)
      ✓ − − [∃x] (Ax & [y] − Bxy)
       ✓ [∃x] (Ax & [y] − Bxy)
         ✓ (Aa & [y] −Bay)
             Aa
          [y] − Bay
        ✓ (Aa → [∃y] Bay)
      −Aa   ✓ [∃y] Bay
      ⊗   Bab
               −Bab
                 ⊗

2.i

[x] (Ax → Bx)

✓ [∃x] [∃y] (Ax & Cxy)

[x] [y] (Cxy → Dyx)

✓ − [∃x] (Bx & [∃y] Dyx)

[x] − (Bx & [∃y] Dyx)

✓ [∃y] (Aa & Cay)

✓ (Aa & Cab)

Aa

Cab

✓ (Aa → Ba)

  −Aa   Ba

   ⊗   [y] (Cay → Dya)

        ✓ (Cab → Dba)

     −Cab   Dba

      ⊗ ✓ − (Ba & [∃y] Dya)

        −Ba   ✓ − [∃y] Dya

        ⊗   [y] −Dya

              −Dba

               ⊗

2.k

✓ [∃x] (Ax & [y] (By → Cxy))

✓ ([∃x] Ax → [∃y] By)

✓ − [∃x] [∃y] Cxy

✓ (Aa & [y] (By → Cay))

Aa

[y] (By → Cay)

✓ −[∃x] Ax   ✓ [∃y] By

[x] −Ax   Bb

  −Aa   ✓ (Bb → Cab)

   ⊗ −Bb   Cab

       ⊗   [x] − [∃y] Cxy

         ✓ − [∃y] Cay

         [y] − Cay

          −Cab

           ⊗

2.m

[x] [y] ((Fx & Gy) → Hxy)
✓ [∃x] [∃y] ((Fx & Iy) & −Hxy)
✓ −[∃x] (Ix & −Gx)
[x] − (Ix & −Gx)
✓ [∃y] ((Fa & Iy) & −Hay)
✓ ((Fa & Ib) & −Hab)
✓ (Fa & Ib)
−Hab
Fa
Ib
✓ −(Ib & −Gb)

```
        −Ib        ✓ − −Gb
         ⊗            Gb
                [y] ((Fa & Gy) → Hay)
                ✓ ((Fa & Gb) → Hab)

        ✓ −(Fa & Gb)      Hab
      −Fa        −Gb       ⊗
       ⊗          ⊗
```

2.o

✓[∃x] (Ax & [y] (By → Cxy))
✓ −[∃x] (Ax & [∃y] (Dy & Cxy))
✓ − −[∃x] (Bx & Dx)
✓ [∃x] (Bx & Dx)
✓ (Ba & Da)
Ba
Da
✓ (Ab & [y] (By → Cby))
Ab
[y] (By → Cby)
✓ (Ba → Cba)

```
−Ba         Cba
 ⊗       [x] − (Ax & [∃y] (Dy & Cxy))
         ✓ −(Ab & [∃y] (Dy & Cby))

      −Ab        ✓ −[∃y] (Dy & Cby)
       ⊗         [y] − (Dy & Cby)
                 ✓ − (Da & Cba)

              −Da        −Cba
               ⊗          ⊗
```

2.q   [x] (Fx → ([∃y] Gxy → [∃z] Gzx))

[x] ([∃z] Gzx → Gxx)

✔ −[∃x] Gxx

✔−[x] (Fx → [y] −Gxy)

✔ [∃x] −(Fx → [y] − Gxy)

✔ −(Fa → [y] −Gay)

Fa

✔ −[y] −Gay

✔ [∃y] − −Gay

✔ − −Gab

Gab

✔(Fa → ([∃y] Gay → [∃z] Gza))

    −Fa   ✔((∃y] Gay → [∃z] Gza)

    ⊗

     ✔ −[∃y] Gay   [∃z] Gza

     [y] −Gay   ✔ ([∃z] Gza → Gaa)

     −Gab   −[∃z] Gza   Gaa

     ⊗   ⊗   [x] −Gxx

                   −Gaa

                   ⊗

2.s   ✔ ([x] [∃y] Axy → [x] [∃y] Bxy)

✔ [∃x] [y] −Bxy

✔ −[∃x] [∃y] −Axy

[y] −Bay

✔−[x] [∃y] Axy   [x] [∃y] Bxy

✔ [∃x] − [∃y] Axy   ✔ [∃y] Bay

✔ −[∃y] Acy   Bab

[y] −Acy   −Bab

[x] − [∃y] −Axy   ⊗

✔ −[∃y] −Acy

[y] − − Acy

− −Acd

−Acd

⊗

Index to Definitions